Check for abbreviations that should be spelled out (189–190)
Use adverb form to modify verbs and other m̶o̶d̶i̶f̶i̶e̶r̶s̶ (64–66)
Check agreement of subject and verb, pronc̶u̶n̶ ̶a̶n̶d̶ ̶ (̶ )
Check for omission or misuse of apostrophe
Rewrite sentence to make it clearer or more r
Check for use of subject form or object form
Check for words that should be capitalized (1
Revise for clearer or more effective overall plan (248, 254–262, 323–325)
Revise excessive coordination (135)
Use semicolon (not comma) between two independent clauses (97)
Check for awkward, inaccurate, inappropriate wording (198–208, 215–222, 227–229)
Develop—support, explain, illustrate (236–238, 242–246, 266–268)
Check dictionary for syllabication of the word (187)
Rewrite sentence to show what the modifier modifies (66–67)
Focus more clearly on unifying idea or key point (238–242)
Put items joined by *and, but, or* in same grammatical category (82)
Do not punctuate as a separate sentence (91–94)
Break up into two separate sentences (94–95)
Check standing of debatable usage in glossary
Recognize sentence parts and constructions (14–28)
Check for missing or misused hyphen (182–185)
Complete incomplete construction (74–78)
Expression is too informal for serious writing (36–38, 211–213)
Italicize word or expression (188)
Check for unnecessary capitalization
Shift modifier to more appropriate position (66–70)
Observe conventional manuscript form (185–187)
Rewrite sentence
Change nonstandard to standard form (35–36, 211)
Follow convention when using numbers (190)
Make overall organization clearer or more effective (289–295, 299–308)
Check reference of pronouns (53–59)
Avoid unnecessary or awkward repetition (153–155)
Check for shift in time or use of pronouns or shift to passive (78–82)
Expression is too slangy for its context (213–215)
Check for spelling errors (159–174)
Check incomplete or mixed construction (70–74, 133–135, 137–138)
Revise awkward or ineffective subordination (136)
Help reader follow from point to point (246–248, 325–326)
Revise for more varied sentence structure (141–145)
Use right verb form (46–53)
Remove deadwood or unnecessary duplication (226–227)

# NEW
# ENGLISH
# HANDBOOK

Hans P. Guth

**San Jose State University**

**Wadsworth Publishing Company**
**Belmont, California**
**A Division of Wadsworth, Inc.**

*New English Workbook* has been specially designed to help students master the concepts presented in this textbook. In addition, there is an Instructor's Manual for teachers.

English Editor: Kevin Howat
Production Editors: Sally Schuman and
Donna Oberholtzer
Managing Designer: Cynthia Bassett
Interior Design: Cynthia Bassett, Pat Friday
Copy Editor: Dorothy Ohliger Conway
Cover Design: Steve Osborn

Printed in the United States of America

2  3  4  5  6  7  8  9  10———86  85  84  83  82

Library of Congress Cataloging in Publication Data

Guth, Hans Paul, 1926–
    New English handbook.

    Bibliography: p.
    Includes index.
    1. English language—Grammar—1950–
2. English language—Rhetoric.  I. Title.
PE1112.G87      808'.042      81-16128
ISBN 0-534-01122-5          AACR2

Acknowledgments are listed on pp. 493–494.

# Preface

## To the Teacher

The *New English Handbook* is designed to help today's students achieve the proficiency in written communication expected of them as college students. It is designed to help teachers work productively in today's classrooms. The aim of the author and the editors has been to fill needs widely felt by teachers of composition:

• **REALISTIC PRIORITIES**  To be effective in today's classrooms, a handbook should set realistic priorities for today's students and focus clearly on essentials. The opening chapters of *New English Handbook* address themselves directly to the students' most basic needs: an understanding of basic sentence structure; help with basic features of written English (verb forms, pronoun forms); help with basic sentence problems (agreement, pronoun reference); help with basic sentence punctuation (complete sentences and fragments, comma splices).

• **EXPLANATIONS ACCESSIBLE TO TODAY'S STUDENTS**  To be widely usable, a handbook should provide clear step-by-step explanations of basic concepts and avoid the teaching of terminology as an end in itself. The author and editors of *New English Handbook* have made a special effort to avoid the overuse of traditional technical terms that defeats many average and below-average students. Where simpler or more nearly self-explanatory terms have become widely established in modern textbooks, this book uses the modernized "plain-English" alternatives: *coordinator* for "coordinating conjunction," *subject form* for "nominative case."

- **EMPHASIS ON POSITIVE WRITING SKILLS** A handbook should combine a program for teaching positive writing skills with an effective guide to revision. *New English Handbook* provides constructive writing practice for the sentence, the paragraph, and the whole theme. Sentence work that includes sentence-completion, sentence-combining, and sentence-imitation exercises provides the "missing link" between grammar and composition.

- **A BALANCED TREATMENT OF THE WRITING PROCESS** In *New English Handbook*, the treatment of the whole theme pays special attention to the *gathering* of material during the prewriting stage and to the subsequent *structuring* of material, with many sample outlines. The treatment of the research paper pays special attention to legitimate and illegitimate uses of quoted material and to the process of integrating source material in the finished paper.

- **EFFECTIVE TEACHING HELPS** The *New English Handbook* provides effective teaching helps, including diagnostic tests at the beginning of most chapters, many helpful charts, and models from a wide range of sources. An accompanying "Back-to-Basics" workbook goes beyond the routine provision of additional exercises to give realistic help to students with special needs.

- **SUPPORT FOR AN EFFECTIVE COMPOSITION PROGRAM** A 100-item objective placement test, suitable for use during a *single class period*, is available to the instructor and is accompanied by instructions and essay topics for a diagnostic essay. In the handbook itself, the chapter on The Whole Theme includes six sets of theme topics geared to the student's progress in mastering different stages of the writing process. The Instructor's Manual for *New English Handbook* is more than an answer key; it provides professional background and discussion of current issues in composition for both the beginning and the experienced teacher.

In preparing this book I have profited greatly from visits to composition programs and talks with teachers at schools throughout the country, including especially the University of

Iowa, Ohio State University, Sinclair Community College, Miami University of Ohio, Texas Tech University, University of Houston, University of New Orleans, University of Cincinnati, University of Dayton, Wright State University, Fresno City College, West Valley College, South Dakota State University, and Henry Ford Community College. I have learned much from the students in my composition classes at San Jose State University, who have shared with me the frustrations and rewards of writing and whose good humor and honest effort have cheered me over the years.

H. Guth

The author and the editors of this book wish to acknowledge gratefully the contributions of reviewers and consultants and the assistance of those who facilitated our visits to their institutions.

Peter Neumeyer
San Diego State

Mary Boseman
Pensacola Junior College

Joseph Trimmer
Ball State University

George Haich
Georgia State University

George Findlen
Northwest Missouri State University

Jack White
Mississippi State University

George Hayhoe
Virginia Polytechnic and State University

Richard Verrell
Boston University

Katherine Scully
Tulsa Junior College

Philip Boshoff
Skidmore College

Kenneth Risdon
University of Minnesota, Duluth

Jim Hanlon
Shippensburg State University

Celest Martin
University of Rhode Island

Dorothy Vella
University of Hawaii, Manoa

Beth Stiffler
Western Illinois University

John Reuter
Florida Southern College

Leota Palmer
William Rainey Harper College

Robert Cosgrove
Saddleback College

Charles Wagner
Sinclair Community College

Mary Beth Pringle
Wright State University

William Gracie
Miami University of Ohio

Alma Bryant
University of South Florida,
Tampa

William Pixton
Oklahoma State University

Jeanette Morgan
University of Houston

Eileen Evans
Western Michigan University

Ed Chute
University of North Dakota

Douglas Butturff
University of Central Arkansas

Jeffrey Gross
University of Mississippi

Frank O'Hare
Ohio State University

Edgar Slotkin
University of Cincinnati

Lorraine Murphy
University of Dayton

Joseph Kolpake
Henry Ford Community College

Richard Hespin
Henry Ford Community College

Elizabeth Penfield
University of New Orleans

Peter Dingus
University of Houston

Barbara Johnston

# Contents
## in Brief

# Contents

# 1

## Introduction
## to Composition

As a college student, you are expected to express yourself effectively in writing. You are expected to write effective **expository** prose—the kind of writing that we use to explain, to inform, to argue, or to persuade. Expository prose is the kind of writing we use when we explain how solar energy works, or when we report on the status of an endangered species. We use it when we try to show the need for fairer taxes, better bicycle paths, or more effective control of handguns. We use it in letters of application to show our qualifications for a job, and we use it on written tests to show our knowledge of a subject. We use it in memos and reports when we describe the progress of a project.

This book is designed to help you improve your ability to write this kind of prose. When you improve your skill as a writer, you learn to make your meaning clear. You learn to organize your thinking. You learn to support a point, following through with explanations and examples. You learn to meet the standards of educated written English, so that your readers will give your ideas at least a respectful hearing.

Your improved ability to handle written English will benefit you both in and out of school. Whether as a student, as a citizen, or as a private individual, you will profit from the ability to express yourself purposefully and forcefully in plain English. As for a future career, few occupations are left that do not require a constant stream of forms, memos, reports, and studies. Paperwork of all kinds plays an ever-growing role in all our lives. Customer, jobholder, and voter alike profit from the ability to make competent and confident use of the written word.

## A HANDBOOK OF COMPOSITION

This book is basically a guide to written composition. *Composition* is an ancient Latin word that means "putting it together." In this book, it means getting a piece of writing into shape. This book is intended for the kind of composition course that has a strong positive emphasis—that focuses attention on the process of putting ideas into words. The instructions in this book are designed to help you make the process of writing a paper a productive and satisfying task. In writing a typical paper, ask yourself four basic questions:

(1) *"What do I know?"* To be worth reading, a paper has to have substance. Suppose you are writing a paper about how our society treats the handicapped. Be sure to ask yourself: "What handicapped people have I known? What do I remember about them? What were their problems? How did they cope with them? What have I read that confirms or modifies some of my own observations?" To give your papers substance, draw on what you have observed, experienced, and read. The crucial part of the pre-writing stage is to call to mind the specifics that will make your subject real for your reader.

(2) *"What do I think?"* A successful paper has a point. As you explore your subject, you have to begin asking yourself how things add up. How do the different parts of the picture fit together? What overall conclusion does your material suggest? In a successful paper, the writer has pulled things together. As your paper takes shape, sum up in one sentence your answer to a reader who asks: "What is the point?" We call such a summing up of the key idea the **thesis** of a paper. The thesis is a claim or general point that is supported by the rest of your paper. Suppose that in thinking about the role of the handicapped in our society you have come to focus on the *changes* you have observed. Your thesis may look like this:

THESIS: Everywhere in American life, handicapped people are beginning to play a more visible and independent role.

(3) *"How am I going to proceed?"* A successful paper has structure. It has a ground plan that the reader can follow. As you explore material you might use in a paper, prepare a scratch outline or rough working outline. Adjust it as necessary as you think more about your subject. In reading your finished paper, your readers need a kind of mental road map that tells them: "We are tracing this process through three major stages." Or "We are going to look at three key qualities that make a job satisfying or worthwhile." Or "This paper about the handicapped is going to have one major section about the situation *then*, and another about the contrasting situation *now*."

(4) *"How well am I reaching my reader?"* Writing is meant to be read. To write effectively, you have to be able to imagine yourself in the reader's shoes. If you make a claim on your readers' time and attention, your part of the bargain is to provide a piece of writing that they can understand and that they can follow. Take time to find the right word. Take time to rewrite an awkward sentence. Provide signals that show where you are headed. Remember that when you introduce readers to new information or new ideas, you are building a bridge. It is your task to take your readers from here to there.

Remember that the ability to write well is not a simple one-dimensional skill. Competence and confidence come with practice. The important thing is that you learn something from every writing task you undertake. At the same time, become more aware of what other writers do—how they approach a subject, how they structure their material. Learn from advice, practice, and example.

## A GUIDE TO REVISION

The guidelines for revision provided in this handbook serve a double purpose. First, they provide you with help in final editing and polishing of your paper before you turn it in. Second, they help you with final revision after your paper has been read and commented on by your instructor.

The standards set in this book apply to effective modern prose that is meant to be taken seriously—both inside and outside the English classroom. At the one extreme, the instructions in this book steer you away from features that would make your writing too informal, too shapeless, too improvised. At the other extreme, this book encourages you to keep your writing from becoming so formal as to turn wooden and artificial. The standards set in this book will help you make your writing acceptable to a fairly conservative reader with a respect for living modern prose.

In helping you locate help with familiar writing problems, this handbook uses a combined *letter-and-number* system. The letter lets you see at a glance what kind of problem you are dealing with: *G* stands for grammatical usage, *P* for punctuation,

*S* for sentence style, *D* for diction (or word choice), *SP* for spelling, *PA* for paragraph, *C* for the whole composition, or the whole theme. The letter together with the guide number directs you to the right section of this book for detailed help in correcting the problem. **G 5c**, for instance, deals with vague uses of *this* and *which*; **S 3b** with awkward uses of the passive.

A complete chart of these guide numbers is the *Handbook Key* printed on the inside back cover, at the end of this book. Your instructor may prefer to use the familiar correction symbols listed alphabetically in the *Guide to Revision* printed on the inside front cover, at the beginning of this book: *cap* for a word that should be capitalized, *lc* for a capitalized word that should be lower case, and the like. By checking the symbol in the Guide to Revision, you will find a general explanation of the symbol and page numbers for specific instructions.

## A CHECKLIST OF FAMILIAR PROBLEMS

The following is a checklist for revision and proofreading of your papers. At the same time, it will help guide you in final revision of papers marked by your instructor:

(1)  *Proofread carefully for spelling to avoid the "unforgivables."* Never misspell the following words:

| | | | | |
|---|---|---|---|---|
| receive | believe | separate | definite | similar |
| perform | probably | used to | writing | occurred |

Watch out for other familiar spelling problems: Check **SP 1c** for words often confused, such as *accept* (take on) and *except* (take out). Check **SP 2b** for doubling of the final consonant before the added ending in *planned* and *referred*.

(2)  *Watch out for features of our writing system that have no equivalent in speech.* Capital letters and apostrophes do not stand for something we can hear in the spoken language. Study the chart with section **SP 5** to make sure you use capitals correctly for names, including especially names of nationalities and languages: *English, Spanish, Chinese.* Review section **SP 4b** to make sure you use the apostrophe correctly for the possessive of nouns—the form that tells us *whose*:

| SINGULAR (BELONGS TO ONE) | PLURAL (BELONGS TO SEVERAL) |
|---|---|
| a friend's bicycle | the spectators' cars |
| my brother's nose | my brothers' noses |
| one country's history | other countries' problems |
| a week's wage | two months' salary |

Remember the major exception to the use of the apostrophe for the possessive: the possessive pronoun *its* (*its* price, *its* roof, *its* number). Use *it's* only as a shortened form of *it is* (*it's* hot; *it's* late).

(3) *Check for basic sentence punctuation.* Be sure to avoid the sentence fragment (*frag*) and the comma splice. See **P 1a** on how to revise fragmentary sentences—groups of words that do not make a complete statement on their own:

FRAGMENTS:   Later than usual.
Without good reason.
Starting at an early age.

Check for fragments caused by a *which, if, because,* or *whereas.* Often these words start a part of the sentence that needs to be linked to a main statement, or main clause. The following are sentence fragments when added after a period as afterthoughts:

FRAGMENTS:   *Which* lost them many friends.
*If* the proposal succeeds.
*Because* the lease had expired.
*Whereas* labor costs are high.

Study **P 2a** on how to avoid the comma splice, often marked *CS.* The comma splice uses only a comma to link, or splice together, two statements that could be separate independent sentences:

COMMA SPLICE:   My sister keeps an old picture on her dresser, its color has faded completely.
REVISED:   My sister keeps an old picture on her dresser; its color has faded completely.

(4) *Check your sentences for agreement between subject and verb.* The most basic relationship in the English sentence is the tie between subject and verb. Look at pairs like "The *bird* / *has*

6

left" and "The *birds* / *have* left," or "The *lake* / *is* cool" and "The *lakes* / *are* cool." Both basic parts of each sentence in each pair include a signal for singular (one) or plural (more than one). We say that both basic parts of the sentence agree in number: *bird* is matched with *has* (singular); *birds* is matched with *have* (plural).

When subject and verb are separated by other material, or when their usual order is changed, agreement problems result. The following is an example of blind agreement (**G 3d**). The verb is matched not with its true subject but with part of the wedge that came between the subject and the verb:

FAULTY:   The accuracy of these *reports* / *are* questionable.
REVISED:   The *accuracy* of these reports / *is* questionable.
             (What is questionable? Their *accuracy* is.)

(5) *Check for other basic relationships in a sentence.* Clarify the relationship between a pronoun and what it stands for, or between a modifier and what it modifies. The guide number **G 5d** may alert you to a pronoun with vague reference (often marked *ref*):

VAGUE:   In my hometown, *they* are building a new city hall.
            (Who are *they*?)
REVISED:   The *people* of my hometown are building a new city hall.

The guide number **G 7b** may alert you to a dangling modifier (often marked *DM*)—a modifier pointing to something that is merely implied and that is left out of the sentence:

DANGLING:   *When contemplating marriage,* the decision should not be made in haste. (Who is contemplating marriage?)
REVISED:   When contemplating marriage, *young people* should not decide in haste.

(6) *Revise awkward or roundabout sentences.* Guide numbers starting with the letter *S* will guide you to handbook sections helping you to make your sentences more forceful and direct. For instance, section **S 1a** will show you how to rewrite a vague, indirect sentence by following the "Who-does-what?" model:

AWKWARD:   Awareness of the need for gun control usually occurs when someone guns down an important public figure. (Who becomes aware?)

REVISED:  *The public* usually becomes aware of the need for gun control when someone guns down an important public figure.

(7)  *Revise inaccurate or inappropriate words.* Sections dealing with diction, or word choice, will encourage you to use exact words, forceful or expressive words, or words that are serious enough for your subject. A guide number like **D 5a** may alert you to a word you have confused with another:

CONFUSED:  Jean was not fully *convicted* [should be *convinced*] of the truth of the report.

The guide number **D 1e** may alert you to a misused idiom, or customary expression:

UNIDIOMATIC:  Millions of immigrants have *stepped* [should be *set*] *foot* on this land of opportunity.

(8)  *Strengthen poorly focused or poorly developed paragraphs.* A rambling paragraph may need a unifying topic sentence that clearly sums up the key idea (**PA 1b**). A thin paragraph may need to be bolstered by additional examples (**PA 1c**). When you see the symbol *dev* (for "develop"), remember the following rule of thumb: If you have only a general statement, add a detailed example. If you have only one example, provide one or two more for added force. If you are describing a person or a scene, move closer for a more detailed look.

(9)  *Clarify or strengthen the overall outline of your paper.* Guide numbers starting with the letter *C* will lead you to sections asking you to reconsider the structure or strategy of your composition as a whole. In a paper on the pro's and con's of divorce, you may have given various reasons why in your opinion many Americans today take divorce too lightly. You may have talked about the difficult readjustments and the psychological and economic difficulties that often follow. But your arguments may be hard to take in because they follow one another in no particular order. In your revision, try to establish several clear overall divisions for your paper. In your final outline, make sure they follow in a logical or sensible order. Perhaps you will identify several major *kinds* of separation that divorce brings about, and present them roughly in the order in which they follow in time:

**The American Way of Divorce**

   I. *Emotional* estrangement and conflict
  II. Dissolution of the *legal* bond
 III. *Economic* consequences of the separation
 IV. Dissolution of the larger *family unit* (especially if there are children)
  V. Disruption of a circle of *friends and acquaintances*

(10) *Strengthen coherence or transition.* The guide number **PA 1d** will lead you to instructions for inserting the missing links in a paragraph: a *for example* or *however* or *on the contrary* that helps the reader see the connection between one part of the paragraph and the next. The subsections under **C 6** will provide hints on how to make a paper as a whole more coherent—to make it move smoothly from point to point.

## A FINAL WORD

For the student writer in a composition course, the grading system or the need to fulfill a requirement furnishes an incentive to do well. But the most important incentive for any writer is the satisfaction that comes from a job well done. Your reward comes when you feel that you have done an honest job of putting a paper together, when you feel you have accomplished something that is truly yours. The hard work you have to put into a composition course will be worthwhile if several times during the course you feel you have written a paper that was worth writing and worth reading.

# 2

# Grammar and Usage

# DIAGNOSTIC TEST

## INSTRUCTIONS:

Look at the blank in each of the following sentences. Of the three possible choices that follow the sentence, which would be right for *serious written English*? Put the letter for the right choice after the number of the sentence.

1. If she had had a chance, she would have _____ to college.
   a. went            b. gone                c. going

2. A new judge took over and _____ him to appear in court.
   a. orders          b. order               c. ordered

3. She went to the bank, but _____ denied her the loan.
   a. it              b. they                c. them

4. In my school, there _____ not enough things to interest me.
   a. was             b. were                c. being

5. Many students do not take their education _____.
   a. real serious    b. really serious      c. very seriously

6. My best friends are those _____ have a sense of humor.
   a. who             b. which               c. whom

7. When we lost, I was upset because I _____ very hard.
   a. working         b. have worked         c. had worked

8. There was ill feeling between _____ and his mother.
   a. he              b. him                 c. hisself

9. As we enter, the first thing that _____ is a large poster.
   a. is seen         b. we saw              c. we see

10. Average drivers became aware of how much gas _____ used.
    a. you            b. they                c. one

11. We read several articles about _____ kind of accident.
    a. this           b. these               c. them

12. Miraculously, last week's explosion _____ no real harm.
    a. done           b. did                 c. doing

13. When _____ our bicycles, thoughtless motorists are a menace.
    a. riding         b. we riding           c. we are riding

14. Vacationers were warned to watch out for sharks and _____ gradually.
    a. should tan     b. to tan              c. tanning

12

**15.** Eskimos always _____ and still are hunting whales for food.
   a. have          b. have hunted          c. had

**16.** The accuracy of her predictions _____ always amazed us.
   a. has          b. have          c. having

**17.** My aunt and her daughters knew how to take care of _____.
   a. themself          b. themselves          c. theirselves

**18.** None of my brothers did _____ in high school.
   a. very well          b. very good          c. real good

**19.** No growth is a new concept for _____ Americans.
   a. us          b. we          c. ourself

**20.** The boy and girl in the front seat _____ hit by flying debris.
   a. being          b. was          c. were

# G1   AN OVERVIEW OF GRAMMAR

**Grammar is the study of how words work together in a sentence.**

Words carry only fragmentary meanings as long as they are loosely strung together. Tourists abroad can make some crude sense to foreigners after picking up some important words. Foreign visitors to the United States can make some headway by taking words from a dictionary. But they will not be speaking English until they can work words into meaningful patterns like the following:

| ACTOR | ACTION VERB | TARGET | |
|---|---|---|---|
| The agent | scrutinized | my passport. | |

| SENDER | ACTION VERB | ADDRESS | MISSIVE |
|---|---|---|---|
| The travel bureau | sent | me | a brochure. |

| ACTOR | ACTION VERB | TARGET | LABEL |
|---|---|---|---|
| Maurice | called | the trip | a disaster. |

13

Our language uses several basic means of combining isolated words in meaningful patterns. The following are the major grammatical devices that help us fit words into a complete sentence:

(1) *Different arrangements of words in a sentence produce different meanings.* In a complete sentence, the right words appear in the right order. Changes in **word order** account for the differences in the following pairs:

> The batter hit *the ball*.
> *The ball* hit the batter.
>
> Craig was looking for *a police officer*.
> *A police officer* was looking for Craig.
>
> Her study dealt with children *only*.
> Her study dealt with *only* children.

(2) *Many words change their forms depending on how they fit into a sentence.* For instance, a word may add an ending like *-s*, *-ed*, or *-ing*. Or it may change from *sing* to *sang*, or *tooth* to *teeth*. Such changes in **word form** account for the differences in the following pairs:

> Stops annoy*ed* our passenger.
> Stop annoy*ing* our passenger.
>
> The physician stud*ied* burns.
> The physician's study burn*ed*.

(3) *Several kinds of linking words help us fit different sentence parts into a sentence.* A major function of such words is to make the sentence as a whole run smoothly. Such **function words** account for the differences in meaning in the following pairs:

> George set *a* poor example.
> George set *the* poor *an* example.
>
> He left *his* friends *the* estate.
> He left *with his* friends *for the* estate.

## G1a   Basic Sentence Parts                    *gr*

**Study the basic building blocks of the English sentence.**

We assign words to major word classes (or **parts of speech**) according to the functions they perform. The same word may serve different functions, and belong to different word classes, in different sentences. The word *light* performs a different function in each of the following:

Turn off the *light.*
Let's *light* a candle.
She had *light* hair.

The basic model of the English sentence has only two basic parts. A complete sentence normally has at least a **subject** and a **predicate**:

| SUBJECT | PREDICATE |
|---------|-----------|
| The boy | reads. |
| A car | stopped. |
| Dogs | bark. |

Look at the words that make up these two basic parts:

(1) *The subject of a sentence calls something to our attention.* It brings something into focus, so that the rest of the sentence can make a statement about it. The most important part of the subject is usually a **noun**: *car, student, bulldog, college, education.* We use nouns to name or label things, places, people, animals, ideas. The consumer looking up entries in the Sears catalog, the chemist giving names to new plastics, the advertiser naming new products—all rely on the naming function of the noun.

The following clues will help you recognize nouns:

• Many nouns stand for things we can count. We can usually add the *-s* ending to change a noun from one (**singular**) to several (**plural**): one *car*, several *cars*; one *boy*, several *boys*; one *airplane*, several *airplanes*; one *idea*, several *ideas*. Not all nouns use the *-s* ending for the plural:

| IRREGULAR PLURALS: | men, women, mice, children |
| UNMARKED PLURALS: | sheep, deer, offspring, people |

Some nouns are used only in the singular: *chaos, courage, rice.*

• Nouns often follow a noun marker like *a, this, my,* or *your*: a *dog,* this *car,* my *friend,* your *neighborhood.* We use three kinds of noun markers over and over:

ARTICLES: *the, a, an*
> the tide, a tree, an apple, a riot, the bill

DEMONSTRATIVE ("POINTING") PRONOUNS: *this, these; that, those*
> this street, these tickets; that detour, those requests

POSSESSIVE PRONOUNS: *my, your, his, her, its, our, their*
> my hat, your gloves, his directions, their surprise

- Nouns often have noun-making endings (**suffixes**) like *-acy*, *-ance*, *-dom*, *-ness*, or *-hood*:

  | | |
  |---|---|
  | *-acy:* | literacy, celibacy, delicacy |
  | *-ance:* | importance, attendance, remittance |
  | *-dom:* | wisdom, kingdom, Christendom |
  | *-ness:* | happiness, darkness, illness |
  | *-hood:* | neighborhood, childhood, adulthood |

- The place of nouns may be taken by noun substitutes, such as the personal pronouns: *I, you, he, she, it, we, they*.

  | | |
  |---|---|
  | *He* | reads. |
  | *It* | stopped. |
  | *They* | bark. |

> See **G 5** for an overview of pronouns.

(2)  *The predicate makes a statement about the subject.* (Sometimes the predicate asks a question about the subject.) The most important word, or group of words, in the predicate is the **verb**: *reads, stopped, has left, will return, is reprimanded, has been elected.* The verb signals the performance of an action, the occurrence of an event, or the presence of a condition. A noun may *name* an action: *theft, arrival, movement, investigation.* A verb refers to present, future, past, or possible performance: *steals, will arrive, has moved, may investigate.*

Verbs set things in motion; they often stand for something we can do: *eat* your food; let us *celebrate*; we should *notify* him. The following clues will help you recognize verbs:

- Verbs are words that can show a *change in time* by a change in the word itself: *steals* (now), *stole* (then); *lies* (now), *lied* (then); *eat* (now), *ate* (then). This change in time is called a change in **tense**. We can change many verbs from present tense to past tense by adding the ending *-d* or *-ed*:

## VERB TENSES

**PRESENT (NOW OR USUALLY):**
　I *work* at home.

**PAST (OVER AND DONE WITH):**
　We *sold* the house.

**PERFECT (COMPLETED RECENTLY OR TRUE UP TO NOW):**
　I *have received* your invitation.
　She *has* always *supported* us.

**PAST PERFECT (BEFORE OTHER PAST EVENTS):**
　His mother *had worked* in a factory.

**FUTURE (STILL TO COME):**
　Your friends *will help* you.

| | | | |
|---|---|---|---|
| **PRESENT:** | ask | arrive | request |
| **PAST:** | asked | arrived | requested |

In the present tense, most verbs add *-s* when *he, she,* or *it* could substitute for the subject (**third person singular**):

My brother *works.*　　(He *works.*)
Jean *travels.*　　　　(She *travels.*)
The phone *rings.*　　　(It *rings.*)

* Verb forms often consist of several words. The main part of the verb follows a word like *can, will, have,* or *was.* Such words are called **auxiliaries,** or helping verbs. If there are several auxiliaries, they typically appear in the following order: An auxiliary like *will (would), shall (should), can (could), may (might)* comes first. After these (or first if none of these appears), there may be a form of *have (has, had).* In the next slot, there may be a form of *be (is, am, are, was, were, be, been).* Here are some possible combinations:

| | (HAVE) | (BE) | MAIN VERB |
|---|---|---|---|
| can | | | happen |
| | has | | arrived |
| could | have | | called |
| | | is | waiting |
| may | | be | canceled |
| will | have | been | sold |
| should | have | been | revised |

**17**

By changing the form of a verb or by using auxiliaries, we can show the major differences in tense (see chart on page 17).

• Verbs often have verb-making suffixes like *-fy*, *-en*, or *-ize*:

| | |
|---|---|
| *-fy:* | notify, magnify, ratify, indemnify |
| *-en:* | darken, weaken, redden, sharpen |
| *-ize:* | organize, synchronize, sympathize |

## G1b  Basic Sentence Patterns                                  *gr*

**Study the basic patterns of the complete English sentence.**

Some English sentences need only two basic parts: a subject and a complete verb. But many sentences need one or two additional basic parts to be complete. We call these added essential parts completers, or **complements**.

| | |
|---|---|
| INCOMPLETE: | The carpenter fixed _____ (What?) |
| INCOMPLETE: | Her grandmother had been _____ (What?) |

We can sort out English sentences according to whether they use one or more completers, and according to the kinds of completers they use. In the simplest sentence pattern, the verb alone makes up the predicate; it tells the whole story:

| SUBJECT | VERB |
|---|---|
| Planes | fly. |
| The victims | suffered. |
| Your letter | has arrived. |

In several typical sentence patterns, the predicate is completed by one or more complements. These become essential parts of the basic structure. An action verb may carry its action across to a target or result (**direct object**):

| SUBJECT | ACTION VERB | OBJECT |
|---|---|---|
| The student | reads | a book. |
| Dudley | made | sandals. |
| A storm | had delayed | the plane. |

In other sentences, the verb is a **linking verb**, which intro-duces a description of the subject. A linking verb pins a label on the subject. The label may be a noun: This noun is often called the **predicate noun** to distinguish it from a noun used as an object:

| SUBJECT | LINKING VERB | NOUN |
|---------|--------------|------|
| Barnes | is | a custodian. |
| He | may be | your brother. |

Or the label may be an **adjective**, a word like *small, cheap, expensive, reasonable,* or *wonderful.* Most adjectives are degree words; they fit in after *very*: very *tall*, very *long*, very *famous*, very *useful*. When an adjective is used to complete the predicate, it is called a **predicate adjective**:

| SUBJECT | LINKING VERB | ADJECTIVE |
|---------|--------------|-----------|
| Our bus | was | crowded. |
| The price | seemed | reasonable. |
| The food | tasted | good. |

For more on adjectives, see **G 1d**.

An action verb like *give, send,* or *write* may carry the pattern first to the destination (**indirect object**) and then go on to what was given or sent (direct object):

| SUBJECT | VERB | INDIRECT OBJECT | OBJECT |
|---------|------|-----------------|--------|
| Hannah | gave | the travelers | directions. |
| My aunt | will send | us | the money. |
| The boy | wrote | his parents | a letter. |

A verb like *name, elect,* or *call* may carry the pattern first to a direct object and then pin a label on the direct object. (The second completer is then called an **object complement**.)

| SUBJECT | VERB | OBJECT | OBJECT COMPLEMENT |
|---------|------|--------|-------------------|
| Eric | called | his friend | a liar. |
| The voters | elected | Reagan | President. |
| The mayor | made | Jim | her assistant. |

The final label in such a sentence may be an adjective instead of a noun:

| SUBJECT | VERB | OBJECT | ADJECTIVE |
|---------|------|--------|-----------|
| Jean | called | her work | monotonous. |
| Textiles | had made | the town | famous. |
| The tenants | painted | the walls | green. |

## G1c  Basic Transformations

**Study the basic transformations that help us adapt simple sentences to different uses.**

Transformations are changes or adaptations that help us go beyond the simple bare-bones sentence. Several simple transformations rearrange (and sometimes remove or expand) basic sentence parts. For instance, to change a statement to a question, we can move all or part of the verb in front of the subject. "You *are* his friend" becomes "*Are* you his friend?"

| | SUBJECT | VERB | COMPLETER |
|---|---------|------|-----------|
| *Have* | our guests | arrived? | |
| *Is* | the package | | ready? |
| *Will* | your friend | pay | the bill? |

Or we add a form of *do* (*does, did*) and place it in front of the subject:

| | | | |
|---|---|---|---|
| *Do* | your friends | agree? | |
| *Did* | the officer | write | a ticket? |

A second transformation changes the verb to the form used in requests or commands (**imperative**). It omits the subject. "You should pay your dues" becomes "Pay your dues!"

| VERB | COMPLETER |
|------|-----------|
| Shut | the door. |
| Be | my friend. |
| Keep | quiet. |

A third transformation changes the way we look at what happens in a sentence. It produces the **passive**, which makes the original object the subject of a new sentence. The passive reverses the order of the original active sentence, which goes from the actor or "doer" through the action to the target. "The manager caught the thief" becomes "The thief was caught by the manager."

In a passive sentence, the original subject appears after *by* at the end of the pattern. But it may also be left out altogether. The verb appears in its passive form, which uses a form of *be* and the form that usually follows *have* (have *caught*, had *brought*, has *admired*). This form is called the past participle—see **G 4**.

| SUBJECT | PASSIVE VERB | |
|---------|--------------|---|
| The book | was read | (by the student). |
| A letter | has been sent | (by my friend). |

For weak or awkward passive, see **G 10c** and **S 3b**.

A fourth transformation brings in the word *there* at the beginning of the sentence and postpones the subject:

| | VERB | SUBJECT |
|---|------|---------|
| There | is | hope. |
| There | was | no time. |
| There | were | few survivors. |

# G1d Modifiers                                    *gr*

**Recognize the modifiers that flesh out the basic patterns.**

The basic sentence patterns include only the parts needed for a complete English sentence. In actual sentences, we usually add **modifiers**—words that tell us more about the basic sentence parts. In a typical sentence, such additional words (or groups of words) develop, narrow, or otherwise modify the meaning of the basic sentence parts.

We divide modifiers into two main groups: The modifiers in the first group modify nouns. Those in the second group modify verbs, and sometimes other parts of a sentence:

(1) *Different kinds of modifiers may cluster around a noun.* All of the modifiers italicized in the following examples modify the noun *dog*:

> A *shaggy* dog barred my way.
> A *big, yellow* dog was chewing the rug.
> A *police* dog tracked me down.
> A dog *with droopy eyes* dozed in the sun.

Of these modifiers, the first three (*shaggy, big, yellow*) are true adjectives. (The others serve the same function as adjectives.) Adjectives answer questions like "Which one?" or "What kind?" They appear in typical adjective positions: "a *reasonable* price," "The price is *reasonable*," "a very *reasonable* price." Most adjectives fit in after words that show differences in *degree*: very *cold*, fairly *tall*, extremely *dangerous*. Most adjectives have distinctive forms for use in comparisons: *small—smaller—smallest; good—better—best; reasonable—more reasonable—most reasonable.* Suffixes that help us derive adjectives from other words are *-ic, -ish, -ive,* and *-ous*:

> *-ic:*   basic, tragic, allergic, synthetic
> *-ish:*  foolish, Spanish, lavish, squeamish
> *-ive:*  expensive, representative, normative
> *-ous:*  famous, enormous, anonymous

Other words or groups of words may modify a noun and serve the same function as an adjective. These include prepositional phrases—see (3) below. They also include verbal phrases—see **G 1f**.

(2) *Different kinds of modifiers may cluster around a verb.* All of the modifiers italicized in the following examples modify the verb *rang*:

> The bell rang *twice.*
> *Suddenly* the bell rang.
> The bell rang *loudly.*
> The bell rang *at intervals.*

Twice, *suddenly*, and *loudly* belong to a class of words called **adverbs**. Many of these show the *-ly* ending. Adverbs answer questions like "When?" "Where?" or "How?"

WHEN?    now, then, tomorrow, yesterday, immediately
WHERE?    there, upstairs, downtown, everywhere
HOW?    carefully, cautiously, silently

See **G 7a** for problems with adverb forms.

(3) *Prepositional phrases may serve the same function as either adjectives or adverbs.* Combinations introduced by *with, at, on,* and similar words may modify either nouns or other parts of a sentence:

The girl *from Chicago* disappeared.    (modifies noun)
The girl disappeared *from Chicago*.    (modifies verb)

---

**A CHECKLIST OF PREPOSITIONS**

The following words may all be used as prepositions. Many point out relationships in *time* or in *space*:

| | | | |
|---|---|---|---|
| about | behind | from | since |
| above | below | in | through |
| across | beneath | inside | to |
| after | beside | into | toward |
| against | between | like | under |
| along | beyond | near | until |
| among | by | of | up |
| around | despite | off | upon |
| as | during | on | with |
| at | except | outside | within |
| before | for | over | without |

The following *combinations* are also used as prepositions:

| | | |
|---|---|---|
| aside from | in spite of | on behalf of |
| as to | instead of | out of |
| as well as | in view of | regardless of |
| because of | on account of | |

23

*With, at, on,* and *from* are **prepositions**. They tie a noun (or equivalent) to the rest of the sentence. Other common prepositions are *about, by, during, in, of, through, to, under, until,* and *without.* A preposition plus the noun it introduces is a **prepositional phrase**. Remember that a prepositional phrase alone cannot make up a complete sentence:

FRAGMENT:   The travelers crossed the river. *On a raft.*
COMPLETE:   The travelers crossed the river *on a raft.*

## G1e   The Combined Sentence        *gr*

**Recognize the units that make up the larger combined sentence.**

Two or more statements may join in a larger combined sentence. When a short sentence becomes part of the larger whole, we call it a **clause**. A clause has its own subject and verb (unless it is a request, with the subject omitted or understood). The following sentences show different ways of joining one clause to another:

The climber slipped; *however,* the rope held.
The company had sent the bill, *but* the mail was slow.
Sue will notify us *if* her plans change.
We need a mechanic *who* knows this kind of car.

In the first two examples, the two clauses remain self-sufficient enough to stand by themselves. They could still be punctuated as complete separate sentences. We call such clauses **independent** clauses. In the last two examples, the second clause cannot stand by itself. Like a two-wheel trailer, it depends on something else. It is subordinated to the main clause. We call such clauses **dependent** clauses. A complete English sentence contains at least one independent clause.

Look at the different links we use in joining two or more clauses:

(1) *Clauses are still considered independent when they are joined by an adverbial connective.* **Adverbial connectives** are such words as *however, therefore, moreover, nevertheless,* and *besides.*

24

Notice the semicolon that is the typical punctuation with this type of connective. (The older term for this kind of connective is "conjunctive adverb.")

> The assembly passed the law; *however,* the governor vetoed it.
> The price of gas went up; *therefore,* we bought a smaller car.
> We warned them of the dangers; *nevertheless,* they continued.

Like adverbs, these connectives may change their position in the sentence:

> We warned them; they continued *nevertheless.*

(2) *Clauses remain independent when they are joined by a coordinator.* **Coordinating connectives** (coordinators, for short) are *and, but, so, for, yet, or,* and *nor.* The comma is the typical punctuation when a coordinator joins two clauses.

> Our team scored, *and* the crowd roared.
> Many are called, *but* few are chosen.
> I was badly prepared, *so* I failed the exam.

See **P 2b** and **P 2c** for punctuation of independent clauses.

(3) *A clause becomes a dependent clause when it is joined to the main clause by a subordinator.* **Subordinating connectives** (subordinators) are words like *if, when, while, as, unless, where, because, though, although,* and *whereas.* The kind of dependent clause that starts with a subordinator is called an **adverbial clause.** (It gives the same kind of information as many adverbs.) Either no punctuation at all or a comma separates the two clauses, depending on how essential the added clause is to the meaning of the whole sentence.

In each of the following examples, the added clause states an essential *if* or *when:*

NO COMMA:   Customers get a discount *if* they buy now.
               You will be arrested *unless* you pay the fine.
               Nobody knows you *when* you are down and out.

In each of the following examples, the first half of the combined sentence is true *regardless* of what is added:

COMMA:    We have a phone, *although* we are not in the phone book.
Sharks are fish, *whereas* whales are mammals.

With this type of connective, we can *reverse* the order of the two clauses:

*If* they buy now, customers get a discount.
*Although* we are not in the phone book, we have a phone.

Remember that a dependent clause alone cannot be a complete sentence:

FRAGMENT:    *Although* I have never tried it.
FRAGMENT:    *Whereas* coal was in plentiful supply.

---

See **P 2d** for punctuation of dependent clauses.

---

(4)   *A clause becomes a dependent clause when it is joined to the main clause by a relative pronoun.* **Relative pronouns** are *who* (*whom, whose*), *which*, and *that*. The clause that follows a relative pronoun is called a **relative clause**. Such clauses relate to one of the nouns in the main clause. They may either follow or interrupt the main clause:

The tickets went to people *who signed up early.*
The company shut down the reactor, *which had been built in 1972.*
A friend *who recognized me* called out my name.

Note that the relative pronouns *whom* and *that* are often left out:

The speaker [*whom*] *we had invited* failed to appear.
The support [*that*] *we received* was inadequate.

Remember that a relative clause alone cannot be a complete sentence:

FRAGMENT:    *Which* reminds me of another teacher.
FRAGMENT:    *Whose* disappearance was never explained.

---

See **P 2e** for punctuation of relative clauses.

---

---

## A CHECKLIST OF CONNECTIVES

| | |
|---|---|
| **ADVERBIAL CONNECTIVES:** | however, therefore, moreover, furthermore, nevertheless, besides, indeed, consequently, instead, in fact, otherwise |
| **COORDINATING CONNECTIVES:** | and, but, for, or, nor, yet, so |
| **SUBORDINATING CONNECTIVES:** | when, whenever, while, before, after, since, until, as, if, because, unless, provided, though, although, whereas; so that, no matter how, no matter what |
| **RELATIVE PRONOUNS:** | who, whom, whose; which, that |
| **SPECIAL CONNECTIVES:** | that, why, whether, how, where, who, what, whoever, whatever |

---

(5) *A special type of dependent clause is not joined to the main clause but rather replaces one of its nouns.* Such a clause-within-a-clause is called a **noun clause**. Noun clauses often start with words like *who, what, why, where,* and *how*:

| | |
|---|---|
| NOUN: | *The thief* returned my documents. |
| NOUN CLAUSE: | *Whoever stole my wallet* returned my documents. |
| NOUN: | She was excited by *the news.* |
| NOUN CLAUSE: | She was excited by *what she had heard.* |

*That,* frequently used as a relative pronoun, is also used to introduce a noun clause:

Osbert denied *that he had forged the check.*
*That Osbert forged the check* has not been proved.

Words like *who, what, where,* and *that* all have other uses. They make up a group of **special connectives** when they introduce noun clauses.

(6) *Remember that many of the connectives we use in combining sentences also have other uses.* Coordinators like *and, or,* and *but* may also join single words. They also join groups of words that do not have a subject and verb. We call such groups of words **phrases**:

WORDS: The villagers danced *and* sang.
PHRASES: We will look for you in the theater *or* at the exit.

Connectives like *for, before, after, since,* and *until* do double duty as prepositions:

COORDINATOR: We had no choice, *for* the lease had expired.
PREPOSITION: He needed a license *for* his pretzel stand.

SUBORDINATOR: We left *before* the movie reached its gory ending.
PREPOSITION: We left *before* the end of the movie.

SUBORDINATOR: The stranger pleaded with us *until* we relented.
PREPOSITION: She worked in the shop *until* dark.

# G1f   Appositives and Verbals   *gr*

**Recognize special sentence resources like appositives and verbals.**

We can greatly extend our sentence resources by putting familiar sentence parts to special uses. Many of the words we use do double duty. They serve more than one kind of purpose. Nouns and verbs, for instance, both have special uses:

(1) *Recognize nouns used as modifiers.* A noun alone often replaces an adjective that modifies another noun: a *group* effort, our new *track* coach, a special *sales* tax. But a noun may also come *after* another noun to modify that noun and bring added information into the sentence. We call such an added noun an **appositive**. The appositive may bring its own noun marker (*a, the, our*) along with it. It may in turn be modified by other material:

Her best friend, *a sophomore,* finished second.
The book was about Margaret Mead, *the world-famous anthropologist.*
Aunt Minnie, *a vigorous woman of fifty-five,* had come in to help. (Dorothy Canfield Fisher)

An appositive alone cannot be a complete sentence:

FRAGMENT: She was driving the same car. *An old station wagon.*
COMPLETE: She was driving the same car, *an old station wagon.*
COMPLETE: She was driving the same car. *It was an old station wagon.*

See **G 8e** on faulty appositives.

(2)  *Know the difference between verbs and verbals.* **Verbals** are parts of verbs or special forms of verbs, but they cannot by themselves be the complete verb of a sentence. For instance, "he *writing*" and "the letter *written*" are not complete sentences. We would have to add an auxiliary to turn each verbal into a complete verb: "He *was writing*"; "The letter *had been written.*"

Two kinds of verbals can take the place of a noun in a sentence. The first kind is the *to* form, or **infinitive.** The second is the *-ing* form, called a **verbal noun** (or gerund) when used instead of a noun. In the following examples, infinitives and verbal nouns serve as subjects or complements, taking the place of nouns:

| SUBJECT | VERB | COMPLETER |
|---|---|---|
| *Speeding* | causes | accidents. |
| He | refused | *to pay.* |
| Teachers | discourage | *cheating.* |

Though used instead of nouns, such verbals do keep important features of verbs. For instance, they are often followed by objects:

| Studying *grammar* | inspires | me. |
|---|---|---|
| Joan | refused | to pay *her dues.* |
| Courtesy | forbids | calling *a police officer* a cop. |

Two kinds of verbals can take the place of an adjective and serve as a modifier. The first kind is a form like *burning, falling, hiding* (**present participles**). The second kind is a form like *burnt, fallen,* and *hidden* (**past participles**):

The spectators fled the *burning* hall.
*Fallen* leaves make me feel sad.
She looked for *hidden* meanings.

Again, such verbals may carry along other material, making up a **verbal phrase**:

*Hiding in the cellar,* he heard the officers *searching the house.*
Nobody had found the papers *hidden in the attic.*

**29**

Infinitives have many other uses besides taking the place of nouns. For instance, we use them in combinations like the following. They then become part of extended verb phrases:

OBLIGATION:   We *ought to go.*
                    Aliens *had to register.*
FUTURE:         It *is going to rain.*
                    I was *about to call* you.

We also use infinitives to modify various other parts of a sentence:

We were looking for a place *to stay.*
The truck driver was ready *to leave.*
The thing *to do* is to stay calm.

Infinitives and other verbals alone cannot be complete sentences:

FRAGMENT:   We stopped at a gas station. *To make a phone call.*
COMPLETE:   We stopped at a gas station *to make a phone call.*

FRAGMENT:   I met Joan. *Walking alone.*
COMPLETE:   I met Joan, *walking alone.*
COMPLETE:   I met Joan. *She was walking alone.*

> See **G 7b** for dangling or misplaced verbals.

# EXERCISES

A. (G 1a, 1d) Test your ability to recognize four major *word classes,* or parts of speech. In each of the following sentences, one word has been italicized. What kind of word is it? After the number of the sentence, put the right abbreviation:

N   for noun
V   for verb (or part of the complete verb)
AJ  for adjective
AV  for adverb

1. These *coupons* came in the mail.
2. Our relatives lived on a *quiet* street.
3. The patient *forgot* the appointment.
4. My sister opened the letter *eagerly.*

5. She used a *small* computer in her business.
6. The earthquake had *weakened* the foundations.
7. Our meeting was a very *fortunate* coincidence.
8. He always sent me stamps for my *collection*.
9. Our guide will *explain* the procedure.
10. The tour buses *rarely* stop here anymore.
11. The winds were stronger at the *higher* elevations.
12. The *women* in the shop demanded higher pay.
13. The club may *organize* a trip to Utah.
14. The fishing season begins *tomorrow.*
15. We expected a more *reasonable* proposal.
16. The police should have *investigated* the incident.
17. The commission will *soon* finish its report.
18. The article described plans for a new *engine.*
19. *Complaints* had come in from many sources.
20. Our guides were used to extremely *cold* weather.

B. (G 1b-c) Test your ability to recognize basic *sentence patterns* and simple *transformations*. In each of the following sets, two sentences are very similar in their basic structure. They follow the same basic pattern, or else they have been adapted or transformed in the same way. The remaining sentence is different. Write the letter for the *different* sentence after the number of the set.

1. (a) Camels survive with little water.
   (b) Whales need air for their lungs.
   (c) Birds migrate in huge swarms.

2. (a) My parents were immigrants.
   (b) The newcomers became citizens.
   (c) The judge asked simple questions.

3. (a) Reports from the field arrived daily.
   (b) Take your complaints to the manager.
   (c) Report the incident in detail.

4. (a) Lenders charge customers interest.
   (b) Teachers ask students questions.
   (c) Reporters called his answers ridiculous.

5. (a) Paper is made from wood pulp.
   (b) The documents had been hidden in a suitcase.
   (c) The tenants will pay by the month.

6. (a) The school board has banned our humor magazine.
   (b) Malnutrition had become a national menace.
   (c) Bromo-Seltzer will cure that headache.

7. (a) The father gave the pair his blessing.
   (b) The Russian authorities denied his wife a passport.
   (c) Her actions kept the voters happy.

8. (a) Corruption was common in high places.
   (b) The apartment was searched by the police.
   (c) His sister looked different without her wig.

9. (a) Leonard lent strangers money.
   (b) The voters elected the actor governor.
   (c) My parents named their child Miranda.

10. (a) Charitable people give generously to charities.
    (b) Please contribute freely to our special fund.
    (c) My father contributed reluctantly to the heart fund.

C. (G 1e) Test your ability to recognize different ways of *combining sentences* in a larger whole. In each of the following sets, two of the combined sentences are very similar in the way they have been put together. They use the same kind of connective. The third combined sentence is different. Write the letter for the *different* sentence after the number of the set.

1. (a) They bought bottled water when the well ran dry.
   (b) She denied the charges that the paper had printed.
   (c) We used kerosene lamps before electricity became available.

2. (a) Robert was a realist, whereas his friends were dreamers.
   (b) Clara remained a candidate, although the interview had been a disappointment.
   (c) The device was an infrared camera, which her roommate had used in experiments.

3. (a) I think; therefore, I am.
   (b) I talk, but my friends never listen.
   (c) She objected, for his arguments were silly.

4. (a) A man who kicks his dog will beat his child.
   (b) You can't tell by the looks of a cat how far it can jump.
   (c) Cars that use much gasoline drain our resources.

5. (a) He can count to twenty after he takes his shoes off.
   (b) If you save one person from hunger, you work a miracle.
   (c) When the cat leaves the house, the mice have a ball.

6. (a) Children love excitement, but they also need stability.
   (b) She had a perfect alibi, which made things easy for her lawyer.
   (c) Sewage pollutes the water, and exhaust fumes poison the air.

7. (a) He forgot where he had hidden the money.
   (b) She owned the car that had stalled in the driveway.
   (c) We had found a mechanic who worked on Sundays.

8. (a) If she is there when I come home from work, I'll call you.
   (b) If you are hungry, we should meet at a place where we can eat.
   (c) When the session ended, they agreed on times when they would meet again.

9. (a) The guide explained how the recorders worked.
   (b) Mary asked why our friends had left.
   (c) Reporters questioned the suspect who had been released.
10. (a) You should repair the awning, or it will collapse.
    (b) We may take the train, though the fares have gone up.
    (c) They have received an inheritance, so their situation has improved.

D. (G 1e) In the following *sentence-combining* exercise, join each pair of short statements in a larger combined sentence. Of the connectives given as choices, use the one that seems to fit best. Be prepared to explain or defend your choices.

(Choose one: *therefore, however, moreover, nevertheless, besides, indeed, in fact.* Use a semicolon.)

1. Roads and freeways were deteriorating.
   The state budget included little money for maintenance.

2. The university was a huge impersonal institution.
   New students often felt isolated.

3. People no longer want to be like everyone else.
   Many Americans are rediscovering their ethnic roots.

(Choose one: *and, but, so, for, yet, or.* Use a comma.)

4. Students have lost interest in political issues.
   Attendance at political rallies is low.

5. Students studied hard.
   Competition for grades was keen.

6. Some critics protest against our overreliance on tests.
   Students take more tests every year.

(Choose one: *if, when, while, as, unless, where, because.* Use no comma.)

7. Unions complain.
   Imported goods take over a market.

8. The accused will go to jail.
   A higher court overturns the conviction.

9. Our energy worries would be over.
   Solar energy could be harnessed on a large scale.

(Choose one: *although, though, whereas.* Use a comma.)

10. For a time, fantasy books topped the bestseller list.
    Today readers buy diet books and job-seeking manuals.

E. (G 1d, 1f) The following *sentence-building* exercise tests your ability to recognize and use a variety of familiar building blocks for the English sentence.

**33**

1. Look at the way *adjectives and adverbs* add information to the two sample sentences. Fill in similar modifiers in the blank spaces left in the next two sentences.

   a. The *handsome* cowboy *slowly* mounted his *magnificent* horse.
   b. The *tired* detective *again* questioned the *uncooperative* suspect.
   c. The _____ gentleman _____ proposed to the _____ lady.
   d. The _____ traveler _____ asked the _____ guide _____ questions.

2. Look at the way *prepositional phrases* add information to the two sample sentences. Fill in similar modifiers in the blank spaces left in the next two sentences.

   a. The girl *in the Cadillac* approached the locked gate *at high speed.*
   b. *At the other end of the swamp,* Leroi was wrestling *with a huge alligator.*
   c. The stranger _____ had hidden the suitcase _____.
   d. _____, the campers were sitting _____.

3. Look at the way *appositives* add information to the two sample sentences. Fill in similar modifiers in the blank spaces left in the next two sentences.

   a. Godzilla, *the fire-breathing reptile,* was fighting two giant caterpillars.
   b. Clark Gable, *an unforgettable screen star,* played in *Gone with the Wind, a great but controversial movie.*
   c. Marilyn Monroe, _____, experienced both success and failure in Hollywood, _____.
   d. Tarzan, _____, travels through the forest with Cheetah, _____.

4. Look at the way *verbal phrases* add information to the two sample sentences. Fill in similar modifiers in the blank spaces left in the next two sentences.

   a. The man *holding the gun* had stopped, *taking careful aim* at the animal.
   b. *Fighting the storm,* the little boat, *lifted by each wave,* plowed on.
   c. The fans _____ mobbed the rock star, _____.
   d. _____, the woman, _____, waved to her audience.

# G2 GRAMMAR AND USAGE

**Use the kind of English that is right for serious writing.**

The language that educated adults use in serious discussion and in writing differs from the language they use in casual talk. Students learn early that often they should say "is not" rather than "ain't," "can hardly wait" rather than "can't hardly wait," and "this kind of car" rather than "these kind of cars." Differences such as these are differences in **usage**. The study of usage investigates choices among alternative words, word forms, and constructions. Effective writers have learned to make the choices that will prove acceptable to their readers.

## G2a   Standard and Nonstandard                    *NS*

**Use standard English in all your written work.**

**Standard** English is the language of education, business, journalism, and government. You will use it in your written work except when you record or deliberately imitate **nonstandard** speech. Historically, nonstandard speech has often been associated with a way of life that required little formal schooling or with jobs that required little reading of instructions and writing of reports. Speakers of nonstandard English often had few dealings with teachers, lawyers, journalists, office workers, and others whose work kept them in daily contact with books, records, forms, memos, notes, and other uses of the written word.

The chart below provides an overview of familiar forms and constructions of nonstandard English.

Nonstandard English is for many people the natural speech of home, neighborhood, or job. However, standard English is

| NONSTANDARD | |
|---|---|
| **VERB FORMS:** | he *don't*, you *was*, I *says* <br> *knowed, growed, brang* <br> I *seen* him, had *went*, has *wrote* |
| **PRONOUN FORMS:** | *hisself, theirself* <br> *this here* book, *that there* car <br> *them* boys, *them* barrels |
| **CONNECTIVES:** | *without* you pay the rent <br> *on account of* he was sick <br> *being as* they missed the plane |
| **DOUBLE NEGATIVES:** | we *don't* have *no* time <br> it *never* hurt *no* one <br> *wasn't nobody* there |

essential to success in school and office. In any dealings with public officials, insurance agents, social workers, or business people of all kinds, the person who does not have an adequate command of standard English is already at a disadvantage.

Many of the features of nonstandard speech stand out and seem clearly out of place in writing. Some expressions are on the borderline between nonstandard and standard. In your writing, however, a simple principle applies: *When in doubt, be safe.* Readers who consider you half educated because you use *irregardless* will seldom give you a chance to prove them wrong.

*Note*: See the Glossary of Usage for items like the following:

| | |
|---|---|
| a/an | hadn't ought to |
| as | irregardless |
| being as | learn/teach |
| couple of | off of |
| double comparative | used to could |
| double negative | without |

# G 2b   Formal and Informal                               *inf*

**Use different kinds of standard English for different occasions.**

We use **informal** English in casual conversation, but also in writing designed to sound chatty or familiar. We find **formal** English in books on serious subjects and articles in serious magazines. We hear relatively formal English in lectures, speeches, and discussions.

In *informal* English, our sentences often keep some of the loose, improvised quality of speech. We may start one pattern and then shift to another in midsentence. We may rethink what we are saying while we are saying it. In *formal* English, grammatical relationships in a sentence are carefully and accurately worked out. Predicates logically fit their subjects. Modifiers are clearly related to what they modify. The advice given in this chapter is designed to help you write formal English—English appropriate for serious writing, but not so extremely formal as to become stilted or affected.

Here are some features of informal English:

| INFORMAL | |
|---|---|
| **CONTRACTIONS:** | *don't, doesn't, isn't, won't, can't; I'm, you've, they're* |
| **CONVERSATIONAL TAGS:** | *well, . . . ; why, . . . ; now, . . .* |
| **PRONOUN FORMS:** | it's *me*, that's *him*<br>*who* did you invite |
| **PRONOUN REFERENCE:** | everybody took *theirs*; somebody left *their* gloves |
| **INTENSIFIERS:** | *so* glad, *such* a surprise<br>*real* miserable, *awful* fast |

*Note*: See the Glossary of Usage for the following items:

| | |
|---|---|
| apt/liable | like I said |
| between/among | most everybody |
| blame on | possessives with verbal nouns |
| can and may | preposition at the end of a sentence |
| cannot help but | providing |
| couple of | reason is because |
| different than | split infinitives |
| due to | these kind |
| each other/one another | used to/didn't use to |
| it's me | where at |
| less/fewer | you with indefinite reference |

For a discussion of formal and informal words, see **D 3.**

# EXERCISE

In each of the following pairs, which is the right choice for *serious written English*? Put the letter for the right choice after the number of the pair.

1. (a) They wanted results regardless of the cost.
   (b) They wanted results irregardless of the cost.

2. (a) We have never had no doubts about him.
   (b) We have never had any doubts about him.

3. (a) She was bitter on account of her complaint had been ignored.
   (b) She was bitter because her complaint had been ignored.

4. (a) My cousin had wrote an angry letter to the mayor.
   (b) My cousin had written an angry letter to the mayor.

5. (a) He arrived early, as he had promised.
   (b) He arrived early, like he had promised.

6. (a) My sister disapproves of this kind of book.
   (b) My sister disapproves of these kind of books.

7. (a) The letter had fallen off the desk.
   (b) The letter had fallen off of the desk.

8. (a) They had always been real kind to strangers.
   (b) They had always been really kind to strangers.

9. (a) The game was canceled because of the rain.
   (b) The game was canceled due to the rain.

10. (a) The visitors had created a ugly scene.
    (b) The visitors had created an ugly scene.

11. (a) Almost everybody in the class knew the play.
    (b) Most everybody in the class knew the play.

12. (a) Nobody comes to see them no more.
    (b) Nobody comes to see them anymore.

13. (a) It was they who first settled the valley.
    (b) It was them who first settled the valley.

14. (a) My cousins always took good care of theirself.
    (b) My cousins always took good care of themselves.

15. (a) We should have gone straight to the sheriff.
    (b) We should have went straight to the sheriff.

# G3   AGREEMENT                  *agr*

**Make the subject and its verb agree in number.**

Most nouns and pronouns have one form for one of a kind (**singular**), another form for more than one (**plural**). Often verbs also offer us two choices: *is/are, was/were, has/have, asks/ask.* When subject and verb are both either singular or plural, they are said to agree in number. To make the verb agree with its subject, we choose the matching form:

| SINGULAR | PLURAL |
|---|---|
| The boy *goes* home. | The boys *go* home. |
| Love *makes* fools. | Fools *make* love. |
| My friend *was* pleased. | My friends *were* pleased. |

Note that for nouns the *-s* ending is a plural signal: boy*s*, fool*s*, car*s*, tree*s*, ticket*s*, house*s*, promotion*s*. But with verbs, the *-s* ending is a signal for singular. We use it when we talk about one single thing or person (**third person singular**), with action now (**present tense**):

| | | |
|---|---|---|
| He talk*s*. | She write*s*. | It bark*s*. |
| They talk. | They write. | They bark. |

See **G 5e** for agreement of a pronoun with its antecedent.

# G 3a  Irregular Plurals                                        *agr*

**Know which nouns borrowed from other languages have kept irregular plurals.**

Most English nouns use the familiar *-s* plural (car*s*, buildings, trees, books, petition*s*). But some words borrowed from Greek and Latin have irregular plural forms:

| SINGULAR | PLURAL | SINGULAR | PLURAL |
|---|---|---|---|
| crisis | crises | criterion | criteria |
| thesis | theses | phenomenon | phenomena |
| analysis | analyses | medium | media |
| hypothesis | hypotheses | stimulus | stimuli |
| curriculum | curricula | | |

Note the following:

(1) *Some anglicized plurals are becoming acceptable.* Most people use "ind*exes*" rather than "ind*ices*," "formul*as*" rather than "formul*ae*." Often the earlier irregular plural survives in a special or technical use: the *antennae* of insects.

**39**

(2)  *Use* data *as a plural to be safe.* "Data" are items of information, and "bacteria" are very small organisms. (The singular forms of these two words—*datum* and *bacterium*—are rarely used, with the result that *data* now often occurs as a singular.)

(3)  *A few foreign words have separate forms for the two sexes* (**gender**). A boy who graduates from college becomes an "alumn*us*," a girl an "alumn*a*." Several male graduates are "alumn*i*," several female graduates "alumn*ae*."

## G 3b  Confusing Singulars and Plurals                    *agr*

**Know how to handle expressions not clearly either singular or plural.**

Agreement problems may result when form points one way and meaning the other. Remember:

(1)  Each, neither, either, *and* everybody *or* everyone (***indefinite pronouns***) *are singular.* They seem to point to more than one person or thing. But they are treated as singulars in formal written English:

SINGULAR:    Each of the students *is* going to receive a diploma.
SINGULAR:    Either of the plans *sounds* all right.
SINGULAR:    Everybody *approves* of your decision.

(2)  *A* number of *is treated as a plural if it means "several" or "many"*:

PLURAL:    A number of people *were* standing in the hallway.

(3)  *Expressions showing the whole amount may be treated as singulars even when they seem plural in form.* They are singular if the sentence is concerned with the sum or total rather than with the individual units:

In those days two dollars *was* much money.

It is the most imperative social truth of our age that about one third of the world is rich and two thirds of the world *is* poor.—C. P. Snow, "On Magnanimity," *Harper's*

(4) *Words like* audience, committee, family, group, jury, police, *and* team *may be used as singular or plural.* We use these **collective nouns** as singulars when we are thinking of the group as a whole. We sometimes use them as plurals when we are thinking of the individual members of the group:

SINGULAR:  The family *is* a crucial social unit.
PLURAL:    The family *were* seated around the dinner table.

(5) *Words ending in -ics look like plurals but are often singular.* Singular are *aeronautics, mathematics, physics,* and similar names for a branch of knowledge or field of study:

SINGULAR:  Mathematics *is* an indispensable tool of modern science.

Other words ending in -*ics* are singular in some senses and plural in others. We say "Statistics *doesn't* appeal to me" when speaking of the *science* of statistics. We say "Statistics *don't* convince me" when speaking of statistical *data*.

# G 3c  Compound Subjects                                    *agr*

**Check for agreement in clauses that contain more than one subject.**

A word like *and* or *or* may join several words to serve together as subjects for the same verb. After such a **compound subject**, the verb may be plural even if each of the subjects is singular when taken by itself:

PLURAL:  The heat and the humidity *were* unbearable.
PLURAL:  Tom and Sue *don't* smoke.
PLURAL:  Hiking and canoeing *are* fun.

*And* actually adds one possible subject to another. *Or* merely gives us a choice between two possible subjects (each of which may be singular). We say "Both his father and his mother *are* to blame" but "Either his father or his mother *is* to blame."
Note some special difficulties:

(1) As well as, together with, *and* in addition to *do not add one subject to another.* They merely show that what is said about the subject applies also to other things or persons:

SINGULAR:     Aunt Sue, together with her children, *is* leaving town.
SINGULAR:     The money, as well as some documents, *has* disappeared.

(2)   *Two nouns joined by* and *may be merely different parts of the description of a single thing or person*:

Pork and beans *is* one of my favorite dishes.
My closest friend and associate *was* a cocker spaniel.

(3)   *In some sentences, an* or, *an* either . . . or, *or a* neither . . . nor *gives the reader a choice between a singular subject and a plural one*. Make the verb of such a sentence agree with the subject closer to it:

Either laziness or excessive social obligations *have kept* him from his work.

# G3d   Blind Agreement                                          *agr*

**Do not make the verb agree with a word that stands in front of it but is not its subject.**

Avoid **blind agreement**. Check especially for *a plural noun* that comes between a singular subject and its verb. Disregard anything that comes in like a wedge between subject and verb:

*An ad* [in these small local papers] *produces* results.

Beware of blind agreement whenever the subject of a sentence is one thing singled out among several, one quality shared by several members of a group, or one action affecting different things or persons:

SINGULAR:     Only *one* of my friends *was* ready in time.
              (not "*were* ready")
SINGULAR:     The *usefulness* of these remedies *has been* questioned.
              (not "*have been* questioned")
SINGULAR:     Understanding the opponent's motives *is* important.
              (not "*are* important")

When for some reason *the subject follows the verb*, do not make the verb agree with a stray noun that stands in front of it:

PLURAL:     Inside the yellowed envelope *were* several large bills.
            (What was inside? *Bills* were inside.)

# G3e  Agreement After *There* and *It*  *agr*

**Check for agreement in sentences starting with "there is," "there are," "it is," and the like.**

After *there*, the verb agrees with the **postponed subject**—with whatever is "there":

SINGULAR:   There *was* much *work* to be done.
PLURAL:   There *were* scattered *rumblings* of dissent.

In formal usage, the plural verb is required even when followed by a compound subject of which each part is singular:

There *were* a bed and a chair for each patient.

On the crown of the hill, there *are* a miniature plaza, miniature cathedral, and miniature governor's palace.—Arnold J. Toynbee, "The Mayan Mystery," *Atlantic*

*It* is a pronoun and can function as the subject. After *it*, the verb is *always* singular:

It *is* their last chance.
It *was* the Joneses.

# G3f  Agreement After *Who, Which,* and *That*  *agr*

**Check for agreement problems caused by relationships among several clauses.**

*Who, which,* and *that* often serve as subjects in **adjective clauses**—that is, dependent clauses that modify a noun or pronoun. The verb following the *who, which,* or *that* agrees with the *word being modified*:

SINGULAR:   I hate a person who *stares* at me.

PLURAL:   I hate people who *stare* at me.

Watch for agreement in combinations like "one of those who *know*" and "one of those who *believe*." Look at the contrast in the following pair:

PLURAL:          Jean is one of *those girls who go* to classes after work.
                 (Many girls go to classes—and Jean is one of them.)

SINGULAR:        Jean is *the only one* of those girls *who goes* to classes after work.
                 (One girl goes to classes—the others don't.)

## G3g  Logical Agreement                                                    *agr*

**Where meaning requires it, observe agreement in other sentence elements in addition to verbs.**

Often you have to carry through agreement in number from the subject not only to the verb but also to the remainder of the sentence:

ILLOGICAL:       Average newspaper *readers* go through their whole *life* knowing
                 a little about everything but nothing well.
REVISED:         Average newspaper *readers* go through their whole *lives* knowing
                 a little about everything but nothing well.

ILLOGICAL:       My more studious *friends* are wise like *an owl.*
REVISED:         My more studious *friends* are wise like *owls.*

See the Glossary of Usage for *these kind.*

# EXERCISES

A. In each of the following sentences, solve an *agreement problem* by changing a single word—usually the verb or first auxiliary. Write the changed form of the word after the number of the sentence.

1. Each of these activities are equally exciting.
2. Much work, skill, and knowledge is involved in assembling a successful exhibit.
3. The description of his appearance and manners hint at his hidden emotions.
4. For these people, the years spent in the armed forces has been a waste of time.
5. My sister and older brother belongs to my mother's church.
6. As one walks farther up the street, the style of the buildings change.
7. The responsibilities of the future lies in our hands.

8. In the display window, there is two old sewing machines and a tailor's dummy dressed in a faded white dress.
9. The deep thinkers among the students attempt to solve all the world's problems by the use of their powerful mind.
10. The weak chemical bonds among oxygen atoms in ozone allows the molecules to break apart.
11. Many crime shows make the viewers feel tough by association and boosts their egos.
12. Youth or good health alone are not enough to assure someone's happiness.
13. There are a daily diet of banal news stories designed to entertain the viewers.
14. The qualifications for a sales representative is much different from those for a manager.
15. That kind of television drama, with nonstop action, fast dialogue, and no message, bore me to tears.
16. I am not one of those who believes in indiscriminate force to restore law and order.
17. A sharp increase in thefts are occurring on the beaches and in the campgrounds of this area.
18. The general attitude of the people I asked were very evasive.
19. The political science courses one takes in college often shows that the nation's great thinkers were people with human failings.
20. One of the first situations that challenge the reader's stereotypes arise as Elisa is working at a drive-in restaurant.

B. Choose the right forms, paying special attention to common sources of *faulty agreement.* Put the letter of the right form after the number of the sentence.

1. In many of my classes, the attitude of the students *(a) was / (b) were* very poor.
2. The benefits that the city has derived from its new industries *(a) is / (b) are* negligible.
3. Cooking, as well as sewing or cleaning, *(a) has / (b) have* always bored me.
4. I was raised in a home where smoking and excessive drinking *(a) was / (b) were* not permitted.
5. Getting along with one's neighbors *(a) is / (b) are* not always easy.
6. The qualities that we look for in a spouse *(a) is / (b) are* determined in part by our family backgrounds.
7. The World's Fair dazzled everyone who *(a) was / (b) were* there.
8. The ability to talk about something other than money and children *(a) is / (b) are* important if a marriage is to last.
9. Colleges have to make provision for students who are below average academically but who nevertheless *(a) wants / (b) want* a college education.
10. Using words like *dichotomy* and *schizophrenia* *(a) is / (b) are* no sign of superior intelligence.

**45**

11. He was one of those hosts who *(a) makes / (b) make* no attempt to entertain the guests.
12. His father felt that five dollars *(a) was / (b) were* more than sufficient as a monthly allowance.
13. According to the judge, neither of the witnesses *(a) was / (b) were* guilty of perjury.
14. We soon realized that our supply of food and fuel *(a) was / (b) were* dangerously low.
15. Weapons like the bow and arrow, the spear, or the knife *(a) was / (b) were* among the first major human inventions.

C. In a college dictionary, look up the plural forms of the following nouns: *antenna, appendix, beau, cactus, cello, cherub, nucleus, oasis, stigma, vertebra.* Check whether the following forms are singular or plural or both: *addenda, agenda, apparatus, candelabra, deer, dice, Saturnalia, series, species, strata.*

# G4  VERB FORMS

**Use verb forms appropriate to serious written English.**

Some of the most noticeable differences between nonstandard and standard English are differences in the forms of verbs. Make sure your writing is free of nonstandard forms like the following:

NONSTANDARD:     A big tree *grow* in our garden.
STANDARD:     A big tree *grows* in our garden.

NONSTANDARD:     Many pioneer families *perish* in the desert.
STANDARD:     Many pioneer families *perished* in the desert.

NONSTANDARD:     Richard *had went* to see a friend.
STANDARD:     Richard *had gone* to see a friend.

# G4a  Regular Verbs        *vb*

**Use the standard forms of regular verbs.**

The most important verb forms are those traditionally grouped together to form the system of tenses. The **tenses** of a verb are forms that show different relationships of events in time:

| ACTIVE VERBS | | |
|---|---|---|
| | **NORMAL** | **PROGRESSIVE** |
| *Present* | I ask, he (she) asks | I am asking |
| *Past* | I asked | I was asking |
| *Future* | I shall (will) ask | I shall be asking |
| *Perfect* | I have asked | I have been asking |
| *Past Perfect* | I had asked | I had been asking |
| *Future Perfect* | I shall (will) have asked | I shall have been asking |

| PASSIVE VERBS | | |
|---|---|---|
| *Present* | I am asked | I am being asked |
| *Past* | I was asked | I was being asked |
| *Future* | I shall (will) be asked | ——— |
| *Perfect* | I have been asked | ——— |
| *Past Perfect* | I had been asked | ——— |
| *Future Perfect* | I shall (will) have been asked | ——— |

In proofreading your writing, look for the following especially:

(1) *Distinguish between present and past.* Most English verbs, the **regular** verbs, have two basic forms. The first form is the plain form of the verb (*consent, smoke, depart, investigate, organize*). Standing by itself, it can form the **present tense**. This "simple present" may point to something happening now, something done regularly or habitually, or something about to happen in the immediate future:

PRESENT:  We *consent.*
PRESENT:  I *exercise* every day.
PRESENT:  They *depart* tonight.

The second basic form of a verb can stand by itself as the **past tense**. It shows that an action took place in the past and came to an end in the past. To form this "simple past," regular verbs add -*ed* or -*d* to the plain form:

PAST:   He *consented.*
PAST:   We *asked* him.
PAST:   They *investigated* him thoroughly.

(2)   *Use the special* -s *form for the third person singular of the present tense.* The "first person" is the person speaking: *I* or *we.* The "second person" is the person spoken to: *you.* The "third person" is a third party (or parties) that we are speaking about: *he, she, it, they.* Make sure you use the special -*s* ending when talking about one *single* person or thing, with action now:

THIRD PERSON:   My uncle *likes* you. (*He* likes you.)
THIRD PERSON:   Marcia *works* downtown. (*She* works there.)
THIRD PERSON:   Inflation *continues.* (*It* continues.)

(3)   *Know the forms that require an auxiliary (or helping verb) to be complete.* The plain form plus -*ing* makes up the present participle. This form is used in the various tenses of the **progressive** construction. The progressive construction normally shows an action or event in progress, still going on:

PROGRESSIVE:   We *are considering* your request.
PROGRESSIVE:   Her cousin *was painting* the house.

Regular verbs make the -*ed* form do double duty as a verbal (past participle) combining with the various forms of *have* to make up the **perfect tenses**. The present perfect describes something that may have happened in the fairly recent past and that has a bearing on the present: "They *have* already *left.*" The past perfect describes something that had already happened when *other* events in the past took place: "They *had* already *left*" when we arrived."

See **G 10a** for sequence of tenses and shifts in tense.

# G4b Irregular Verbs *vb*

**Know the standard forms of irregular verbs.**

**Irregular** verbs often have not two but three basic forms. The simple past is often different from the past participle: *run—ran—run; know—knew—known; go—went—gone.* Pay special attention to verbs whose basic forms are confusing in spelling or in sound. The chart on page 50 contains groups of irregular verbs. (Some regular verbs are included because they have irregular forms in nonstandard English.) Study one of the groups at a time.

Remember the following points:

(1) *Use the right past tense of irregular verbs.* Use the right forms in sentences like the following:

STANDARD: The wind *blew* all night.
We spent all day but *caught* few fish.
We *knew* them when we lived in Texas.

(2) *Use the right forms after forms of* have *and* be. The third of the three listed forms is the one used after *have (has, had).* It is the form for the perfect tenses:

STANDARD: Our neighbors *had gone* to church.
Your sister *has* already *eaten.*
We *should have taken* your advice.
She *had* already *written* to the manager.

The same form (past participle) is used in all passive verbs after a form of *be (am, are, is, was, were, has been,* and so on):

STANDARD: The fish *is frozen* and shipped by plane.
The bicycle *was stolen* during the night.
The bolt *had been worn* out.

(3) *Sometimes we have a choice of two acceptable forms.* In the following examples, either choice would be right:

They gracefully *dived* (or *dove*) into the pool.
She *dreamed* (or *dreamt*) of a vacation in the sun.
He *lighted* (or *lit*) his cigarette.
Your prediction *has proved* (or *has proven*) wrong.

|         | **PRESENT** | **PAST** | **PERFECT** |
|---------|-------------|----------|-------------|
| *Group 1* | begin  | began   | have begun |
|         | bend   | bent    | have bent |
|         | blow   | blew    | have blown |
|         | break  | broke   | have broken |
|         | bring  | brought | have brought |
|         | burst  | burst   | have burst |
|         | buy    | bought  | have bought |
|         | catch  | caught  | have caught |
|         | choose | chose   | have chosen |
|         | come   | came    | have come |
| *Group 2* | dig    | dug     | have dug |
|         | do     | did     | have done |
|         | drag   | dragged | have dragged |
|         | draw   | drew    | have drawn |
|         | drink  | drank   | have drunk |
|         | drive  | drove   | have driven |
|         | drown  | drowned | have drowned |
|         | eat    | ate     | have eaten |
|         | fall   | fell    | have fallen |
|         | fly    | flew    | have flown |
| *Group 3* | freeze | froze   | have frozen |
|         | get    | got     | have gotten (got) |
|         | go     | went    | have gone |
|         | grow   | grew    | have grown |
|         | know   | knew    | have known |
|         | prove  | proved  | have proved (proven) |
|         | ride   | rode    | have ridden |
|         | run    | ran     | have run |
|         | say    | said    | have said |
|         | see    | saw     | have seen |
| *Group 4* | sing   | sang    | have sung |
|         | speak  | spoke   | have spoken |
|         | steal  | stole   | have stolen |
|         | swim   | swam    | have swum |
|         | swing  | swung   | have swung |
|         | take   | took    | have taken |
|         | tear   | tore    | have torn |
|         | throw  | threw   | have thrown |
|         | wear   | wore    | have worn |
|         | write  | wrote   | have written |

The ship *sank* (or *sunk*) within minutes.
Business *thrived* (or *throve*) as never before.
The sleepers *waked* (or *woke*) refreshed.

*Note*: Sometimes we have two different forms with *different meanings*: "The picture was *hung*" but "The prisoner *was hanged*." "The sun *shone*" but "I *shined* my shoes."

# G4c   *Lie, Sit,* and *Rise*                                   *vb*

**Know the standard forms of *lie, sit,* and *rise*.**

Some verbs have doubles just different enough to be confusing:

(1)  *Lie—lay—lain* shows somebody or something situated somewhere. The same basic forms are used in the combination *lie down*:

PRESENT:   On hot days, the animals *lie* in the shade.
PAST:       A letter *lay* on the floor.
PERFECT:   They *have lain* down.

*Lay—laid—laid* shows that somebody is placing something somewhere. It is followed by an object. Use it when you can substitute *place* or *put*:

I wish I *could lay* my hands on him.
The weary travelers *laid down* their burdens.
You *should have laid aside* some money for emergencies.

(2)  *Sit—sat—sat* shows that someone is seated. *Sit down* follows the same scheme:

Though he told me that he seldom *sat* while at work, he *has sat* for an hour exactly where he *sat down* when he looked for a place to *sit*.

*Set—set—set*, one of the few verbs with only one basic form, belongs with *lay* as a possible substitute for *place* or *put*. You, yourself, *sit*, or *sit down*; you *set*, or *set down*, something else:

When you *have set* the alarm, *set* it down by the cot I *set* up.

(3) *Rise—rose—risen* means "get up" or "go up." *Raise—raised—raised* refers to lifting something or *making* it go up:

Since you *rose* this morning, the tax rate *has risen* ten cents.
Though they are always *raising* prices, they have not *raised* the salaries of the employees.

# EXERCISES

A. Test your knowledge of *regular and irregular verbs*. What form of the word in parentheses would be right for the blank space in each of the following sentences? Put the right form after the number of the sentence. (Use a single word each time.)

1. (steal)        Several sticks of dynamite had been _____ from the shed.
2. (throw)        We spotted the swimmer and _____ her a lifeline.
3. (tear)         Someone had _____ open the envelope.
4. (go)           He might have _____ in someone else's car.
5. (choose)       Last year, the party _____ a new leader.
6. (know)         Without the ad, she would not have _____ about the job.
7. (drive)        The car has been _____ too fast and too carelessly.
8. (see)          Several years ago, we _____ a road company production of *Hair.*
9. (break)        Her cabin had been _____ into several times.
10. (grow)        Everything had _____ well in the moist climate.
11. (develop)     Our friendship changed and _____ over the years.
12. (write)       She would have _____ if she were planning to join us.
13. (know)        When we came home, she already _____ what had happened.
14. (choose)      Our candidate has not yet _____ a running mate.
15. (take)        Someone has _____ the papers from the file.
16. (investigate) Last year, a grand jury _____ their dealings.
17. (speak)       You should have _____ to the manager.
18. (drown)       Several vacationers have _____ in the lake.
19. (ride)        You never should have _____ in a stranger's car.
20. (wear)        Coats like these are _____ by construction workers in Alaska.

B. Choose the *right verb forms* for formal written English. Put the numbers for the right forms after the number of each sentence.

1. If a teacher *(1) lays / (2) lies* a hand on an unruly student, he or she is likely to be sued by the student's parents.

2. In discussions touching on religious issues, many perplexing questions can be *(3) raised / (4) risen.*
3. After the class *(5) sat / (6) set* down, the teacher wanted to know who had *(7) wrote / (8) written* "The Student's Lament."
4. The picture showed two elderly gentlemen *(9) setting / (10) sitting* at a table and playing chess.
5. While my cousins *(11) swam / (12) swum* in the clear, cold water, I *(13) sat / (14) set* in the canoe watching them.
6. While *(15) setting / (16) sitting* up a new filing system, we must have *(17) mislaid / (18) mislain* your letter.
7. The report has been *(19) laying / (20) lying* on her desk all summer; at least it *(21) lay / (22) laid* there last week.
8. When I *(23) saw / (24) seen* the deserted entrance, I *(25) knew / (26) knowed* that the performance had already *(27) began / (28) begun.*
9. The park department finally *(29) sat up / (30) set up* benches for visitors who might want to *(31) set down / (32) sit down.*
10. Satisfied with the conditions *(33) sat / (34) set* by the negotiators, the rebels *(35) laid down / (36) lay down* their arms.

# G5 PRONOUN REFERENCE                    *ref*

**To make a pronoun stand for the right noun, place the right pronoun in the right position.**

Pronouns often take the place of something mentioned earlier. When you use a pronoun like *he, it,* or *this,* it should be clear who or what *he, it,* or *this* is. A pronoun has to refer clearly to its **antecedent**, the thing or person that "went before."

# G5a Ambiguous Reference               *ref*

**Do not let a pronoun point to more than one possible antecedent.**

Look at the use of *he* and *him* in the following example: "Jim was friendly to my brother because *he* wanted *him* to be *his* best man." Who was getting married, and who was going to be best man? The sentence is **ambiguous**; it confuses the reader because of an unintended double meaning. Rearrange the material in such a sentence:

53

AMBIGUOUS: After Mother brought Sue back, we took pictures of *her*.
CLEAR: We took pictures of *Sue* after Mother brought *her* back.
CLEAR: We took pictures of *Mother* after *she* brought Sue back.

If a *they* follows two plural nouns, you can sometimes avoid ambiguity by *making one of them singular*. (Similarly, one of two singular nouns might be changed into a plural.)

AMBIGUOUS: *Students* like *science teachers* because *they* are realistic and practical.
CLEAR: A *student* usually likes *science teachers* because *they* are realistic and practical.
(*They* can no longer be mistakenly referred to *students*.)

*Note*: The farther removed a pronoun is from its antecedent, the greater the danger of ambiguous reference. Do not make a reader go back through several sentences in a paragraph to check what *he, this,* or *they* stands for.

## G5b   Reference to Modifiers                    *ref*

**Make pronouns refer to one of the basic parts of a sentence rather than to a modifier.**

The following sentence would sound absurd: "During the summer, Grandfather worked on a river boat, but in the winter *it* usually froze over." The *it* seems to refer to the boat, but boats do not freeze over. Similar doubletakes result when a pronoun points to a **possessive**—a form of a noun that shows where something belongs: the *child's* rattle, the *horse's* bridle.

AMBIGUOUS: I reached for the *horse's* bridle, but *it* ran away.
(The bridle seems to be running away.)
CLEAR: The *horse* ran away after I reached for *its* bridle.
(The possessive has been changed to a pronoun, and the noun put where it is needed to prevent confusion.)

*Note*: Reference to a possessive accounts for the awkwardness of sentences like the following: "In *John Steinbeck's* novel *The Grapes of Wrath*, he describes the plight of the marginal farmer." Better: "In *his novel . . . John Steinbeck* describes . . ."

# AN OVERVIEW OF PRONOUNS

|  | SUBJECT FORM | OBJECT FORM |
|---|---|---|
| *Personal pronouns* | I<br>you<br>he<br>she<br>it<br>we<br>you<br>they | me<br>you<br>him<br>her<br>it<br>us<br>you<br>them |

|  | FIRST SET | SECOND SET |
|---|---|---|
| *Possessive pronouns* | my<br>your<br>his<br>her<br>its<br>our<br>your<br>their | mine<br>yours<br>his<br>hers<br>its<br>ours<br>yours<br>theirs |

|  | SINGULAR | PLURAL |
|---|---|---|
| *Reflexive pronouns*<br>(also "intensive"<br>pronouns) | myself<br>yourself<br>himself<br>herself<br>itself | ourselves<br>yourselves<br>themselves |

|  | SINGULAR | PLURAL |
|---|---|---|
| *Demonstrative pronouns*<br>("pointing" pronouns) | this<br>that | these<br>those |
| *Indefinite pronouns* | everybody (everyone), everything<br>somebody (someone), something<br>nobody (no one), nothing<br>anybody (anyone), anything<br>one | |
| *Relative pronouns* | who (whom, whose)<br>which<br>that | |
| *Interrogative pronouns*<br>("question" pronouns) | who (whom, whose)<br>which<br>what | |

## G 5c  Vague *This* and *Which*                               *ref*

**Avoid ambiguity caused by idea reference.**

Vague idea reference results when a *this* or *which* refers to the overall idea expressed in an earlier statement:

AMBIGUOUS:   I knew that Bob was cheating, but the other students were not aware of *this*.
(Were they unaware of the *cheating*, or of my *knowing* about it?)
CLEAR:   I knew that Bob was cheating, but the other students did not realize *that I knew*.

We can often make a vague *this* more specific: "this *assumption*," "this *practice*." A vague *which* is more difficult to improve. You may have to rewrite the sentence without it:

AMBIGUOUS:   I have received only one letter, *which* frightens me.
CLEAR:   *Receiving* only one letter frightened me.
CLEAR:   *The letter* (the only one I received) frightened me.

## G 5d  Implied Antecedents                               *ref*

**Eliminate indirect reference.**

In informal conversation, we often make a pronoun point to something that we have not actually mentioned. We expect its identity to be understood. We say, "In Nebraska, *they* grow mostly wheat." *They* means the people farming there. In writing, spell out the implied antecedent:

CLEAR:   In Nebraska, *the farmers* grow mostly wheat.

Avoid the orphaned *it* or *they*, which refers to an implied idea in sentences like the following:

AMBIGUOUS:   My mother was a musician; therefore, I have also chosen *it* as my profession.
(The *it* stands not for "musician" but for "music.")
REVISED:   My mother was a *musician*; therefore, I have also chosen *music* as my profession.

AMBIGUOUS:   The prisoner's hands were manacled to a chain around his waist, but *they* were removed at the courtroom door.
(What was removed? The prisoner's hands?)

REVISED:     The prisoner's hands were manacled to a chain around his waist, but *the manacles* were removed at the courtroom door.

# G 5e   Indefinite Antecedents                    *ref*

**Treat expressions like *everybody, somebody,* and *a person* as singulars.**

Informal English often switches to a plural pronoun after expressions that are technically singular: "Everybody received *their* copy of the test." Handbooks used to require the singular pronoun *he, him,* or *his* in such sentences: "*Everybody* received *his* copy of the test." In recent years, many people have pointed out that *he or she,* or *his or her,* would usually be more accurate in such situations: "*Everybody* received *his or her* copy of the test." Since the double pronoun can make a sentence awkward, the best solution is often to make the original expression plural in form as well as in meaning:

INFORMAL:     *Everybody* I knew was getting more serious about *their* future careers.
FORMAL:     *All my friends* were getting more serious about *their* future careers.

INFORMAL:     *A person* can be successful if *they* set realistic goals for *themselves.*
FORMAL:     *People* can be successful if *they* set realistic goals for *themselves.*

Watch for the following:

(1)   *Look out for the* **indefinite pronouns**. These are pronouns that do not point to one particular person or group of people: *everybody (everyone), somebody (someone), nobody (no one), anybody (anyone), one.* If you use one of these, treat it consistently as a singular:

RIGHT:     *Everybody* on the team did *her* best.
RIGHT:     *Nobody* should meddle in affairs that are none of *his or her* business.
RIGHT:     It was part of the knight's code that *one* must value *his* (or *one's*) honor more than life.
RIGHT:     *Someone* had left *her* (or *his*) car parked in the driveway.

(2)   *Look out for expressions that stand for one representative person.* Treat as singular such expressions as *a person, an individual, the typical student,* or *an average American.* These may

**57**

seem to refer to more than one person, but they are singular in form:

WRONG: A person can never be too careful about *their* use of language.
RIGHT: A person can never be too careful about *his or her* use of language.

WRONG: A *student* is here in college to study, but *they* are usually poorly prepared for this task.
RIGHT: A *student* is here in college to study, but *he* (or *she*) is usually poorly prepared for this task.

*Note: None* started as the equivalent of "no one," but today either singular or plural forms after it are acceptable:

None of the students *has his* (or *her*) books ready [or "*have their* books ready"].

On shifts in pronoun reference, see **G 10b**.

# EXERCISES

A. In each of the following sentences, you can solve a problem of *pronoun reference* by changing one pronoun. Write the changed pronoun after the number of the sentence.

1. Universities provide many services to the community surrounding it.
2. Each woman has their own reason for getting an education.
3. The bear feeds primarily on roots; to attack livestock, they would have to be desperate.
4. All his clothes looked tailor-made, and it gave him an air of distinction.
5. Women among medical students are still a minority, although admission policies are now more favorable toward her.
6. In most cases, given time, the new brother will learn their responsibilities quickly.
7. A girl who follows my advice should find themselves doing well in school.
8. Everyone entered in the men's singles had proved themselves in tough competition.
9. Our society, while asserting the rights of the individual, did not practice what they preached.
10. No one in my father's fraternity had ever forgotten their old friends.

B. Check *pronoun reference* in the following sentences. Write *S* for satisfactory or *U* for unsatisfactory after the number of each sentence. (Be prepared to explain what is wrong with each unsatisfactory sentence and how it could be revised.)

1. Each person runs differently, depending on their body size.
2. Good advice and much practice can help debaters improve their style.
3. The average individual respects the wishes of the group because they hate to be considered odd.
4. My father is extremely intelligent, though he does not always express it in a verbal form.
5. Although most Americans were in support of the Allies, they tried to remain neutral.
6. Our teachers told us we should learn for our future and not for the grades.
7. I feel bad when I'm in a market and they look at me as if I were a criminal.
8. The uniformed guards look very official, but they are employed by a private company.
9. Since Mary's father coaches the basketball team, she tried to attend some of them.
10. We always assumed that someone's religion was his or her own business.
11. People must learn to have faith in themselves.
12. The English taught in elementary school included a weekly spelling test, but they did little to improve my oral use of language.
13. Newspapers give prominence to youths who get into trouble, which pins a bad label on all young people.
14. Average students often need more explanation than they get in class.
15. Everyone wants to be the sole owner of their property.
16. In order for a person to be an individual, he or she must be themself.
17. The book's title sounded interesting, but when I read it I found it boring.
18. Teachers should have longer office hours so that they can help their students.
19. In today's world, the sight of a parent spending enough time with their child is rare indeed.
20. When a person leaves home and goes to school, they are on their own.

# G6 PRONOUN CASE                                     *pr*

**Use the right pronoun forms for written English.**

Some pronouns have different forms, used depending on the function of the pronoun in the sentence. *I* and *he* are **subject forms**. They identify the person that the predicate says something about. *Me* and *him* are **object forms**, identifying the object of a verb or preposition. Only half a dozen pronouns have a separate object form: *I—me*; *we—us*; *he—him*; *she—her*; *they—them*; *who—whom*. These differences in form are traditionally called differences in **case**.

| SUBJECT | OBJECT | OBJECT OF PREPOSITION |
|---|---|---|
| *I* congratulated | *him.* | |
| *He* recommended | *me* | to *them.* |
| *They* prejudiced | *her* | against *me.* |

A third possible form shows that the object of an action is the same as the performer. *Himself, themselves, myself, ourselves,* and similar forms are **reflexive forms**.

> He cut *himself.*
> They asked *themselves* what had gone wrong.
> We introduced *ourselves* to the interviewer.

They are also used as **intensives**, for emphasis:

> The dean told me so *herself.*
> We should also weigh the testimony of the accused men *themselves.*

---

For an overview of pronouns, see **G 5**.

---

## G 6a  Subject and Object Forms                    *ca*

**Use the right pronoun forms for subject and object.**

Formal use of these forms differs from what we commonly hear in informal and nonstandard speech.

(1)  *Choose the standard form when a pronoun is one of several subjects or objects*:

SUBJECT:  My brother and *I* [not "*me* and my brother"] were reading comic books.
(Who was reading? *I* was reading.)

OBJECT:  She asked my brother and *me* [not "my brother and *I*"] to dry the dishes.
(Whom did she ask? She asked *me.*)

(2)  *Be careful with pronoun-noun combinations.* Choose between *we girls—us girls* or *we Americans—us Americans*:

SUBJECT:  *We scouts* are always eager to help. (*We* are eager.)
OBJECT:  He told *us scouts* to keep up the good work. (He told *us.*)

(3)   *Use object forms after prepositions*: with *her*; because of *him*; for *me*. Use the object form for a pronoun that is the second or third object in a prepositional phrase:

OBJECT:   This kind of thing can happen to you and *me* [not "to you and *I*"].
OBJECT:   I knew there was something between you and *her* [not "between you and *she*"].
OBJECT:   She had bought tickets for Jim, Laura, and *me* [not "for Jim, Laura, and *I*"].

(4)   *Use the right pronoun after* as *and* than. Often the part of the sentence they start has been shortened. Fill in enough of what is missing to see whether the pronoun would be used as subject or object:

SUBJECT:   He is as tall as *I* (*am*).
           His sister was smarter than *he* (*was*).
OBJECT:    I owe you as much as (I owe) *them*.
           I like her better than (I like) *him*.

(5)   *In formal usage, use subject forms after linking verbs.* These introduce not an object of an action but a description of the subject:

The only ones not invited were *she* and a girl with measles.

The need for this use of the subject form seldom arises except after "it is," "it was," "it must be," and so on. (See the Glossary of Usage for *it's me* / *it is I*.)

*Note*: Formal English avoids the reflexive pronoun as a substitute for the plain subject form or object form:

SAFE:   My friend and *I* [not "and *myself*"] were the last ones to leave.
SAFE:   I asked both his friend and *him* [not "and *himself*"] to come over after dinner.

# G 6b   *Who* and *Whom*                                    *ca*

**Know how to use *who* and *whom*.**

*Who* and *whom* are easily confused. How they fit into a sentence is not always obvious. Furthermore, *who* is increasingly replacing *whom* in speech.

SPOKEN: Tell me *who you are thinking of.*
WRITTEN: It is good for the sanity of all of us to have someone *whom we continue to think of* as Mister even though we address him by his given name.—Philip M. Wagner, "Mencken Remembered," *The American Scholar*

Observe the following guidelines in your writing:

(1) *Choose* who *or* whom *at the beginning of a question.* Who asks a question about the subject. *Whom* asks a question about an object:

SUBJECT: *Who* did it? *He* did.
OBJECT: *Whom* did you meet? I met *him.*
OBJECT: To *whom* should I write? To *him.*

In more complicated questions, it may not be obvious whether a *who* asks about a subject or about an object. However, the *he*-or-*him* test will always work:

*Who* do you think will win? (I think *he* will win.)
*Whom* did you expect to come? (I expected *him* to come.)

(2) *Choose* who *or* whom *at the beginning of a dependent clause.* To apply the *he*-or-*him* test to a dependent clause, separate it from the rest of the sentence. In the following examples, *who* (or *whoever*) is the subject of a verb:

SUBJECT: Ask her / *who* wrote the letter.
(*He* wrote the letter.)
SUBJECT: We approached the man / *who* was waiting.
(*He* was waiting.)
SUBJECT: Here is a nickel for / *whoever* gets there first.
(*He* gets there first.)

In the following examples, *whom* is the object of a verb or of a preposition:

OBJECT: *Whom* we should invite / is a difficult question.
(We should invite *him.*)
OBJECT: She knew my brother, / *whom* I rarely see.
(I rarely see *him.*)
OBJECT: He knew few people / on *whom* he could rely.
(He could rely on *them.*)

---

See the Glossary of Usage for *who, which,* and *that.*

# EXERCISES

A. Which of the italicized *pronoun forms* are right for written English? Which are inappropriate? After the number of each sentence, write the revised form of one pronoun that should be changed.

1. Teachers should not be condescending just because *they* know more than *us* students.
2. Jack constantly enriched the conversation of *my* friends and *I* with brilliant comments.
3. People *who* are asked to "play *themselves*" in a movie often find that a good actor can portray their type more effectively than *them*.
4. My brother and *me* had no respect for the people with *whom* we worked, and soon we had no respect for *ourselves*.
5. *I* am tired of the rumors about a rift between the board and *I*.
6. People *who* I had not seen for months or *whom* I knew very slightly telephoned to advise *me* to get off the newly formed committee.
7. People *who* cannot suffer can never grow up or discover *whom* they are.
8. Grandmother disapproved of John, *who* showed little respect for his grandfather and *she*.
9. *We* occasionally encounter a fictional character with *who* we can immediately identify.
10. *We* would argue for hours with *whoever* was willing to listen to *we* newcomers.

B. In each of the following sentences, change *one pronoun* to the form that is right for written English. Write the changed form after the number of the sentence.

1. After dinner, us children would go to the first floor to play, explore, and talk.
2. When my mother punished my sister and I, she always suffered more than we did.
3. My cousin, who I had not seen for several years, worked there and knew how to get things done.
4. My sister is better than me at learning foreign languages.
5. I stopped at Jane's house because I had some letters for she and her mother.
6. I recognize the man's face; it was him who started the riot.
7. Every year, my parents take my sister and I on a camping trip.
8. This information should remain strictly between you and I.
9. The new ruler surrounded himself with subordinates on who he could rely.
10. Visitors from outer space might smile at the technology that us Earthlings possess.

# G7 MODIFIERS

**Check the form and position of modifiers.**

Modifiers help us build up bare-bones sentences. Modifiers range from single words to long prepositional or verbal phrases:

| | |
|---|---|
| ADJECTIVES: | The *dutiful* son obeyed his *angry* parents. |
| ADVERBS: | Jean will *probably* leave *early*. |
| PREP. PHRASE: | A woman *in overalls* was standing *on a ladder*. |
| VERBAL PHRASE: | The man *waiting in the dark doorway* was an old friend. |

## G7a Adjectives and Adverbs                     *ad*

**In formal English, use the distinctive adverb form.**

Written English observes the distinction between adjectives and adverbs more consistently than spoken English does. **Adjectives** modify nouns. They tell us which one or what kind: the *dutiful* son, a *difficult* exam, an *easy* answer, the *angry* driver. After a **linking verb**, an adjective points back to the subject; it pins a label on the subject:

| | |
|---|---|
| ADJECTIVE: | These bottles are *empty*. (*empty* bottles) |
| | The speaker seemed *nervous*. (a *nervous* speaker) |
| | The rains have been *heavy*. (*heavy* rains) |

The most common linking verb is *be* (*am, is, are, was, were, has been,* and so on). Here are some other verbs that may function as linking verbs and may then be followed by adjectives:

| | |
|---|---|
| Genevieve *turned* pale. | Honeysuckle *smells* sweet. |
| The heat *grew* oppressive. | The soup *tasted* flat. |
| He *became* rich overnight. | His hands *felt* moist. |
| Your fears *will prove* silly. | Sirens *sound* scary. |
| The accused *remained* silent. | Your friend *looks* ill. |

**Adverbs** modify verbs. They tell us where, when, and how something is done:

| | |
|---|---|
| WHERE? | We ate *outside*. |
| | The guests went *upstairs*. |

**64**

WHEN?  The bus will leave *soon.*
Your brother called *yesterday.*

HOW?  The engine ran *smoothly.*
She answered *reluctantly.*
We lifted the lid *cautiously.*

Remember:

(1) *Whenever you have a choice, use the adverb form to modify a verb.* Very often, we can turn an adjective into an adverb by adding the *-ly* ending: *bright—brightly, cheerful—cheerfully, considerable—considerably, frequent—frequently, happy—happily, rapid—rapidly, rare—rarely, single—singly.* Use the distinctive adverb form to tell the reader how something was done or how something happened:

ADVERB:  The inspectors examined every part *carefully.*
ADVERB:  We have changed the original design *considerably.*
ADVERB:  No one took the new policy *seriously.*

Some adverbs, such as *fast, much, thus,* and *well,* have no distinctive adverb ending. For words like *fast, much,* and *early,* the adjective and the adverb are the same:

ADJECTIVE:  The incident had caused *much* trouble.
ADVERB:  I want to thank you very *much.*

ADJECTIVE:  The *early* bird gets the worm.
ADVERB:  Perhaps the worm should not get up *early.*

*Note*: Some words ending in *-ly* are not adverbs but adjectives: a *friendly* talk, a *lonely* life, a *leisurely* drive.

(2) *Use* well *and* badly *as adverbs instead of* good *and* bad. *Good* and *bad* used as adverbs are often heard in informal speech but are unacceptable in writing. Change "I don't hear *good*" to "I don't hear *well*." Change "I write pretty *bad*" to "I write *badly*."

WRONG:  This morning, the motor was running *good.*
RIGHT:  This morning, the motor was running *well.*

The adverb *well*, however, may do double duty as an adjective, in the sense of "healthy," "not ill": "He looks *well*"; "I don't feel *well*."

(3) *Avoid informal adverbs like* slow, quick, *and* loud. Formal usage prefers "talks *loudly*" to "talks loud," "go *slowly*" to "go slow," or "come *quickly*" to "come quick," though both the long form and the short form of these adverbs have long been standard English.

(4) *Use adverbs to modify other modifiers.* In formal usage, use the adverb form to modify either an adjective or another adverb. In the phrase "our *usually* polite waiter," *usually* is an adverb modifying the adjective *polite*.

ADVERB + ADJECTIVE:   a *surprisingly* beautiful bird
a *hopelessly* retarded student
an *impressively* versatile actor

ADVERB + ADVERB:   You sang *admirably* well.
He answered *surprisingly* fast.
She worked *incredibly* hard.

(5) *Avoid informal expressions like* real scared, awful expensive, *and* pretty good. Many everyday expressions use adjective forms instead of adverb forms as informal **intensifiers**: "He speaks *awful* fast." "Dean Howard is *real* popular." "I am *dreadful* sorry." Substitute a formal intensifier like *really, very, fairly,* or *extremely*:

FORMAL:   Dean Howard is *extremely* popular.
FORMAL:   The city hall is *fairly* old.

## G7b  Misplaced Modifiers      *Dm, mm*

**Place modifiers so that they point clearly to what they modify.**

Changes in meaning result from changes in the position of modifiers:

ADVERB:   The car *almost* broke down on every trip we took.
(It never quite did.)
The car broke down on *almost* every trip we took.
(It did frequently.)

PREP. PHRASE:   The man *with the ax* opened the door.
The man opened the door *with the ax*.

| | |
|---|---|
| VERBAL: | Jerry married a wealthy woman *yearning for high social status.* |
| | *Yearning for high social status,* Jerry married a wealthy woman. |

Watch out for the following:

(1) **Misplaced modifiers** *seem to point to the wrong part of the sentence.* Usually you can simply shift the modifier to a more appropriate position. Sometimes you may have to recast the sentence as a whole:

| | |
|---|---|
| MISPLACED: | I looked at the tree I had felled *with my hands in my pockets.* |
| | (It is hard to fell trees with your hands in your pockets.) |
| REVISED: | *With my hands in my pockets,* I looked at the tree I had felled. |
| | |
| MISPLACED: | *Being made of stone,* the builder expected the house to stand for a century. |
| REVISED: | Since *the house* was made of stone, the builder expected it to stand for a century. |

(2) *A* **dangling modifier** *is left dangling—what it points to is not part of the sentence.* A dangling modifier is usually a verbal— a *to* form (infinitive) or an *-ing* form (participle). Revise by bringing back into the sentence what the verbal is supposed to modify:

| | |
|---|---|
| DANGLING: | *To do well in college,* good grades are essential. |
| REVISED: | To do well in college, *a student* needs good grades. |
| | |
| DANGLING: | Sometimes, *after convincing a friend to finish school,* she finds few openings in the field of her choice. |
| REVISED: | Sometimes, after *her friends* have convinced her to finish school, a woman finds few openings in the field of her choice. |

(3) *A* **squinting modifier** *seems to point two ways at once:*

| | |
|---|---|
| SQUINTING: | I feel *subconsciously* Hamlet wanted to die. |
| | (Are you talking about *your* subconscious feelings—or Hamlet's?) |
| REVISED: | I feel that Hamlet *subconsciously* wanted to die. |

*Note:* Some verbal phrases are not intended to modify any one part of the main sentence. These are called **absolute constructions**. The most common ones are expressions that *clarify the attitude or intention of the speaker:*

| | |
|---|---|
| RIGHT: | *Generally speaking,* traffic is getting worse. |
| | They had numerous children—seven, *to be exact.* |
| | *Considering the location,* the house is not a bad bargain. |

**67**

Formal English, more frequently than informal English, uses verbals that *carry their own subjects along with them*:

RIGHT:   *The air being warm,* we left our coats in the car.
         *Escape being impossible,* we prepared for the worst.

# EXERCISES

A. In each of the following sentences, one word should be changed to the distinctive *adverb form*. Write the changed word after the number of the sentence.

1. When the witness began to talk, she spoke nervously and very defensive.
2. He was tired and unable to think logical.
3. I read the questions as careful as the time allowed.
4. Toward the end of the story, the events unfold very sudden, as they sometimes do in real life.
5. My father regarded life more serious than most people do.
6. Macbeth interpreted the prophecies of the weird sisters very literal.
7. During the time Judy spent in France, her French improved considerable.
8. I had to talk fast and furious before the householder could slam the door in my face.
9. An experienced cryptographer can decipher a simple code very easy.
10. My father didn't do very good in school because he had to work on my grandfather's farm.

B. In the following *sentence-combining* exercise, lift the italicized part from the second sentence of each pair. Then add that part as a modifier to the first sentence of the pair. Make sure the added modifier points clearly to what it modifies. (Use the punctuation indicated to set off the modifier.)

EXAMPLE:   The little girl made her mother very angry.
           The little girl was *sloshing through the puddles.*
(RESULT)   Sloshing through the puddles, the little girl made her mother very angry.

1. The coach lectured the girls on the team.
   The coach was *raising her voice.*
   (comma or commas)
2. The officer arrested the suspects.
   The suspects were *writing graffiti on the station wall.*
   (no comma)
3. Our guide found the travelers a place to stay.
   The travelers were *without hotel rooms.*
   (no comma)

4. The kindly peasants raised the children.
   The children had been *abandoned by their parents.*
   (no comma)
5. The bride stood next to her father.
   The bride was *dressed in white.*
   (comma or commas)

C. Rewrite each of the following sentences to eliminate unsatisfactory *position of modifiers.*

1. Having run for an hour, the food tasted great.
2. The car was towed away by John, having exploded on Interstate 59.
3. Unsure of my future, the army was waiting for me.
4. After ringing for fifteen minutes, the president's secretary answered the phone.
5. Several reporters sat with coffee cups discussing the day's events.
6. After graduating from high school, my parents asked me what I planned to do.
7. When traveling during the night without sufficient lighting, other motorists will have difficulty seeing the vehicle.
8. These magazines appeal to immature readers with stories about torrid love affairs.
9. Sometimes a student studies only so that she can prove in class the professor is wrong just to be showing off.
10. I just wrote to my family for the first time since I came here on the back of a postcard.

D. (Review) Check *form and position of modifiers* in each of the following sentences. After the number of the sentence, write *S* for satisfactory or *U* for unsatisfactory. (Be prepared to explain how you would revise unsatisfactory sentences.)

1. The counselor tried hard to treat everyone fair and equal.
2. He was hit by a rotten egg walking back to the dorm.
3. Brushing the aides aside, the reporter insisted on the promised interview with the senator.
4. All the girls performed admirably, but Judy did exceptionally well.
5. No matter what dish George prepared, it tasted flat.
6. Having walked for four hours, the car looked wonderful.
7. Whenever my parents fight, they try to talk quiet but usually fail.
8. The children were becoming less cautious and more brave on their bicycles.
9. The pay was good, but the food was awful bad.
10. To play tennis properly, the racket must be held firmly.
11. The survey was as complete as the time allowed.
12. When cooking Chinese food, the vegetables have to be very fresh and crisp.
13. We opened the door very cautious and looked around.

**69**

14. Being forever late to meetings, the committee had finished its business before I arrived.
15. Such magazines as *Argosy, Adventure,* and *True* have on their covers brightly colored pictures of hunters in wild country.

# G 8   CONFUSED SENTENCES                                        *st*

**Revise confusing sentences.**

When a sentence seems garbled or confused, straighten out basic relationships by asking: "Who does what? What is being described as what? What caused what?"

## G 8a   Omission and Duplication                               *st*

**Check your sentences for omitted or duplicated elements.**

Check for omission or duplication that results from hasty writing, inaccurate copying, or careless typing.

(1)  *Check for parts of a sentence that have been left out.* Make sure you have written each sentence in full. Do not leave out minor sentence elements like *a, the, has, be,* or *am.* Many hastily written sentences lack some essential part:

INCOMPLETE:  My grandparents moved to Hawaii and have often visited them since.
(Who has often visited?)
COMPLETE:  My grandparents moved to Hawaii, and *I* have often visited them since.

INCOMPLETE:  As a child, she contracted polio, but did not cause paralysis.
(What did not cause paralysis?)
COMPLETE:  As a child, she contracted polio, but *the disease* did not cause paralysis.

(2)  *Check for duplicated words.* Check especially for duplication of words like *of* and *that*:

DUPLICATED:  They had built a model plane *of* which they were very proud *of.*
REVISED:  They had built a model plane *of* which they were very proud.

| | |
|---|---|
| DUPLICATED: | I think *that* because he is ill *that* he will not come. |
| REVISED: | I think *that* because he is ill he will not come. |
| | Because he is ill, I think *that* he will not come. |

# G 8b   Mixed Construction                                   *st, mx*

**Do not confuse different ways of expressing the same idea.**

You may sometimes start a sentence one way and finish it another. To revise such mixed sentences, retrace your steps. Choose one of the two possible ways of putting the sentence together. The revised sentence will be *consistent*—it will stay with one possible way of saying what you have in mind:

| | |
|---|---|
| MIXED: | In case of emergency should be reported to the head office. |
| CONSISTENT: | *In case of emergency, report* to the head office. |
| CONSISTENT: | *Emergencies should be reported* to the head office. |

| | |
|---|---|
| MIXED: | The department manager rejected him to be one of her assistants. |
| CONSISTENT: | The department manager *rejected his application.* |
| CONSISTENT: | The department manager *did not want him* to be one of her assistants. |

| | |
|---|---|
| MIXED: | The course was canceled because of not enough students registered. |
| CONSISTENT: | The course was canceled *because not enough students registered.* |
| CONSISTENT: | The course was canceled *because of insufficient enrollment.* |

*Note*: In informal English, an adverbial clause starting with *because* sometimes appears as the subject of a verb. Formal English requires a noun clause starting with *that*:

| | |
|---|---|
| MIXED: | *Because* we listened to his proposal *does not mean* we approve of it. |
| CONSISTENT: | *That* we listened to his proposal *does not mean* that we approve of it. |

# G 8c   Faulty Predication                                   *st*

**Make sure that what the predicate says can logically apply to the subject.**

The subject of a sentence calls our attention to something. The predicate then makes a statement about the subject: "Birds (subject) *fly* (predicate)." "The choice (subject) *was difficult* (predicate)." Make sure the statement made by the predicate can apply logically to the subject of the sentence:

ILLOGICAL: *The choice* of the new site *was selected* by the mayor.
(What was selected? The site, not the choice)
LOGICAL: *The new site was selected* by the mayor.
LOGICAL: *The choice* of the new site *was made* by the mayor.

ILLOGICAL: *The participation* in our club meetings *is always overcrowded.*
(What is overcrowded? The meetings, not the participation)
LOGICAL: *Our club meetings are always overcrowded.*
LOGICAL: *The participation* in our club meetings *is always very strong.*

# G 8d  Faulty Equation                                            *st*

**Use a linking verb to join two things that are logically equal.**

In sentences like the following, a form of the linking verb *be* joins two labels for the same person or thing: "The manager is *a Southerner.*" "Dinosaurs were *giant reptiles.*" Such equations become illogical when they link two labels that do not really stand for the same thing:

ILLOGICAL: Her job was a mail carrier.
(A mail carrier is a person, not a job.)
LOGICAL: She was employed *as* a mail carrier.
LOGICAL: Her job was *that of* a mail carrier.

ILLOGICAL: A student with a part-time job is a common cause of poor grades.
(A student is not a cause.)
LOGICAL: A student's *part-time job* is a common cause of poor grades.

Faulty equation often occurs in "is-when" or "was-when" sentences. Children will say, "A zoo *is when* you go to look at animals." Logically, a zoo is not a time when something happens, but a place *where* something happens.

ILLOGICAL: Parole *is when* a prisoner is set free on condition of good behavior.
LOGICAL: Parole *is the practice* of setting prisoners free on condition of good behavior.

*Note*: Linking verbs often cause faulty equation when they introduce **prepositional phrases**. Such phrases typically tell us not what something is but how, when, or where it is done. Use an infinitive (or a similar noun equivalent) instead:

> Our only hope *is to convince* your parents [not "*is by convincing* your parents"].
> Their method of selection *was to question* the candidates carefully [not "*was by questioning* the candidates"].

## G8e Faulty Appositives *st*

**Make sure that your appositives can be equated with the nouns they modify.**

An **appositive** is a noun placed next to another noun: "John, *a sophomore*, came to see me." Here, John and the sophomore are identical. However, it does not make sense to say, "There was only *one telephone call, a friend* of yours." A friend can *make* a telephone call, but we would not say that he *is* one.

FAULTY: We have only one *vacancy, a mathematics teacher.*
(A teacher is not a vacancy, and a vacancy is not a teacher.)
REVISED: We have only one *vacancy,* a *position* for a mathematics teacher.
(What is actually vacant is a *position* for a teacher.)

# EXERCISES

A. Check *sentence structure* in the following sentences. Look for examples of hasty writing, mixed construction, faulty predication, and faulty appositives. Label each sentence *S* (satisfactory) or *U* (unsatisfactory). Be prepared to explain how you would revise unsatisfactory sentences.

1. In an era of dwindling resources, we will all have to give up conveniences to which we are used to.
2. Divorce is the official, legal termination of a marriage.
3. Parents view sex as sacred and should be reserved for marriage alone.
4. By cutting the number of jurors in half greatly reduces the time used in selecting a jury.
5. He was watched by the owner, a little man who peeped over the counter with a wrinkled face.

6. Committing suicide in the story pointed out that the weak cannot survive in this world.
7. Scientists know how to distill drinking water from salt water, but the cost of such a project is too unprofitable.
8. One good example of romantic love triumphing against odds is when people with different religions marry.
9. I saw him eat three hot dogs and drank three cokes.
10. I suddenly realized that we were no longer on level ground and that the road was tilting upward on great concrete stilts.
11. In these novels, the older a man is, the more chivalrous and the more gallantry he possesses.
12. Nowadays the idea of love is begun at a very tender age.
13. One major reason for increased job opportunities for women is the threat of successful law suits against companies that discriminate.
14. Because little of the pledged money actually came in, the repertory company had to give up its experiment.
15. My father first met his business partner in the army, for whom he drove a jeep and was his immediate supervisor.

B. Revise each of the following *confused sentences.*

1. Usually it takes a minimum of effort and concentration to watch TV than it does to read a book.
2. She tried to promote peace among each individual.
3. The individual pieces of this complex problem makes it nearly impossible for anyone to find the solution.
4. Our government, both state and federal, are bound by the Constitution to educate the citizenry.
5. Typical playground equipment fails to keep in mind the needs of children.
6. A woman is more likely to understand another woman's feeling better than a man.
7. The players up for the team were about even in ability and was a hard decision to make.
8. A person who fails in various things might give him an inferior feeling.
9. Radical opinions are too biased and will not accept realistic compromise.
10. Assimilation is when we try to make everyone as similar as possible.

# G 9   INCOMPLETE CONSTRUCTIONS                    *st*

**In formal English, spell out relationships merely implied in various informal constructions.**

In written English, we avoid shortcuts common in informal speech. Check constructions like the following for logical completeness.

# G 9a   Incomplete Comparison                                    *inc*

**Complete incomplete comparisons.**

Normally, *more, better,* and *whiter,* the **comparative forms**, establish a comparison between two elements:

*Carpenters* make more money than *teachers.*
*Half a loaf* is better than *a slice.*

*Most, best,* and *whitest,* the **superlative forms**, establish a comparison within a group of at least three elements:

The annual classic at Le Mans is the most dangerous *automobile race in Europe.*

In formal English, observe the following guidelines:

(1)   *Spell out what is being compared with what.* Watch for incomplete comparisons resulting from the use of *more* and *the most* as intensifiers: "That girl has *more* luck" (than who or than what?). "I had *the most* wonderful experience" (of the day? of the year? of a lifetime?). "I saw *the most* exciting play" (the most exciting play of the season? the most exciting play ever produced?).

(2)   *Compare things that are really comparable.* Revise sentences like the following: "The *fur* was as soft as a *kitten*." Actually, the *fur* was as soft as a *kitten's* (fur), or as soft as *that* of a kitten. Check for logical balance in sentences like the following:

ILLOGICAL:   *Her personality* was unlike *most other people* I have known in the past.
LOGICAL:   *Her personality* was unlike *that of* most other people I have known in the past.

ILLOGICAL:   *The teachings* of Horatio Alger reached a wider audience than Whitman.
LOGICAL:   *The teachings* of Horatio Alger reached a wider audience than *those of* Whitman.—Saul Bellow, "The Writer as Moralist," *Atlantic*

(3)   *Clarify three-cornered comparisons.* Some comparisons mention *three* comparable items without making it clear which two are being compared:

CONFUSING: *We* distrusted the *oil companies* more than the *Arabs.*
CLEAR: We distrusted the oil companies more than *we did* the Arabs.
CLEAR: We distrusted the oil companies more than the Arabs *did.*

*Note*: Sometimes the absurdity of an illogical comparison is not immediately obvious: "Their fullback was heavier than *any player on their team.*" Their fullback is part of their team, and he cannot be heavier than *any player* on the team, including himself. He can be heavier than *other* players on the team:

LOGICAL: Their fullback was heavier than *any other player* on their team.

See the Glossary of Usage for informal *so* and *such.*

# G9b Contraction of Coordinate Elements *inc*

**In shortening coordinate elements, leave out only identical items.**

When several items of the same kind are coordinated by a connective like *and* or *but,* we often leave out forms that would cause unnecessary duplication. When we leave out too much, we may cause truncated sentences. Check for excessive shortcuts in the following situations:

(1) *Check for completeness when shortening one of several similar verbs.* Leave out only words that would be duplicated exactly. In the following sentence, *be done* appears twice: "It can *be done* and will *be done.*" You can therefore leave out the first *be done* and write: "It *can* and *will be done.*" However, an unacceptable shortcut appears in "It *can* and *has been done.*" The complete verbs would be *can be done* and *has been done.* The words omitted do not duplicate those in the second verb exactly.

INCOMPLETE: The patient *was given* an injection and the instruments *made* ready.
COMPLETE: The patient *was given* an injection, and the instruments *were made* ready.

(2) *Check for unsatisfactory shortcuts in comparisons of the as-good-if-not-better type.* The following example is incomplete:

"My theme is *as good* if not *better than* yours." The complete forms would be *as good as* and *better than*. Formal English would require "My theme is *as good as*, if not *better than*, yours." Less awkward is shifting the second part of the comparison to the end of the sentence:

RIGHT:   My theme is as good as yours, *if not better.*

(3)   *Check several linked prepositional phrases.* Keep prepositions that are not identical but merely express a similar relationship:

WRONG:   I have great *respect and faith* in her.
         (Taken up separately, the two phrases would require different prepositions: "respect *for* her" and "faith *in* her.")
RIGHT:   I have great *admiration and respect* for her.
         (Taken up separately, the two prepositions would be identical: "admiration *for* her" and "respect *for* her.")

Notice the use of different prepositions in the following examples:

RIGHT:   He was jealous *of* but fascinated *by* his rival.
RIGHT:   Her behavior during the trial adds *to* rather than detracts *from* my admiration for her.

# EXERCISES

A. Check the following sentences for *incomplete construction.* Label each sentence *S* (satisfactory) or *U* (unsatisfactory). Your teacher may ask you to revise unsatisfactory sentences.

1. In much of Europe, American films are more popular than any other country.
2. Children on the whole understand other children better than adults.
3. The light at the intersection of Sixth and Grove will turn green exactly six seconds after the intersection of Wright and Grove.
4. Our present prison system has neither prevented nor deterred people from returning to crime.
5. Children seem to like the so-called adult Westerns as much as adults do.
6. Unlike America, traveling abroad is a rare luxury in many foreign countries.

7. Marsha never has and never will succeed in making her restaurant something more than a place to eat food.
8. The United States has more television sets to the square mile than any other country in the world.
9. Year after year, American colleges produce more physical education teachers than mathematics.
10. The secretary of state usually attracts more criticism than any member of the President's cabinet.
11. Critics of our schools must realize that they can and are doing great harm by indiscriminate attacks.
12. Unlike a track coach, history teachers seldom have newspaper articles written about them when their students do exceptional work.
13. Most young children learn a second language more readily than an older person does.
14. The impact of American books, magazines, and comics in Great Britain is much greater than British publications in the United States.
15. A good background in the liberal arts is excellent preparation for such practical professions as engineers and lawyers.

B. Make each of the following *incomplete sentences* more complete by rewriting the italicized part. Write the rewritten part after the number of the sentence.

1. People today use more resources and live longer *than the previous century.*
2. *Juries have always and will always be swayed* by the eloquence of a lawyer.
3. An older person's need for love is *as big as a child.*
4. Taxpayers are already *familiar and hostile to the usual explanations.*
5. The population of China is already *bigger than any country.*
6. *The club had in the past and was still barring* certain kinds of people from membership.
7. I thought the Sears Building in Chicago was *as tall or taller than any building in New York City.*
8. People in show business *seem to have more bad luck.*
9. The statistics for rape are much less complete *than robberies or similar crimes.*
10. Few of my friends were *preoccupied or even interested in making a living.*

# G10  CONSISTENCY

**Do not confuse your readers by shifts in tense, reference, or grammatical perspective.**

The need for consistency makes a writer guard against confusing shifts in perspective. Like a road full of unexpected twists and turns, sentences that lack consistency slow down and confuse the reader.

# G10a   Shifts in Tense                                    *sf*

**Be consistent in your use of verb forms that show the relationship of events in time.**

Verbs are words that have a built-in reference to time: We *agree* (now). We *agreed* (then). The forms that show time relationships are called **tense** forms. When describing a situation or telling a story, be aware of the tense forms you are using to show time:

| | |
|---|---|
| PRESENT: | Nuclear energy *poses* a serious problem for political leaders. (action now) |
| PAST: | The U.S. *exploded* the first atom bomb in Nevada. (action happening and concluded in the past) |
| PRESENT PERFECT: | The President *has called* for a new look at the nuclear arms race. (action in the recent past or with special relevance for the present) |
| PAST PERFECT: | By then, the two countries *had agreed* on a moratorium on tests. (action in the more distant past, before other past events) |

Watch out for confusing shifts in time:

(1) *Avoid shifting from past to present.* Do not switch to the present when something becomes so real that it seems to be happening in front of you:

| | |
|---|---|
| SHIFT: | We *were waiting* for the elevator when suddenly all lights *go* out. |
| REVISED: | We *were waiting* for the elevator when suddenly all lights *went* out. |

| | |
|---|---|
| SHIFT: | The pedestrians *scattered* as the car *comes* careening around the corner. |
| REVISED: | The pedestrians *scattered* as the car *came* careening around the corner. |

(2) *Show differences in time as needed to avoid confusion:*

| | |
|---|---|
| SHIFT: | The poor grade *disappointed* me, because I *studied* very hard. |
| CONSISTENT: | The poor grade *disappointed* me, because I *had studied* very hard. (Studying came before the disappointment.) |

| | |
|---|---|
| SHIFT: | Linda *was* only a messenger, but she *was* now the supervisor of the whole floor. |

**79**

CONSISTENT: Linda *had been* only a messenger, but she *was* now the supervisor of the whole floor.
(Working as a messenger came before promotion.)

SHIFT: My uncle always *talked* about how farming *has changed.*
CONSISTENT: My uncle always *talked* about how farming *had changed.*
(about how it had changed up to the time when he talked)

(3)  *Use consistent forms when dealing with possible events.* In the following sentences, note the differences between factual reference to a possibility and the **conditional**, which makes the same possibility seem less probable, or contrary to fact:

SHIFT: If they *come* to this country, the government *would* offer them asylum.
FACTUAL: If they *come* to this country, the government *will* offer them asylum.
CONDITIONAL: If they *came* to this country, the government *would* offer them asylum.

(4)  *Use different tense forms in direct and indirect quotation.* What the speaker felt or observed at the time would be in the present tense in direct quotation: He said, "I *feel* fine." It would be in the past tense in indirect quotation: He said that he *felt* fine. What the speaker felt *before* he spoke would occur in the past when quoted directly: He said, "I *felt* fine." It would occur in the past perfect when quoted indirectly: He said that he *had felt* fine.

DIRECT: Roosevelt said, "We *have* nothing to fear but fear itself."
INDIRECT: Roosevelt said that the nation *had* nothing to fear but fear itself.

Failure to adjust the tenses in indirect quotations can lead to sentences like the following:

SHIFT: Her husband admitted that he *was* [should be "*had been*"] a confirmed bachelor.
SHIFT: Mr. Chamberlain said that there *will be* [should be "*would be*"] peace in our time.

*Note*: When a statement made in the past *states a general truth*, the present tense is acceptable:

Galileo said that the earth *moves* and that the sun *is* fixed; the Inquisition said that the earth *is* fixed and the sun *moves*; and Newtonian astronomers, adopting an absolute theory of space, said that both the sun and the earth *move.*—A. N. Whitehead, *Science and the Modern World*

> For an overview of verb tenses, see **G 4.**

## G 10b  Shifts in Reference                                        *sf*

**Be consistent in the way you refer to yourself and others.**

The pronoun you use to refer to yourself is *I*, *me*, or *my* (**first person singular**). Writers who want to speak directly to their readers can call them *you* (**second person singular** and **plural**). They can use *we* to refer to both the readers and themselves:

> *You* will agree that *we* must do everything in our power.
> As *you* no doubt remember, *we* have witnessed several similar incidents.

However, *you* also appears as an informal equivalent of *one* or *a person*, referring not so much to the reader as to people in general. In formal writing, use *you* only to mean "you, the reader":

INFORMAL:  Sailing to the colonies, *you* had to worry about pirates.
FORMAL:    Sailing to the colonies, *travelers* had to worry about pirates.

Avoid shifts like the following:

(1) *Avoid shifts to the indefinite, generalized* you. Revise sentences that shift to *you* after the person involved has already been identified in some other way:

SHIFT:       *I* would not want to be a celebrity, with people always knowing what *you* are doing.
CONSISTENT:  *I* would not want to be a celebrity, with people always knowing what *I* am doing.

SHIFT:       When questioned by police, *a person* should be willing to identify *yourself.*
CONSISTENT:  When questioned by police, *people* should be willing to identify *themselves.*

(2) *Avoid shifts to the request form.* In giving directions or instructions, we naturally use the form for requests or commands (**imperative**): "*Sift* the flour." "First *remove* the hubcaps."

**81**

Avoid shifting to the request form when giving general advice to the public:

| SHIFT: | High schools *should stop* educating all students at the same rate. *Give* aptitude tests for placement and then *separate* the students. |
| CONSISTENT: | High schools *should stop* educating all students at the same rate. They *should give* aptitude tests and then *separate* the students. |

(3) *Avoid shifts in references to groups.* Make up your mind whether you are talking about all members or one typical member:

| SHIFT: | Some *nonsmokers* might not patronize a restaurant because of the smoke *he* might inhale. |
| CONSISTENT: | Some *nonsmokers* might not patronize a restaurant because of the smoke *they* might inhale. |

# G10c  Shifts to the Passive                                    *sf*

**Avoid shifting to the passive when the person in question is still the active element in the sentence.**

Some sentences confuse the reader by shifting from an **active** construction ("*He built* the house") to a **passive** one ("*The house was built* by him"):

| SHIFT: | He *returned* to the office as soon as *his lunch had been eaten.* (This sounds as though his lunch might have been eaten by somebody else.) |
| CONSISTENT: | He *returned* to the office as soon as he *had eaten* his lunch. |

Unsatisfactory shifts to the passive are especially frequent after an impersonal *one* or *you*:

| SHIFT: | As *you scan* your yard, a small patch of unused earth *is located.* |
| CONSISTENT: | As *you scan* your yard, *you locate* a small patch of unused earth. |

See **S 3b** on the awkward passive.

# G10d  Faulty Parallelism                                    *FP* or ‖

**Use parallel grammatical structure for elements serving the same function in a sentence.**

Sentence parts joined by *and, or,* and *but* have to be **parallel**. They should fit into the same grammatical category. If you put an *and* after *body,* your readers expect another noun: "body and *chassis,*" "body and *soul.*" If you put an *and* after *swore,* they expect another verb: "swore and *affirmed,*" "swore and *raved.*" The same principle applies to sentence parts like the following:

INFINITIVES: Two things that a successful advertisement must accomplish are *to be noticed* and *to be remembered.*

PARTICIPLES: I can still see my aunt *striding* into the corral, *cornering* a cow against a fencepost, *balancing* herself on a one-legged milking stool, and *butting* her head into the cow's belly.

CLAUSES: The young people *who brood* in their rooms, *who forget* to come down to the dining hall, and *who burst out* in fits of irrationality are not worrying about who will win the great game.—Oscar Handlin, "Are the Colleges Killing Education?" *Atlantic*

Faulty parallelism results when the added part does not fit the expected pattern. For instance, "*ignorant* and *a miser*" is off balance because it joins an adjective and a noun. You could change *ignorant* to a noun ("He was an *ignoramus* and a miser") or *miser* to an adjective ("He was ignorant and *miserly*").

FAULTY: He liked *the country* and *to walk* in the fields.
PARALLEL: He liked *to live* in the country and *to walk* in the fields.

FAULTY: She told me of *her plans* and *that she was leaving.*
PARALLEL: She *informed* me of her plans and *told* me that she was leaving.

Look especially for the following:

(1) *Avoid linking a noun with an adjective as the modifier of another noun:*

FAULTY: The schools must serve *personal and society* needs as they evolve.
PARALLEL: The schools must serve *personal and social* needs as they evolve.

(2) *Check for parallelism when using paired connectives.* These are words like *either . . . or, neither . . . nor, not only . . . but also,* and *whether . . . or:*

FAULTY: I used to find him either *on the porch* or *dozing* in the living room.
PARALLEL: I used to find him either *sitting* on the porch or *dozing* in the living room.

**83**

| FAULTY: | We wondered whether *to believe* him or *should* we try to verify his story. |
|---|---|
| PARALLEL: | We wondered whether we should *believe* him or *try* to verify his story. |

(3) *Avoid faulty parallelism in a series of three or more elements.* Do not lead your readers into what looks like a series, only to make the last element snap out of the expected pattern:

| FAULTY: | He liked *to swim, relax,* and *everything peaceful.* |
|---|---|
| PARALLEL: | He liked *swimming, relaxation,* and peaceful *surroundings.* |

If the elements in a faulty series are not really parallel in *meaning*, the revision might break up the series altogether:

| FAULTY: | My new friend was *polite, studious,* and *an only child.* |
|---|---|
| PARALLEL: | My new friend was *a gentleman, a scholar,* and *an only child.* |
| BROKEN UP: | My new friend, *an only child,* was a gentleman and a scholar. |

(4) *Repeat structural links as needed to reinforce parallel structure.* Repeating a preposition like *for* or *to*, or a connective like *when* or *whether*, can help you improve parallelism in a sentence:

| FAULTY: | The story focuses on whether *the old man will capture* the large fish or *will the fish elude* him. |
|---|---|
| PARALLEL: | The story focuses on *whether* the old man will capture the large fish or *whether* the fish will elude him. |

# EXERCISES

A. Check the following passages for unnecessary or confusing *shifts in perspective.* Label each sentence *S* (satisfactory) or *U* (unsatisfactory). Be prepared to explain how you would revise unsatisfactory sentences.

1. Things like this make people face reality and wonder what their destiny is going to be.
2. We gathered some old rags, and a bucket and soap were placed near the car.
3. The harder I push, the tighter I grip the wrench, the more the blood dripped from my scraped knuckles, and the angrier I became.
4. The more I think about the accident, the more one question kept entering my mind.

5. It was soon discovered by the students that if you didn't work fast you were put in the slow group.
6. Suddenly the sky darkens, a breeze springs up, and thunder rolls across the lake.
7. Only when one faces the decision of whether to have an abortion can you really feel what a tough issue it is.
8. A true gentleman behaves the way he does because courtesy has to him become second nature.
9. As the world grew dark, he dreams of a place he will never see.
10. To the early Christians, endurance meant seeing one's loved ones thrown to wild beasts without losing faith in your God.
11. Parents must take an active interest in what their children are doing. Coach a ball team or be a counselor to a scout group.
12. As I walk by the shop, the owner, not having anything to do, was looking out of the window.
13. The police were warning us that if the crowd did not calm down arrests will be made.
14. My favorite television program was already in progress. Right in the middle of a dramatic scene, the station goes off the air.
15. Millions of people every day rush off to jobs they detest.

B. Check the following sentences for *parallel structure.* Label each sentence *S* for satisfactory, or *FP* for faulty parallelism. Be prepared to explain how you would revise the unsatisfactory sentences.

1. Her parents kept telling her Joe was poor, lazy, and his hair was too long.
2. The affluent American has a large income, a nice house, and lives in the nice part of town.
3. The book made me remember the bombings, the dismembered bodies, and the fire and fury of war.
4. The boy described how he was beaten by his masters, taken advantage of by the older servants, and the meager meals of bread and porridge he received.
5. To most readers, the word *home* suggests security and comfort as well as a place to live.
6. The success of a television program depends on how well the program has been advertised, the actors taking part, and is it comedy or serious drama.
7. Students come to college to have fun, find a husband or wife, and many other ridiculous reasons.
8. Objective tests can never be a true measure of ability or an accurate prediction of future success.
9. My father thought that girls should not go to dances, see boys only in the company of a chaperone, and many other old-fashioned prejudices.
10. In many gangster movies, the hero deceives the police, moves in the best society, and shows brazen courage when finally cornered by the police.

C. (Review) Make each of the following sentences *more consistent* by rewriting the italicized part. Write the rewritten part after the number of the sentence.

1. I had been waiting for more than three hours *when finally help arrives.*
2. During the summer, they planned to hitchhike, stop at interesting places, *and taking side trips whenever they felt like it.*
3. The rain fell for thirteen days; *then suddenly the sun shines.*
4. People wonder at times *if others try to make you feel bad on purpose.*
5. Teenagers assert their independence through the way they dress, comb their hair, *and their tastes in music.*
6. He blamed me for not giving him a chance to succeed *and I ruined his big chance for him.*
7. We are not qualified to speak of good *if evil has never been examined.*
8. She got her opinions by listening to her teachers *and then evaluate their ideas.*
9. If voters understood the true extent of environmental pollution, *they will vote for the necessary cleanup measures.*
10. Few newspaper readers understand the subtle ways *in which advertisers appeal to your fears and prejudices.*

# 3

# Sentence Punctuation

# DIAGNOSTIC TEST

## INSTRUCTIONS:

Look at the blank in each of the following sentences. Of the three possible choices that follow the sentence, which would be right for serious written English? Put the letter for the right choice after the number of the sentence.

1. The weather had _____ was raining heavily.
   a. changed it        b. changed, it        c. changed; it

2. Our friends had a fishing _____ converted navy boat.
   a. trawler, a        b. trawler. A        c. trawler; a

3. The offer has _____ we are returning your check.
   a. expired therefore    b. expired; therefore,    c. expired, therefore,

4. We put everything in the back of the _____ wear, fishing gear, and coils of rope.
   a. truck, rain        b. truck: rain        c. truck. Rain

5. Lillian _____ as a playwright, also wrote *An Unfinished Woman*.
   a. Hellman, known    b. Hellman known    c. Hellman; known

6. Dudley had been the second _____ the first.
   a. child not        b. child; not        c. child, not

7. We had moved to _____ when I was three.
   a. El Paso, Texas,    b. El Paso Texas    c. El Paso Texas,

8. An attendant came in and asked: "Who is _____
   a. next?        b. next"?        c. next?"

9. The handicapped were _____ new legislation.
   a. helped. By        b. helped by        c. helped; by

10. She urged her daughters to take difficult _____ calculus.
    a. subjects, such as    b. subjects. Such as    c. subjects, such as,

11. "Be careful," my aunt _____ cannot be trusted."
    a. said, she        b. said, "she        c. said. "She

12. Traditional cars—big, showy, _____ on the way out.
    a. uneconomical were        b. uneconomical—were
    c. uneconomical, were

13. We lived in a small _____ of the people were farmers.
    a. town most        b. town; most        c. town, most

**14.** To speed up _____ sent the money in advance.
   a. delivery, we          b. delivery we          c. delivery; we

**15.** The store sold fishing supplies: _____ and beer.
   a. bait, tackle,          b. bait tackle          c. bait; tackle

**16.** According to the biographer, "Walt Whitman always dreamed of 'the true _____
   a. America."          b. America".          c. America.'"

**17.** There will be no diplomas for _____ fail the tests.
   a. students, who          b. students. Who          c. students who

**18.** People applying for _____ to fill in long forms.
   a. loans have          b. loans, have          c. loans; have

**19.** Who first said, "Less is _____
   a. more?"          b. more"?          c. more."

**20.** Many settlers had _____ the year was over.
   a. died. Before          b. died, before          c. died before

# P1  END PUNCTUATION

**Use end punctuation to mark off complete sentences.**

End punctuation brings what we are saying to a complete stop. We use it to separate complete sentences—units that can stand by themselves. Here are three kinds of complete sentences:

STATEMENTS:    We hear much about solar energy.
               Many Canadians speak French.
               Space probes have landed on Venus.

QUESTIONS:     Do our big cities have a future?
               Why has your policy changed?
               What should we do next?

# PUNCTUATION MARKS
## Reference Chart

**COMMA**
before coordinators   P 2b
with nonrestrictive adverbial clauses   P 2d
after introductory adverbial clauses   P 2d
with nonrestrictive relative clauses   P 2e
with nonrestrictive modifiers   P 3b
after introductory modifiers   P 3c
with adverbial connectives   P 2c
with *especially, namely, for example*   P 1a
with *after all, of course,* and other sentence   P 3c
   modifiers
between items in a series   P 4a
in a series of parallel clauses   P 2a
between coordinate adjectives   P 4b
with dates, addresses, and measurements   P 4c
with direct address and other parenthetic   P 5c
   elements
between repeated or contrasted elements   P 4d
with direct quotations   P 6a

**SEMICOLON**
between closely related sentences   P 2a
before adverbial connectives   P 2c
before coordinators between clauses
   containing commas   P 2b
in a series with items containing commas   P 4a

**COLON**
to introduce a list or an explanation   P 1a
to introduce a formal quotation   P 6a

**PERIOD**
at end of sentence   P 1a
for ellipsis   P 6c
with abbreviations   M 2a

**DASH**
to show a break in thought   P 1a, P 5a
before summary at end of sentence   P 5a

**QUOTATION MARKS**
with direct quotations   P 6a
for quotation within quotation   P 6a
with terminal marks   P 6b
with technical terms   P 6e
to set off titles   M 1d, P 6f

**EXCLAMATION MARK**   P 1c

**QUESTION MARK**   P 1c

**PARENTHESES**   P 5b

| REQUESTS | Send in your coupon now! |
|---|---|
| OR | Turn down the radio! |
| COMMANDS: | Sell real estate in your spare time! |

## P1a  Sentences and Fragments                    *frag*

**Use the period at the end of a simple statement.**

A complete statement normally needs at least a subject and a complete verb. Look at the complete verbs that help turn each of the following into a separate sentence:

Linda *works* downtown.
My insurance *will pay* for the damage.
Her friends *are studying* in the library.
My baggage *was left* behind.

Do not use a period to set off a unit that is not a complete sentence but merely a **sentence fragment**. Most fragments merely register in writing the many fragmentary sentences we hear in speech. The most common kind adds an afterthought to the main statement. Each of the following sentence fragments adds an explanation or a comment:

| FRAGMENT: | I left home. *To go to college.* |
|---|---|
| FRAGMENT: | They pulled up in their new car. *A gray Mercedes.* |
| FRAGMENT: | The office was closed. *Because of a strike.* |
| FRAGMENT: | They promised to deliver the car. *Tomorrow.* |

Sometimes a sentence fragment is a single word. However, most sentence fragments are **phrases**—groups of words that cannot appear as separate statements. They lack either a subject, or all or part of the verb. All of the following are typical sentence fragments:

| ADJECTIVES AND ADVERBS: | Early in the morning. |
|---|---|
| | Late as usual. |
| | Beautiful but dangerous. |
| PREPOSITIONAL PHRASES: | In an old station wagon. |
| | For my brothers and me. |
| | Without a valid permit. |

**91**

| APPOSITIVES: | Her ex-husband. |
| | A dear old friend. |
| | The next turn after this. |

| VERBALS: | Basking in the sun. |
| | Being a holiday. |
| | Having studied all night. |
| | Written on a napkin. |

Other sentence fragments are dependent clauses. A clause has its own subject and verb. But a dependent clause starts with a connective that *subordinates* the clause to the main part of the sentence. Such connectives are **subordinators** like *if, because, when, unless, although,* and *whereas.* Or they are **relative pronouns**: *who, which,* and *that.* The following dependent clauses are typical fragments:

| SUBORDINATORS: | *If* you arrive in time. |
| | *Because* the motor was running. |
| | *Whereas* Lyle pays all her own bills. |

| RELATIVE | *Which* had never happened before. |
| PRONOUNS: | *Who* lived in the house next door. |

Do the following to eliminate sentence fragments:

(1) *Try joining the fragment to the main statement without any punctuation at all.* Whenever a fragment is pointed out to you, try first to connect it with the main idea in such a way that the sentence flows smoothly, without interruption. Most prepositional phrases and infinitives can be joined to the main statement without a break.

| FRAGMENT: | Be sure to be there. *At seven o'clock.* |
| REVISED: | Be sure to be there *at seven o'clock.* |

| FRAGMENT: | He bought a used car. *In spite of my warnings.* |
| REVISED: | He bought a used car *in spite of my warnings.* |

| FRAGMENT: | His sister had gone back to school. *To study medicine.* |
| REVISED: | His sister had gone back to school *to study medicine.* |

(2) *Use a* **comma** *as required when an appositive, a verbal phrase, or the like adds optional or nonessential information.* Additions like the following require a slight break, signaled by a comma:

We had coffee with Henry, *a dear old friend.*
I slept through most of the day, *having worked all night.*
He collected South American snakes, *beautiful but dangerous.*

> See **P 2** and **P 3** for situations that require a comma.

(3)   *Use a* **colon** *to introduce a list or an explanation.* Such a colon means "as follows." It introduces a list or description of something that has already been mentioned in a more general way. Note that a complete statement precedes the colon in each of the following examples:

We have two excellent players this year: *Phil and Tom.*

They served an old-fashioned breakfast: *fishballs, brown bread, and baked beans.*

Your friend lacks an essential quality: *tact.*

(4)   *Use a* **comma** *when an explanation or example follows a familiar transitional expression.* Added explanations or examples often follow expressions like *especially, such as, namely,* or *for example.* When they introduce material that is not a complete sentence, these expressions usually come after a comma:

The school attracted many foreign students, *especially* Arabs.
Our laws protect religious minorities, *such as* Mormons or Quakers.

In formal usage, a second comma often separates *namely, for example, for instance,* and *that is* from what they introduce. (This second comma is *not* used with *especially* and *such as.*)

She objected to my system of punctuating, *for example,* my use of dashes.

(5)   *Use a* **dash** *to show a definite break in thought:*

These are my relatives—*a motley crew.*
He would close his eyes and talk into the dictaphone—*a strange way to write an English theme.*

> For more on uses of the dash, see **P 5a.**

(6)   *Turn the fragment into a separate statement.* If the fragment cannot become part of the preceding statement, develop it into a complete separate sentence:

**93**

FRAGMENT: She appealed to a higher court. *Being a futile effort.*
REVISED: She appealed to a higher court. *The effort was futile.*

*Note*: Experienced writers use **permissible fragments** for special effects. The following examples illustrate the most common of these:

- Common *transitional expressions*:

  *So much for* past developments. *Now for* a look at our present problems.

- *Answers to questions*, suggesting the give-and-take of conversation:

  What did we gain? *Nothing.*

- *Descriptive passages*, especially when designed to give a static, pictorial effect:

  We stood in the hot dry night air at one in the morning, waiting for a train at an Arizona station. *Nothing but the purple arc of sky and at the end of the platform the silhouette of a cottonwood tree lapped by a hot breeze. The stars big as sunflowers.*—Alistair Cooke, *One Man's America*

- Narrative passages suggesting *random, disconnected thought*:

  There he is: the brother. *Image of him. Haunting face.*—James Joyce, *Ulysses*

Most teachers discourage their students from experimenting with such incomplete sentences. To be safe, avoid all fragments in ordinary expository writing.

# P1b   Fused Sentences                                    *FS*

**Make sure you do not run together two complete sentences without any punctuation.**

Sometimes a second sentence ties in closely with what has gone before. If there is no punctuation to separate the two statements, the result is a **fused sentence**:

| | |
|---|---|
| FUSED: | Fred no longer lives here *he left for Alaska.* |
| REVISED: | Fred no longer lives here. *He left for Alaska.* |
| | |
| FUSED: | She took the exam over *this was her last chance.* |
| REVISED: | She took the exam over. *This was her last chance.* |

> For the semicolon between closely related sentences, see **P 2a.**

## P1c Exclamations and Questions                    *?/!/*

**Signal exclamations and questions by adding the appropriate marks.**

(1) *Use an exclamation mark to give an utterance unusual emphasis.* Such utterances range from a groan, curse, or shout to an order or a command. The **exclamation mark** can signal excitement, insistence, surprise, indignation, or fear:

> Ouch!
> Silence! Get up! Close the book!
> They like me!
> And this person wants to be President!

Note that exclamation marks rarely appear in ordinary expository prose.

(2) *Use a question mark whenever an utterance is worded as a request for information.* Whenever you raise your voice inquiringly at the end of something you say, terminate the written equivalent with a **question mark** (*He sent you a check?*). Not all questions, however, are marked by intonation, or changes in the tone of voice. Use the question mark nevertheless:

> Who are you?
> What did he want?

Do not forget to use question marks at the end of questions that are *long or involved*:

> How is a new student supposed to find her way through the maze of instructions printed in small print in the college catalog?

**95**

# EXERCISES

A. In which of the following passages is the second unit a *sentence fragment*? Write *frag* after the number of each such passage. In which of the following passages is the second unit a complete separate sentence? Write *S* for satisfactory after the number.

1. The United States has always been a rich country. Free from serious starvation problems and devastating diseases.
2. Christmas time in prison is a sad time. Grimy walls like any other time of the year.
3. The cry for law and order has changed nothing. Crimes are still as numerous as before.
4. Americans were considered materialists. Interested only in money.
5. The story begins like a typical short story. A story about a small town having a drawing once a year.
6. The smart students bragged about their grades. The athletic stars treated other people as inferiors.
7. The article is aimed at the twenty- to twenty-seven-year-old group. Male and female college juniors, seniors, and recent graduates trying to find employment with little luck.
8. Moviegoers are tired of sex and violence. They can get those on the evening news.
9. The school was very poor. Most of the time, we shared books.
10. I want to be able to write a good essay. Something with facts and important details.
11. She left school after two years. To take over her father's business.
12. Many minority students went out for sports. Because it gave them their only real chance.
13. People used to grow up in larger families. For example, a family consisting of parents, grandparents, and three or four children.
14. The place was called the loft. It was a big room at the top of the building.
15. We got a new teacher. She was a deeply concerned and dedicated woman.
16. The veterinarian told us the animal had died of a heart attack. While he was preparing to operate.
17. A regulation target resembles an upside-down saucer. Measuring no more than five inches in diameter.
18. She simply could not satisfy anybody's standards. Not those of her superiors and not those of her co-workers.
19. The ocean has always beckoned to people. Daring them to risk all to sail the seas.
20. Felipe has never washed a dish in his life. He does not mind cooking.

B. Check the following for sentence fragments and other *problems with end punctuation*. Write down the italicized part of each example, adding or changing punctuation as necessary. (Use a period followed by a capital letter to separate two complete sentences.)

1. There were jobs for *the newcomers the rent was reasonable.*
2. That morning I *had been late. Because of the wait in the bus line.*
3. The mother had hiked *down into the valley. To get help.*
4. They were studying the marvels of *Indian architecture. Such as Aztec pyramids and Mayan temples.*
5. Men once had clearly *defined roles. Hunting and fishing.*
6. One woman was a *jockey the other woman interviewed was a commercial pilot.*
7. We tried a new *sales technique. With good results.*
8. What good does it do to kill *a person for taking someone else's life.*
9. He was attacking his *favorite target. Public money for private schools.*
10. American schools are neglecting the major languages *of the modern world. Especially Russian and Chinese.*
11. When will people realize that *the resources of this planet are not inexhaustible.*
12. Her favorite authors were always experimenting with *impossible new ideas. For example, robots with human emotions.*
13. In the old sentimental stories, the desperate unwed mother would *leave her child on someone's doorstep. In a wicker basket.*
14. He began to consider *the unthinkable. Turning himself in.*
15. The prime suspect had spent the evening *conducting a symphony orchestra. A perfect alibi.*

# P2    LINKING PUNCTUATION

**Use commas or semicolons as required when several clauses combine in a larger sentence.**

Several short statements may combine to become part of a larger sentence. We call each subsentence in the new combined sentence a **clause**. Independent clauses are still self-contained. They could easily be separated again by a period. Dependent clauses have been linked in a more permanent way. They would sound incomplete if separated from the main clause.

# P2a   Comma Splice            *cs*

**Use a semicolon between complete sentences that are closely related.**

A **semicolon** may replace the period between two complete sentences. Often two statements go together as related pieces of information. Or they line up related ideas for contrast. When a semicolon replaces the period, the first word of the second statement is *not* capitalized:

> Sunshine was everywhere; orchards were in bloom.
> Some librarians circulate books; others hoard them.
> He had long and wavy hair; it made him look young.

Remember:

(1) *Do not use a comma alone to join two independent clauses.* Notice that there is no connective between the two clauses in each of the following pairs. The clauses remain independent. A **comma splice** runs on from one independent clause to the next with only a comma to keep them apart:

COMMA SPLICE:   I loved London, it is a wonderful city.
REVISED:        I loved London; it is a wonderful city.

COMMA SPLICE:   Carol is twenty-eight years old, she might go back to school.
REVISED:        Carol is twenty-eight years old; she might go back to school.

(2) *Never merely put two independent clauses next to each other without any punctuation.* A **fused sentence** results when two such clauses are simply run together without a connective:

FUSED:     I am not sick I just like to sit in a chair and think.
REVISED:   I am not sick; I just like to sit in a chair and think.

(3) *Use commas if you wish to separate three or more parallel clauses.* Note that the clauses in the following examples are closely related in meaning and similar in structure:

> Be brief, be blunt, be gone.
> Students in India demonstrate against the use of English, African nationalists protest against the use of French, young Israelis have no use for the languages once spoken by their parents.

*Note*: Some writers use the comma between *two* independent clauses when the logical connection or similarity in structure is especially close:

> Rage cannot be hidden, it can only be dissembled.—James Baldwin, *Notes of a Native Son*

Many teachers and editors object to this practice; avoid it in your own writing.

# P 2b Coordinators

*⬦ or ⬦*

**Use a comma when a coordinator links two clauses.**

Coordinating connectives typically require a comma. *And, but, for, or, nor, so,* and *yet* link two clauses without making the one more important than the other. There are only seven of these coordinators. Put a **comma** where the first clause ends, *before* the connective:

The bell rang, *and* George rushed out of the room.
She saw me, *but* she did not recognize me.
We went inside, *for* it had started to rain.
You had better apologize, *or* she will not speak to you again.
The singer was ill, *so* the performance was canceled.
Everyone knew the truth, *yet* no one spoke up.

After *nor,* the usual order of subject and verb is changed:

We cannot let key industries die, *nor can we subsidize* every business in trouble.

Remember the following exceptions and variations:

(1)  *Do not use a comma with a coordinator when it merely joins two words or two phrases:*

NO COMMA:  A truck driver came in *and* sat down at the counter.
NO COMMA:  We usually picnicked in the park *or* on the beach.

(2)  And, but, *and* or *often appear without a comma when the clauses they join are short.* Yet *and* so *are frequently used with a* **semicolon**:

The wind was blowing *and* the water was cold.
The critics praised Oliver's work; *yet* no one bought his paintings.

(3)  *Any coordinator may be used with a* **semicolon** *between clauses that already contain commas or that are unusually long:*

Now in the Big Bend the river encounters mountains in a new and extraordinary way; *for* they lie, chain after chain of them, directly across its way.—Paul Horgan, "Pages from a Rio Grande Notebook," *New York Times Book Review*

**99**

**(4)** *Coordinators leave the clauses they join self-sufficient or independent grammatically.* Thus, the clauses they connect may still be kept separate from each other by a **period**:

I called your office twice. *But* nobody answered. *So* I left without you.

See Glossary on **and** or **but** beginning a sentence.

## P2c    Adverbial Connectives           *p* or *;/*

**Use a semicolon with adverbial connectives.**

Adverbial connectives are words like *therefore, however, nevertheless, consequently, hence, accordingly, moreover, furthermore, besides, indeed,* and *in fact.* (The older term for these words is **conjunctive adverb**.) The two statements they join are often linked by a **semicolon** rather than by a period. A period, nevertheless, would still be possible and acceptable:

Business was improving; *therefore,* we changed our plans.
Business was improving. *Therefore,* we changed our plans.

The hall was nearly empty; *nevertheless,* the curtain rose.
The hall was nearly empty. *Nevertheless,* the curtain rose.

Remember:

**(1)** *Do not use just a comma with adverbial connectives.* If a comma replaces the semicolon, the sentence turns into a **comma splice**:

COMMA SPLICE:     French Canadians insisted on preserving their language, *therefore* federal employees were being taught French.
REVISED:         French Canadians insisted on preserving their language; *therefore,* federal employees were being taught French.

**(2)** *Put the semicolon at the point where the two statements join, regardless of the position of the connective.* The adverbial connective itself often appears *later* in the second clause:

English is required; *therefore,* students have no choice.
English is required; students, *therefore,* have no choice.
English is required; students have no choice, *therefore.*

Use this possible shift in position to help you identify members of this group. They share their freedom of movement with adverbs (and are therefore called "*adverbial* connectives" or "conjunctive *adverbs*").

(3) *In formal writing, separate the adverbial connective from the rest of the second statement.* Use one or two **commas** as required. Make sure that there is a punctuation mark both before and after the connective:

FORMAL:    We liked the area; the food, *however,* was impossible.
FORMAL:    Demand had dropped off; prices, *nevertheless,* remained high.

*Note*: These additional commas are *optional*. Informal writing and journalistic writing tend toward **open punctuation**, using fewer commas than formal writing does. Accordingly, the authors of popular books and magazine articles tend not to separate adverbial connectives from the rest of a clause.

# P2d    Subordinators        *p* or ⌖

Use either commas or no punctuation as required with subordinators.

Subordinating connectives are words like *if, when, because, although,* and *whereas.* An *if* or a *because* changes a self-sufficient, independent clause into a **dependent clause**, which normally cannot stand by itself. "If I were in charge" does not become a complete sentence until you answer the question "If you were in charge, *then what*?" Beware of dependent clauses added to a main statement as an afterthought:

FRAGMENT:    He failed the test. *Because he did not study.*
REVISED:    He failed the test *because he did not study.*

Subordinators normally start dependent clauses that tell us when, where, why, or how (**adverbial clauses**). Here is a list of subordinators, sorted out according to the kind of information they bring into a sentence:

| | |
|---|---|
| TIME AND PLACE: | when, whenever, while, before, after, since, until, as long as, where, wherever |
| REASON OR CONDITION: | because, if, unless, provided |
| CONTRAST: | though, although, whereas, no matter how |

**101**

In some situations, subordinators require *no punctuation*. In others, they require *commas*. Observe the following guidelines:

(1)   *Use no punctuation to set off restrictive adverbial clauses.* Adverbial clauses often restrict or limit the meaning of the main clause. They *narrow* the possibilities. They state essential conditions. Suppose an employer tells you, "I'll raise everyone's wages *after I strike oil.*" Without the proviso about striking oil, the sentence would sound like an immediate promise of more money. With the proviso, it means that you will get more money only by a remote chance.

When they *follow* the main clause, such **restrictive** clauses are not set off by punctuation:

> Hundreds will perish *if* the dam breaks.
> The firm will fail *unless* business improves.
> Do not sign *until* you hear from me.
> Check for leaks *before* you light the pilot.
> I will follow *wherever* you go.

(2)   *Use commas to set off nonrestrictive adverbial clauses.* Occasionally the time, place, or condition for an action or event is already shown in the main clause. In that case, the dependent clause may merely *elaborate* on the information already given. Such dependent clauses are called **nonrestrictive**. They are separated from the main clause by a **comma**:

> She went back to *Georgia, where* she was born.
> Bats were well developed *as far back as the Eocene, when* our ancestors were still in the trees.

(3)   *Set off an adverbial clause that establishes a contrast.* *Though, although,* and *whereas* usually introduce nonrestrictive material. They usually require a **comma**. Rather than adding essential conditions, these words establish a *contrast* between the statements they connect. Both statements are separately true:

> I like the work, *though* the salary is low.
> Her friend wore a sports shirt and slacks, *whereas* the other men wore tuxedos.

Combinations like *whether or not* and *no matter how* show that the main statement is true *regardless*:

We are canceling the lease, *whether you like it or not.*
She will never forgive you, *no matter what you do.*

(4) *Set off an adverbial clause that comes before the main clause.* When a subordinator joins two statements, we can reverse their order. After an introductory adverbial clause, a **comma** normally indicates where the main clause starts:

Vote for me *if you trust me.*
*If you trust me,* vote for me.

I drove more slowly *after I noticed the police car.*
*After I noticed the police car,* I drove more slowly.

(5) *Go by the meaning of the sentence when using connectives like* because *and* so that. Some subordinators introduce either restrictive or nonrestrictive material, depending on the meaning of the sentence:

NO COMMA: Why are you going to town?
I am going to town *because I want to do some shopping.*
(The reason for your trip is the essential part of the sentence.)
COMMA: What are you going to do?
*I am going to town,* because I want to do some shopping.
(The reason for your trip is added, nonrestrictive explanation.)

*Note*: Some connectives belong to *different groups*, and are punctuated differently, depending on their meaning in the sentence. *However* is normally an adverbial connective and requires a semicolon. It sometimes takes the place of the subordinating connective *no matter how* and requires a comma:

ADVERBIAL: I cannot please him; *however, I am trying hard.*
SUBORDINATOR: I cannot please him, *however hard I try.*

*Though*, normally a subordinator, is used in informal English as an adverbial connective placed in the middle or at the end of a clause:

ADVERBIAL: I needed more freedom; *my parents, though, didn't agree with me.*

# P 2e   Relative Clauses

𝄒 or ⌃

**Use either commas or no punctuation as required with relative clauses.**

Relative clauses start with a relative pronoun: *who (whose, whom), which,* or *that.* Such clauses add information about one of the nouns (or pronouns) in the main part of the sentence. They can, therefore, appear at different points in the sentence. They may *interrupt* as well as follow the main clause:

> The odds favored candidates *who applied early.*
> The address *that they gave us* does not exist.
> Those *who know how to talk* can buy on credit. (Creole proverb)

Observe the following guidelines:

(1)   *Use no punctuation to set off restrictive relative clauses.* The added information is essential when we need it to know "Which one?" or "What kind?" Such relative clauses narrow the possibilities; they help us identify something. Such clauses are **restrictive**. They are *not* separated from the rest of the sentence by commas:

> People *who live in glass houses* should not throw stones.
> (applies only to special people)
> People love animals *that are furry and cuddly.*
> (applies only to this special kind)
> Call the woman *whose name appears on this card.*
> (identifies the person)

The pronoun *that* almost always introduces a restrictive clause:

> The forms *that we sent in* were lost in the mail.
> We are looking for something *that works.*

Shortened relative clauses with a pronoun like *that* or *whom* left out are always restrictive:

> The forms *we sent in* were lost in the mail.
> The lawyer *she recommended* was out of town.

(2)   *Use commas to set off nonrestrictive relative clauses.* A relative clause is **nonrestrictive** if we already know which one or

**104**

what kind. Such nonessential information answers the question "What *else* about it?"

> Sharks differ from whales, *which surface to breathe.*
> (applies to all whales)
> We drove down Main Street, *which leads to City Hall.*
> (we already know which street)
> I called Aunt Sue, *to whom the letter was addressed.*
> (we already know which person)

When a nonrestrictive clause interrupts the main clause, *two* commas are needed:

> Computers, *which perform amazing feats,* do break down.
> Karen, *who was studying law,* seldom wrote.

(3) *Punctuate other clauses that modify nouns as you would relative clauses.* Sometimes a clause starting with *when, where,* or *why* modifies a noun:

RESTRICTIVE:     The place *where I work* has no heat.
NONRESTRICTIVE:  Minnesota, *where I was born,* has cold winters.

*Note:* Watch out for commas used mistakenly to set off a relative clause that is really restrictive:

WRONG:   Ex-convicts, *who carry guns,* should be sent back to jail.
RIGHT:   Ex-convicts *who carry guns* should be sent back to jail.
         (not all ex-convicts, only those who carry guns)

# P2f  Noun Clauses                                                        *p*

**Use no punctuation to set off noun clauses from the rest of the sentence.**

Use no punctuation when the place of one of the nouns in a sentence is taken by a *clause within a clause.* Clauses that take the place of a noun are called **noun clauses.** Do not set them off from the rest of the sentence by punctuation:

NOUN:         The mayor announced *her plans.*
NOUN CLAUSE:  The mayor announced *that she would retire.*

NOUN:         Irma told me *the story.*
NOUN CLAUSE:  Irma told me *why she had changed jobs.*

NOUN: *The writer* knew your name.
NOUN CLAUSE: *Whoever wrote it* knew your name.

Watch out for commas used mistakenly to set off noun clauses:

WRONG: I finally remembered**,** *that the store had moved.*
RIGHT: I finally remembered *that the store had moved.*

---

# EXERCISES

A. Each of the following sentences combines *two independent clauses.* In each case, the two clauses simply stand next to each other, without a connective. Write down the last word of the first clause and the first word of the second, with a semicolon to join them.

EXAMPLE: His hair was very neat every strand was in place.
(Answer) neat; every

1. A pawnshop is on the ground floor above it is a hotel.
2. The old man has stepped out of the lobby he is walking down the street.
3. I enjoy running it becomes an almost unconscious act.
4. People were shouting ridiculous commands everyone with a flashlight began directing traffic.
5. The building has two stories there are two big display windows on the ground floor.
6. At first we were afraid later we learned to trust each other.
7. Poverty is a major problem in our world it is found in every city in the United States.
8. The church is usually completely quiet a few people come in to pray.
9. John wasn't going to school anymore he was a photographer.
10. Being an officer in today's army is not easy it is a challenging but rewarding job.
11. I entered the office it was a very modern one with plants around the room.
12. We were once urged to buy and spend urgent messages to conserve are now coming at us from all directions.
13. This job was the most important thing in her life it was her chance to make it into the big time.
14. We fished in the stream until midnight it was illegal really to fish after dark.
15. She had just come out of the movie theater her face showed her satisfaction.

B. Each of the following examples *combines two clauses* in a larger sentence. How are the two clauses related, and what would be the right punctuation for the combined sentence? Choose the right answer for the blank space left in each sentence. After the number of the sentence, write *C* for comma, *SC* for semicolon, or *No* for no punctuation.

1. My parents never pressured me about getting married _____ in fact, they wanted me to finish college first.
2. She wasn't a big-time photographer _____ but she had enough work to keep up her studio.
3. Students who need financial aid _____ have to meet definite requirements.
4. He always talked about Chicago _____ which he called the Windy City.
5. Before we knew it _____ the party was over.
6. Some store clerks had the disgusting habit of waiting on whites before blacks _____ no matter how long the blacks had been waiting for service.
7. Lawmakers must rid the country of crime _____ before it reaches epidemic proportions.
8. My father fought with Pancho Villa _____ he was, in fact, the only private in Villa's army.
9. My friends were the sons of captains or colonels _____ though a few fathers were admittedly mere sergeants and corporals.
10. The dean never explained _____ why the application was denied.
11. Freedom of speech includes freedom for those _____ whose views we find offensive.
12. Jobs were scarce and insecure _____ so my parents left town.
13. The sun, which is the final source of most of our energy _____ is a gigantic nuclear furnace.
14. The furniture was all glass and steel _____ and the walls were painted a bright red.
15. Human beings could not survive on other planets _____ unless they created an artificial earthlike environment.
16. Many Spanish-speaking Americans are called Mexican-Americans _____ some parts of New Spain, however, were never a part of Mexico.
17. The whole crowd in the theater cheered _____ when the cavalry came to the rescue at the end of the movie.
18. When meteors hit the surface _____ they form craters like those made by volcanoes.
19. My parents never became thoroughly Americanized _____ but they had also become strangers in their native land.
20. Space exploration is incredibly expensive _____ therefore, only a few of the richest nations take part.

C. Check the punctuation in the following combined sentences. Pay special attention to the difference between *restrictive and nonrestrictive.* Put *S* after the number of the sentence if punctuation is satisfactory. Put *U* if punctuation is unsatisfactory.

1. Nations often change place names that carry an unwanted legacy from the past.
2. The name Stalingrad, which acquired a symbolic meaning in World War II, later disappeared from the map.
3. St. Petersburg which was the capital of Czarist Russia is now Leningrad.
4. English and French names were widely used in Africa until the new nations became independent.
5. After the Belgians left the Congo, names like Leopoldville disappeared.
6. Maps no longer show Rhodesia, which was named after a British explorer.
7. Older names usually survive only, if they are not linked with the colonial past.
8. Similar changes took place in the Far East, where Batavia turned into Jakarta many years ago.
9. A Malaysian city had been named after Jesselton who was a British empire builder.
10. The city that bore his name is now called Kinabalu.

# P3   PUNCTUATING MODIFIERS   *p*

**Distinguish between modifiers set off by commas and those requiring no punctuation.**

Often nouns and verbs carry along further material that develops or modifies their meaning. How we punctuate such modifiers depends on the role they play in the sentence. The following sections deal with punctuation that may be required for modifiers that become part of one single clause.

## P3a   Unnecessary Commas   *p*

**Do not use commas between basic sentence elements.**

Do not use a comma between the subject and its verb, or between the verb and one or more objects. In addition, do *not* set off the many modifiers that blend into a simple sentence without a break. These include many single-word modifiers: adjectives and adverbs. They also include most prepositional phrases:

> *Perhaps* he will call *again.*
> Forms *with unanswered questions* will be returned.
> They had traveled *to California in 1981.*

# P3b   Restrictive and Nonrestrictive Modifiers   *p* or ⌃

**Know when to use commas with modifiers.**

Punctuation may be required when a modifier follows a noun (or a pronoun). A noun may be followed by an **appositive**—a second noun that modifies the first. It may be followed by a **verbal phrase**—starting with a form like *running, explaining, starting,* or with a form like *dressed, sold, taken.* Or it may be followed by an **adjective phrase**—made up of several adjectives, or of an adjective and other material:

APPOSITIVES:   Her aunt, *a lawyer,* lived in Boston.
We visited the place, *a vegetarian restaurant.*

VERBALS:   The person *running the place* was a friend.
We saw the bride, *dressed in white.*

ADJECTIVES:   The climbers, *weary but happy,* started down.
We approached the lake, *smooth as a mirror.*

Observe the following guidelines:

(1)   *Use no punctuation with restrictive modifiers.* Modifiers that follow a noun become an essential part of the statement if they are used for the purpose of identification. In that case, they are **restrictive**: They limit or narrow a general term like *student* to single out one particular student or one particular kind:

RESTRICTIVE:   A student *showing a valid I.D.* will enter free.
(Others pay.)
RESTRICTIVE:   We collected containers *suitable for recycling.*
(We discarded the others.)

(2)   *Use commas to set off nonrestrictive modifiers.* Often a modifier merely gives further information about something already identified. It is **nonrestrictive**. Nonrestrictive material is set off from the rest of the sentence by a **comma**. Use a comma both before and after if the nonrestrictive material occurs in the middle of the sentence:

She talked to her lawyer.
(What else about that person?)
She talked to her lawyer, *a well-known attorney.*

**109**

The applicant requested an interview.
(What else about her?)
The applicant, *a recent graduate,* requested an interview.

(3) *Remember that a proper name is usually adequate identification.* A modifier following a name is usually nonrestrictive. It is usually set off:

She joined the Actors' Theater, *a repertory company.*
Uncle Max, *smiling broadly,* stood in the doorway.

H. J. Heinz, *the Pittsburgh pickle packer,* keeps moving up in the food-processing industry.

However, a *restrictive* modifier occasionally is needed to help the reader distinguish between several people of the same name:

I find it hard to distinguish between Holmes *the author* and Holmes *the Supreme Court justice.*

(4) *Occasionally a modifier already contains one or more commas.* Use **dashes** to set such a modifier off from the rest of the sentence:

My sister—a *tough, stubborn, hard-driving competitor*—won many prizes.

# P3c   Sentence Modifiers   *𝒑* or ⌃

**Set sentence modifiers off by commas.**

Modifiers may modify sentence elements other than nouns. They may also modify the sentence as a whole rather than any part of it. Look for the following:

(1) *Verbals and verbal phrases modifying a verb may be either restrictive or nonrestrictive.* Notice the **comma** showing the difference:

RESTRICTIVE:     He always came into the office *carrying a shirt box full of letters under his arm.*

NONRESTRICTIVE:  Deadline newspaper writing is rapid because it cheats, *depending heavily on clichés and stock phrases.*

(2) *Always set off verbal phrases modifying the sentence as a whole.* Such phrases are often called **absolute constructions**:

*To tell you the truth,* I don't even recall his name.
*The business outlook being rosy,* he invested his savings in highly speculative stocks.
Our new manager has done well, *considering her lack of experience.*

(3)  *Set off long introductory modifiers.* If a sentence is introduced by a long modifying phrase, use a **comma** to show where the main sentence starts. Use this comma after prepositional phrases of three words or more:

*After a solemn Sunday dinner,* Father called me into his study.

*Like many good reporters,* they had long fumed at the low status of the journalistic rank and file.

Set off *introductory verbals and verbal phrases* even when they are short:

*Smiling,* she closed the cash register.
*To start the motor,* turn the ignition key.

(4)  *If you wish, use the optional commas with transitional expressions.* Expressions like *after all, of course, unfortunately, on the whole, as a rule,* and *certainly* often do not modify any one part of a sentence. Instead, they help us go on from one sentence to another. Depending on the amount of emphasis you would give such a modifier when reading, make it stand out from the rest of the sentence by a **comma**:

*After all,* we are in business primarily for profit.
*On the other hand,* the records may never be found.
You will submit the usual reports, *of course.*

Sentence modifiers that are set off require *two* commas if they do not come first or last in the sentence:

We do not, *as a rule,* solicit applications.
A great many things, *to be sure,* could be said for him.

# EXERCISES

A.  Check the following sentences for conventional punctuation of *modifiers*. After the number of each sentence, put *S* for satisfactory, *U* for unsatisfactory. Be prepared to explain how you would revise unsatisfactory sentences.

**111**

1. Faced with sympathy or kindness, we reply with reserve. (Octavio Paz)
2. A young woman in California failed to "come down" after ingesting STP, a powerful hallucinogen.
3. My teachers in both high school and college gave me pointers on academic success.
4. Looking straight ahead you see a body of polluted water the Monongahela River.
5. Overdoses of the hardest drug, heroin, killed some 900 people in New York City alone.
6. Joe apparently not having any customers was sitting in his own barber chair and smoking a cigar.
7. For Chinese-speaking children in American schools, English used to be the only approved language of instruction.
8. A person leasing a car still has to pay for repairs and maintenance.
9. On the main island of Britain, the Welsh, hearing English constantly, are now mostly bilingual.
10. Having swallowed enough water to last me all summer I decided to leave water skiing alone.
11 A good example of our neglect of public health problems, is the lack of therapy for the mentally ill.
12. Spain once experienced a strong Arab influence, reflected in its architecture.
13. People, coming from Latin American countries, stand closer to each other in conversation than North Americans do.
14. Owen Nielsen, my godfather, was a passionate man, often shouting at his family at the dinner table.
15. Everyone, sitting at a desk, should have some exercise each day.

B. What punctuation, if any, should appear at the blank space in each of the following sentences? After the number of the sentence, write *C* for comma, *NC* for no comma, or *D* for dash.

1. In spite of repeated promises _____ the shipment never arrived.
2. The agency collected debts _____ from delinquent customers.
3. Whipped by the wind _____ five-foot swells splash over the deck.
4. The book told the story of Amelia Earhart _____ a true pioneer.
5. A printed receipt will be sent to all students _____ sending in their fees.
6. I looked with amazement at the pots _____ filled with large snapping Dungeness crabs.
7. Working on the pitching and rolling deck _____ we hauled up the heavy nets.
8. The owner, a large woman with mean eyes _____ watched us the whole time.
9. Back at the wharf _____ we sipped hot coffee, trying to get warm.
10. The city, on the other hand _____ has shown no interest in the project.
11. The mechanics working on a competitor's car _____ are racing against the clock.

12. The wooden benches, bolted to the planks _____ were torn loose by the waves.
13. My uncle—a jovial, fast-talking man _____ used to sell insurance.
14. Their performance has been unsatisfactory _____ to say the least.
15. The lawyer opened his briefcase _____ full of closely printed documents.

# P4    COORDINATION        *p* or ⌄

**Use the comma (and sometimes other marks) when several elements of the same kind appear together.**

When we coordinate parts of a sentence, we make several similar or related elements work together.

## P4a   Series

**Use commas to separate three or more items of the same kind in a series.**

A **series** is made up of three or more sentence parts of the same kind. The most common pattern separates the elements in a series by **commas**. The last comma is followed by an *and* or *or* that ties the whole group together:

> After dinner, *we talked, laughed, and sang.*
> The hills were bright with *red, white, and brown* poppies.
>
> Only 18 percent of this country's 56 million families are conventionally "nuclear," with *breadwinning fathers, homemaking mothers, and resident children.*—Jane Howard, *Families*

This basic *A, B, and C* pattern can be expanded to four or more elements:

> The stand sold *nuts, raisins, apples, and every other kind* of organic lunch.
> Many students worked as *cooks, dishwashers, janitors, or messengers.*

The following variations are possible:

(1) *The items in a series may be groups of words that already contain commas.* To prevent misreading, use **semicolons** to show the major breaks:

**113**

Three persons were mentioned in her will: *John, her brother; Martin, her nephew;* and *Helen, her faithful friend.*

(2) *A writer may leave out the* and *or the* or *for variety or for special effect.* The following example uses commas only:

The idea was to pool all the needs of all those who had in one way or another been bested by their environment—*the crippled, the sick, the hungry, the ragged.*—John Lear, "The Business of Giving," *Saturday Review*

*Note*: In informal or journalistic writing, the last comma is often left out. Most teachers, however, require the use of the last comma. Use it to be safe:

I *took* out my license, *laid* it on the table, and *watched* the agent pick it up.

## P4b  Coordinate Adjectives                    *p* or ⌃

**Separate coordinate adjectives by a comma.**

Two adjectives that work together to modify the same noun are called **coordinate** adjectives. Coordinate adjectives are interchangeable adjectives. Use a **comma** between them when you can reverse their order:

| a *tall, handsome* stranger | a *handsome, tall* stranger |
| a *foggy, drizzly* day | a *drizzly, foggy* day |

With true coordinate adjectives, an *and* could take the place of the comma:

a *black* and *shaggy* dog ⟶ a *black, shaggy* dog
a *starved* and *exhausted* stranger ⟶ a *starved, exhausted* stranger
a *grand* and *awe-inspiring* sunset ⟶ a *grand, awe-inspiring* sunset

Not every pair of adjectives falls into this pattern. Often an adjective combines with a noun to indicate a type of person or object: a *public* servant, a *short* story, a *black* market. An adjective that comes before such a combination modifies the combination as a whole. Do *not* separate such adjectives by a comma. Use the comma only if you could use *and* instead:

NO COMMA:  a *long* short story (not "long *and* short")
a *lively* black market (not "lively *and* black")
a *dedicated* public servant (not "dedicated *and* public")

# P4c  Dates and Addresses                    *p* or ↗

Use commas with dates, addresses, measurements, and similar information that has three or four parts.

Dates, addresses, page references, and the like often come in several parts. The different parts are kept separate from each other by a **comma**. The last item is followed by a comma unless it is at the same time the last word of the sentence:

DATE:       The date was *Tuesday, December 3,* 1981.
ADDRESS:    Please send my mail to *483 Tulane Street, Jackson, Oklahoma,* starting the first of the month.
REFERENCE:  The quotation is from *Chapter V, page 43, line 7,* of the second volume.

Commas are also used to keep separate the different parts of *measurements* employing more than one unit of measurement. Here the last item is usually *not* separated from the rest of the sentence:

The boy is now *five feet, seven inches* tall.
*Nine pounds, three ounces* is an unusual weight for this kind of fish.

# P4d  Repetition and Contrast                *p* or ↗

Use commas between repeated or contrasted elements.

Use commas between expressions that are identical or that give two different versions of the same meaning. Use the **comma** after a word or phrase to be repeated or to be followed by a definition or paraphrase:

*Produce, produce!* This is the law among artists.
We were there in the nine days before Christmas, *the Navidad.*

Undergraduate education must prepare the student *not to walk away from choices, not to leave them to the experts.*—Adele Simmons, "Harvard Flunks the Test," *Harper's*

Use commas also to separate words or groups of words that establish a *contrast*:

> His wife, not his brother, needs the money more.
> The days were warm, the nights cool.

Many entering freshmen and their parents seek an education that leads to *job security, not critical and independent thinking.*—Adele Simmons, "Harvard Flunks the Test," *Harper's*

# EXERCISES

A. Check the following sentences for punctuation of *coordinate or closely related elements.* After the number of each sentence, put *S* for satisfactory, *U* for unsatisfactory. Be prepared to explain how you would revise unsatisfactory sentences.

1. It was economics that altered the condition of slavery, not *Uncle Tom's Cabin.*
2. Mexicans have in them the placidity the gentleness and the patience of the Indian as well as the violence of the Spaniard.
3. He remembered the arenas with their intricate grillwork gates; the beautiful girls in festive gowns of red, purple, and every hue imaginable; and the excited crowds shouting "Bravo" to the fierce-eyed matador.
4. My cousin was always flying off to places like Chattanooga Tennessee or Missoula Montana.
5. The editorial offices of the magazine were located at 235 East 45th Street, New York, New York.
6. Aaron thought of himself as a noble, dedicated person persecuted by callous, materialistic teachers and employers.
7. Lee was known as a strategist not as a tactician.
8. The marooned astronauts came to know hunger, thirst, cold, and the continual throbbing headache of oxygen deprivation.
9. Ralph ran stumbling along the rocks, saved himself on the edge of the pink cliff, and screamed at the ship. (William Golding)
10. After a while, the messenger arrives with a large box full of breakfast: coffee, steaming hot; a triple order of bacon; two fried eggs; and bagels, split and buttered.
11. She had last been seen leaving church on Sunday, April 7, 1978, in Cleveland, Ohio.
12. The floor of the office was gritty with cigarette butts torn handbills and crushed cartons.
13. We had not expected to find such honest, public servants among such poor pessimistic people.

14. For them, yoga was a way of life, a cause, and a religion.
15. One corner of the room is fitted with three worn turntables, a huge electric clock, and a cantilevered microphone that hangs over a console of switches, buttons, and dials.

B. What should be the punctuation at the blank space in each of the following sentences? Put *C* for comma or *NC* for no comma after the number of the sentence.

1. Prosperity as we know it depends heavily on oil _____ coal, and natural gas.
2. The company had moved its offices to Atlanta _____ Georgia.
3. Young journalists dream of exposing corrupt _____ public officials.
4. Seven feet, two inches _____ was unusual even for a basketball player.
5. The information appears in Chapter 3 _____ page 48.
6. They had started their shop as a hobby _____ not as a business.
7. Kidnappings _____ bombings, and armed attacks had become commonplace.
8. They had come to Jamestown, Virginia _____ from Liverpool, England.
9. We joined hands _____ and sang the old nostalgic songs.
10. The new mayor owed much to her loyal _____ confident supporters.

# P5   PARENTHETIC ELEMENTS

**Use dashes, parentheses, or commas to set off parenthetic elements.**

To some extent, conventions of punctuation follow the rhythms of speech. This is true of conventional ways of setting off parenthetic elements—elements that interrupt the normal flow of thought. Parenthetic elements may appear in a sentence without becoming grammatically a part of it.

# P5a   Dashes                                              *p* or —/

**Use the dash—sparingly—to signal a sharp break in a sentence.**

A speaker may pause for dramatic effect. Or a speaker may stop in the middle of a sentence to supply some preliminary detail or additional clarification. In writing, set such material off from the rest of a sentence by **dashes**. Use dashes for the following situations:

(1) *A word or phrase is made to stand out for emphasis.* The dash produces a dramatic or climactic effect:

After twenty-three years, he was leaving Newston jail—*a free man.*
Every time we look at one of the marvels of modern technology, we find a by-product—*unintended, unpredictable, and often lethal.*

(2) *A complete sentence interrupts another sentence.* There is no connective or relative pronoun to provide a smooth transition:

The cranes—*these birds were last sighted three years ago*—settled down on the marsh.

(3) *A modifier that would normally require commas already contains internal commas.* Dashes then signal the stronger breaks:

The old-style family—*large, closely knit, firmly ruled by the parents*—is becoming rare.

(4) *A list interrupts rather than follows a clause.* Dashes take the place of the colon that would normally signal that a list follows:

The group sponsored performers—*dancers, poets, musicians*—from around the world.

(5) *After an introductory list, the sentence starts over with a summarizing* all, these, *or* those:

*Arabs, Japanese, Vietnamese, South Americans*—all these are a familiar part of the campus scene.

(6) *A humorous afterthought or an ironic aside follows after a pause*:

Traditionally, novels are read in the United States by 1.7 percent of the population—*which somewhat reduces their clout.*—Richard Condon, "That's Entertainment!" *Harper's*

# P5b  Parentheses

*p* or *( )* /

Use parentheses to enclose unimportant data (or mere asides).

**Parentheses** are most appropriate for facts or ideas mentioned in passing:

> The University of Mexico was founded in 1553 (*almost a century before Harvard*).

> Kazan directed the rest of his considerable steam into studying English (*he graduated with honors*), waiting on tables, and joining as many extracurricular campus clubs as he could.—Thomas B. Morgan, "Elia Kazan's Great Expectations," *Harper's*

Use parentheses around dates, addresses, page references, chemical formulas, and similar information if it might be of interest to some readers but is not an essential part of the text. Here are some typical examples: *(p. 34) (first published in 1910) (now called Market Street).*

*Note*: When a sentence in parentheses begins *after* end punctuation, end punctuation is required inside the final parenthesis:

> Select your purchases with care. (*No refunds are permitted.*)

# P5c  Commas for Parenthetic Elements

*p* or ⌃

Use commas for parenthetic elements that blend into a sentence with only a slight break.

Sometimes we interrupt a sentence for clarification or comment, with only a minor break. Sometimes we pause at the beginning or the end of a sentence to comment or to turn to the reader. Use **commas** to set off such slight interruptions in the flow of thought:

> I do not believe that gifts, *whether of mind or character,* can be weighed like sugar and butter. (Virginia Woolf)

Note especially the following:

(1)  *Use commas when you address the reader or comment on*

**119**

*what you are saying.* Use these commas when you seem to be turning to your audience for special attention or for agreement:

DIRECT ADDRESS:    Marriage, *my friends,* is a serious business.
COMMENT:    Politicians, *you will agree,* were never popular in this part of the country.
Our candidate, *it seems,* is not well known.

(2) *Use commas to set off introductory tags.* These may include greetings and exclamations, as well as an introductory *yes* or *no.* Such introductory tags frequently precede a statement in conversation and in informal writing:

TAG OPENING:    *Why,* I don't even know that man.
*Yes,* you can now buy Pinko napkins in different colors.
*Well,* you can't have everything.

(3) *Use commas to set off echo questions.* Such "tag questions" are often added to a statement to ask for agreement or confirmation:

TAG QUESTION:    You are my friend, *aren't you?*
So he says he is sick, *does he?*

(4) *Use commas for slight breaks caused by unusual word order.* In sentences like the following, the italicized parts have changed their usual position in the sentence:

Laws, *to be cheerfully obeyed,* must be both just and practicable.
The Spaniards, *at the height of their power,* were great builders of towns.

(5) *Use commas to suggest a thoughtful pause.* Commas may take the place of dashes to set off a word for emphasis. They suggest a thoughtful pause rather than a dramatic break:

We should act, *and suffer,* in accordance with our principles.
People cannot, *or will not,* put down the facts.

# EXERCISES

A. Check the following passages for punctuation of *parenthetic elements.* After the number of each passage, write *S* for satisfactory, *U* for unsatisfactory. Explain why satisfactory passages were punctuated the way they were.

1. Well, you have made your point, Danny. The rest of us, you will agree, have the right to our own opinions.
2. Many discoveries though first made in wartime, were later put to peacetime uses.
3. Hard as it is for many of us to believe, women are not really superior to men in intelligence or humanity—they are only equal. (Anne Roiphe)
4. Most of the energy we use—whether from coal, oil, or water—ultimately derives from the sun.
5. Why if I were you I would return the whole shipment to the company.
6. Geothermal power in one's backyard, unless there is a geyser on the property, just cannot be achieved.
7. Most energy (as leaders of the ecology movement have told us for years) comes from fossil fuels.
8. Nuclear fuel would create an enormous waste problem (as indeed there is already with our existing uranium plants.
9. Many people would agree, offhand, that every creature lives its life and then dies. This might, indeed, be called a truism. But, like some other truisms, it is not true. The lowest forms of life, such as the amoebae, normally (that is, barring accidents) do not die. (Susanne K. Langer)
10. Fashions (especially adolescent fashions) do not, as a rule outlast their generation.

   B. Copy the following sentences, adding all punctuation needed for *parenthetic elements.*

1. Why this town my friends has weathered far worse storms.
2. My aunt headstrong quick-witted and deeply religious ruled the family with an iron hand.
3. To change the rules all the time we revised them twice last year does not make sense does it?
4. Well this theory it seems to me was rejected long ago.
5. Law and order a balanced budget and no foreign entanglements these it would appear were his favorite slogans.

# P6 QUOTATION

**Know how to punctuate different kinds of quoted material.**

Often you will need to show that you are reproducing information or ideas derived from a specific source. You will need to show that you are quoting something first said or observed by someone else.

## P6a Direct Quotation

*p* or *"/*

**In repeating someone's exact words, mark them off clearly from your own text.**

Direct quotations are enclosed in **quotation marks**. They are usually separated by a **comma** from the credit tag (the statement identifying the source):

> She said, "Leave me alone."
> "I don't care," he said.

> I once asked her what she would like her epitaph to read. She replied, "She lived long enough to be of some use."—Jean Houston, "The Mind of Margaret Mead," *Quest*

The following variations are important:

(1) *Often the credit tag interrupts the quotation.* Use **commas** both before and after the credit tag if it splits *one* complete sentence:

> "Both marijuana and alcohol," *Dr. Jones reports*, "slow reaction times on a whole spectrum of tasks."

Use a comma before and a **period** (or semicolon) after the credit tag if it comes between *two* complete sentences:

> "Your payment is overdue," the letter said. "This is a final warning."
> "The light is on," she said; "they must be inside."

(2) *No comma is required with very short quotations.* We leave out the introductory comma especially when a short quotation is part of a long sentence that is not a mere credit tag:

> He always said "Good day" when he left.
> Your saying "I am sorry" was not enough to soothe his wounded pride.

> The clatter of dishes and tableware, mingled with lusty shouts of "Seconds here!" and "Please pass the butter!", will resound across the country.—John Crawford, "A Plea for Physical Fatness," *Atlantic*

No comma is required when the credit tag follows a question or an exclamation:

> "Is everybody all right?" he shouted at the top of his voice.

(3) *A* **colon** *often replaces the comma before long or formal quotations.* Whether you use a comma or a colon, capitalize the first word of the quotation if it was capitalized in the original source (or if it would have been capitalized if written down):

The rule says: "No tools will be taken from this building."

(4) *Long quotations often appear as* **block quotations.** Long quotations (more than four or five typed lines) should be set off from the rest of a paper *not* by quotation marks but by special indenting. The same applies to quotations consisting of more than a full line of poetry. Quoted lines of poetry are usually set off the same way, although one or two lines may be run in with the continuous text. A slash then shows where a new line of poetry begins. (See the sample research paper in Chapter 9 for examples of such **block quotations.**)

(5) *Special* **single quotation marks** *signal a quotation within a quotation.* Show when the person you are quoting is quoting someone else in turn. In a quotation marked by conventional double marks, the single marks signal the quote within the quote:

She said, "Everywhere today we hear the familiar cry: *'Cut that budget!'*"
He said, "People who say *'Let me be honest with you'* seldom are."

# P6b Terminal Marks in Quotations ℗ or "/

**Observe conventional order when quotation marks coincide with other marks of punctuation.**

Observe the following guidelines:

(1) *Keep commas inside, semicolons outside a quotation.* Commas conventionally come before the final quotation mark; semicolons and colons conventionally follow it:

As he said, "Don't worry about me," the ship pulled away from the quay.
You said, "I don't need your sympathy"; therefore, I didn't offer any.

(2) *End punctuation usually comes before the final quotation marks.* Sometimes, however, you will have to use a question mark

or an exclamation mark after the quotation has formally ended. This means that the quotation itself is not a question or an exclamation. Rather, you are asking a question or exclaiming about the quotation:

QUOTED QUESTION:    He said, "Where are they now?"
QUESTIONED QUOTE:   Who said, "To err is human"?

QUOTED SHOUT:       She shouted: "The dam broke!"
SHOUTED QUOTE:      He actually said: "You don't count"!

(3) *A terminal mark is not duplicated at the end of a quotation*—even when logic might seem to require its repetition. For instance, use only one question mark when you are asking a question about a question:

Were you the student who asked, "Could we hold class on the lawn?"

# P6c   Insertions and Omissions                              *p* or *"/*

**In direct quotation, show clearly any changes you make in the original text.**

Use special marks as follows:

(1) *Identify explanations or comments of your own.* Set them off from the quoted material by **square brackets**. Use these brackets for material that was not part of the original quotation:

As Dr. Haben observes, "Again and again, they [the Indians] saw themselves deprived of lands of whose possession they had been assured with solemn oaths."

The note read: "Left Camp B Wednesday, April 3 [actually April 4]. Are trying to reach Camp C before we run out of supplies."

(2) *Show that you have left out unnecessary or irrelevant material from a quotation.* Indicate the omission by three spaced periods (called an **ellipsis**). If the omission occurs after a complete statement in the original text, use a sentence period and then add the ellipsis:

The report concluded on an optimistic note: "All three patients . . . are making remarkable progress toward recovery."

"To be a bird is to be alive more intensely than any other living creature, man included. . . . They live in a world that is always present, mostly full of joy." So wrote N. J. Berrill, Professor of Zoology at McGill University.—Joseph Wood Krutch, "If You Don't Mind My Saying So," *The American Scholar*

*Note*: To indicate *extensive omissions* (a line or more of poetry, a paragraph or more of prose), you may use a single typed line of spaced periods.

# P 6d   Indirect Quotation                                    *p* or "/

In indirect quotations, reproduce someone else's ideas or thoughts but translate them into your own words.

Indirectly quoted statements often take the form of noun clauses introduced by *that*. Indirectly quoted questions take the form of noun clauses introduced by words like *whether, why, how,* and *which*. Such clauses are *not* separated from the statement indicating the source by a comma or colon. They are *not* enclosed in quotation marks:

DIRECT:      The mayor replied, "I doubt the wisdom of such a move."
INDIRECT:    The mayor replied *that she doubted the wisdom of such a move.*

DIRECT:      The artist asked, "Which of the drawings do you like best?"
INDIRECT:    The artist asked *which of the drawings I liked best.*

Note two exceptions:

(1)  *We sometimes make the source statement go with the indirect quotation as parenthetic material.* We may then need **commas**:

> *As Gandhi remarked,* the first consequence of nonviolent action is to harden the heart of those who are being assaulted by charity. But, *he continued,* all the while they are being driven to a frenzy of rage, they are haunted by the terrible knowledge of how wrong they are.—Michael Harrington, "Whence Comes Their Passion," *The Reporter*

(2)  *Even in an indirect quotation, you may want to keep part of the original wording.* Use **quotation marks** to show you are repeating selected words or phrases exactly as they were used:

> Like Thackeray's daughters, I read *Jane Eyre* in childhood, carried away "as by a whirlwind." (Adrienne Rich)

**125**

# P6e  Words Set Off from Context  *p* or "/

Use quotation marks to indicate words and phrases that are not part of your normal vocabulary.

Mark expressions that are not your own, even though you may not be quoting them from any specific source:

(1)  *Quotation marks may identify words used for local color or ironic effect.* They enable you to hold an expression, as it were, at arm's length:

> It would seem that every modern child's pleasure must have its "constructive aspects."—Lois Phillips Hudson, "The Buggy on the Roof," *Atlantic*
>
> The argument that these taboos exist only because of "sexual hang-ups" ignores a much more likely explanation.—Barbara Lawrence, "Four-Letter Words Can Hurt You," *New York Times*

(2)  *Quotation marks may identify technical terms or words discussed as words.* Use such marks when a technical term is probably new to the reader. Use them when you look at the history, meaning, or grammatical use of a word. **Italics** (italicized print, shown by underlining in typed manuscript) often serve the same purpose:

> She wore a "Mother Hubbard," a loose, full gown long since out of fashion.
>
> The word *mob* was attacked as slang by some eighteenth-century writers.

(3)  *Italicized print often identifies foreign words.* **Italics** (or underlining) rather than quotation marks identify words that have been borrowed from foreign languages and have not yet become part of the general vocabulary of English:

> Young Latin American men are very touchy these days about *machismo*, best translated as "an emphasis on masculinity."—Linda Wolfe, "The Machismo Mystique," *New York*

Many legal and scientific terms borrowed from Latin belong in this category:

> A writ of *certiorari* is used by a superior court to obtain judicial records from an inferior court or a quasi-judicial agency.

The word "comet" comes from the Greek *aster kometes,* meaning long-haired star.

# P 6f   Titles or Names Set Off                    *"/* or *ital*

**Use quotation marks or italics as required to set off titles or names.**

We put quotation marks around the titles of poems, articles, songs, and the like that would normally be *part* of a larger publication. We italicize (underline in typing) the title of a complete publication—a magazine, a newspaper, or a book:

> The index to the *New York Times* devoted three column inches to the heading "Sex" in 1952.
>
> Her poem "Fields" appeared in *Poet's Corner.*

Italicize (underline) the titles of plays, major musical works including operas and ballets, movies, television and radio programs, and such works of art as paintings and sculptures:

> My aunt wanted us to watch *Romeo and Juliet* or *Swan Lake* rather than *I Love Lucy* or *The Price Is Right.*
>
> Every summer, an army of tourists troops past Leonardo da Vinci's *Mona Lisa.*

Italicize (underline) the names of ships and of other specially named craft, including space vehicles, planes, or trains: the *Queen Mary, Apollo IX,* the *Hindenburg.*

> The ill-fated *Titanic* became one of the best-known ships of all time.
>
> Soon the *California Zephyr* and the other great trains will live only in legend.

*Note*: The name of the Bible and the names of its parts are usually not italicized:

> She opened the Bible and read to us from the Book of Job.

---

For more on italics, see **M 1d**.

# EXERCISES

A. Check the following passages for conventional punctuation of *quoted material*. After the number of each passage, write *S* for satisfactory, *U* for unsatisfactory. Explain why the satisfactory passages were punctuated the way they were.

1. Tillie Olsen wrote about what she called "unprivileged lives."
2. "That was sweet of you," my cousin said.
3. The student's voice was loud and angry when she asked the dean, "What do you think we are, little kids."
4. "We've completely crossed the void," he told Ichor. "We are approaching the outer limits of a planetary system."
5. Stan Steiner has said, "The Chicano can rightly claim that he has been humiliated by the textbooks, tongue-tied by teachers, de-educated by the schools."
6. The man from Buffalo kept asking the guide "what he meant by primitive?"
7. This "ardent and avowed rebel," as she described herself to her friend Benjamin Franklin, had other schemes to keep her busy. (Miriam Troop)
8. The *Daily News,* in an editorial headed "We Beg to Differ," labeled the calling out of the National Guard "ill-advised and dangerous."
9. "Something is wrong here," she said, "people are not following their instructions."
10. When she came back from Mexico, she kept using words like *paseo* and *abrazo.*
11. She thought for a while and said, "All I remember is the announcement: 'Follow Code 305.'"
12. Would you have had the heart to tell him: "Time is up?"
13. The speaker charged "that the television audience resembled the ancient Romans, who liked to see the gladiators do battle to the death."
14. The speaker quoted Jefferson as saying that "our new circumstances" require "new words, new phrases, and the transfer of old words to new objects."
15. The constant war cry of my high school English teachers was give an example!

B. What punctuation, if any, is missing at the blank space in each of the following passages? Write it after the number of the passage. Write *No* if no punctuation is necessary. (Make no changes in capitalization.)

1. The chief psychologist said _____ The accidents will be simulated."
2. The lecturer was explaining what is meant by "total recall _____
3. Where does it say, "No minors are allowed _____
4. According to Rachel Carson, "Sir James Clark Ross set out from England in command of two ships 'bound for the utmost limits of the navigable globe _____

5. Restaurant owners were used to offering local police "something for their trouble _____

6. "The main problem," the commission said _____ is insufficient training of personnel."

7. "The main problem is not mechanical defects," the report said _____ it is human error."

8. "Where is the money going to come from _____ the governor asked.

9. He just mumbled _____ Excuse me" and walked on.

10. He carefully explained _____ why the regulations had not been followed.

# 4

# Sentence Style

# DIAGNOSTIC TEST

## INSTRUCTIONS:

Which of the sentences in each of the following pairs is clearer, more direct, or more effective? Write the letter of the better sentence after the number of the pair.

1. (a) The government continued its disregard of the wishes of the inhabitants of that region.
   (b) The government continued to disregard the wishes of the people in that region.

2. (a) Over 20,000 people participated in an antinuclear demonstration.
   (b) There was a nuclear demonstration participated in by over 20,000 people.

3. (a) As a salesclerk, one should show an interest in the customer.
   (b) A salesclerk should show an interest in the customer.

4. (a) People eating mussels out of season may become victims of severe poisoning.
   (b) If mussels are eaten out of season, a severe case of poisoning may be contracted.

5. (a) The mayor's office will investigate the unauthorized distribution of this information.
   (b) There will be an investigation by the mayor's office of the unauthorized distribution of this information.

6. (a) Both sides of this form are to be completed by every applicant.
   (b) Every applicant should complete both sides of this form.

7. (a) If people are willing to learn, they will usually get the job, if there are any vacancies.
   (b) A person willing to learn will usually get the job, provided one is available.

8. (a) I felt that the speaker was deliberately deceiving the audience.
   (b) I felt that an element of deliberate deception was present in the speaker's words.

9. (a) Students may take a test and pass it, and they will then be exempted from taking the course.
   (b) Students will be exempted from taking the course if they pass a test.

**10.** (a) We watched the officer who questioned the suspects who had been apprehended.

(b) We watched the officer questioning the suspects who had been apprehended.

# S 1 EFFECTIVE SENTENCES

**Write sentences that clearly signal important relationships.**

When you work on sentence style, you focus on what helps your sentences carry their message. You work on what makes sentences effective. You practice writing sentences that come right to the point. You learn to choose the sentence resources that are right for the job.

Many simple sentences are built on the "Who does what?" model. When such a sentence moves with few or no modifiers from subject to verb and from there to any complements, we are likely to encounter few problems of clarity or proper perspective:

*My friend waited* outside the restaurant.
*The relatives* of the deceased *crowded the room.*
*The heavens declare the glory* of God.

Learn how to keep your sentences equally clear and direct when they carry more complicated information.

See **G 1** for a review of basic sentence elements.

## S 1a Effective Predication                                      *st*

**Rewrite weak sentences to make them follow the "Who does what?" model.**

The subject and the predicate are the two basic structural supports of a sentence. The subject brings something to our attention. The predicate then makes a statement about it. The core of the predicate is a verb. Often the verb sets things in motion or brings action into the sentence:

The car / *swerved.*
The judge / *stayed* the order.
The building / *collapsed.*

In many effective sentences, subject and predicate together answer our basic question: "Who does what?" You can often strengthen weak sentences by bringing them closer to this basic model. Try to make the subject name the key agent. Then make the predicate state the key point:

WEAK:        *One crucial factor* in the current revolution in our social structure *is the relationship* between the white policeman and the black community. (Subject and predicate carry little of the meaning.)
STRONGER:    *The white policeman* standing on a Harlem street corner *finds himself at the very center* of the revolution now occurring in the world.—James Baldwin, *Nobody Knows My Name*
             (The "crucial factor"—the *policeman*—is now the subject of the sentence.)

In revising weak sentences, remember the following guidelines especially:

(1) *Strengthen weak sentences by shifting the action from a noun to a verb.* Look for sentences in which nouns ending in *-ment, -ion, -ism,* and the like serve as the subject of the sentence. Often these nouns refer to actions, events, and activities that could be more vigorously expressed by a verb. Make the agent or "doer" the subject of the sentence:

WEAK:        Violent *arguments* frequently *took place.*
REVISED:     *We* often *argued* violently.

WEAK:        A certain *element* of confusion *was present.*
REVISED:     The speaker *confused* us.

WEAK:        A *criticism* which is prevalent against modern poetry *is* that *its appeal is* only to the sophisticated.
REVISED:     *Many critics complain* that *modern poetry appeals* only to the sophisticated.

(2) *Do without tag statements that shift the main point to a dependent clause.* To make the subject and predicate of a main

clause carry your main point, eliminate tag statements like "The simple fact is that . . ." and "The question now confronting us is whether . . .":

WEAK: *The question* now confronting us *is* whether we should yield to intimidation, and thus encourage other groups to resort to the same tactics.

REVISED: *Should we yield* to intimidation and thus encourage other groups to resort to the same tactics?

## S1b Effective Coordination                                     *coord*

**Use coordination when two ideas are about equally important.**

When we coordinate two things, we make them work together. In sentences like the following, both clauses are about equally important. A simple *and* or *but* coordinates the two ideas:

We tried to locate the files, *but* we were unsuccessful.

Matthew was a subeditor on a large London newspaper, *and* Susan worked in an advertising firm. (Doris Lessing)

Our press is essentially provincial in this country, *and* except for a few syndicated columnists the reputation of our newspaper reporters is mainly local.

A simple *and* is also appropriate when events follow each other as they happen, without emphasis on cause and effect or other logical relations:

There was a shock, *and* he felt himself go up in the air. He pushed on the sword as he went up and over, *and* it flew out of his hand. He hit the ground *and* the bull was on him.—Ernest Hemingway, "The Undefeated"

*Excessive coordination* results from the overuse of *and*. Note that it merely says "more of same," without showing any specific relationship. Avoid *and* when it merely makes a sentence ramble on, without preparing the reader for what is coming:

RAMBLING: A member of the reserve has to participate in weekly drills, *and* he may be called up in emergencies, which came as an unpleasant surprise to me, *and* you would do better to stay away from it.

If you doubt the appropriateness of a coordinator like *and* or *but*, test the sentence by inserting "equally important":

EFFECTIVE: Under one of the plans, reservists spend only six months on active duty, *but* [equally important] they remain in the ready reserve for seven and a half years.

EFFECTIVE: Radioactivity is a threat to workers at nuclear plants, *and* [equally important] radioactive wastes are a threat to the environment.

## S1c   Effective Subordination                              *sub*

**Use subordination when details, reasons, or qualifications accompany a main point.**

Subordinating connectives (*when, while, since, because, if, though*) and relative pronouns (*who, which,* and *that*) add a **dependent** clause to the main clause. They can make the material they subordinate seem less important. They fit well when the main clause states a major point, with the dependent clauses establishing relations in place, time, or logic:

The edge of the cape was wet with blood *where* it had swept along the bull's back as he went by.—Ernest Hemingway, "The Undefeated"

Subordination helps the main idea stand out in a larger combined sentence:

SIMPLE: The term *democracy* originated in ancient Greece. Different people have used it to describe quite different political systems. Often the person who uses the word thinks it has only one meaning.

COMBINED: *Democracy*, a term that originated in ancient Greece, *has been used to describe quite different political systems,* though the person who uses it usually thinks it has only one meaning.

Remember the following points:

(1) *Effective subordination clarifies relationships in a sentence.* Merely placed next to each other, the following two statements may seem disjointed: "Kroger organized a counterfeiting ring. He had studied printing in Germany." When one is subordinated to the other, the connection between them becomes more obvious:

EFFECTIVE: Kroger, *who had studied printing in Germany,* organized a counterfeiting ring.

(2)  *Unskillful subordination blurs emphasis. "I was ten* when we moved to Alaska" focuses the reader's attention on you and your age. "When I was ten, *we moved to Alaska"* focuses the reader's attention on Alaska. **Upside-down subordination** results when the wrong item seems to stand out. When tucked away in a subordinate part of a sentence, important information may catch the reader unaware. It may, as a result, have an ironic effect. Avoid upside-down subordination when no irony is intended:

UPSIDE-DOWN:    The salary was considered good by local standards, *though* it was not enough to feed and clothe my family.

IMPROVED:    *Though* considered good by local standards, my salary was not enough to feed and clothe my family.

UPSIDE-DOWN:    He had a completely accident-free record up to the last day of his employment, *when* he stepped on a power line and almost lost his life.

IMPROVED:    On the last day of his employment, *after* ten years without a single accident, he stepped on a power line and almost lost his life.

# S1d  Effective Modifiers                                            *st*

**Use modifiers to help a sentence carry added freight.**

A skillful writer often uses modifying words and phrases where an inexperienced writer might use separate clauses. Observe the tightening of relationships when separate statements are combined in a compact sentence:

SEPARATE:    Dolphins can send distress signals to other members of their group. They communicate by beeps and clicks.

COMBINED:    Dolphins, *communicating by beeps and clicks,* can send distress signals to other members of their group.

SEPARATE:    I lay on the couch in the kitchen. I was reading *The Last Days of Pompeii.* How I wished I could have been there.

COMBINED:    I lay on the couch in the kitchen, reading *The Last Days of Pompeii* and wishing I were there. (Alice Munro)

SEPARATE:    We caught two bass. We hauled them in briskly, as though they were mackerel. After we pulled them over the side of the boat, we stunned them with a blow on the back of the head.

COMBINED:    We caught two bass, *hauling them in briskly* as though they were mackerel, *pulling them over the side of the boat* in a businesslike manner without any landing net, and *stunning them with a blow on the back of the head.* (E. B. White)

Remember:

(1) *Use the full range of modifying phrases.* In addition to single words, we use the following modifiers to make a sentence carry added freight:

PREPOSITIONAL PHRASE: They crossed the swollen river *in a small rubber raft.*

ADJECTIVE PHRASE: The climbers, *weak from days without food,* gave up the attempt.

APPOSITIVE: The rhinoceros, *an animal built like a tank,* faces extinction.

VERBALS: *Goaded beyond endurance,* Igor turned on his pursuers, *shaking his fists.*

ABSOLUTE CONSTRUCTIONS: *Her face drawn, her lips tight,* the mayor announced her decision.

(2) *Use the full range of possible positions for added modifiers.* The following sentences, from a bullfighting story by Ernest Hemingway, illustrate the effective use of one or more modifiers *at different positions* in the sentence:

• Breaking up subject and verb:

The horse, *lifted and gored,* crashed over with the bull driving into him.

Manuel, *facing the bull, having turned with him each charge,* offered the cape with his two hands.

• At the end of the sentence:

Manuel walked towards him, *watching his feet.*

The bull was hooking wildly, *jumping like a trout, all four feet off the ground.*

• At the beginning of the sentence:

Now, *facing the bull,* he was conscious of many things at the same time.

*Heads up, swinging with the music, their right arms swinging free,* they stepped out.

• More than one position:

The bull, *in full gallop,* pivoted and charged the cape, *his head down, his tail rising.*

# EXERCISES

A. Rewrite the following sentences for *more effective predication*. If possible, make the subject and the predicate tell the reader who does what.

1. Vigorous discussion of current political events often took place among the customers.
2. It is very probable that intimidation of witnesses will result from such threatening remarks.
3. A recent development is the encouragement of new technology for extracting oil by the Canadian government.
4. There has been much support among voters for rent control measures of different kinds.
5. A conscientious teacher's satisfaction is incomplete unless she reaches a full realization of her goals.
6. As the result of unruly demonstrations, repeated interruptions of the committee's deliberations took place.
7. The conclusion is inevitable that considerable impairment of our country's military strength has come about as the result of these cuts.
8. A plan for safe driving is of no use if the cooperation of the individual driver is not present.
9. The pressure of society to conform is so great that the student is in constant awareness of its presence.
10. The contribution of the alumni to the growth of the college will be in proportion to their information about its educational needs.

B. Rewrite the following passages, making effective use of *subordination*. In each passage, use at least one dependent clause, starting with a subordinator (*if, when, because, where, although, whereas,* or the like) or with a relative pronoun (*who, which,* or *that*).

1. Campus elections are ridiculous. Nobody qualified runs. I refuse to have anything to do with them.
2. Piloting a boat is easy. It is like driving a car. The controls are about the same.
3. Monkeys are of low intelligence. They are imitative. They can be trained to perform simple tasks.
4. My father came from a wealthy family, and my mother came from a very poor home, and it was strange that she held the purse strings in the family.
5. Many high school teachers follow a textbook word for word, and they go over each page until everyone understands it. In college, many teachers just tell the student to read the textbook, and then they start giving lectures on the material covered in the text, but they don't follow it word for word.

C. Combine the separate statements in each of the following groups. Keep the first statement as the main part of the sentence. Use the information in the additional statements as *modifiers* in the larger combined sentence. Example:

**139**

SEPARATE:   The lizard watched me.
            It was basking in the sun.
            It had beady eyes.
COMBINED:   The lizard *basking in the sun* watched me *with beady eyes.*

1. Lake Tahoe is America's largest mountain lake.
   It is surrounded by snow-capped peaks.

2. Horses changed the Indians' way of life.
   The horses had been brought to the New World by the Spaniards.

3. The tidal wave hit the island.
   The wave had been caused by the earthquake.
   The wave hit with tremendous force.

4. Ronald Reagan was elected President.
   He was a former governor of California.

5. Scientists are studying dolphins.
   Dolphins are warm-blooded, intelligent mammals.
   They are able to communicate by a complex set of signals.

6. The *Amsterdam News* condemned the violence.
   It is the nation's largest newspaper.

7. Her friends were hoping for a more natural way of life.
   They were leaving the congested city.

8. Thousands of migrants came into California.
   They were often called "Okies."
   They came from Midwestern farms.
   Their farms had been ruined by drought.

9. The people watched the ship leave.
   They were standing on the pier.
   Tears were streaming down their faces.

10. The band marched onto the playing field.
    The trumpets were blaring.
    The banners were flying.

   D. Use *modifiers* to build up the following simple sentences with additional details. Use different kinds of modifiers in various positions. Example:

SIMPLE:    A girl plays "Silent Night."
MODIFIED:  A small, skinny girl plays "Silent Night" with two fingers on an
           untuned piano in a garage.

1. A woman runs.

2. A dog crossed the road.

3. The rider mounted the horse.

**140**

4. Energy is in short supply.

5. Her cousin bought a new car.

    E.  Study the following examples of *effective sentences.* They make exceptionally full use of the sentence resources that we can draw on to help load a sentence with information. For each of the model sentences, write a sentence of your own on a subject of your own choice. As much as you can, follow the sentence structure of the original. Try to come close—you need not follow the model sentence in every detail.

MODEL 1:    Your photographs will be more artistic if you use the film that has chromatic balance.

IMITATION:    Your checks will be more welcome if you draw them on an account that has money in it.

MODEL 2:    Everyone is a moon and has a dark side which he never shows to anybody. (Mark Twain)

MODEL 3:    Lonnie wore the composed, politely appreciative expression that was her disguise in the presence of grown-ups. (Alice Munro)

MODEL 4:    Using their dreams alone, creative people have produced fiction, inventions, scientific discoveries, and solutions to complex problems. (Jean Houston)

MODEL 5:    The fullback held the ball lightly in front of him, his knees pumping high, his hips twisting as he ran toward the end zone.

# S2  SENTENCE VARIETY

**Keep your sentences from becoming plodding and monotonous.**

An effective writer uses sentences of different length and structure for variety and emphasis.

# S2a  Sentence Length      *var*

**Use short sentences to sum up a point; use long sentences for detailed explanation and support.**

A short sentence is often appropriate for summing up a key idea or for giving pointed advice. The following short sentences are quotable, emphatic, to the point:

Economy is the art of making the most of life. (G. B. Shaw)

You should write, first of all, to please yourself. (Doris Lessing)

A long, elaborate sentence is often appropriate for detailed description, explanation, or argument. The following sentences are carefully worked out, with all details in place and all if's and but's fully stated:

As the pastor paused to gather his thoughts—hair falling to the wrong side of its part, tie clashing more loudly than last week, and his smile slightly twisting his face—he seemed a little more human to us all.

There will never be a really free and enlightened State until the State comes to recognize the individual as a higher and independent power, from which all its own power and authority are derived, and treats him accordingly.—Thoreau, "Civil Disobedience"

Remember the following points:

(1)  *Avoid excessive use of short, isolated sentences.* They can easily make your writing sound immature:

CHOPPY:  Many teachers can give students information. Very few can inspire students to learn. Information is of little use to students. Soon they will leave college. Then they will forget what they have memorized. They must be inspired to learn on their own.

IMPROVED:  Many teachers can give students information, but few can inspire them to learn. When students leave college, the information they have memorized will be of little use and will soon be forgotten. What they need most is the ability to learn on their own.

(2)  *Learn how to make a short summary sentence and a long elaborating sentence work together.* We often use a short, pointed sentence as the opening sentence or topic sentence of a paragraph. Then we follow up in longer sentences that fill in details:

*Newspapers give a distorted view of life.* They overemphasize the unusual, such as a mother's giving birth to quintuplets, the development of a Christmas tree that grows its own decorative cones, the minting of two pennies which were only half engraved, gang fights, teenage drinking, or riots. . . .

(3)  *Occasionally make your reader stop short at a brief, memorable statement of an important point.* A short sentence can be especially effective if it sets off an important conclusion or a key observation at the end of a passage:

**142**

With the great growth in leisure-time activities, millions of Americans are turning to water sports: fishing, swimming, water skiing, and skin diving. *Clean water exhilarates and relaxes.*—Vance Packard, "America the Beautiful—and Its Desecraters," *Atlantic*

# S2b Varied Word Order *var*

**Vary normal word order to keep your sentences from being too much alike.**

Though most of your sentences will follow the subject-verb sequence, there will usually be enough variety in the remaining sentence elements to prevent tiring repetition. Monotony is most likely to result when a number of sentences start with the same subject, especially a pronoun like *I* or *he* or *she*:

MONOTONOUS:   A good example of a topic drawn from personal experience is a bus accident I once had. I wrote a paper about this experience of mine. I remembered the events that took place during the accident. I could describe them well. After all, I had experienced them. It was a shocking experience. I will never forget it. The facts stand out in my memory because it was so shocking.

Do the following to give your sentences variety:

(1) *Make a modifier that usually occurs later in the sentence precede the subject.* The **introductory modifier** can bring variety into a group of plodding sentences:

VARIED:   He reversed the direction of the canoe. *After a few seconds,* he stopped paddling. *Slowly* he made the canoe drift to the bank. *When within a yard of the shore,* he grabbed one of the overhanging branches.

VARIED:   The Trans World Terminal stems from the work of contemporary architects like Corbusier of France and Nervi of Italy, masters of the curve in concrete. *Like a true eagle,* this building is all curves and muscle, no right angles. *Built of reinforced concrete,* the whole structure swoops and turns and rises.—Ken Macrorie, "Arriving and Departing," *The Reporter*

(2) *Shift a complement to a more emphatic initial position.* The **introductory complement** is normal in exclamations beginning with *what* or *how*: "*What stories* that man told!" "*What a*

**143**

*liar* you are!" *"How true* that is!" In other sentences, this turning around (or **inversion**) of the usual pattern is especially effective when it takes up something mentioned earlier:

EFFECTIVE:    The committee has asked me to resign. *That* I will never do.
EFFECTIVE:    Mr. Schlumpf fried two small pieces of fish. *One of these* he fed to his cat. *The other* he ate himself.
EFFECTIVE:    We really should not resent being called paupers. *Paupers* we are, and *paupers* we shall remain.

*Note*: Like other attention-getting devices, the introductory complement sometimes attracts attention to the speaker rather than to what he or she is saying. Sometimes the construction smacks of old-fashioned oratory:

*More patient wife* a husband never had.
*Gone* are the days of my youth.
*Such deeds of glory* we shall see no more.

(3)  *Shift the predicate of the main clause toward the end.* Work some of the modifiers into the sentence earlier. Such treatment may strengthen a sentence especially if a **final modifier** is a belated qualification or concession, unexpectedly weakening the main point:

WEAK:       Richard Wagner became one of the most successful composers of all time in spite of the jeers of his contemporaries. (This version may make your readers remember the jeers rather than the man's success.)
IMPROVED:   Richard Wagner, *though jeered at by his contemporaries,* became one of the most successful composers of all time.

*Note*: A **loose** sentence finishes one major statement *early* but then leads on to further points or further detail. It is an expandable or cumulative sentence that looks as if it had been built in stages:

LOOSE:     She liked a simple life and simple people, and would have been happier, I think, if she had stayed in the backlands of Alabama riding wild on the horses she so often talked about, not so lifelong lonely for the black men and women who had taught her the only religion she ever knew. (Lillian Hellman)

In a **periodic** sentence, an essential part of the main statement is *held in suspense* until the end. The sentence ends when the main statement ends. Everything else is worked into the sentence along the way:

PERIODIC:    *Comedy,* though often showing us cranks or eccentrics, nevertheless *aims its ridicule,* as many critics have said, *at common failings of human nature.*

# EXERCISES

A. Choose five of the following *short, memorable statements* as model sentences. For each, write a sentence of your own that follows as closely as possible the structure of the original. (Sample imitations follow two of the model sentences.)

MODEL 1:    Love is as necessary to human beings as food and shelter. (Aldous Huxley)

MODEL 2:    The man with a new idea is a crank until the new idea succeeds. (Mark Twain)

IMITATION:  The person with two-inch soles is considered crazy until two-inch soles become fashionable.

MODEL 3:    Those who cut their own wood are twice warmed.

MODEL 4:    A nail that sticks out will be hammered down. (Japanese saying)

MODEL 5:    Curiosity, like all other desires, produces pain as well as pleasure. (Samuel Johnson)

IMITATION:  Marriage, like many other institutions, brings restrictions as well as benefits.

MODEL 6:    Work expands so as to fill the time available for its completion. (C. Northcote Parkinson)

MODEL 7:    Perversity is the muse of modern literature. (Susan Sontag)

B. Study the following examples of *long, elaborate sentences* carrying along many details. Choose three of these as model sentences. For each, write a similar sentence of your own, carrying nearly as much freight as the original. (You need not follow the structure of the original in all details.)

1. (a news event) On an early January day in 1968, a volcanic eruption pushed some steaming rocks above the surface waters of the South Pacific, adding a new island to the remote Tonga Archipelago.
2. (a snapshot of a person) A dirty, long-haired young man in a faded army fatigue jacket, weary from walking, reached through the barbed-wire fence to pet a mud-covered Jersey milk cow grazing in a field alongside the country road.
3. (a sentence that traces a process) We begin as children; we mature; we leave the parental nest; we give birth to children who, in turn, grow up, leave, and begin the process all over again. (Alvin Toffler)

**145**

4. (a sentence that explains an important requirement) An interview need not be an ambush to be good, but it should set up a situation in which the subject can be surprised by what he says—that is, a situation in which he has to do some audible thinking. (Richard Todd)

C. Study the following example of how a *short summary sentence and a long elaborating sentence* can work together. Then write three pairs of your own that similarly give your reader "the long and the short of it."

*Training is everything.* The peach was once a bitter almond; cauliflower is nothing but cabbage with a college education. (Mark Twain)

D. Each of the following model sentences starts with a *variation* from the usual subject-verb order. For three of these, write a similar sentence of your own. A sample imitation follows the first of the model sentences.

**MODEL 1:**  Stronger than the mighty sea is almighty God.
**IMITATION:**  Bleaker than a misspent youth is life without experience.
**MODEL 2:**  On a huge hill, cragged and steep, truth stands. (John Donne)
**MODEL 3:**  To describe with precision even the simplest object is extremely difficult. (Aldous Huxley)
**MODEL 4:**  A trim, clear-eyed, self-assured woman, she sometimes runs the five miles to and from her office at the Institute of Medical Sciences.
**MODEL 5:**  What makes democratic politics different from most other professions is that, occasionally, the politician has a duty to risk his job by performing it conscientiously. (George F. Will)

E. Describe the variations in *sentence style* in the following passages. Describe the functions performed or the effects produced by sentences of different length. Point out variations in word order.

1. Why conform to a group? Why throw away your birthright for a Greek pin or a peace button, for security and nonentity? This goes especially for the typical college student, who merely wants to do what "everyone else is doing." What everyone else is doing isn't best. It's merely common. One of the synonyms of "common" is "vulgar."

2. The dictionary can neither snicker nor fulminate. It records. It will offend many, no doubt, to find the expression *wise up,* meaning to inform or to become informed, listed in the *Third International* with no restricting label. To my aging ears, it still sounds like slang. But the evidence—quotations from the *Kiplinger Washington Letter* and the *Wall Street Journal*—convinces me that it is I who am out of step, lagging behind. (Bergen Evans)

3. Some people believe that it is easier today for a woman to achieve whatever she wants simply because the idea that all fields are open to women is more widely accepted, and therefore many more opportunities exist. But this is only partly true. Having chosen what she wants to become, a woman must be prepared to commit herself over a long period to reach her goal.

She must work hard and be ready to meet the unexpected; and she must face the fact that she will have to put up with a lot to make her dreams come true. (Margaret Mead)

# S3    AWKWARD CONSTRUCTION      *awk*

**Avoid constructions that make for an indirect, awkward, wooden style.**

Sentences may be long and complicated and yet say clearly what the writer had in mind. On the other hand, the grammatical equipment even in short sentences may become so heavy that it interferes with communication.

## S3a    Deadwood      *awk*

**Prune your sentences of deadwood.**

Often a sentence runs more smoothly after it has been trimmed down. Avoid unnecessary *there are*'s and *who were*'s:

AWKWARD:    *There are* many farmers in the area *who are* planning to attend the meeting *which is* scheduled for next Friday.

BETTER:    Many farmers in the area plan to attend the meeting scheduled for next Friday.

Other sentences can be cleared of deadwood by effective use of pronouns:

AWKWARD:    A child of preschool age often shows a desire to read, but the *child's* parents often ignore this *desire.*

BETTER:    A child of preschool age often shows a desire to read—*which* the parents ignore.

Some connectives, prepositions, and pronouns are unnecessary or unnecessarily heavy:

AWKWARD:    I wrote little, *because of the fact that* my childhood had been *an* uneventful *one.*

BETTER:    I wrote little, because my childhood had been uneventful.

**147**

## S3b  Awkward Passive                                        *awk*

**Avoid the passive when it makes sentences awkward or roundabout.**

An active sentence is modeled on the "agent-action-target" relationship: "The woodcutter *felled* the tree." A passive sentence reverses this perspective and looks at the action from the point of view of the original subject: "The tree *was felled* by the woodcutter." As a result, the passive is appropriate when the target or result of an action seems more important than the performer:

> The *dusky,* a subspecies of the seaside sparrow, *has never been found* anywhere except on Merritt Island and along the St. John's River.

> Among the Ibo, *the art of conversation is regarded* very highly, and proverbs are the palm oil with which *words are eaten.*—Chinua Achebe, *Things Fall Apart*

The passive is also appropriate when the doer or performer of an action is beside the point or hard to identify:

> Some of John's *brain cells were damaged* when he was a small child.
> In World War II, *millions* of people *were driven* from their homes.

Avoid unnecessary or awkward uses of the passive:

(1) *Avoid the pretentious passive.* Do not use the passive under the mistaken impression that it will make your sentences more formal or impressive. Learn to convert weak passives back to the active:

| | |
|---|---|
| WEAK PASSIVE: | Although Bradley Hall *is* regularly *populated* by students, close study of the building as a structure *is* seldom *undertaken.* |
| ACTIVE: | The students *passing* through Bradley Hall seldom *pause to study* its structure. |
| | |
| WEAK PASSIVE: | My experiences at writing *were* greatly *increased* due to two long essays due each week. |
| ACTIVE: | I *wrote* more than ever, *having to turn in* two long essays each week. |

(2) *Avoid the evasive passive.* Since the doer or performer is often omitted from a passive sentence, we may find it hard to identify the person responsible for an action or idea:

**148**

| EVASIVE: | A plan for popular election of Supreme Court justices *is* now *being advanced.* (By whom?) |
|---|---|
| EVASIVE: | The racial problem is clearly one that *could and should have been solved* long ago. (By whom?) |

On *shifts* to the passive, see **G 10c.**

## S 3c Impersonal Constructions *awk*

**Revise impersonal constructions to make your sentences more direct.**

Familiar props can make a sentence awkward or roundabout. The impersonal *one*, the *it* without antecedent, and *there-is* or *there-are* sentences are most appropriate when the people or forces behind an action are of secondary importance. We naturally say "It rains" or "It snows"—what matters is the process, not its causes. Guard against the unnecessary use of such constructions:

(1) *Avoid using the pronoun* one *as an unnecessary prop in a sentence.* The **impersonal** *one* is often a tiresome substitute for the people concerned, especially if their identity is indirectly shown by modifiers:

| ROUNDABOUT: | *When teaching, one* should be patient. |
|---|---|
| DIRECT: | *Teachers* should be patient. |

| ROUNDABOUT: | *As a father, one* should not spoil his children. |
|---|---|
| DIRECT: | *Fathers* should not spoil their children. |

| ROUNDABOUT: | *If one is a citizen of a democracy, she* should exercise her voting rights. |
|---|---|
| DIRECT: | *A citizen of a democracy* should vote. |

(2) *Avoid unnecessary use of sentence openers that postpone the main point.* In **it-is** and **there-is** sentences, the first two words are mere props, which can make the sentences sound lame and indecisive. Sometimes the main topic of a sentence receives needed emphasis if it is introduced by *it is* or *there is*:

| EMPHATIC: | It is *his competence* that we question—not his honesty. |
|---|---|

**149**

More often, however, the reshuffling of sentence elements made necessary by *it is* or *there is* causes awkwardness:

AWKWARD:    In 1979, *there was* a strike participated in by five thousand union members.
DIRECT:     In 1979, five thousand union members participated in a strike.

## S 3d   Excessive Subordination                              *awk*

**Avoid overburdened sentences caused by excessive subordination.**

Excessive subordination causes various types of overburdened sentences. One common type dovetails several dependent clauses into each other, thus making a subordinating connective follow another subordinator or a relative pronoun. The resulting **that-if**, **if-because**, **which-when** constructions are often awkward:

AWKWARD:    I think *that if* there were less emphasis on conformity in high school, college students would be better prepared for independent thinking.
IMPROVED:   In my opinion, college students would be better prepared for independent thinking *if* there were less emphasis on conformity in high school.

Look out for the following:

(1)  *Avoid "house-that-Jack-built" sentences.* Several dependent clauses of the same type follow each other, making the sentence trail off into a confusing succession of modifiers:

AWKWARD:    When I was in Mexico City, I visited Jean, *who* was living with a Mexican girl *who* posed for the local artists, *who* are usually too poor to pay their rent, let alone the model's fee.
IMPROVED:   When I was in Mexico City, I visited Jean. She was living with a Mexican girl *who* posed for the local artists but seldom received any money for her work. Most artists there are too poor to pay their rent, let alone the model's fee.

(2)  *Avoid an awkward string of introductory clauses.* Sometimes too many similar dependent clauses delay the main point:

AWKWARD:    *When* children are constantly watched *when* they are born and *while* they are babies, the reason is that mothers want to see whether their children are developing as the books say they should.

IMPROVED: Some mothers constantly watch young children to see whether they are developing as the books say they should.

(3) *Avoid seesaw sentences.* These start with a dependent clause, go on to the main clause, and then add a second dependent clause that in a confusing way changes the meaning of the first:

CONFUSING: *Because many teenagers marry hastily,* their marriages end in divorce, *because they are too immature to face adult responsibilities.*

CLEARER: Many teenagers are too immature to face adult responsibilities. They marry hastily, and often their marriages end in divorce.

# S3e  Awkward Modifiers                                    *awk*

**Revise when awkwardly placed modifiers overburden or weaken a sentence.**

Do the following to revise sentences with awkward modifiers:

(1) *Keep lengthy modifiers from breaking up the pattern of a clause.* Lengthy appositives, verbal phrases, or dependent clauses sometimes separate elements that belong together:

AWKWARD: The pilot told his friends that he had flown Clinton Morris, *a resident of New York City sought by the government for income tax evasion,* out of the United States.

REVISED: The pilot told his friends about a passenger he had flown out of the United States: Clinton Morris, *a resident of New York City sought by the government for income tax evasion.*

AWKWARD: Our club treasurer, *being the daughter of parents constantly stressing the importance of maintaining a proper sense of the value of money,* refused to pay our expenses.

REVISED: *As the daughter of parents who had constantly lectured her about the value of money,* our club treasurer refused to pay our expenses.

(2) *Keep tagged-on modifiers from weakening a strong sentence.* Avoid the kind of lame ending that results when a writer adds a qualification or reservation as an unexpected afterthought:

LAME:     A threatening epidemic can be prevented if the proper authorities take firm action from the start, *usually*.

REVISED:  *Usually* a threatening epidemic can be prevented if the proper authorities take firm action from the start.

# EXERCISES

A. Rewrite the following sentences to clear them of *deadwood and impersonal constructions*.

1. As a skier, it is essential to stay in good physical shape.
2. When one owns a farm, there is a constant stream of forms and question-naires to fill out.
3. There are many ways in which a student who is interested in meeting a foreign student may come to know one.
4. My friend badly needed a government loan, but the income level of this friend's parents made her ineligible for the loan.
5. This year has been a discouraging one for those who are committed to the cause of better public health services.

B. Rewrite the following sentences to convert *awkward or unnecessary passives* back to active statements.

1. Our food was carried in sturdy backpacks, and many a simple but nour-ishing meal was enjoyed along the trail.
2. All instructions should be read carefully and all blank spaces filled in before this form is signed by the applicant.
3. If any experimenting endangering human lives is to be done by the gov-ernment, the voters should be consulted first.
4. When information about summer school is received, the necessary dead-lines may have already passed.
5. Various ways of living are being tested today and experimented with by youth whose dominant characteristic is the desire for flexibility.

C. Read the following sample sentences to find *awkward sentences* in need of revision. Which of the sentences seem awkward, overburdened, or confusing? Put *U* for unsatisfactory after the number of the sentence. Which sentences seem clear and well built? Put *S* for satisfactory after the number of the sentence. (Your instructor may ask you to rewrite the unsatisfactory sen-tences.)

1. Conservationists can tell many stories of conflicting goals and missed opportunities.

2. The camp counselor, talking on and on and without noticing anything wrong or hearing the laughter, finally turned around.
3. From small incidents, like receiving too much change and pocketing it, to larger issues, like cheating on a test, a lifelong pattern may be established.
4. We read about the passenger pigeon, once darkening the skies in untold numbers, now extinct.
5. When people are constantly under supervision when at work and asked immediately where they are going when they leave their station, a feeling of harassment is experienced.
6. Saturday mornings used to be my best time for studying, because I knew nothing was due the next morning (which was Sunday), until I started working.
7. From across the dinner-littered dining table, my father blinks myopically and asserts that current conflicts are no different from any other conflicts and that my dissent is no different from what his dissent used to be.
8. Motorists are quickly informed of the whereabouts of restaurants, motels, and, of course, speed traps set by the police, by other CB operators.
9. The dreary weather, mainly rain, that never seemed to stop, and my problems with my parents, which were serious, upset me.
10. The Texas-born, Boston-trained lawyer, who has rung up many firsts in just three years on Capitol Hill, has plain-spoken her way to national prominence.
11. A child's first impressions of people and places shape the course of her future life, frequently.
12. All electric appliances, far from being labor-saving devices, are new forms of work, decentralized and made available to everybody. (Marshall McLuhan)
13. Knowing the right answers is sometimes less important than asking the right questions.
14. As we left the city, we approached a range of hills which seemed like giant waves which were about to break.
15. If someone is exercising his slightly off-key singing voice and a friend mockingly plugs her ears and winces in agony, the singer might well take the gesture as a personal insult if he didn't have a sense of humor.

# S4  REPETITION                                              *rep*

**Learn to make effective use of repetition and parallelism.**

Unintentional repetition can make a passage sound clumsy. Deliberate repetition can emphasize important points and give continuity to a sentence or a paragraph.

## S4a   Awkward Repetition           *rep*

**Avoid unintentional repetition of sounds, syllables, words, or phrases.**

Carelessly repeated sounds or sentence elements can grate on the reader's ears. Revise for awkward repetition like the following:

AWKWARD:     Commercials seldom make for entertain*ing* and relax*ing* listen*ing*.
BETTER:     Commercials seldom entertain and relax the listener.

AWKWARD:     Close examina*tion* of the results of the investiga*tion* led to a reorganiza*tion* of the department.
BETTER:     Close study of the results of the inquiry caused the company to reorganize the department.

AWKWARD:     We listened to an account *of* the customs *of* the inhabitants *of* the village.
BETTER:     We listened to an account of the villagers' customs.

Unintentional repetition is especially annoying when the similarity in sound covers up a *shift in meaning or relationship*:

My father lost his savings during the depression because he had *banked on* [better: "relied on"] the well-established reputation of our hometown *bank*.

## S4b   Emphatic Repetition           *rep*

**Use intentional repetition for clarity and continuity.**

A writer may repeat important words and phrases for emphasis:

EMPHATIC:     When I returned to State, *I studied* as I have never studied since. *I studied* before classes. *I studied* after classes. *I studied* till English, history, and zoology merged into one blurry mass of incoherent erudition.

EMPHATIC:     In my mother's world, *no one ever* shrugged his shoulders; *no one was ever* bored and lazy; *no one* was *ever* cynical; *no one ever* laughed.—Alfred Kazin, "The Bitter 30's," *Atlantic*

Notice the cumulative effect of intentional repetition in the following passage from Stephen Crane's "The Open Boat":

In the meantime, the oiler *rowed*, and then the correspondent *rowed*, and then the oiler *rowed*. Gray-faced and bowed forward, they mechanically, turn by turn, plied the leaden oars.

# S4c  Parallel Structure

**‖**

**Use parallel structure to help channel the reader's attention.**

Parallel structure pulls together related ideas through the repetition of similar grammatical patterns. The following passages make effective use of parallelism:

The only advice that one person can give another about reading is
> *to take no advice,*
> *to follow your own instincts,*
> *to use your own reason,*
> *to come to your own conclusions.* (Virginia Woolf)

The air *must be* pure
> *if we are to* breathe;
the soil *must be* arable
> *if we are to* eat;
the water *must be* clean
> *if we are to* drink.

*The more* things you love,
*the more* you are interested in,
*the more* you enjoy,
*the more* you are indignant about—
> *the more* you have left when anything happens. (Ethel Barrymore)

Remember:

(1) *Parallel structure helps us line up related ideas.* It helps the reader see that several things are part of the same picture or the same story:

> *Together we* planned the house, *together we* built it, and *together we* watched it go up in smoke.

> I have *thought* about their remarks, *tried* to put myself in their place, *considered* their point of view. (Nora Ephron)

> It was much worse for them, *they tell me.* They had a terrible time of it, *they assure me.* I don't know how lucky I was, *they say.* (Nora Ephron)

(2)   *Parallel structure helps us line up different ideas for comparison or contrast*:

> Her remarks provoked much comment, *self-righteous from her enemies, apologetic from her friends.*
>
> Whereas *it is desirable that* the old *should treat with respect* the wishes of the young, *it is not desirable that* the young *should treat with respect* the wishes of the old.

We call the neat balancing of two direct opposites an **antithesis**. Note the antithetical style of the following passage:

> India *is a poetic nation, yet it demands* new electrical plants. It *is a mystical nation, yet it wants* new roads. It *is* traditionally *a peaceful nation, yet it could,* if misled, *inflame* Asia.—James A. Michener, "Portraits for the Future," *Saturday Review*

(3)   *Parallel structure helps us make a series of parallel sentences build up to a* **climax**. The author of the following passage starts with a general point and then gives two examples from areas of life other than his own. He then closes in on the area that is of special concern to him:

> Institutions *must be judged by* their end products. A government *is judged by* the way it administers justice and equity to all its citizens. A corporation *is judged by* the goods it sells in the market. A university *must be judged not by* its success in turning out Olympic sprinters or Rose Bowl elevens *but by* whether or not it produces educated citizens for the republic.— James E. Odenkirk, "Intercollegiate Athletics: Big Business or Sport?" *Academe*

On *faulty* parallelism, see **G 10d**.

# EXERCISES

A. Study the use of *repetition and parallelism* in the following passages. Choose five of these as model sentences. For each, write a passage of your own on a subject of your own choice. Follow the structure of the original as closely as you can.

MODEL 1:              Studies serve for delight, for ornament, and for ability. (Sir Francis Bacon)

| | |
|---|---|
| **SAMPLE IMITATION:** | Cars serve for transportation, for relaxation, and for ostentation. |
| **MODEL 2:** | Courage is not the absence of fear; it is the control over fear. (Dickie Chapelle) |
| **MODEL 3:** | To assign unanswered letters their proper weight, to free us from expectations of others, to give us back to ourselves— there lies the great, the singular power of self-respect. (Joan Didion) |
| **MODEL 4:** | My lack of excitement, of curiosity, of surprise, of any sort of pronounced interest, began to arouse his distrust. (Joseph Conrad) |
| **MODEL 5:** | Women feel just as men feel; they need exercise for their faculties and a field for their efforts as much as their brothers do; they suffer from too rigid a restraint, too absolute a stagnation, precisely as men would suffer. (Charlotte Brontë) |
| **MODEL 6:** | Young people believe that by remaining individuals, by avoiding the marriage vows, by living together only as long as love lasts, they will avoid the togetherness demanded of the married; they will avoid the staleness of being taken for granted. |
| **MODEL 7:** | While there is a lower class, I am in it; while there is a criminal element, I am of it; while there is a soul in prison, I am not free. (Eugene Debs) |

B. Study the following passages. Point out any features that make for *effective sentence style*. Examine such features as sentence length, variety, emphasis. Point out any special or unusual effects.

1. We go to our libraries in order to read and take advantage of the experiences of others. I think we all realize that not every written word in a library is entirely true. Many different authors have here written what they think, what they have experienced, what they believe is true, and sometimes what they wish were true. Some are wrong, a few are right, and many are neither entirely wrong nor entirely right.

2. This is not a Utopian tract. Some of those who complain about the quality of our national life seem to be dreaming of a world in which everyone without exception has talent, taste, judgment, and an unswerving allegiance to excellence. Such dreams are pleasant but unprofitable. The problem is to achieve some measure of excellence *in this society,* with all its beloved and exasperating clutter, with all its exciting and debilitating confusion of standards, with all the stubborn problems that won't be solved and the equally stubborn ones that might be.—John W. Gardner, *Excellence*

3. We are informed that marriage should be a place where we can grow, find ourselves, be ourselves. Interestingly, we cannot be entirely ourselves even

with our best friends. Some decorum, some courtesy, some selflessness are demanded. As for finding myself, I think I already know where I am. I'm grown up; I have responsibilities; I am in the middle of a lifelong marriage; I am hanging in there, sometimes enduring, sometimes enjoying.—Suzanne Britt Jordan, "My Turn," *Newsweek*

# 5

# Spelling and Mechanics

# DIAGNOSTIC TEST

## INSTRUCTIONS:

Look at the blank in each of the following sentences. Of the three choices that follow the sentences, which is the right one? Put the letter for the right choice after the number of the sentence.

---

**1.** We were _____ a trip to Wyoming.
   a. planing        b. planning        c. plannyng

**2.** Everyone re _____ ved a printed notice.
   a. cei        b. cie        c. cea

**3.** The two _____ houses had both been burglarized.
   a. family's        b. families        c. families'

**4.** I hesitate to say _____ to blame.
   a. who's        b. whose        c. whos

**5.** We usually took our vacation in Feb_____.
   a. uary        b. ruary        c. uerry

**6.** A political leader needs _____.
   a. self-confidance        b. self confidents        c. self-confidence

**7.** What happened to the old-fashioned _____?
   a. Forth Of July        b. fourth of july        c. Fourth of July

**8.** The ambulance _____ arrived sooner.
   a. should have        b. should of        c. shoudve

**9.** We were both taking a course in _____ literature.
   a. womans        b. women's        c. womens'

**10.** The rule _____ apply to people over sixty-five.
   a. doesnt        b. dosent        c. doesn't

**11.** The decision was _____ a mistake.
   a. definately        b. definitely        c. definitly

**12.** The organization included both teachers and _____.
   a. principles        b. principal's        c. principals

**13.** When the subsidy ran out, _____ was felt everywhere.
   a. its absence        b. it's absence        c. its absents

**14.** The design was bas _____ sound.
   a. ically        b. icly        c. icaly

**15.** The researchers were stud _____ the documents.
    a. yng                b. ying                c. ing

**16.** My uncle just had his _____ birthday.
    a. fourty-fourth      b. forty fourth      c. forty-fourth

**17.** The _____ debts had doubled during the year.
    a. city's            b. cities           c. citys

**18.** They were reluctant to _____ handouts from us.
    a. except          b. acept          c. accept

**19.** The neighborhood had many _____ families.
    a. polish american    b. Polish-american    c. Polish-American

**20.** The mansion looked like something out of *Gone* _____.
    a. *With The Wind*    b. *with the Wind*    c. *with the wind*

# SP 1   SPELLING PROBLEMS      *sp*

**Improve your spelling by developing good spelling habits.**

Merely looking up misspelled words has little long-range effect. The following procedure has a good chance of producing results:

(1) *Master the true "unforgivables."* A handful of common words are misspelled again and again by poor spellers. No matter how intelligent or capable you are, misspelling one of these will make you look ignorant. Make absolutely sure that you master the words in the following list. Watch out for them in your writing. *Never* misspell one of these:

| | | |
|---|---|---|
| accept | definite | receive |
| all right | environment | similar |
| a lot | occurred | studying |
| basically | perform | surprise |
| believe | probably | writing |

(2) *Start a record of your own personal spelling problems.* Whenever a piece of writing is returned to you, write down all the words that you misspelled. Work your way through a list of common spelling demons (such as the one printed under **SP 3**). List those that you have found troublesome in your own writing.

(3) *Put in twenty minutes three times a week over a period of time.* Unless you work on your spelling regularly, you will make little progress. You cannot unlearn in two or three hours the spelling habits that you developed over many years.

(4) *Fix each word firmly in your mind.* At each sitting, take up a group of perhaps ten or twenty spelling words. If you are a "visualizer," place your spelling words before you in clear, legible handwriting. Try putting them on a set of small note cards that you can carry around with you. Run your eyes over each word until you can see both the individual letters and the whole word at the same time. If you learn mainly by ear, read each word aloud. Then spell each letter individually: *Receive*—R-E-C-E-I-V-E. If you learn best when you can bring your nerves and muscles into play, try writing each word in large letters. Trace it over several times.

(5) *Make use of memory devices like the following*:

| | |
|---|---|
| acquainted: | MAC got ACquainted. |
| all right: | ALL RIGHT means ALL is RIGHT. |
| beginning: | There's an INNING in begINNING. |
| believe: | Don't beLIEve LIEs. |
| business: | The drive-IN stayed IN busINess. |
| criticism: | There's a CRITIC in CRITICism. |
| environment: | There's IRON in the envIRONment. |
| government: | People who GOVERN are a GOVERNment. |
| library: | The LiBRarians BRought BRicks for the LIBRARY. |
| performance: | He gave a PERfect PERformance. |
| recognition: | There's a COG in reCOGnition. |
| surprise: | The SURfer had a SURprise. |
| villain: | There's a VILLA in VILLAin. |

# SP1a  Spelling and Pronunciation                            *sp*

**Watch for differences between the spoken and the written word.**

Some words become spelling problems because the gap between spelling and pronunciation is unusually wide.

(1) *Watch for sounds not clearly heard in much informal speech.* Be sure to include the italicized letters in the following words:

| | | |
|---|---|---|
| accident*a*lly | can*d*idate | lib*r*ary |
| basic*a*lly | gover*n*ment | prob*a*bly |
| Feb*r*uary | incident*a*lly | quan*t*ity |

(2) *Watch for silent consonants.* Know how to spell the following:

| | | |
|---|---|---|
| condem*n* | de*b*t | mor*t*gage |
| forei*g*n | dou*b*t | sovere*ig*n |

(3) *Watch for vowels in unstressed positions.* The vowels *a*, *e*, and *i* become indistinguishable in the endings -*ate* and -*ite*, -*able* and -*ible*, -*ance* and -*ence*, -*ant* and -*ent*. If you can, choose the right ending by associating the word with a closely related one: *definite* (finish, defin*i*tion); *separate* (separa*tion); *ultimate* (ultim*a*tum); *indispensable* (dispens*a*ry). Watch out for the following:

*a:*  accept*able*, accept*ance*, advis*able*, attend*ance*, attend*ant*, brilli*ant*, perform*ance*

*e:*  consist*ent*, excell*ence*, excell*ent*, exist*ence*, experi*ence*, independ*ent*, persist*ent*, tend*ency*

*i:*  irresist*ible*, plaus*ible*, poss*ible*, suscept*ible*

(4) *Watch for* have *in combinations like* could have been, should have been, *and* might have been. Never substitute *of*:

| | | |
|---|---|---|
| WRONG: | could of been | should of known | might of failed |
| RIGHT: | could *have* been | should *have* known | might *have* failed |

**163**

# SP1b  Variant Forms          *sp*

**Watch for different forms of the same word.**

Some words are confusing because they appear in different forms.

(1)  *Watch out for different spellings of the same root*:

| | | |
|---|---|---|
| ti*ll* | — | unti*l* |
| f*ou*r, f*ou*rteen | — | f*o*rty |
| ni*n*e, ni*n*ety | — | ni*n*th |
| prec*ede* | — | proc*eed* |

(2)  *Watch out for spelling differences in pairs representing different parts of speech.* The spelling of a noun may be different from that of the corresponding verb or adjective:

| | |
|---|---|
| absor*b*—absor*p*tion | dissen*t*—dissen*s*ion |
| advi*s*e (v.)—advi*c*e (n.) | gener*ous*—gener*o*sity |
| conscien*ce*—conscien*t*ious | geni*us*—ingeni*ous* |
| courte*ous*—courte*sy* | proc*eed*—proc*edure* |
| curi*ous*—curi*o*sity | pron*ounce*—pron*un*ciation |

(3)  *Watch out when spelling changes because of a change in grammatical form.* For instance, we "choose" and "lead" in the present, but we "chose" and "led" in the past. Some plural forms cause spelling difficulties: one *man* but several *men*, one *woman* but several *women*. Remember these especially:

| | | | | | |
|---|---|---|---|---|---|
| **SINGULAR:** | hero | Negro | potato | tomato | wife |
| **PLURAL:** | hero*es* | Negro*es* | potato*es* | tomato*es* | wi*ves* |
| | | | | | |
| **SINGULAR:** | freshman | Irishman | life | veto | calf |
| **PLURAL:** | freshm*en* | Irishm*en* | li*ves* | veto*es* | cal*ves* |

Be sure to add the *-ed* for *past tense* or *past participle* in words like the following:

| | |
|---|---|
| used to: | He us*ed* to live here. |
| supposed to: | She was suppos*ed* to write. |
| prejudiced: | They were prejudic*ed* (bias*ed*) against me. |

*Note*: Your dictionary lists the correct spelling of plural forms that are difficult or unusual. Sometimes it lists two acceptable forms: *buffalos* or *buffaloes*, *scarfs* or *scarves*.

# SP1c Confusing Pairs

**Watch for words that sound similar or alike.**

Some words need attention because they *sound* similar but differ in spelling or in meaning. Try to apply tests like the following:

| | |
|---|---|
| WHOSE? | *their* car; they and *their* parents |
| WHERE? | here and *there*; it wasn't *there* |

| | |
|---|---|
| TAKE ON: | I *accepted* the job. |
| TAKE OUT: | The law *excepts* students. |

Know the following pairs:

| | |
|---|---|
| accept: | to *acc*ept a bribe; to find something *acc*eptable; to make an *acc*eptance speech (take on) |
| except: | everyone *exc*ept Judy; to make an *exc*eption; to *exc*ept (exempt, exclude) present company |
| capital: | unused capit*al*; modern capit*al*ism; the capit*al* of France; capit*al* letters |
| Capitol: | the cupola of the Capit*ol*; remodeling the façade of the Capit*ol* (a building) |
| cite: | *c*ited for bravery; to *c*ite many different authorities; a *c*itation for reckless driving (name or quote) |
| site: | the *s*ite of the new school (where it is *sit*uated or located) |
| sight: | knew him by *sight* (vision) |
| conscious: | she was consc*ious* of it (aware) |
| conscience: | her cons*cience* bothered her (moral sense) |
| council: | members of the city coun*cil*; Coun*ci*lor Brown (group) |
| counsel: | the coun*sel*ing staff of the college; camp coun*sel*ors (advice) |
| desert: | we lost our way in the de*sert*; he de*sert*ed (abandoned) his family; he got his just de*sert*s (what was earned) |
| dessert: | the dinner did not include a de*ss*ert |
| effect: | to *effect* (produce, bring about) a change; immediate *effects* (results); an *effect*ive speech (produces results) |
| affect: | it *affect*ed (influenced) my grade; he spoke with an *affect*ed (artificial) British accent |
| loose: | l*oose* and fast; l*oose*n your grip |
| lose: | win or l*ose*; a bad l*ose*r |

| personal: | a personal appeal; speak to her personally (in person) |
| personnel: | a personnel bureau; hire additional personnel (employees) |

| presents: | visitors bearing presents (gifts) |
| presence: | your presence is requested; presence of mind (being there) |

| principal: | his principal (main) argument; the principal of the school; principal (main sum) and interest |
| principle: | principles (rules, standards) of conduct; the principles of economics |

| quiet: | be quiet; a quiet neighborhood (silent) |
| quite: | quite so; not quite (entirely) |

| than: | bigger than life; more trouble than it is worth (comparison) |
| then: | now and then; until then (time) |

| there: | here and there; there you are; no one was there (where?) |
| their: | they lost their appetite; mental ills and their cure (whose?) |

| to: | go to bed, cut to pieces; easy to do, hard to deny |
| too: | too good to be true (excess); bring your children, too (also) |

| whether: | whether good or bad (choice) |
| weather: | bad weather; to weather the storm (climate) |

# EXERCISES

A. After the number of each sentence, write down the choice that fits the context.

1. Everyone *accepted/excepted* our invitation.
2. The injury *effected/affected* her hearing.
3. The *presence/presents* of heavily armed troops quieted the crowd.
4. The teachers shouted down the surprised *principle/principal*.
5. The new rules applied to all *personal/personnel*.
6. He loved the town, but staying *their/there* had become impossible.
7. She cherished the *quiet/quite* moments between visits.
8. The speaker had antagonized most of the *woman/women* in the audience.
9. Seymour was *too/to* short-tempered to work in public relations.
10. Anything was better *then/than* going back down the mountain.
11. Three members of the city *council/counsel* had resigned.
12. Most farms were *then/than* family-owned.
13. He always lectured us about sound business *principles/principals*.
14. The test was given to all incoming *freshman/freshmen*.
15. Her grandparents had been *prejudice/prejudiced* against poor immigrants.
16. Ever since he found the money, he has been bothered by his *conscious/conscience*.

17. Her mother *use/used* to run a store in a small Southern town.
18. Somebody should *of/have* called the police.
19. Several people had parked *their/there* motorcycles in the driveway.
20. No one knew *whether/weather* we could meet the deadline.

B. Insert the missing letter or letters in each of the following words: accept__nce, attend__nce, brilli__nt, consist__ncy, curi__sity, defin__te, excell__nt, exist__nce, experi__nce, independ__nt, indispens__ble, occurr__nce, irresist__ble, perform__nce, persist__nt, prec__ding, proc__dure, pron__nciation, separ__te, tend__ncy.

C. Look up the plural of *cargo, Eskimo, hoof, mosquito, motto, piano, solo, soprano, wharf, zero.*

D. In available dictionaries, check the status of simplified spellings like thr*u*, an*e*sthetic, th*o*, catal*og*, or any others you have encountered.

# SP2 SPELLING RULES                                                      *sp*

**Let a few simple spelling rules help you with common errors.**

The purpose of spelling rules is to help you memorize words that follow a common pattern. Spelling rules provide a key to a group of words that you would otherwise have to study individually.

## SP2a  *I* Before *E*

**Put *i* before *e* except after *c*.**

The same sound is often spelled differently in different words. For instance, *ie* and *ei* often stand for the same sound. If you sort out the words in question, you get the following:

*ie:*   achieve, believe, chief, grief, niece, piece (of pie), relieve
*cei:*  ceiling, conceited, conceive, perceive, receive, receipt

In the second group of words, the *ei* follows the letter *c*. In other words, it is *i* before *e* except after *c*. Exceptions:

*ei:*   either, leisure, neither, seize, weird
*cie:*  financier, species

**167**

## SP 2b   Doubled Consonant                                    *sp*

**Know when to double a single final consonant before an added vowel.**

In many words, a single final consonant is doubled before an ending (or **suffix**) that begins with a vowel: *-ed, -er, -est, -ing*. The word *plan* has a single final *n*, but we double the *n* in *planned*, *planning*, and *planner*. The word *big* has a single final *g*, but we double the *g* in *bigger* and *biggest*.

Double the final letter only under the following conditions:

(1)   *The vowel before the final consonant must be a "short" or single vowel.* It cannot be a "long" or double vowel (**diphthong**). Long or double vowels are shown in writing by combinations like *oa, ea, ee,* and *ou* (b*oa*t, r*ea*d) or by a silent final *e* (k*i*t*e*, h*o*p*e*, h*a*t*e*). Note the differences in pronunciation and in spelling in the following pairs:

| DOUBLING | NO DOUBLING |
|---|---|
| bar—ba*rr*ed | bare—bared |
| bat—ba*tt*ed | boat—boating |
| hop—ho*pp*ing | hope—hoping |
| plan—pla*nn*ed | plane—planed |
| red—re*dd*er | read—reading |
| scrap—scra*pp*ed | scrape—scraped |
| slip—sli*pp*ed | sleep—sleeping |
| stop—sto*pp*ed | stoop—stooped |

(2)   *The last syllable before the suffix must be the one stressed in pronunciation.* Sometimes a shift in stress will be reflected in a difference in the spelling of different forms of the same word. Compare the following groups:

| DOUBLING | NO DOUBLING |
|---|---|
| ad*mit*, admitted, admittance | *ed*it, edited, editing |
| for*get*, forgetting, forgettable | *ben*efit, benefited |
| be*gin*, beginning, beginner | *har*den, hardened |
| re*gret*, regretted, regrettable | pro*hib*it, prohibited, prohibitive |
| over*lap*, overlapping | de*vel*op, developing |
| pre*fer*, preferred, preferring | *pref*erence, preferable |
| re*fer*, referred, referring | *ref*erence |

# SP 2c   *Y* as a Vowel   *sp*

**Change *y* to *ie* before *s*.**

*Y* is sometimes used as a consonant (*year, youth*), sometimes as a vowel (*my, dry; hurry, study*). As a single final vowel, the *y* changes to *ie* before *s*. It changes to *i* before all other endings except *-ing*.

*ie:*  family—families, fly—flies, study—studies, try—tries, quantity—quantities
*i:*  beauty—beautiful, bury—burial, busy—business, copy—copied, dry—drier, lively—livelihood, noisy—noisily
*y:*  burying, copying, studying, trying, worrying

When it follows another vowel, *y* is usually preserved: *delays, joys, played, valleys.* Exceptions: *day—daily, gay—gaily, lay—laid, pay—paid, say—said.*

# SP 2d   Final *E*   *sp*

**Drop the final silent *e* before an added vowel.**

A silent *e* at the end of a word is dropped before an ending that begins with a vowel. It is preserved before an ending that begins with a consonant:

|  | DROPPED *e* | KEPT *e* |
|---|---|---|
| bore | boring | boredom |
| hate | hating | hateful |
| like | liking, likable | likely |
| love | loving, lovable | lovely |

Exceptions: *argue—argument, due—duly, dye—dyeing* (as against *die—dying*), *mile—mileage, true—truly, whole—wholly, judge—judgment, acknowledge—acknowledgment.*

*Note*: A final *e* may signal the difference in pronunciation between the final consonants in *rag* and *rage*, or in *plastic* and *notice*. Keep such a final *e* not only before a consonant but also before *a* or *o*:

*ge:*  advantage—advantageous, change—changeable, courage—courageous, outrage—outrageous
*ce:*  notice—noticeable, peace—peaceable

# EXERCISES

A. Insert *ei* or *ie*: ach___vement, bel___ver, dec___tful, f___ld, inconc___ vable, misch___f, perc___ve, rec___ving, rel___f, s___ze, w___rd, y___ld.

B. Select the appropriate word in each of the numbered pairs.

1. (a) *bared* / (b) *barred* from office
2. his (a) *bating* / (b) *batting* average
3. (a) *caned* / (b) *canned* meat
4. (a) *biding* / (b) *bidding* their time
5. (a) *hoping* / (b) *hopping* for the best
6. (a) *pined* / (b) *pinned* to the mat
7. a (a) *well-planed* / (b) *well-planned* outing
8. (a) *robed* / (b) *robbed* in white
9. a boy (a) *spiting* / (b) *spitting* his parents
10. (a) *taped* / (b) *tapped* him on the shoulder

C. Combine the following words with the suggested endings: accompany ___ed, advantage___ous, argue___ing, benefit___ed, carry___s, come___ing, confide___ing, differ___ing, excite___able, friendly___ness, lively___hood, occur___ing, prefer___ed, remit___ance, sad___er, satisfy___ed, shine___ing, sole___ly, study___ing, tragedy___s, try___s, use___ing, valley___s, whole___ly, write___ing.

D. For each blank space, what would be the right form of the word in parentheses? Put the right form after the number of the sentence.

1. (family)     Several _____ were having a picnic.
2. (plan)       The holdup had been _____ carefully.
3. (study)      My friends were _____ in the library.
4. (regret)     I have always _____ this oversight.
5. (city)       We visited three _____ in one week.
6. (pay)        They had already _____ the bill.
7. (love)       They never stopped hating and _____ each other.
8. (quantity)   Great _____ of food had been consumed.
9. (beauty)     She always described her aunts as famous _____.
10. (occur)     The thought had _____ to us.
11. (begin)     My patience was _____ to wear thin.
12. (copy)      He had _____ the whole paragraph.
13. (refer)     Your doctor should have _____ you to a specialist.
14. (stop)      You should have _____ at the light.
15. (lay)       We had _____ the tile ourselves.
16. (admit)     Marcia had _____ her mistake.
17. (refer)     She was _____ to a famous incident.
18. (bore)      The speaker was _____ the audience.
19. (forget)    She kept _____ my name.
20. (apply)     Sue had _____ to several colleges.

# SP 3 WORDS OFTEN MISSPELLED

*sp*

**Watch for words frequently misspelled.**

The following are among the words most frequently misspelled in student writing. Take up one group of twenty or twenty-five at a time. Find the ones that would cause you trouble.

| | | |
|---|---|---|
| absence | amount | beginning |
| abundance | analysis | belief |
| accessible | analyze | believe |
| accidentally | annual | beneficial |
| acclaim | anticipate | benefited |
| accommodate | anxiety | boundaries |
| accompanied | apologize | breath |
| accomplish | apology | brilliant |
| accumulate | apparatus | Britain |
| accurately | apparent | buses |
| accuses | appearance | business |
| accustom | applies | |
| achievement | applying | calendar |
| acknowledgment | appreciate | candidate |
| acquaintance | approach | career |
| acquire | appropriate | careless |
| acquitted | approximately | carrying |
| across | area | category |
| actuality | argue | ceiling |
| address | arguing | cemetery |
| adequate | argument | challenge |
| admit | arising | changeable |
| adolescence | arrangement | character |
| advantageous | article | characteristic |
| advertisement | artistically | chief |
| afraid | ascend | choose |
| against | assent | chose |
| aggravate | athlete | clothes |
| aggressive | athletic | coarse |
| alleviate | attendance | column |
| allotted | audience | comfortable |
| allowed | authority | comfortably |
| all right | | coming |
| already | balance | commission |
| altar | basically | committed |
| altogether | basis | committee |
| always | beauty | companies |
| amateur | becoming | competition |
| among | before | competitive |

**171**

completely
comprehension
conceivable
conceive
concentrate
condemn
confident
confidential
conscience
conscientious
conscious
considerably
consistent
continually
continuous
control
controlled
convenience
convenient
coolly
courageous
course
courteous
criticism
criticize
cruelty
curiosity
curriculum

dealt
deceit
deceive
decision
definite
definitely
definition
dependent
describe
description
desirability
desirable
despair
desperate
destruction
devastate
develop
development
device

difference
different
difficult
dilemma
dining
disappear
disappearance
disappoint
disastrous
discipline
disease
disgusted
dissatisfaction
dissatisfied
doesn't
dominant
due
during

ecstasy
efficiency
efficient
eighth
eliminate
embarrass
embarrassment
eminent
emphasize
endeavor
enforce
enough
entertain
environment
equipped
especially
etc.
exaggerate
excellent
exceptionally
exercise
exhaust
exhilarate
existence
experience
explanation
extraordinary
extremely

familiar
families
fascinate
finally
financial
financier
foreign
forward
friend
fulfill
fundamentally
further

gaiety
generally
genius
government
governor
grammar
guaranteed
guidance

happily
happiness
height
heroes
heroine
hindrance
hopeful
huge
humorous
hundred
hurriedly
hypocrisy
hypocrite

ignorant
imaginary
imagination
immediately
immensely
incidentally
indefinite
independent
indispensable
inevitable
influence
ingenious

insight
intellectual
intelligence
interest
interpret
interrupt
involve
irrelevant
irresistible
itself

jealous

knowledge

laboratory
laid
leisure
likelihood
literature
livelihood
loneliness
losing

magnificence
maintain
maintenance
manageable
manufacturer
marriage
mathematics
meant
medieval
merely
mileage
miniature
minute
mischievous
muscle
mysterious

naive
necessarily
necessary
ninety
noticeable

obstacle
occasion
occasionally
occurred
occurrence
omit
operate
opinion
opponent
opportunity
optimism
original

paid
parallel
paralysis
paralyze
particularly
passed
past
peace
peculiar
perceive
perform
performance
permanent
persistent
persuade
pertain
phase
phenomenon
philosophy
physical
piece
pleasant
possess
possession
possible
practical
precede
prejudice
prepare
prevalent
privilege
probably
procedure
proceed

professor
prominent
propaganda
prophecy
psychology
pursue

quantity

really
recommend
regard
relief
relieve
religion
repetition
representative
resource
response
rhythm
ridiculous
roommate

safety
satisfactorily
schedule
seize
sense
separate
sergeant
shining
significance
similar
sincerely
sophomore
speech
sponsor
strength
stretch
strictly
studying
subtle
succeed
successful
summarize
surprise

| temperament | transferred | various |
|---|---|---|
| tendency | tries | vengeance |
| therefore | | villain |
| thorough | undoubtedly | |
| together | unnecessary | weird |
| tragedy | useful | writing |
| | using | |

# EXERCISE

Use the following to test your knowledge of words often misspelled. Have someone dictate these sentences to you. Make a list of the words that give you trouble.

1. *Amateurs benefited* more than other *athletes.*
2. The *committee* heard every *conceivable opinion.*
3. *Manufacturers developed* a new *device.*
4. We kept all *business decisions confidential.*
5. Her *appearance* was *definitely* a *surprise.*
6. She *accused* her *opponent* of *hypocrisy.*
7. The *absence* of *controls* proved *disastrous.*
8. We met a *prominent professor* of *psychology.*
9. Their *marriage succeeded exceptionally* well.
10. These *privileges* are *undoubtedly unnecessary.*
11. The *sponsor* was *dissatisfied* with the *performance.*
12. Their *approach* was *strictly practical.*
13. *Companies* can seldom just *eliminate* the *competition.*
14. A *repetition* of the *tragedy* is *inevitable.*
15. This *subtle difference* is *irrelevant.*

## SP4 THE APOSTROPHE

**Use the apostrophe for contractions and possessives.**

The **apostrophe** has no exact equivalent in speech and is therefore easily omitted or misplaced.

## SP4a Contractions

**Use the apostrophe in informal contracted forms.**

Use the **apostrophe** to show that one or more letters have been left out. Use it in contractions, or shortened forms, like the following:

| | |
|---|---|
| we *are* ready | *we're* ready |
| she *is* a friend | *she's* a friend |
| he *will* be back | *he'll* be back |
| they *are* late | *they're* late |
| you *are* right | *you're* right |
| it is *not* true | it *isn't* true |

Look for the following especially:

(1) *Use the apostrophe in combined forms that include a shortened form of* not:

| | |
|---|---|
| we *cannot* leave | we *can't* leave |
| she *will not* say | she *won't* say |
| he *could not* stay | he *couldn't* stay |
| they *have not* paid | they *haven't* paid |
| you *are not* safe | you *aren't* safe |

Make sure not to misspell *don't* and *doesn't*. These are shortened forms of *do not* and *does not*:

| | |
|---|---|
| *do not:* | We *don't* usually hire in the summer. |
| *does not:* | The new converter *doesn't* work. |

(2) *Know familiar confusing pairs.* Use *it's, who's,* and *they're* only if something has been left out:

| | |
|---|---|
| *it's* (it *is,* it *has*) | *it's* true, *it's* raining |
| | *it's* expired |
| *its* (of it) | took *its* course |
| | *its* size, *its* results |
| *who's* (who *is*) | *who's* to blame? |
| | the one *who's* guilty |
| *whose* (of whom) | *whose* turn is it? |
| | one *whose* car stalled |
| *they're* (they *are*) | *they're* late |
| | if *they're* here |
| *their* (of them) | *their* belongings |
| | *their* parents |

*Note*: Contractions are common in informal speech and writing. Avoid them in formal reports, research papers, and letters of application. Use them sparingly in ordinary prose.

# SP 4b Possessives *ap*

**Use the apostrophe for the possessive of nouns.**

The **possessive** is a special form of nouns. We use it to show who owns something or where something belongs. We usually make up the possessive form by adding an apostrophe plus *s* to the plain form:

| WHOSE? | | |
|---|---|---|
| my *sister's* car | | Mr. *Smith's* garage |
| her *aunt's* house | | the *student's* name |
| the *family's* debts | | my *doctor's* address |
| our *mayor's* office | | one *person's* opinion |

Besides ownership or possession, the possessive form shows other relationships. However, with most of these the possessive form still tells us "whose?": the *girl's* friends, a *child's* innocence, the *general's* dismissal, the *children's* activities. The possessive usually comes before another noun but is sometimes separated from it:

The fault was not *Dan's.*
It is either *Marcia's* car or *Sue's.*

Remember the following points:

(1) *Know the difference between singular and plural possessives.* If a plural noun already ends with *-s*, we add *only* the apostrophe. We do not add a second *s.* Study contrasting pairs like the following:

| SINGULAR | PLURAL |
|---|---|
| my *sister's* face | my *sisters'* faces |
| a *parent's* duties | both *parents'* duties |
| a *worker's* pay | the *workers'* strike |
| one *family's* home | both *families'* homes |
| a *peasant's* hut | the *peasants'* revolt |

However, use the regular possessive when a plural noun does not end with the plural *-s.* Examples of such unusual plurals are *children, women, men,* and *people*:

| | |
|---|---|
| *children's* toys | *women's* rights |
| *men's* wear | *people's* prejudices |

**176**

(2) *Use the apostrophe in familiar expressions dealing with time or value.* Distinguish between singular and plural:

| SINGULAR | PLURAL |
|---|---|
| a *week's* pay | two *weeks'* pay |
| an *hour's* drive | three *hours'* drive |
| a *dollar's* worth | two *dollars'* worth |

Expressions like the following are possessive forms and require an apostrophe:

a *moment's* notice     *today's* paper     a *day's* work

(3) *Know when to use the apostrophe with pronouns.* Use the apostrophe with the possessive forms of **indefinite pronouns**: *everyone* (*everybody*), *someone* (*somebody*), *anyone* (*anybody*), *no one* (*nobody*), and *one*:

to *everybody's* surprise
at *someone's* suggestion
(also: at someone *else's* house)
*one's* best friends

Do *not* use the apostrophe with **possessive pronouns**: *its, hers, ours, yours, theirs*:

both *its* ears     it was *hers*     this is *yours*

(4) *Follow your preference when the singular form of a noun already has a final* -s. After the apostrophe that signals the possessive, you may or may not add another *s*, depending on whether you would expect an extra syllable in pronunciation. With words like the following, the additional syllable seems clearly required: the *boss's* office, the *waitress's* tip. But with many proper names, either form would be right:

| BOTH RIGHT: | *Dolores'* trip | *Dolores's* trip |
|---|---|---|
| | *Jones'* raise | *Jones's* raise |
| | *Dickens'* novel | *Dickens's* novel |

*Note*: Many combined words or phrases form the possessive as if they were single words: the *commander in chief's* orders, a *father-in-law's* hopes, *Simon & Schuster's* spring list. But sometimes we want to show that something belongs to several people: a *mother's and father's* worries, *Simon's and Adele's* marriage.

## SP 4c   Plurals of Letters and Symbols                    *ap*

**Use the apostrophe in special situations.**

Use the **apostrophe** to separate the plural *s* from the name of a letter or a symbol, or from a word named as a word (two large 7's; if's and but's):

> Those great big beautiful A's so avidly sought, those little miserly C's so often found, were meant for another time and another student body.—Oscar Handlin, "Are the Colleges Killing Education?" *Atlantic*

# EXERCISES

A. Change each of the following to the possessive form. Examples: pay for a month—a *month's* pay; the wedding of my brother—my *brother's* wedding.

1. the playground for children
2. the budget of the President
3. wages for two weeks
4. the members of her family
5. the homes of many families
6. the pay of an officer
7. the future of America
8. the locker room for girls
9. a vacation of three months
10. the worth of a dollar
11. the employment record of a person
12. the fringe benefits of the employees
13. the vote for women
14. the retirement of the coach
15. the working hours of our custodians

B. Choose the right spelling in each of the following pairs.

1. When the mother and the father respect each *(1) other's / (2) others'* opinions, children learn to live harmoniously by following their *(3) elders / (4) elders'* example.
2. Since the *(5) treasurers / (6) treasurer's* resignation, the *(7) members / (8) member's* have been speculating about *(9) whose / (10) who's* going to succeed her.
3. *(11) Mrs. Beattys / (12) Mrs. Beatty's* husband still sends her *(13) flowers / (14) flower's* on *(15) Valentines / (16) Valentine's* Day.

4. We were all overjoyed when my *(17) brother's / (18) brothers'* baby took *(19) its / (20) it's* first steps.
5. A *(21) student's / (22) students'* lack of interest is not always the *(23) teachers / (24) teacher's* fault.
6. *(25) Its / (26) It's* the *(27) parents / (28) parents'* responsibility to provide for their *(29) children's / (30) childrens'* religious education.
7. *(31) Lets / (32) Let's* borrow *(33) someones / (34) someone's* car and go for an *(35) hour's / (36) hours'* drive.
8. *(37) Charles / (38) Charles's* father murmured audibly that the assembled *(39) relatives / (40) relative's* had consumed at least ten *(41) dollars / (42) dollars'* worth of food.

---

# SP 5    CAPITALS        *cap*

**Capitalize proper names and words in titles.**

We capitalize the first word of a sentence and the pronoun *I*. In addition, we use capitals for proper names and for words in titles.

## SP 5a   Proper Names        *cap*

**Capitalize proper names.**

Proper names are always capitalized. Capitalize the names of persons, places, regions, countries, languages, historical periods, ships, days of the week, months (but not seasons), organizations, religions: *James, Brazil, Italian, the Middle Ages, S.S. Independence, Sunday, February, Buddhism.*

Remember the following:

(1) *Capitalize words derived from proper names.* In particular, capitalize words that make use of the name of a country, nationality, place, or religion: *English grammar, French pastry, Mexican nationals, Spanish names, German beer, Parisian fashions, Christian charity, Marxist ideas.*

*Note*: In some words, the proper name involved has been lost sight of, and a lower-case letter is used: *guinea pig, india rubber, pasteurized milk.*

## A CHECKLIST OF CAPITALIZED NAMES

**PEOPLE:** Eleanor Roosevelt, Langston Hughes, Albert Einstein, Edna St. Vincent Millay

**TITLES:** Dr. Brothers, Senator Kennedy, Queen Elizabeth, Pope John Paul, the President

**CONTINENTS:** Asia, America, Europe, Australia, the Antarctic

**COUNTRIES:** United States of America, Canada, Great Britain, Mexico, Denmark, Japan

**LANGUAGES:** English, Spanish, Chinese, Russian, French

**REGIONS:** the South, the East, the Near East, the Midwest

**STATES:** Kansas, North Dakota, Louisiana, Rhode Island

**CITIES:** Oklahoma City, Dallas, Baltimore, Los Angeles, Washington, D.C.

**SIGHTS:** Lake Erie, Mount Hood, Death Valley, the Grand Canyon

**ADDRESSES:** Park Lane, Fleet Avenue, Oak Street

**MONTHS:** January, March, July, October

**WEEKDAYS:** Monday, Wednesday, Saturday, Sunday

**HOLIDAYS:** Labor Day, Thanksgiving, Easter, the Fourth of July

**INSTITUTIONS:** the Supreme Court, the Department of Agriculture, the U.S. Senate

**BUSINESSES:** Ford Motor Company, General Electric, Sears

**SCHOOLS:** Oakdale High School, Las Vistas Junior College, University of Maine

**GROUPS:** the Democratic Party, the American Legion

**FAITHS:** Christian, Muslim, Jewish, Buddhist

**DENOMINATIONS:** Methodist, Mormon, Unitarian, Roman Catholic

(2) *Capitalize general words that become part of a proper name.* The general term for a title, family relationship, institution, or geographic feature is capitalized when it combines with a proper name: *Major Brown, Aunt Augusta, Sergeant Barnacle, Campbell High School, Indiana University, Tennessee Valley Authority, Medora Heights, Institute for the Blind, Lake Erie.* Some titles refer to only one person and can take the place of the person's name: *the Pope, the Queen* (of England), *the President* (of the United States).

(3) *Capitalize a general word that is put to special use as a proper name.* The same word may serve as a general term but also as a proper name for one person, institution, or place:

| GENERAL WORD | PROPER NAME |
|---|---|
| democratic (many institutions) | Democratic (name of party) |
| orthodox (many attitudes) | Orthodox (name of church) |
| history (general subject) | History 31 (specific course) |
| west (general direction) | Middle West (specific area) |
| my mother (common relationship) | Mother (name of the person) |

## SP 5b Titles of Publications *cap*

**Capitalize major words in titles.**

A capital letter marks the first and last words and all major words in the title of a book, other publication, or work of art. The only words not counting as major are articles (*a, an,* and *the*), prepositions (*at, in, on, of, from, with*), and connectives (*and, but, if, when*). Prepositions and connectives are usually capitalized when they have five or more letters.

Observe these conventions in writing the titles of a theme:

```
Goalie Without a Mask
Travels with a Friend Through Suburbia
How to Lose Friends and Become a Public Enemy
```

The same conventions apply to titles of publications cited in a sentence:

Several generations of Americans read *Sink or Swim, Phil the Fiddler, Mark the Match Boy,* and *From Canal Boy to President,* records of achievement which rewarded personal goodness with happiness and goods.—Saul Bellow, "The Writer as Moralist," *Atlantic*

# EXERCISE

Which of the words in the following sentences should be capitalized? After the number of each sentence, write down and capitalize all such words.

1. A yale graduate, baird worked at chase manhattan and smith, barney & co.
2. Pistol shots crackled in dearborn, the detroit suburb that is home to the ford motor company's sprawling river rouge plant.
3. Last october, a huge and very ugly statue of sir winston churchill was unveiled in parliament square, london.
4. As he was helped aboard, egyptian mohammed aly clutched a small blue-bound koran that had been given to him by the arab mayor of hebron.
5. The sprawling city of canton, 110 miles by rail from hong kong, has for centuries been china's principal gathering place for asian and european traders.
6. The american tourist cashing her traveler's check at tokyo's hotel okura got a bundle of good news.
7. Last week, 3,500 delegates met in manhattan to celebrate the centennial of the union of american hebrew congregations, founded in cincinnati by rabbi isaac wise.
8. At columbia and barnard, at atlanta's morehouse college and the university of virginia, economics was suddenly the subject to take.
9. Seven novels by mickey spillane are among the thirty best-selling novels of all time, along with *gone with the wind, peyton place, lady chatterley's lover,* and *in his steps,* by charles monroe sheldon, 1897.
10. Like other newspapers, the *new york journal-american* had learned the art of catering to the irish catholics.

## SP 6   THE HYPHEN                                *hy*

**Use the hyphen where required by current practice.**

Use of the **hyphen** is the least uniform and the least stable feature of English spelling. In doubtful cases, use the most recent edition of a good dictionary as your guide.

# SP 6a   Compound Words   *hy*

**Know which compound words require a hyphen.**

Treatment varies for words used together as a single expression. Some **compound words** are clearly distinguished from ordinary combinations by differences in both writing and pronunciation: *black bird* (black BIRD) but *blackbird* (BLACKbird), *dark room* (dark ROOM) but *darkroom* (DARKroom). Such unmistakable compounds are *headache, highway,* and *stepmother.* In many similar compounds, however, the parts are kept separate: *high school, labor union, second cousin.* Still other compound words conventionally require a hyphen: *cave-in, great-grandfather, mother-in-law, President-elect.*

ONE WORD: *bellboy, bridesmaid, stepfather, checklist, highlight, headquarters, blackout, bittersweet*

TWO WORDS (OR MORE): *commander in chief, goose flesh, vice versa, off year, high command*

HYPHEN: *able-bodied, bull's-eye, drive-in, court-martial, merry-go-round, six-pack, in-laws, vice-president, Spanish-American, one-sided, off-season, in-group*

Remember:

(1) *Hyphenate compound numbers from twenty-one to ninety-nine.* Also hyphenate fractions used as modifiers:

There were *twenty-six* passengers.
The plane was *one-third* empty.
The tank was *three-quarters* full.

Practice varies for other uses of fractions:

Two thirds (or two-thirds) remained poor.

(2) *Be sure to spell* today, tomorrow, nevertheless, *and* nowadays *as single words.* Be sure *not* to spell as single words *all right, a lot* (a lot of time), *be able,* and *no one.*

## SP 6b Prefixes

*hy*

**Know which prefixes require a hyphen.**

Many hyphenated compounds combine a word and its prefix. A prefix can be attached at the beginning of different words. Watch for the following:

(1)   All-, ex- *(in the sense of "former")*, quasi-, self-, *and sometimes* co- *require a hyphen*: all-knowing, ex-husband, quasi-judicial, self-contained, co-worker.

(2)   *All prefixes require a hyphen before words beginning with a capital letter*: all-American, anti-American, pro-British, un-American, non-Catholic.

(3)   *Often a hyphen prevents the meeting of two identical vowels or three identical consonants*: anti-intellectual, semi-independent, fall-like.

*Note*: Sometimes a hyphen distinguishes an unfamiliar use of a prefix from a familiar one: *recover—re-cover* (make a new cover), *recreation—re-creation* (creating again or anew).

## SP 6c Group Modifiers

**Use the hyphen with group modifiers.**

Several words may temporarily combine as a modifier preceding a noun. They are then usually joined to each other by hyphens: a *flying-saucer* hat, a *middle-of-the-road* policy, a *question-and-answer* period, a *step-by-step* account, a *devil-may-care* attitude. No hyphens are used when the same combinations serve some other function in a sentence: tend toward the *middle of the road*; explain a process *step by step*.

*Note*: No hyphen is used when a modifier before a noun is in turn modified by an adverb ending in -*ly*: a *fast-rising* executive, a *well-balanced* account; but a *rapidly growing* city, a *carefully documented* study.

# EXERCISE

After the number of each sentence, write all combinations that should be hyphenated or written as one word.

1. She had won a hard fought grass roots campaign that toppled a well entrenched incumbent.
2. The room was only about two thirds full, with seventy five people in attendance.
3. Though at times her son in law seemed self conscious, he never the less had a well balanced personality.
4. He was the kind of law and order candidate who promises to crack down on ex convicts.
5. Several players from these Italian American families had gone on to become all Americans.
6. Those who denounced the parking privileges for out of town students were obviously not from out of town.
7. Both pro British and anti British Arabs were united in their contempt for ex king Farouk.
8. The anti intellectual local news paper had called our candidate an absent minded ex professor and a tool of the labor unions.
9. Now a days few self respecting candidates conduct old fashioned campaigns taking them into out of the way places.
10. Jane Andrews and her co author have written a well documented account of the un democratic procedures followed by quasi judicial agencies.

# M1 MANUSCRIPT MECHANICS

**Submit neat and competently prepared copy.**

Whenever you hand in a theme or a report, the outward appearance of your manuscript is the first thing to strike your reader. A good first impression is likely to put the reader in a receptive mood.

# M1a Penmanship and Typing *ms*

**Make sure all copy, whether handwritten or typed, is neat and legible.**

Remember the following guidelines:

(1) *Write legibly.* To produce legible handwritten copy, use composition paper of standard size, preferably ruled in wide lines. Use a reliable pen. Prune your writing of flourishes; avoid excessive slanting or excessive crowding. Unconventional handwriting is likely to annoy rather than impress the reader.

(2) *Type neatly.* To prepare typewritten copy, use unlined paper of standard size. Onionskin paper or semitransparent sheets are for carbon copies. *Double-space* all material. Leave two spaces after a period or other end punctuation. Use two hyphens—with no space on either side—to make a dash.

(3) *Leave adequate margins.* Leave about an inch and a half on the left and at the top. Leave about an inch on the right and at the bottom. *Indent* the first line of a paragraph—about an inch in longhand, or five spaces in typed copy.

(4) *Proofread carefully.* Last-minute corrections are permissible on the final copy, provided they look neat and are few in number:

• *To take out a word or phrase,* draw a line through it. Do not use parentheses or square brackets for this purpose:

```
We hear the complaints to which we are accustomed to.
```

• *To correct a word,* draw a line through it and insert the corrected word in the space immediately above. Do not cross out or insert individual letters:

```
                                    collected
The officer has to stay calm, cool, and collective.
```

• *To add a missing word,* insert a caret ( ∧ ) and write the word immediately above:

```
              not
Thou shalt∧steal.
```

• *To change the paragraphing of a paper,* insert the symbol ¶ to indicate an additional paragraph break. Insert "*no* ¶" in the margin to indicate that an existing paragraph break should be ignored.

> . . . was finished. ⁋The second part of the
> program . . .

## M1b  Titles of Themes                                    *ms*

**Use standard form for the titles of your themes.**

Titles of themes follow the rules for the capitalization of words in titles of publications (see **SP 5b**). Do *not* underline or put in quotation marks the title that you assign to one of your own themes. Use a question mark or an exclamation mark after it where appropriate, but do *not* use a period even if your title is a complete sentence:

Chivalry Is Dead
Is Chivalry Dead?
Chivalry Is Dead!

## M1c  Dividing Words                                      *div*

**Observe conventional syllabication.**

Leaving a slightly uneven right margin is better than dividing words at the end of every second or third line. Dictionaries generally use centered dots to indicate where a word may conventionally be divided (*com·pli·ment*). Remember:

(1) *When in doubt, check your dictionary*—or carry the whole word to the next line. Here are some typical words as broken up into syllables in a dictionary:

**ad·dress      af·fec·ta·tion      en·vi·ron·ment      mal·ice**

(2) *Do not set off single letters.* Setting off single letters saves little or no space. It tends to confuse the reader. Do not divide words like *about, alone,* and *enough* or like *many* and *via.* Similarly, do not set off the ending *-ed* in words like *complained* or *renewed.*

(3) *Divide hyphenated words at the original hyphen.* Do not break up the *American* in "un-American" or the *sister* in "sister-in-law."

(4) *Do not divide the last word on a page.*

## M1d Italics *ital*

**Use italics to set off special words and phrases from the rest of a sentence.**

**Italics** (or slanted type) are indicated in the handwritten or typed manuscript by underlining.

(1) *Italics identify technical terms and words borrowed from foreign languages.* (See **P 6e**.)

(2) *Italics emphasize.* They call special attention to part of a sentence:

> The judge told me to apologize *in person* to everyone who had sat down in the freshly painted pews.

> The company is not liable for accidents caused by the negligence of employees or *by mechanical defects.*

(3) *Italics set off the title of a publication from the text in which it is cited.* Italicize titles of periodicals and of works published as separate units. Use **quotation marks** to set off titles of articles, chapters, songs, or poems that are merely a part of a complete publication. (See **P 6f**.)

> In *El Laberinto de la Soledad,* Octavio Paz describes the Mexican character.

> The old songs like "The Jolly Ploughboy" and "The Green Glens of Antrim" gave way to "Galway Bay" and "I'll Take You Home Again, Kathleen."

## M2 ABBREVIATIONS AND NUMBERS

**Avoid the overuse of abbreviations in ordinary prose.**

Abbreviations save time and space. Here as in other matters, however, formal written English discourages excessive shortcuts.

# M2a Abbreviations

*ab*

**Spell out inappropriate abbreviations.**

Some abbreviations are generally appropriate in expository writing. Other abbreviations are appropriate only in addresses, invoices, reports, and other special contexts. Most of these have to be written in full in ordinary expository prose.

Observe the following guidelines:

(1) *Use acceptable abbreviations for titles and degrees.* Before and after names, use the titles *Mr., Mrs., Ms., Dr.,* and *St.* (Saint), and the abbreviations *Jr.* (Junior) and *Sr.* (Senior). Use standard abbreviations for degrees: *M.D., Ph.D.* Use *Prof.* only before the full name:

Mr. John J. Smith, Jr.
Dr. Alice Joyce *or* Alice Joyce, M.D.
Prof. Shelby F. Jones *but* Professor Jones

(2) *Use familiar initials for organizations.* Use initials for the names of agencies, organizations, business firms, technical processes, chemical compounds, and the like when the full name is awkward or unfamiliar: *AFL-CIO, FBI, CIA, IBM, UNICEF, PTA, FM radio.*

The ampersand (&) and abbreviations like *Inc.* and *Bros.* occur in ordinary writing only in references to organizations that employ those abbreviations in their official titles: *Smith & Company, Inc.*

(3) *Use familiar abbreviations related to time and number.* Before or after numerals, use *A.D.* and *B.C., a.m.* and *p.m.* (also *A.M.* and *P.M.*), *no.* (also *No.*):

Augustus reigned from 27 B.C. to 14 A.D.
Planes leave at 11 a.m. and 2:30 p.m.
The issue was Volume 7, no. 2.

Some common Latin abbreviations serve as links or tags in ordinary prose: *e.g.* (for example), *etc.* (and so on), *i.e.* (that is). However, the modern tendency is to prefer the corresponding English expressions.

(4) *Spell out addresses and geographic names in ordinary*

*writing.* Use abbreviations like *Md.* and *N.Y.* only when writing an address for a letter or the like. In ordinary writing, spell out the names of countries, states, streets, and the like: *United States; Buffalo, New York; Union Street; Grant Avenue.* Some familiar exceptions are *USSR; Washington, D.C.;* and *U.S.* in combinations like *U.S. Navy.*

(5) *Spell out most measurements in ordinary writing.* In ordinary expository prose, *lb.* (pound), *oz.* (ounce), *ft.* (foot), and *in.* (inch) are usually spelled out. Some units of measurement are more unwieldy and are abbreviated, provided they are used with figures: *45 mph, 1500 rpm.* Spell out % (percent) and ¢ (cent), but use $ for exact figures: $287.55.

# M2b  Numbers                                    *num*

**Use figures in accordance with standard practice.**

In ordinary expository prose, the use of figures is to some extent restricted. They are generally appropriate in references to the day of the month (*May 13*), the year (*1917*), street numbers (*1014 Union Avenue*), and page numbers (*Chapter 7, page 18*). For other uses of numbers, the following conventions are widely observed:

(1) *Spell out round numbers.* Numbers from one to ten, and round numbers requiring no more than two words, are usually spelled out: *three dollars a seat, five hundred years later, ten thousand copies.*

(2) *Use numerals for exact figures.* Numerals are used for exact sums, technical measurements, decimals, and percentages, as well as for references to time using A.M. or P.M.: *$7.22; 500,673 inhabitants; 57 percent; 2:30 p.m.*

(3) *Avoid numerals at the beginning of a sentence.* Write "Fifteen out of 28 replied . . ." or "When questioned, 15 out of 28 replied. . . ." Except in special situations like this one, changes from figures to words (and vice versa) in a series of numbers are generally avoided.

(4)  *Hyphenate compound numbers*. When spelled out, compound numbers from 21 to 99 are hyphenated: *twenty-five, one hundred and forty-six*. (See also **SP 6a**.)

# EXERCISE

Rewrite the following passage, using abbreviations and numerals in accordance with standard practice:

Mister Geo. Brown had resided at Eighteen N. Washington St. since Feb. nineteen-hundred and forty-four. Though he weighed only one hundred and twenty-six lbs. and measured little more than 5 ft., he was an ardent devotee of the rugged life. He did his exercises every A.M. and refused to send for the Dr. when he had a cold. 3 yrs. after he moved here from Chicago, Ill., the Boy Scouts of America made him an honorary member, & he soon became known in scout circles for the many $ he contributed to the Boy Scout movement. One Sat. afternoon B. forgot to spell out the amount on a check for one-hundred and twenty-five dollars intended for a bldg. drive and payable to the B.S. of A. The treasurer, Bernard Simpson of Arlington, Va., wrote in 2 additional figures, spelled out the changed amount, and left the U.S. after withdrawing B.'s life savings of twelve-thousand five-hundred and fifty dollars from the local bank. "Ah," said Geo. when he found 2$ and 36 cts. left in his account, "if I had only spelled out the No.'s and abbrev.!"

# 6

# Words

# DIAGNOSTIC TEST

## INSTRUCTIONS:

Look at the three possible choices for the blank space in each sentence. Which word or phrase would be the best choice for serious written English? Write the letter for the best choice after the number of the sentence.

1. The law prevents the police _____ conducting random searches.
   a. against       b. from       c. in

2. Our present failures will be judged harshly by _____.
   a. posterity       b. prosperity       c. poverty

3. The _____ often scheduled quizzes on Fridays.
   a. professors       b. profs
   c. instructional personnel

4. We tried to comply _____ the court order.
   a. with       b. by       c. to

5. In our ideas about progress, growth has played a central _____.
   a. factor       b. role       c. contribution

6. The group asked the whole community to _____.
   a. chip in       b. attribute       c. contribute

7. She often dissented _____ the majority opinion.
   a. from       b. against       c. of

8. An exclusive trade agreement between two countries is _____.
   a. heterogeneous       b. multilateral       c. bilateral

9. The conductor did not _____ for the concert.
   a. show up       b. appear       c. bother to show

10. We closed the branch office _____ sales had dropped off.
    a. due to the fact that       b. in view of the fact that
    c. because

11. The city eliminated the branch libraries _____.
    a. in one fell swoop       b. in a jiffy
    c. all at once

12. The questionnaire asked about people's _____ origins.
    a. ethical       b. ethnic       c. external

13. The admiring author _____ Napoleon as a great leader.
    a. celebrated          b. exposed          c. decried

14. We should stress the _____ of reading and writing.
    a. basic fundamentals          b. basic essentials
    c. fundamentals

15. The engineers were working on the _____ in the system.
    a. defects          b. bugs          c. goofs

16. Spanish-speaking people were _____ in the area.
    a. predominate          b. predominant          c. predestined

17. In a biblical movie, a steam engine would be an _____.
    a. anachronism          b. anarchy          c. anathema

18. After several days in the desert, we became _____.
    a. defoliated          b. dehydrated          c. indoctrinated

19. Flowers that grow back every year are _____.
    a. annuals          b. perennial          c. biannual

20. In starting her business, she encountered many _____.
    a. hassles          b. occurrences of an obstructive nature
    c. problems

# D1 COLLEGE DICTIONARIES

**To make the best use of your dictionary, familiarize yourself
fully with how it provides information.**

College dictionaries provide information on the full range of
meaning of a word. They also tell us about its history, its uses,
and its possible limitations. The ideal dictionary would tell its
users in plain English what they want to know. In practice, dic-

tionaries try to give information that is technically accurate and yet intelligible to the reader who needs help.

The following dictionaries are widely recommended:

• *Webster's New World Dictionary* (NWD) makes a special effort to explain the meanings of words simply and clearly, using "the simplest language consistent with accuracy and fullness." Historical information *precedes* current meanings, so that the reader is given a sense of how a word developed. Lists of idioms provide an excellent guide to how a word is used in characteristic phrases. Throughout, informal and slang uses of words are so labeled. Sample entry:

> **bi·o·de·grad·a·ble** (-di grā′də b'l) *adj.* [BIO- + DEGRAD(E) + -ABLE] capable of being readily decomposed by biological means, esp. by bacterial action: said of some detergents with reference to disposal in sewage

• *Webster's New Collegiate Dictionary* is published by the G. & C. Merriam Company, whose collection of several million citation slips has been called "the national archives of the language." The *Collegiate* is based on *Webster's Third New International Dictionary*, the most authoritative and comprehensive unabridged dictionary of current American English. Historical information precedes meanings, which are presented in the order of their development. The Merriam-Webster dictionaries have abandoned the practice of labeling words "informal" as too arbitrary or subjective. They make only sparing use of the label "slang." Unlike the NWD, the *Collegiate* lists names of people and places in separate indexes at the end of the book. Sample entry:

> **ex·po·sé** *or* **ex·po·se** \,ek-spō-'zā, -spə-\ *n* [F *exposé*, fr. pp. of *exposer*] **1** : a formal recital or exposition of facts : STATEMENT **2** : an exposure of something discreditable ⟨a newspaper ∼ of crime conditions⟩

• *The Random House College Dictionary* caters to the preferences of conservative readers. Both informal English and slang are marked. Usage notes recognize many traditional restrictions. The most frequently encountered meanings of a word come first.

| | |
|---|---|
| vocabulary entry — pronunciation syllabication dots | **beau·ty** (byoō/tē), *n., pl.* **-ties** for 2–6. **1.** a quality that is present in a thing or person giving intense aesthetic pleasure or deep satisfaction to the senses or the mind. **2.** an attractive, well-formed girl or woman. **3.** a beautiful thing, as a work of art, building, etc. **4.** Often, **beauties.** that which is beautiful in nature or in some natural or artificial environment. **5.** a particular advantage: *One of the beauties of this medicine is the absence of aftereffects.* **6.** a person or thing that excels or is remarkable of its kind: *His black eye was a beauty.* [ME *be(a)ute* < OF *beaute*; r. ME *bealte* < OF, var. of *beltet* < VL *\*bellitāt-* (s. of *\*bellitās*) = L *bell(us)* fine + *-itāt-* -ITY] —**Syn. 1.** loveliness, pulchritude, comeliness, fairness, attractiveness. **2.** belle. —**Ant. 1.** ugliness. |
| synonym lists — | |
| part of speech and — inflected forms | **be·gin** (bi gin/), *v.,* **be·gan, be·gun, be·gin·ning.** —*v.i.* **1.** to proceed to perform the first or earliest part of some action; commence or start. **2.** to come into existence; originate: *The custom began during the Civil War.* —*v.t.* **3.** to proceed to perform the first or earliest part of (some action): *Begin the job tomorrow.* **4.** to originate; be the originator of: *Civic leaders began the reform movement.* [ME *beginn(en)*, OE *beginnan* = *be-* BE- + *-ginnan* to begin, perh. orig. to open, akin to YAWN] —**be·gin/ner,** *n.* |
| etymology — | |
| synonym study — | —**Syn. 3.** BEGIN, COMMENCE, INITIATE, START (when followed by noun or gerund) refer to setting into motion or progress something that continues for some time. BEGIN is the common term: *to begin knitting a sweater.* COMMENCE is a more formal word, often suggesting a more prolonged or elaborate beginning: *to commence proceedings in court.* INITIATE implies an active and often ingenious first act in a new field: *to initiate a new procedure.* START means to make a first move or to set out on a course of action: *to start paving a street.* **4.** inaugurate, initiate. —**Ant. 1.** end. |
| antonym — | |
| | **be·la·bor** (bi lā/bər), *v.t.* **1.** to discuss, work at, or worry about for an unreasonable amount of time: *He kept belaboring the point long after we had agreed.* **2.** to scorn or ridicule persistently. **3.** *Archaic.* to beat vigorously. Also, *Brit.,* **be·la/bour.** |
| variant spelling — | |
| hyphenated entry — | **belles-let·tres** (*Fr.* bel le/tR³), *n.pl.* literature regarded as a fine art, esp. as having a purely aesthetic function. [< F: lit., fine letters] —**bel·let·rist** (bel le/trist), *n.* —**bel·let·ris·tic** (bel/li tris/tik), *adj.* —**Syn.** See **literature.** |
| word element — | **bene-,** an element occurring in loan words from Latin where it meant "well": *benediction.* [comb. form of *bene* (adv.) well] |
| consecutive definition numbers — | **be·neath** (bi nēth/, -nēth/), *adv.* **1.** below; in or to a lower place, position, state, or the like. **2.** underneath: *heaven above and the earth beneath.* —*prep.* **3.** below; under: *beneath the same roof.* **4.** further down than; underneath; lower in place than: *the first drawer beneath the top one.* **5.** inferior in position, rank, power, etc.: *A captain is beneath a major.* **6.** unworthy of; below the level or dignity of: *beneath contempt.* |
| usage note — | **bent**[1] (bent), *adj.* **1.** curved or crooked: *a bent bow; a bent stick.* **2.** determined, set, or resolved (usually fol. by *on*): *to be bent on buying a new car.* |
| example contexts — | **bet·ter**[1] (bet/ər), *adj., compar. of* **good** *with* **best** *as superl.* **1.** of superior quality or excellence: *a better coat.* **2.** morally superior; more virtuous: *He's no better than a thief.* **3.** of superior value, fitness, desirability, acceptableness, etc.: *a better time for action.* **4.** larger; greater: *the better part of a lifetime.* **5.** improved in health; healthier: *Is your mother better?* —*adv., compar. of* **well** *with* **best** *as superl.* **6.** in a more excellent way or manner: *to behave better.* **7.** to a greater degree; more completely or thoroughly: *I probably know him better than anyone else.* **8.** more: *I walked better than a mile to town.* **9. better off, a.** in better circumstances. **b.** more fortunate; happier. **10. go (someone) one better,** to exceed another's effort; be superior to. **11. had better,** would be wiser or more reasonable to; ought to: *We had better stay indoors today.* **12. think better of,** to reconsider and decide more favorably or wisely: *She was tempted to make a sarcastic retort, but thought better of it.* —*v.t.* **13.** to make better; improve; increase the good qualities of. **14.** to improve upon; surpass; exceed: *We have bettered last year's production record.* **15. better oneself,** to improve one's social standing, financial position, or education. —*n.* **16.** that which has greater excellence: *the better of two choices.* **17.** Usually, **betters.** those superior to one in wisdom, social position, etc. **18. for the better,** in a way that is an improvement: *His health changed for the better.* **19. get the better of, a.** to get an advantage over. **b.** to prevail against. [ME *bettre,* OE *betera;* c. OHG *bezziro* (G *besser*), Goth *batiza* = *bat-* (akin to BOOT²) + *-iza* comp. suffix] —**Syn. 13.** amend; advance, promote. See **improve.** |
| idiomatic phrases — | |
| Explanation of Dictionary Entries (From *The Random House College Dictionary*) | |

Like *Webster's Collegiate,* this dictionary is based on a larger unabridged dictionary. Sample entry:

> **e·lite** (i lēt′, ā lēt′), *n.* **1.** (*often construed as pl.*) the choice or best of anything considered collectively, esp. of a group or class of persons: *the elite of the intellectual community.* **2.** (*construed as pl.*) persons of the highest class: *Only the elite were there.* **3.** a group of persons exercising the major share of authority or control within a larger organization: *the power elite in the U.S.* **4.** a type, approximately 10-point and having 12 characters to the inch, widely used in typewriters. Cf. **pica**[1]. —*adj.* **5.** representing the choicest or best. Also, **é·lite′**. [< F *élite,* OF *e(s)lite,* n. use of fem. of *e(s)lit* ptp. of *e(s)lire* to choose; see ELECT]

• *The American Heritage Dictionary,* an ambitious project first published in 1969, is intended as a "sensible" (moderately conservative) guide to the vocabulary of the educated adult. The aim of the editors was to provide a book less forbidding and more readable than traditional dictionaries. The use of abbreviations and symbols is kept to a minimum. Historical information about words, for instance, appears without abbreviations, backed up by a special appendix devoted to the Indo-European roots of many English words. Definitions branch out from a "central meaning" that is not necessarily the earliest historical sense of the word. Sample entry:

> **im·promp·tu** (ĭm-prŏmp′tōō, -tyōō) *adj.* Not rehearsed; extempore. See Synonyms at **extemporaneous.** —*adv.* Without rehearsal or preparation; spontaneously. —*n.* Something made or done impromptu, as a musical composition or remark. [French, from Latin *in promptū,* in readiness, at hand : *in,* in + *promptū,* ablative of *promptus,* ready, PROMPT.]

# D1a Synonyms and Antonyms     *d*

**Use the dictionary to help you distinguish between closely related terms.**

Often a dictionary indicates meaning by a **synonym**, a word that has nearly the same meaning as the word you are looking up. For example, your dictionary may give "sad" or "mournful" as a synonym for *elegiac.* It may give "instructive" as a synonym for *didactic.* Often your dictionary will explain a word by giving an **antonym**, a word of approximately opposite meaning. *Desultory* is the opposite of "methodical." *Hackneyed* is the opposite of "fresh" or "original."

Synonyms are seldom simply interchangeable. Their areas of meaning overlap, but at the same time there are subtle differences. *Burn, char, scorch, sear,* and *singe* all refer to the results of exposure to extreme heat, but whether a piece of meat is charred or merely seared makes a difference to the person who has it for dinner. Look at the way the following entry distinguishes among words like *feeling, passion,* and *emotion*:

> **SYN.—feeling,** when unqualified in the context, refers to any of the subjective reactions, pleasurable or unpleasurable, that one may have to a situation and usually connotes an absence of reasoning [I can't trust my own *feelings*]; **emotion** implies an intense feeling with physical as well as mental manifestations [her breast heaved with *emotion*]; **passion** refers to a strong or overpowering emotion, connoting especially sexual love or intense anger; **sentiment** applies to a feeling, often a tender one, accompanied by some thought or reasoning [what are your *sentiments* in this matter?]

From *Webster's New World Dictionary*

# D1b   Denotation and Connotation   *d*

**Use the dictionary as a guide to the associations of words.**

Many words denote—that is, point out or refer to—very nearly the same objects or qualities. At the same time, they connote—that is, suggest or imply—different attitudes on the part of the speaker. *Cheap* and *inexpensive* both mean low in price. However, we may call an article "cheap" to suggest that we consider it shoddy or inferior. We may call it "inexpensive" to suggest that we consider it a good bargain.

The part of the meaning that points "out there" is the **denotation** of a word. The attitude or emotion that a word suggests is its **connotation**. *Leader* has favorable, flattering connotations. *Demagogue* has unfavorable, derogatory connotations. Words with strong connotations bring into play a wide range of associations. *Dagger* simply denotes a short weapon for stabbing, but it connotes treachery. *Sword* denotes a somewhat longer weapon; it connotes courage and chivalrous adventure.

Here are some sets of words that show differences in connotation:

**199**

| FAVORABLE | UNFAVORABLE | NEUTRAL |
|---|---|---|
| public servant | bureaucrat | government employee |
| financier | speculator | investor |
| law officer | cop | police officer |
| legislative consultant | lobbyist | representative of group interests |
| stage personality | ham | actor |
| labor leader | union boss | union official |
| captain of industry | tycoon | business success |
| investigator | spy | detective |
| captive | jailbird | prisoner |
| soldier of fortune | hired killer | mercenary |

Here is how a dictionary handles the connotations of synonyms of *plan*:

> *SYN.*—**plan** refers to any detailed method, formulated beforehand, for doing or making something *[* vacation *plans];* **design** stresses the final outcome of a plan and implies the use of skill or craft, sometimes in an unfavorable sense, in executing or arranging this *[* it was his *design* to separate us*];* **project** implies the use of enterprise or imagination in formulating an ambitious or extensive plan *[* a housing *project];* **scheme,** a less definite term than the preceding, often connotes either an impractical, visionary plan or an underhanded intrigue *[* a *scheme* to embezzle the funds*]*

From *Webster's New World Dictionary*

# D1c Context *d*

**Use the dictionary as a guide to the context where a given meaning is appropriate.**

If we really want to know a word, we have to know how it is used in **context**. The context of a word may be another word ("*square* meal"), a whole sentence or paragraph ("*Square* your theories with your practice"), a whole article or book (a treatment of squares in a book on plane geometry), or a situation (a police officer directing a pedestrian to a square).

Here is an entry showing a word used in different contexts:

> **apt** (apt), *adj.* 1. inclined; disposed; given; prone: *too apt to slander others.* 2. likely: *Am I apt to find him at home?* 3. unusually intelligent; quick to learn: *an apt pupil.* 4. suited to the purpose or occasion: *an apt metaphor.*

From *The Random House College Dictionary*

In an unfamiliar context, familiar words may have a new or different meaning. For instance, an author praising modesty and thrift may describe them as "homely virtues." Looking up the word, you will find that its original meaning is "associated with the home." Favorable associations of domestic life account for such meanings as "simple," "unpretentious," "intimate." Unfavorable associations account for such meanings as "crude," "unpolished," "ugly."

# D1d  Grammatical Labels  *d*

**Use the dictionary as a guide to the functions a word serves in a sentence.**

Many English words serve different possible functions in a sentence. For instance, *human* is usually labeled both as an **adjective** (adj.) and as a **noun** (n.), with some indication that the latter use ("a human" rather than "a human being") is not generally accepted. *Annoy* is labeled a **transitive verb** (v.t.); it is incomplete without an object. In other words, we usually annoy somebody or something; we don't just annoy. *Set* also is usually transitive ("*set* the bowl on the table"), but it is labeled **intransitive** (v.i.) when applied to one of the celestial bodies. In other words, the sun doesn't set anybody or anything; it just sets.

Here are some other common grammatical labels:

| | |
|---|---|
| *adv.* | adverb |
| *conj.* | conjunction (connective) |
| *pl.* | plural |
| *pp.* | past participle (of verb) |
| *prep.* | preposition |
| *prp.* | present participle (of verb) |
| *sg.* | singular |

# D1e  Idiom  *id*

**Use the dictionary as a guide to idiomatic phrases.**

A word often combines with other words in a set expression that becomes the habitual way of conveying a certain idea. Such

**201**

expressions are called **idioms**. To write idiomatic English, you have to develop an ear for individual ways of saying things. For instance, we *do* a certain type of work, *hold* a job or position, *follow* a trade, *pursue* an occupation, and *engage in* a line of business.

Study the following list of idiomatic phrases using the word *mind*. Can you think of half a dozen similar phrases using the word *eye* or the word *hand*?

**—bear (or keep) in mind** to remember **—be in one's right mind** to be mentally well; be sane **—be of one mind** to have the same opinion or desire **—be of two minds** to be undecided or irresolute **—☆blow one's mind** [Slang] to undergo the hallucinations, etc. caused by, or as by, psychedelic drugs **—call to mind** 1. to remember 2. to be a reminder of **—change one's mind** 1. to change one's opinion 2. to change one's intention, purpose, or wish **—give (someone) a piece of one's mind** to criticize or rebuke (someone) sharply **—have a (good or great) mind to** to feel (strongly) inclined to **—have half a mind to** to be somewhat inclined to **—have in mind** 1. to remember 2. to think of 3. to intend; purpose **—know one's own mind** to know one's own real thoughts, desires, etc. **—make up one's mind** to form a definite opinion or decision **—meeting of (the) minds** an agreement **—never mind** don't be concerned; it doesn't matter **—on one's mind** 1. occupying one's thoughts 2. worrying one **—out of one's mind** 1. mentally ill; insane 2. frantic (*with* worry, grief, etc.) **—put in mind** to remind **—set one's mind on** to be determined on or determinedly desirous of **—take one's mind off** to stop one from thinking about; turn one's attention from **—to one's mind** in one's opinion

From *Webster's New World Dictionary*

A special problem for inexperienced writers is the idiomatic use of **prepositions**. The following list reviews idiomatic uses of some common prepositions:

abide *by* (a decision)
abstain *from* (voting)
accuse *of* (a crime)
acquiesce *in* (an injustice)
adhere *to* (a promise)
admit *of* (conflicting interpretations)
agree *with* (a person), *to* (a proposal), *on* (a course of action)
alarmed *at* (the news)
apologize *for* (a mistake)
aspire *to* (distinction)
assent *to* (a proposal)

attend *to* (one's business)
avail oneself *of* (an opportunity)
capable *of* (an action)
charge *with* (an offense)
collide *with* (a car)
compatible *with* (recognized standards)
comply *with* (a request)
concur *with* (someone), *in* (an opinion)
confide *in* or *to* (someone)
conform *to* (specifications)
deficient *in* (strength)

delight *in* (mischief)
deprive *of* (a privilege)
derived *from* (a source)
die *of* or *from* (a disease)
disappointed *in* (someone's performance)
dissent *from* (a majority opinion)
dissuade *from* (doing something foolish)
divest *of* (responsibility)
find fault *with* (a course)
identical *with* (something looked for)
ignorant *of* (a fact)
inconsistent *with* (sound procedure)
independent *of* (outside help)
indifferent *to* (praise or blame)
infer *from* (evidence)
inferior *to* (a rival product)
insist *on* (accuracy)
interfere *with* (a performance), *in* (someone else's affairs)
jealous *of* (others)

long *for* (recognition)
object *to* (a proposal)
oblivious *of* (warnings)
part *with* (possessions)
partial *to* (flattery)
participate *in* (activities)
persevere *in* (a task)
pertain *to* (a subject)
preferable *to* (an alternative)
prevail *on* (someone to do something)
prevent someone *from* (an action)
refrain *from* (wrongdoing)
rejoice *at* (good news)
required *of* (all members)
resolve *on* (a course of action)
rich *in* (resources)
short *of* (cash)
secede *from* (the Union)
succeed *in* (an attempt)
superior *to* (an alternative)
threaten *with* (legal action)
wait *for* (developments), *on* (a guest)

# EXERCISES

A. Compare *three college dictionaries* by investigating the following:

1. Read the definitions of *cliché, kitsch, graffiti, gobbledygook,* and *guru.* What do they say? Are they clear and informative?
2. Study the order of meanings for *coy, nice, operate.* How does the order differ, and why?
3. Compare the treatment of synonyms (if any) for *dogmatic, prompt,* and *train* (v.).
4. What and where are you told about Dreyfus, Prometheus, Niels Bohr, Tierra del Fuego, Susan B. Anthony?
5. How does the dictionary deal with *Aryan, dago, dame, nazi?*

B. What's *new* in dictionaries? How up to date, or how far behind, is your dictionary in its coverage of the following words? For those that are missing, write a short definition that would help a dictionary editor bring the dictionary up to date.

| | | |
|---|---|---|
| aerospace | Chicano | payload |
| airbag | cosmonaut | residuals |
| anchorman | holding pattern | schlock |
| Black Muslim | hydrofoil | skydiving |
| bluegrass | kibbutz | tax shelter |
| body stocking | minibike | tokenism |
| buzz word | paparazzo | unisex |

C. Study the *synonyms* in the following sets. What meaning do all three words have in common? How do they differ? Which are differences in connotation?

1. gaze—stare—ogle
2. settlement—compromise—deal
3. loyalty—allegiance—commitment
4. obedient—docile—obsequious
5. revolt—revolution—mutiny
6. intelligent—clever—shrewd
7. juvenile—youngster—adolescent
8. severe—strict—punitive
9. imaginary—fantastic—visionary
10. fatherly—paternal—paternalistic

D. How does your dictionary distinguish among the *different meanings* of each of the following words? Show how context determines your choice of the meaning appropriate in each phrase.

1. *bay* leaves, at *bay*, *bayed* at the moon, *bay* window, bomb *bay*, a breeze from the *bay*
2. *head* of lettuce, *head* the procession, a *head* of steam, *heads* or tails, over the listeners' *heads*, went to his *head*, *heads* of government, *head* off complaints, not have a *head* for figures
3. car of recent *make*, *make* the beds, *make* money, *make* excuses, *makes* my blood boil, *make* a speech, *makes* easy reading, *made* him a sergeant
4. *repair* a car, *repaired* to the meeting, in good *repair*, *repair* the damage
5. *straight* to the point, *straight* alcohol, *straight* party line, the comedian's *straight* man, *straight* hair, thinking *straight*

E. Answer the following questions about *grammatical functions* of words after consulting your dictionary.

1. Is *incompetent* used as a noun?
2. Which of the following words are used as verbs: *admonition, loan, lord, magistrate, minister, sacrilege, spirit, war*?
3. Are the following words used as adjectives: *animate, predominate, very*?
4. What idiomatic prepositions go with the following words when they are used as verbs: *glory, care, marvel*?
5. Are the following used as intransitive verbs: *entertain, censure, promote*?

F. Find any *unidiomatic prepositions*. Write a more appropriate preposition after the number of each unsatisfactory sentence. (Write *S* if the sentence is satisfactory.)

1. To seek a good grade at someone else's expense would be a violation to our standards of conduct.
2. Politicians must learn to refrain from making hasty statements.
3. During the past fifty years, deaths caused by highway accidents have been more numerous than those incurred from two world wars and the war in Korea.
4. Plans for cost reduction have been put to action by different agencies of the federal government.
5. Several families volunteered to take care for the children of flood victims.
6. Most of the people on our mailing list complied with our request.
7. The present board will never assent to a radical revision of the charter.
8. Only the prompt help of the neighbors prevented the fire of becoming a major disaster.
9. During the first years of marriage, we had to deprive ourselves from many things that other people take for granted.
10. The arrival of the ship to its destination caused general rejoicing.
11. Though I support Mr. Finchley's candidacy, I take exception with some of his statements.
12. We will not hesitate to expose businesses that deprive their employees from these benefits.
13. The new ordinance was identical with one tried out and rejected in another city.
14. The government seemed indifferent to the suffering caused by its actions.
15. As an instrument of the popular will, the Senate suffers from defects inherent to its constitution.

# D2   WORD HISTORY

**Let the history of a word help you understand its uses, meanings, and associations.**

College dictionaries often summarize the **etymology** of a word. They briefly trace its origin and history. Your dictionary is likely to trace the word *lock* to corresponding words in earlier English (ME = Middle English; AS = Anglo-Saxon or Old English), in other Germanic languages (G = German; ON = Old Norse or Early Scandinavian), and in the common parent language of most European languages (IE = Indo-European). Here is the etymology of a word that came into English from Latin by way of Italian and French:

**pop·u·lace** \'päp-yə-ləs\ *n* [MF, fr. It *popolaccio* rabble, pejorative of *popolo* the people, fr. L *populus*] **1** : the common people : MASSES **2** : POPULATION

From *Webster's New Collegiate Dictionary*

In addition to tracing words to other languages, the etymologist is concerned with **semantic** change—gradual changes in meaning. The most complete record of such changes is the unabridged *New English Dictionary on Historical Principles*, reissued in 1933 as the *Oxford English Dictionary* (OED). This monumental reference work gives the earliest date a word occurs and then provides quotations tracing its development down through the centuries.

The most extensive changes in vocabulary come about through contacts between different cultures. Armed conquest, colonial expansion, and international trade make words move from one language to the other. Roughly three fourths of the words in your dictionary came into English from foreign sources. When the Anglo-Saxon tribes came to England from continental Europe during the period between A.D. 450 and 600, they spoke Germanic dialects, close to the dialects from which modern Dutch and German are derived. The American tourist coming to Germany can still easily recognize the German words for *arm, drink, father, fish, hand,* or *house.* However, the basic Germanic vocabulary of **Anglo-Saxon** or **Old English** was enriched by words from other languages throughout early English history.

# D 2a  Latin and Greek  *d*

**Know some of the most common Latin and Greek roots.**

English has borrowed heavily from Latin and Greek. Latin had been the language of the Roman Empire. It became the official language of the Roman Catholic Church, which established itself in England in the seventh century and remained the supreme spiritual authority until the sixteenth century. English early took over Latin words related to the Bible and to the teachings and rituals of the church:

altar　　　candle　　　mass　　　pope　　　shrine　　　relic

Greek was the language of the literature, philosophy, and science of ancient Hellenic culture, flourishing both in Greece and in other parts of the Mediterranean world. Either in the original Greek or in Latin translation, this body of knowledge helped shape Western civilization during the Middle Ages and Renaissance. Modern English uses thousands of words that came originally from Greek or Latin. Modern scientific and technological terms draw heavily on Greek and Latin roots:

GREEK: anonymous, atmosphere, catastrophe, chaos, climax, crisis, enthusiasm, skeleton

LATIN: contempt, gesture, history, incredible, index, individual, intellect, legal, mechanical, rational

(1) *Know the most common Latin and Greek roots.* A common Latin or Greek root often provides the key to a puzzling word. For instance, the Greek root *phys-* usually refers to the body or to material things. The Greek root *psych-* usually refers to the mind or the soul. This distinction explains pairs like the following: *physician* (heals the body) and *psychiatrist* (heals the mind); *physiology* (study of bodily functions) and *psychology* (study of mental functions); *physical* (characteristic of material reality) and *psychic* (going beyond material reality).

Here is a brief list of common Latin and Greek roots. Explain how each root is used in the sample words given for it:

| ROOT | MEANING | EXAMPLES |
|------|---------|----------|
| arch- | *rule* | monarchy, anarchy, matriarch |
| auto- | *self* | autocratic, autonomy, automation |
| capit- | *head* | capital, per capita, decapitate |
| carn- | *flesh* | carnivorous, incarnation, carnival |
| chron- | *time* | chronological, synchronize, anachronism |
| culp- | *fault* | culpable, culprit, exculpate |
| doc- | *teach* | docile, doctrine, indoctrinate |
| graph- | *write* | autograph, graphic, seismograph |
| hydr- | *water* | dehydrate, hydraulic, hydrogen |
| jur- | *swear* | conjure, juror, perjury |
| man- | *hand* | manacle, manual, manufacture |
| port- | *carry* | portable, exports, deportation |
| phon- | *sound* | euphony, phonograph, symphony |
| terr- | *land* | inter, terrestrial, subterranean |
| urb- | *city* | suburb, urban, urbane |
| verb- | *word* | verbal, verbiage, verbose |
| vit- | *life* | vitality, vitamin, revitalize |
| vol- | *will* | volition, involuntary, volunteer |

(2) *Know common prefixes and suffixes.* Especially useful is a knowledge of the most common Latin and Greek **prefixes** and **suffixes**. These are syllables attached at the beginning or at the end of a word to modify its meaning. A common prefix is *sub-*, meaning "below" or "beneath." It helps explain not only *substandard* and *subconscious* but also *submarine* (below the sea) and *subterranean* (beneath the surface, underground). The suffix *-cide* means "killer" or "killing." It helps explain *homicide* (of a human being), *suicide* (of oneself), *fratricide* (of a brother), *parricide* (of a parent), and *insecticide* (of insects).

Here is a brief list of Latin and Greek prefixes. Explain the meaning of each word given as an example:

| PREFIX | MEANING | EXAMPLES |
|--------|---------|----------|
| bene- | *good* | benefactor, benefit, benevolent |
| bi- | *two* | bicycle, bilateral, bisect |
| contra- | *against* | contraband, contradict, contravene |
| dis- | *away, apart* | disperse, disorganize, discourage |
| ex- | *out* | exclude, exhale, expel |
| extra- | *outside* | extraordinary, extravagant, extrovert |
| mono- | *one* | monarch, monopoly, monolithic |
| multi- | *many* | multicolored, multilateral, multinational |
| omni- | *all* | omnipotent, omnipresent, omniscient |
| per- | *through* | percolate, perforate, permeate |
| pre- | *before* | preamble, precedent, prefix |
| poly- | *many* | polygamy, polysyllabic, polytheistic |
| post- | *after* | postpone, postwar, postscript |
| re- | *back* | recall, recede, revoke, retract |
| tele- | *distant* | telegraph, telepathy, telephone |
| trans- | *across, beyond* | transatlantic, transmit, transcend |

# D 2b  Borrowings from Other Sources  *d*

**Recognize some of the sources of the English vocabulary.**

Here are some kinds of historical information that you will find in a good dictionary:

(1) *Thousands of words came into English from French.* England was conquered by the French-speaking Normans in the

years following 1066. At the beginning of the so-called **Middle English** period (about 1150), the Norman conquerors owned most of the land and controlled the most important offices in state and church. The language of law, administration, and literature was French. When English gradually reestablished itself, thousands of French words were retained. Many of these words were associated with the political and military role of the Norman overlords: *castle, court, glory, mansion, noble, prince, prison, privilege, servant, treason, treasure, war.* But hundreds of other words absorbed into Middle English were everyday words like *avoid, branch, chair, demand, desire, disease, envy, praise, table, uncle.*

*Note*: Many French words passed into English through the hands of English poets who found them in medieval French poetry and romance. Some of these words preserve a poetic and often old-fashioned flavor: *chevalier* for "knight," *damsel* for "girl," *fealty* for "loyalty," *paramour* for "sweetheart," *travail* for "toil."

(2) *Foreign languages have influenced the vocabularies of special fields of interest.* Since the beginning of **Modern English** (about 1500), many words have come into English from French, Italian, Spanish, and various other sources. French supplied words for fashions, the arts, and military organization. Italian supplied words related to opera and music. Spanish supplied words related to the discovery of new continents, often words first brought into Spanish from New World sources.

FRENCH: apartment, ballet, battalion, cadet, caress, corps, façade, infantry, negligee, patrol
ITALIAN: concert, falsetto, sonata, solo, soprano, violin
SPANISH: alligator, banana, cannibal, cocoa, mosquito, potato, tobacco, tomato

(3) *Modern English has a number of foreign words in different stages of assimilation.* If they are still felt to be foreign rather than English, your dictionary may put a special symbol in front of them, or label them "French," "Italian," or whatever is appropriate. How does your dictionary handle the following Russian words: *troika, tovarich, apparatchik*?

# EXERCISES

A. Find the *original meaning* of each of the following words: *attenuate, circumlocution, disaster, egregious, immigrant, paradise, philosophy, premise, recalcitrant, republic.* How does the original meaning help explain the current use of each word?

B. Report on the *history* of five of the following. What language does each term come from? How did it acquire its current meaning?

| | | |
|---|---|---|
| carnival | Halloween | police |
| crescendo | laissez faire | propaganda |
| cynic | millennium | pundit |
| dollar | nirvana | utopia |
| ecology | pogrom | vaudeville |

C. Explain the meaning of the *common element* in each of the following sets. How does the common element help explain each word in the set?

1. anesthetic—anarchy—anemic
2. antibiotic—biography—biology
3. audiovisual—audition—inaudible
4. biennial—centennial—perennial
5. century—centipede—percentage
6. cosmic—cosmopolitan—microcosm
7. disunity—discord—dissent
8. eugenics—eulogy—euphonious
9. heterogeneous—heterosexual—heterodox
10. magnify—magnificent—magnitude
11. prelude—interlude—ludicrous
12. synchronize—symphony—sympathy

D. Explain the basic meaning of each *Latin and Greek prefix* used in the following words: *ambivalent, antedate, antipathy, circumvent, concord, hypersensitive, international, introvert, malpractice, multimillionaire, neofascist, postgraduate, pseudoscientific, retroactive, semitropical, ultramodern, unilateral.*

E. What are the meanings of the following expressions? How many of them does your dictionary consider *foreign* rather than English?

ad hoc, aficionado, blitz, corpus delicti, coup de grace, cum laude, de jure, El Dorado, ersatz, eureka, fait accompli, habeas corpus, hara-kiri, hoi polloi, quod erat demonstrandum, tour de force

# D3  VARIETIES OF USAGE

**Recognize words that are appropriate only to certain situations or limited to specific uses.**

Dictionaries use **restrictive labels** to show that a word is used only under certain circumstances, or that it will seem out of place in the wrong situation. In the following dictionary entry, six of the nine numbered meanings of *brass* carry restrictive labels:

> **brass** (bras, bräs), *n.* **1.** any of various metal alloys consisting mainly of copper and zinc. **2.** an article made of such an alloy. **3.** *Mach.* a partial lining of soft metal for a bearing. **4.** *Music* **a.** an instrument of the trumpet or horn family. **b.** such instruments collectively. **5.** *Brit* **a.** a memorial tablet or plaque incised with an effigy, coat of arms, or the like. **b.** *Slang.* money. **6.** *Furniture.* any piece of ornamental or functional hardware. **7.** *U.S. Slang.* **a.** high-ranking military officers. **b.** any very important officials. **8.** *Informal* excessive assurance; impudence; effrontery. —*adj.* **9.** of or pertaining to brass. [ME *bras*, OE *bræs*; c. OFris *bres* copper, MLG *bras* metal] —**brass′ish**, *adj.*

— subject label

— geographic label

— usage

From *The Random House College Dictionary*

## D3a  Nonstandard Words                     *Ns*

**Recognize words that suggest nonstandard speech rather than educated usage.**

Usage labels provide a guide when roughly synonymous choices have different associations. One choice may suggest the folk speech of street and neighborhood ("nohow"); the other may suggest the standard English of school and office ("not at all"). Words like *anywheres* and *nohow* are either not listed in your dictionary at all or labeled illiterate or **nonstandard**. Like nonstandard grammatical patterns, they are often associated with low social standing or a lack of formal education.

> See **G 2a** for more on nonstandard English.

## D3b  Informal Words                        *inf*

**Recognize words that are too informal for serious writing.**

People use informal language when at ease and with their friends. As a result, it tends to sound relaxed and folksy. But

**211**

people who are comfortable in sports clothes over the weekend put on business clothes when going to the office on Monday morning. Similarly, a writer has to be able to use formal language in formal situations. Some dictionaries label informal words **colloquial**. The word does not mean "local" but "characteristic of informal speech."

| INFORMAL | FORMAL | INFORMAL | FORMAL |
|----------|--------|----------|--------|
| boss | superior | kid | child |
| brainy | intelligent | mean | ill-natured |
| bug | germ | skimpy | meager |
| faze | disconcert | sloppy | untidy |
| flunk | fail | snoop | pry |
| folks | relatives | snooze | nap |
| hunch | premonition | splurge | spend lavishly |
| job | position | stump | baffle |

Other familiar words are generally acceptable in one sense but informal in another. Informal are *alibi* in the sense of "excuse," *aggravate* in the sense of "annoy," *funny* in the sense of "strange," and *mad* in the sense of "angry." Do the following to keep your writing from becoming too informal:

(1) *Avoid catchall words.* Many familiar words of approval or disapproval are too vague or gushy for serious writing. Avoid routine use of words like the following: *nice, cute, terrific, great, wonderful, awful, terrible.*

(2) *Avoid informal abbreviations.* Avoid clipped forms like *bike, prof, doc, math, econ.* (Other shortened forms, like *phone, ad,* and *exam,* are now commonly used in serious writing.)

(3) *Avoid informal combined verbs.* Informal English uses many combined or **phrasal verbs** like the following:

| INFORMAL | FORMAL |
|----------|--------|
| chip in | contribute |
| get across | communicate |
| check up on | investigate |
| come up with | find |
| cut out | stop |
| get on with | make progress |

**212**

(4)  *Do without informal tags.* Informal language uses many tags like *kind of, sort of, a lot, lots.*

(5)  *Improve on tired informal expressions.* The following are among the overused **figurative expressions** of informal speech:

| | |
|---|---|
| have a ball | polish the apple |
| butter up | shoot the breeze |
| hit the road | jump on the bandwagon |
| use elbow grease | call it quits |

On trite expressions, see also **D 5c.**

*Note*: Informal expressions can set a casual, leisurely tone:

> There was a broad streak of mischief in Mencken. He was forever *cooking up* imaginary organizations, having *fake* handbills printed, inventing exercises in pure nonsense.—Philip M. Wagner, "Mencken Remembered," *The American Scholar*

But informal English can also suggest that you are not taking your subject (or your reader) seriously enough.

# D 3c  Slang                              *sl*

**Use slang only in the most informal kinds of writing or for special effects.**

No one can fix the exact point at which informal language shades over into slang. Generally, slang is more drastic in its disregard for what makes language formal and dignified. It often has a vigor missing in more pedestrian diction. The figurative expressions it substitutes for less imaginative formal terms are often apt: *blowhard, gumshoe, drunk tank, downer, spaced out, whirlybird.* Often a slang expression has no very satisfactory formal equivalent: *come-on, eyewash, runaround, stuffed shirt.* Nevertheless, most slang is too crude, extravagant, or disrespectful for use in writing. Avoid expressions like the following: *beat one's brains out, blow one's top, chew the fat, fly off the handle, hit the ceiling, lay an egg.*

TOO SLANGY: What *folks have dumped on marriage* in the way of expectations, selfish interests, and *kinky kicks* needs prompt removal if the institution is to survive.

TOO SLANGY: People didn't live as long, so a spouse could safely assume that the partner would *kick the bucket* in five or ten years and the *one still breathing could have another go at it.*

*Note*: The humor in slang is often callous. Calling a person "fatso" or "skinny" or "bonehead" may be funny, but it also shows a lack of tact or respect.

# EXERCISES

A. Which of the following expressions would you expect to carry *restrictive labels*? Check your answers with the help of your dictionary.

bad-mouth, Brownie point, go Dutch, goof off, hang-up, highfalutin, jalopy, mooch, narc, nit-picking, persnickety, shyster, skin flick, windbag

B. Arrange the expressions in each group in order *from the most formal to the most informal*. Be prepared to defend your decisions. (Your instructor may ask you to check your own judgments against those of your dictionary.)

1. live it up, live on little, live up to a promise
2. dress up for a party, dress down an offender, dress a wound
3. dream up a scheme, a cherished dream, dreamboat
4. tear up the bill, tear into someone, that tears it
5. hook up the microphone, got him off the hook, did it on his own hook
6. crack a book, her voice cracked, crack down on crime
7. have a go at it, go through with it, go for broke
8. skip town, skip a grade, children skipping down the path
9. deal cards, make a deal, big deal!
10. sweat shirt, sweat out a decision, no sweat

C. Much *slang* comes and goes. Which of the following are still current? Select five and write a sentence or two about each to help a dictionary editor complete a coverage of recent slang.

| | | |
|---|---|---|
| cop-out | mickey mouse | uptight |
| rap | jive | bread |
| jock | blast | the man |
| gyp | busted | yak |
| rip-off | dude | flaky |
| bummer | zonked | put-down |

D. Point out *informal words and slang*. Write down a more formal replacement for each informal expression.

1. Travelers who wish to see the true Paris should not go at a time when it is swamped by tourists.
2. Modern medicine has found ways of licking many dread diseases.
3. Psychologists have discovered that many young people get a kick out of cutting up in front of a group.
4. I admired these people because it shows guts to stand up for what is right.
5. When the refugees were told that the train was going to leave in ten minutes, there was a mad rush to the station.
6. Parents only confuse a child by bawling him out every time he commits a minor mistake.
7. When Lovelace fails to suggest a definite date for the wedding, Clarissa begins to suspect that he is only pulling her leg.
8. Sent to size up our new allies, he found most of them in good shape.
9. The concert was scheduled to start at eight o'clock, but unfortunately the soloist did not show up.
10. In view of the late hour, we decided we better shove off and get some shut-eye.

E. Observe the language used by your friends or fellow students to find *six current slang expressions* not listed in your dictionary. Define them and explain their use. Indicate what, if anything, they reveal about the speaker's attitude.

# D4 WORDS IN LIMITED USE *d*

**Recognize words that have only regional currency or are not in general use.**

Dictionaries use restrictive labels to show that a word is not used throughout the English-speaking world, or not current at this time, or familiar mainly to specialists.

# D4a Regional Labels *d*

**Notice geographic labels for words in use mainly in one region.**

During the centuries before travel, books, and finally radio and television exercised their standardizing influence, languages gradually developed regional varieties. Sometimes, as with German and Dutch, they grew far enough apart to become separate languages.

Here are the types of regional variation that you are likely to encounter:

(1) *Vocabulary differs somewhat from one English-speaking country to another.* American travelers in England notice the British uses of *tram, lorry, lift, torch, wireless, fortnight.* Here is a passage with many British terms:

> A scale or two adhered to the *fishmonger's* marble slab; the *pastry-cook's* glass shelves showed a range of interesting crumbs; the *fruiterer* filled a long-standing void with fans of cardboard bananas and a "Dig for Victory" placard; the *greengrocer's* crates had been emptied of all but earth by those who had somehow failed to dig hard enough. . . . In the *confectioner's* windows, the ribbons bleached on dummy boxes of chocolate among flyblown cutouts of prewar blondes. *Newsagents* without newspapers gave out in angry red chalk that they had no matches either.—Elizabeth Bowen, *The Heat of the Day*

(2) *Like most European languages, British English varies greatly from area to area.* Such regional varieties within a country are called **dialects**. Students of English literature usually encounter some dialect writing. For instance, a poet to whom a girl is a "bonny lass," a church a "kirk," and a landowner a "laird" is using one of the dialects of Scotland and Northern England rather than standard British English.

(3) *American speech shows some regional differences.* By and large, the intermingling of settlers from many areas and the rapid growth of mass media have kept these American dialects from drifting very far apart. Here are some of the words that your dictionary may mark **dialectal**: *dogie, poke* (bag), *reckon* (suppose), *tote* (carry), *you all.*

# D 4b   Obsolete and Archaic                                    *d*

**Know how dictionaries label words no longer in common use.**

Some words, or meanings of words, have gone out of use altogether. They are called **obsolete**. Examples of obsolete meanings are *coy* (quiet), *curious* (careful), and *nice* (foolish). Some words or meanings are no longer in common use but still occur in special contexts. Such words and meanings are called **archaic**. The King James version of the Bible preserves many archaisms that were in common use in seventeenth-century England: *thou* and *thee, brethren, kine* (cattle).

In the following dictionary entry, five of the numbered meanings of *brave* are labeled obsolete:

**brave** (brāv) *adj.* **brav·er, brav·est 1.** Having or showing courage; intrepid; courageous. **2.** Making a fine display; elegant; showy. **3.** *Obs.* Excellent. — *v.* **braved, brav·ing** *v.t.* **1.** To meet or face with courage and fortitude: to *brave* danger. **2.** To defy; challenge: to *brave* the heavens. **3.** *Obs.* To make splendid. — *v.i.* **4.** *Obs.* To boast. — *n.* **1.** A man of courage. **2.** A North American Indian warrior. **3.** *Obs.* A bully; bravo. **4.** *Obs.* A boast or defiance.

From *Standard College Dictionary*

Here are some archaisms familiar to readers of poetry and historical fiction:

| | | | |
|---|---|---|---|
| *anon* | (at once) | *fere* | (companion) |
| *brand* | (sword) | *forsooth* | (truly) |
| *childe* | (aristocratic youth) | *methinks* | (it seems) |
| *erst* | (formerly) | *rood* | (cross) |
| *fain* | (glad or gladly) | *sprite* | (ghost) |

# D4c  Neologisms                                        *d*

**Be cautious in using words that have recently come into the language.**

Lexicographers, who at one time resisted the introduction of new words, now compete in their coverage of **neologisms**, or newly coined expressions. Many new words serve a need and rapidly become accepted: *bookmobile, cybernetics, astronaut, fallout, space shuttle, supersonic, transistor.* But many other coined words make conservative readers squirm. Avoid copywriters' words like the following:

| | | |
|---|---|---|
| jumboize | paperamics | outdoorsman |
| moisturize | usership | |

Many new words are part of an impersonal bureaucratic jargon that lacks the life and color of real language. Memos and reports often use words made up, on the model of *escapee, personalize, finalize, socioeconomic.*

> For more on jargon, see **D 6c.**

## D 4d   Subject Labels                                                    *d*

**Watch for technical terms that are not likely to be familiar to outsiders.**

Labels like *Law, Naut.* (nautical), or *Mach.* (machinery) are called subject labels. The **technical terminology** or, on a less formal level, the shoptalk of a trade or profession requires explanation in writing for the general reader. Students majoring in mathematics will have no difficulty with *set, natural number, integer, rational number,* and *number sentence.* But others would want these terms explained.

# EXERCISES

A. Which of the following words have *regional or dialect uses*? (And where are they used?) Which of these words (or which of their uses) are *archaic*? Which are *obsolete*?

| | | |
|---|---|---|
| bloke | cove | hackney |
| bonnet | dogie | petrol |
| boot | favor | quid |
| bower | gentle | thorpe |
| complected | goober | trolley |
| costermonger | goodman | tube |
| coulee | | |

B. In an article on Maine speech, E. B. White discussed the following expressions among others: *tunk* a wedge, *soft* weather, *dozy* wood, people *from away*, a *snug* pasture, *gunkhole, nooning.* Write a paper in which you discuss a number of expressions that you associate with a specific *region or group of people*. For instance, investigate dialect features that set your own native speech apart from that of a region where you now live.

C. The following *new words* have all gained wide currency in recent years. Choose five of these. Explain briefly what each means and why it has become familiar.

| | | |
|---|---|---|
| printout | fast-breeder | bleep |
| subculture | peak load | replay |
| sexism | elitist | multiethnic |
| transplant | laser | recycle |

D. Discuss the use of *newly coined words* in current advertising. Which of these do you think may eventually become standard English? Explain why.

E. What special fields of interest do the following *technical terms* represent? Which of the terms would you expect the average high school graduate to know? *a priori, brochure, calorie, camshaft, crochet, de facto, graupel, lien, solstice, sonata, sprit, symbiosis, thyroid, venire, ventricle.*

F. A student investigating post office *shoptalk* discussed the following terms: *swing room, star route, merry-go-round, tour three, fat stock, confetti, shedders, scheme man, nixie clerk.* Conduct a similar investigation of shoptalk in one of the following areas: railroading, trucking, flying, electronics, journalism.

# D5 EXPRESSIVE LANGUAGE　　*d*

**Use the exact words needed to carry your intended meaning.**

Effective writing is clear, fresh, graphic, and concrete. Learn to revise your writing for more effective, more expressive word choice.

## D5a  Accurate Words　　*d*

**Aim at accurate words and exact shades of meaning.**

Hastily written words often express the intended meaning almost but not quite:

HASTY: *The news* about widespread corruption was first *exposed* by the local press.

REVISED: The news about widespread corruption first *appeared* in the local press. (Evildoers or shortcomings are "exposed," but news about evildoers is "printed," "presented," or "reported.")

Check your papers for the following:

(1) *Watch out for words easily confused.* We sometimes confuse words closely related in sound or meaning:

The work was sheer *trudgery* (should be *drudgery*).
Similar choices *affront* every student (should be *confront*).
He grew up in a *staple* environment (should be *stable*).
Self-control is an *envious* asset (should be *enviable*).

(2) *Watch out for garbled idioms*:

GARBLED:    Unemployment *played* an important *factor*.
SHOULD BE:  Unemployment *played* an important *role*.

GARBLED:    Many young people have *lost their appeal for* fraternities.
SHOULD BE:  Fraternities have *lost their appeal* for many young people.

(3) *Watch out for words with the wrong connotation*:

INEXACT:  Life in the suburbs *subjects* a family to the beauties of nature.
REVISED:  Life in the suburbs *brings* a family *closer* to the beauties of nature. (The connotations of *subject* are unfavorable; it implies that we are exposed to something unwillingly.)

# D 5b   Specific Words     *d*

### Use specific, informative words.

Instead of a colorless, general word like *building,* use a more expressive word like *barn, mansion, warehouse, bungalow, tenement, shack, workshop,* or *cabin. Tenement* carries more information than *building.* It also comes closer to concrete experience, making it possible for the reader to visualize an actual structure. When words remain unnecessarily general, readers are too far removed from what they can see, hear, and feel.

GENERAL:  All the animals of the farm joined in singing "Beasts of England."
SPECIFIC:  The whole farm *burst* out into "Beasts of England" in tremendous unison. The cows *lowed* it, the dogs *whined* it, the sheep *bleated* it, the horses *whinnied* it, the ducks *quacked* it. (George Orwell)

Here are some all-purpose words with the more concrete choices that could take their place. What does each of the concrete words add to the general idea? What does it make you see or hear?

| GENERAL | CONCRETE |
|---------|----------|
| look | gaze, stare, peer, squint, ogle |
| walk | stride, march, slink, trot, shuffle, drag |
| sit | slump, squat, lounge, hunch, crouch |
| take | seize, grab, pounce on, grip |
| cry | weep, sob, sigh, bawl |
| throw | hurl, pitch, toss, dump, flip |

## D5c   Figurative Words                                     *d*

**Use figurative expressions to make writing graphic and colorful.**

Figurative language exploits the similarities between things. A compressed comparison introduced by *as* or *like* is called a **simile.** An implied comparison that uses one thing as the equivalent of another is called a **metaphor.** Literally, *monkey* refers to a small, long-tailed animal. Figuratively, it may mean a person who, like a monkey, is full of tricks and mischief.

Fresh, well-chosen figurative expressions catch our attention and make us see the point:

> In this movie, "understanding" is sprinkled onto both sides of the conflict *like meat tenderizer.* (Peter Rainer)
>
> Getting complete sentences out of him was like trying to put together *Homo sapiens* from a *few bones in a cave.* (Anita Strickland)

Remember the following advice:

(1) *Figurative expressions should be apt.* The implied analogy must fit:

APT:   Putting the hubcap back on the rim is *like putting an undersized lid on an oversized jar.* (As one side of the hubcap is pounded into place, the opposite side pops out.)

INEPT: Lacking the ignition of advertising, our economic engine would run at a slower pace. (An engine without ignition would not run at a slower pace; it would just be dead.)

(2) *Figurative expressions should be consistent.* When several figurative expressions appear close together, they should blend into a harmonious whole rather than clash because of contradictory associations. Avoid the **mixed metaphor:**

CONSISTENT: Fame cannot spread wide or endure long that is not *rooted* in nature, and *manured* by art. (Samuel Johnson)
MIXED: America's colleges are the *key* to national survival, and the future of the country lies in their *hands*. (Keys do not have hands.)
MIXED: Enriched programs give the good student a chance to *dig* deeper into the large *sea* of knowledge. (Most people do their digging on solid ground rather than at sea.)

(3) *Figurative expressions should not call excessive attention to themselves.* Avoid metaphors that are strained enough to become distracting:

EXTRAVAGANT: When the average overmothered college student is removed from parental control, the severance of the umbilical cord causes him or her to bleed to death, psychologically speaking.

# D5d   Fresh Words                                            *d*

**Phrase ideas freshly in your own words.**

Many phrases that may once have been striking have become trite through overuse. Such tired phrases are called **clichés**. They make the reader feel that nothing new is being said and that there is little point in paying attention:

TRITE: He was always *wrapped up* in his own thoughts and feelings.
FRESH: Only the *cocoon* of his own thoughts and feelings existed for him.

TRITE: The dean let us have it, *straight from the shoulder.*
FRESH: The dean spoke to us directly and urgently, *like a scout just returned from the enemy camp.*

To the cliché expert, ignorance is always "abysmal," fortitude "intestinal," and necessity "dire." Daylight is always "broad," silence "ominous," and old age "ripe." People make a "clean break" and engage in "honest toil" till the "bitter end." They make things "crystal clear"; they wait "with bated breath"; they work "by the sweat of their brow."

Avoid clichés like the following:

| | |
|---|---|
| believe it or not | burn the midnight oil |
| better late than never | couldn't care less |
| beyond the shadow of a doubt | crying shame |
| bolt out of the blue | dire straits |

| | |
|---|---|
| easier said than done | nature's glory |
| the facts of life | off the beaten track |
| few and far between | pride and joy |
| fine and dandy | proud owner |
| the finer things | rear its ugly head |
| first and foremost | rude awakening |
| free and easy | a shot in the arm |
| get in there and fight | sink or swim |
| good time was had by all | a snare and a delusion |
| green with envy | sneaking suspicion |
| in one fell swoop | something tells me |
| in the final analysis | straight and narrow |
| it goes without saying | strike while the iron is hot |
| it stands to reason | tender mercies |
| last but not least | to all intents and purposes |
| the last straw | truer words were never spoken |
| let's face it | truth is stranger than fiction |
| malice aforethought | up in arms |

# EXERCISES

A. Make sure you can distinguish between the *confusing words* in the following pairs: *antic—antique; biography—bibliography; clique—cliché; connive—conspire; difference—deference; ethical—ethnic; feudalism—fatalism; gentle—genteel; literal—literary—literate; manners—mannerisms; sensible—sensitive; specie—species.*

B. Write down a *more accurate* word for the word italicized in each sentence.

1. Diane had only a small knowledge of the problem *coherent* in being a woman.
2. Justice prevails when a criminal is *righteously* punished for wrongdoing.
3. The March of Dimes was originally organized to help those *inflicted* with infantile paralysis.
4. My parents were idealists and tried to raise healthy, *opinionated* children.
5. By *defying* to participate in saluting the flag, people are showing disrespect to our country.
6. Abortion is quickly becoming more acceptable but still considered by many *immortal.*
7. In my *analogy* of this essay, I hope to show its strengths and weaknesses.
8. Our next *fiascle* took place in Hollywood.
9. My dilemma is whether to describe the three incidents separately or *incarcerate* them all in one short story.

10. He tried for years to win the *disparaging* strife against alcohol.
11. Many references to his early life *percolate through* Eliot's poetry.
12. The chairman *contributed* the low attendance to poor publicity.
13. A good listener can listen to teachers and retain the knowledge they have *expelled.*
14. Sick people can no longer pay for their hospital costs without a tremendous *drain* being put on their families.
15. Thorough reforms would be hard to *induce upon* our society.

C.  How many different *figurative expressions* can you find in the following passage?

The sixties was the decade when the frightened cry of "Timber!" was everywhere in the unclean air of publishing. The flow of competitive daily newspapers dried up, and magazines great and small fell like the trees chopped down for the paper to print them. Now that the flagship *Life* has joined its lessers in the Sargasso Sea of bestilled publications, some conventional wisdom prevails as to how American publishing became trapped in such an economic rathole: spiraling production costs, quadrupling postage rates, blood-sucking competition for advertising dollars from television, the general malaise of the economy, mass circulations sustained at uneconomical cut rates, the decline of print, et cetera. None of these reasons, to my way of thinking, explains the big picture.—Warren Hinckle, "The Adman Who Hated Advertising," *Atlantic*

D.  Look at the use of *figurative expressions* in the following sentences. Which work well to help the author make a point? Which are mixed or overdone? Which are borderline? (Your instructor may ask you to find more apt figurative expressions to replace the unsatisfactory ones.)

1. Frustration and depression will take over our minds the way bacteria do our bodies if we do not harness them.
2. The new law is a carefully tossed salad of penalties and incentives.
3. Modern society is like a mobile: Disturb it here and it jiggles over there, too. Because every facet of life involves energy, energy policy disturbs everything at once.
4. The story told by Poe's biographers was a tale told by idiots, in which incredible oceans of slushy sentimentality broke in waves of froth over the submerged rocks of fact.
5. The producer and director of the movie have tapped a sensitive nerve in their audiences like a bunch of wildcatters hitting a pool of oil.
6. The President will run down his batteries if he continues issuing high-voltage announcements about energy "catastrophe."
7. When I moved to the new school, many new faces dotted this horizon of experience.
8. Slapping on a price freeze to stop inflation could become a one-way street to a Pandora's box of problems.

9. To be the son of a great man can be a disadvantage; it is like living next to a huge monument.
10. This cat was in our driveway when the kiss of death took him by surprise.
11. Education is certainly not a precise instrument. When you increase the supply, you don't get the same immediate effect as when you press on the accelerator of your automobile.
12. College can supply the appropriate building blocks that make it easier to grow up in the tough world of today.
13. We sat in a circle on the floor, pouring out the paths and roads we had traveled since we graduated.
14. An industrial world thinks it wants only a pinch of intelligence to season a great plateful of mechanical aptitudes. (Jacques Barzun)
15. I was dismayed to find that the place associated with my favorite childhood memories had succumbed to the clutch of change.

E. Rewrite the following sentences to eliminate *clichés*. Try to make your phrasing fresh enough to revive the reader's attention.

1. They will have to get his signature by hook or by crook.
2. Catching the street-corner pusher has become small potatoes. The major effort is now international, and it is a pathway strewn with political pitfalls.
3. Cleopatra squeezes Antony under her thumb, while Octavia pulls the rug from under him in front of Caesar and his troops.
4. After one more defeat, she will have to throw in the sponge.
5. The reporter swallowed their story hook, line, and sinker.
6. The typical organization man knows which side his bread is buttered on.
7. Party platforms never get down to brass tacks.
8. When we try to revitalize our neighborhoods, appealing to self-interest is our best bet.
9. When we are asked to change administrations in the midst of a serious international crisis, we should remember that it is unwise to change horses in midstream.
10. The opposing candidate is a Johnny-come-lately who entered the campaign only at the urging of influential backers.

# D6 DIRECTNESS

**Know how to be blunt and direct.**

At times, a writer will be deliberately indirect for tactical reasons. More common is the kind of careless indirectness that for no good reason slows down the reader. Learn how to say things briefly and directly in plain English.

# D6a Redundancy *w*

**Avoid wordiness.**

The most easily spotted kind of wordiness is **redundancy**, or unnecessary duplication. The phrase *basic fundamentals* is redundant because *basic* and *fundamental* mean nearly the same thing. In the following sentences, one or the other way of expressing the same idea should be omitted:

REDUNDANT:   We left *in the morning* at about six o'clock A.M.
As a rule, the weather was *usually* warm.
There is more to it than *seems apparent*.
*Physically,* he has not grown much *in height*.
*In my opinion, I think* you are right.

Do the following to avoid wordiness other than direct duplication:

(1)   *Avoid familiar wordy tags.* Expressions like the following are unnecessary mouthfuls:

| WORDY | BRIEF |
| --- | --- |
| at the present time | now |
| due to the fact that | because |
| under the prevailing circumstances | as things are |
| in this time and age | today |

(2)   *Use simple, direct transitional expressions.* Roundabout transitions sometimes take the place of simple phrases like *for example, however,* and *therefore:*

WORDY:            *In considering this situation, we must also take into account the fact that* other students do not feel this way.
ECONOMICAL:   Others, *however,* do not feel this way.

WORDY:            *Taking these factors into consideration, we must conclude that* your request is unjustified.
ECONOMICAL:   *Therefore,* your request seems to us unjustified.

(3)   *Avoid awkward introductory tags.* Introductory phrases like *the fact that* or *the question whether* can often be trimmed without loss:

| | |
|---|---|
| WORDY: | *The question of whether* churches should unite has at times been a hotly debated issue. |
| ECONOMICAL: | Whether churches should unite has at times been a hotly debated issue. |

(4) *Avoid vague all-purpose nouns.* Words like *situation, angle, factor, aspect, line, context,* or *element* are often mere padding:

| | |
|---|---|
| PADDED: | When I first came to Smith College, *there was a situation where* some students had better housing than others. |
| PLAIN: | When I first came to Smith College, some students had better housing than others. |
| PADDED: | Another *aspect* that needs to be considered is the consumer relations *angle.* |
| PLAIN: | We should also consider consumer relations. |

# D 6b  Euphemisms                                                      *d*

**Prefer plain English to euphemisms and weasel words.**

Much roundabout diction results from the desire to be elegant. Refined or impressive names for unpleasant or prosaic things are **euphemisms**. The most familiar euphemisms are those for elementary facts of human existence:

| | |
|---|---|
| (birth) | *blessed event, new arrival* |
| (pregnancy) | *to be expecting, to be in a family way* |
| (age) | *senior citizens, the elderly* |
| (death) | *pass on, expire, the deceased, mortal remains, memorial park* |

Euphemisms are "beautiful words"—words more beautiful than what they stand for. Often they are required by politeness or tact. When referring to people you respect, you will prefer *stout* to *fat, intoxicated* to *drunk,* and *remains* to *corpse.* Often, however, euphemisms mislead, or even deliberately deceive. Plumbers become "sanitary engineers," file clerks "research consultants," undertakers "funeral directors," translators "language facilitators," and fortune tellers "clairvoyant readers." In much public-relations prose and political propaganda, euphemisms become "weasel words." They cover up facts that the reader is entitled to know: *straitened financial circumstances* for "bankruptcy"; *planned withdrawal* for "disorganized retreat"; *resettlement* for "forcible removal."

| EUPHEMISM | BLUNT |
|---|---|
| immoderate use of intoxicants | heavy drinking |
| lack of proper health habits | dirt |
| deteriorating residential section | slum |
| below the poverty line | poor |

# D 6c · Jargon                                                    *d*

**Do not try to impress your reader with pretentious pseudo-scientific language.**

Much inflated diction results from a writer's using two highbrow words where one lowbrow word would do. **Jargon** tries to make the trivial seem important. It cultivates an impressive pseudoscientific air by using indirect, impersonal constructions and technical-sounding Latin and Greek terms:

| | |
|---|---|
| JARGON: | He was instrumental in the founding of an Irish national theater. |
| PLAIN ENGLISH: | He helped found an Irish national theater. |
| | |
| JARGON: | Procedures were instituted with a view toward the implementation of the conclusions reached. |
| PLAIN ENGLISH: | We started to put our ideas into practice. |
| | |
| JARGON: | Careful consideration of relevant data is imperative before the procedure most conducive toward a realization of the desired outcomes can be determined. |
| PLAIN ENGLISH: | Look before you leap. |

Jargon addicts say "Reference was made" rather than "I mentioned"; "the hypothesis suggests itself" rather than "I think." They are fond of "factors," "phases," "aspects," "criteria," "data," "facets," "phenomena," "structures," "levels," and "strata." In each of the following pairs, avoid the big word if the simpler word will do:

| FANCY | SIMPLE |
|---|---|
| ameliorate | improve |
| magnitude | size |
| interrelationship | relation |
| methodology | methods |
| residence | home |
| maximize | develop fully |
| insightful | intelligent |
| preadolescence | childhood |

Obviously, many scientific and scholarly subjects call for language that is technical, precise, impersonal. Jargon is the *unnecessary* use of technical language in order to borrow the prestige of science and scholarship.

## D 6d  Flowery Diction  *d*

**Avoid language that is flowery or overdone.**

Flowery and extravagant diction interferes with a writer's doing justice to a subject. Flowery diction results from an attempt to give a poetic varnish to prose. Some writers cannot resist the temptation to call a police officer a "minion of the law," an Irishman a "native of the Emerald Isle," a colonist who served in the War of Independence a "gallant warrior defending our infant republic."

FLOWERY: The respite from study was devoted to a sojourn at the ancestral mansion.
PLAIN ENGLISH: I spent my vacation at the house of my grandparents.

FLOWERY: The visitor proved a harbinger of glad tidings.
PLAIN ENGLISH: The visitor brought good news.

Do not imitate writers who habitually prefer the fancy word to the plain word, the elegant flourish to the blunt phrase. Here is a brief list of words that can make your writing seem affected:

| FLOWERY | PLAIN | FLOWERY | PLAIN |
|---|---|---|---|
| astound | amaze | nuptials | wedding |
| betrothal | engagement | obsequies | funeral |
| commence | begin | presage | predict |
| demise | death | pulchritude | beauty |
| emolument | pay, reward | vernal | springlike |
| eschew | avoid | vista | view |

# EXERCISES

A. What makes each of the following sentences *wordy*? Rewrite each sentence to eliminate wordiness.

1. The war against alcohol lasts enduringly forever.
2. Mormons fleeing persecution founded the beginning of our community.
3. In due time, a new fad will eventually replace this current craze.
4. The central nucleus of the tribe was based around the institution of the family.
5. I feel that I have the personality of a happy, smiling type of person.
6. Some of today's popular music seems to revert back to music popular thirty years ago.
7. The weather bureau announced that at times there would be occasional rain.
8. The reason that married students have high grades academically is that they have a definite goal in the future to come.
9. In the modern world of this day and age, economical operation has become an indispensable condition for business success.
10. I felt honored and lucky to have a chance of taking advantage of the opportunity of getting a good education.

B. Investigate the current use of *euphemisms* in one major area, such as education, medicine, or the funeral industry. Examine such euphemisms for intention, appropriateness, effect.

C. Translate the following examples of *jargon* into plain English.

1. I sincerely believe that the government should divulge more on the subject of socialism and its cohorts, because its impetus has reached a frightening momentum.
2. In camp, cooking is done over open fires, with the main dietary intake consisting of black beans and rice.
3. To be frank about it, today an inadequacy can bring about the ruination of a person in later life when it happens in education.
4. Being in social situations in Washington subjected me to some embarrassing instances due to my deficiency in etiquette, which was superfluous at home because of its nonexistence.
5. The English language and its use have become very important factors in correlation with communication to large audiences.
6. In these two books, there are basic differences in character representation that are accountable only in terms of the individual authors involved.
7. Further insight into the article discovered that the writing insinuated a connection between the conviction of the accused and his working-class background.
8. Advertisements similar to those of Certs and Ultra-Brite are creating a fallacy in the real cause of a person's sex appeal.

9. The fact that we are products of our environmental frame of reference ensures that each of us has deeply ingrained within the fiber of our being preconceived ideas that influence our thoughts, actions, and reactions.
10. We say we believe in democracy while denying the partaking of its first fruits, justice and equality, to diverse members of our society. This is true in many aspects of our lives, but especially so in the context of racial prejudice.

D. Study the language used by your favorite *sports writer, fashion analyst,* or *society editor*. Write a brief report, providing samples of characteristic diction.

# 7

# The Paragraph

# DIAGNOSTIC TEST

## INSTRUCTIONS:

Read each of the three paragraphs carefully. Answer the questions that follow each paragraph. Put the letter for the right answer after the number of the question.

A. Censorship has been on the rise in the U.S. in recent years. Efforts to ban books in public libraries and schools have redoubled, according to recent studies. School boards publish lists of approved books that in effect ban books previously studied but now excluded. Such omitted books often include Richard Wright's classic *Black Boy* and John Steinbeck's *Grapes of Wrath*. One school board banned *Making It with Mademoiselle* but then found out the book was a how-to pattern book for young dressmakers. In fact, several school districts have banned the *American Heritage Dictionary* because it includes the sexual meaning for the word *bed*, used as a transitive verb.

1. What is the overall pattern of this paragraph? (a) key idea—reasons—restatement of key idea; (b) key idea—explanation—examples; (c) key idea—situation then—situation now.

2. The repetition of words like *school board* or *school districts* shows (a) awkward repetition of terms; (b) intentional repetition for emphasis; (c) evidence of continued focus on the same basic topic.

3. The phrase *in fact* at the beginning of the last sentence is (a) a transition leading to an emphatic additional example; (b) a signal that the topic sentence will appear at the end; (c) a change from theory to fact.

4. If the writer had wished to provide additional links between sentences in this paragraph, words or phrases like the following would have been most appropriate: (a) *however* or *nevertheless*; (b) *on the other hand* or *on the contrary*; (c) *for example*.

B. The objection to censorship has deep roots in American history and in the collective memory of Americans. It is true that the pilgrims who sought religious freedom here claimed that right for themselves without granting it to others. However, such leaders of the American revolution as Thomas Jefferson and Thomas Paine vigorously supported the right of others to their own opinions. Nineteenth-century writers like Emerson and Thoreau preached nonconformity and self-reliance. In this century, the book burnings that marked Hitler's rise to power left many Americans with an abhorrence for the suppression of dissent.

5. The major organizing principle in this paragraph is (a) chronology; (b) classification; (c) cause and effect.

**6.** This paragraph uses familiar transitional expressions to signal each of the following *except* (a) concession; (b) summary; (c) counterargument.

**7.** The topic sentence in this paragraph is the (a) first sentence; (b) third sentence; (c) last sentence.

C. What has happened to America's mythical national heroes? For several generations, a legendary figure like Buffalo Bill could serve as a symbol of the gallant, reckless, sturdy independence of the Western frontier. At the same time, he was celebrated as a show business genius who made his Wild West show the most famous spectacle of its kind. Today, however, his name reminds us above all of the reckless destruction of the American buffalo. Whereas the Indians had regarded the animal with almost religious reverence, hunters like Buffalo Bill started the wholesale slaughter that decimated the herds and that destroyed the livelihood of the native Americans. Buffalo Bill is one of many mythical heroes who have been taken down from their pedestals as Americans have critically reevaluated their past.

**8.** What is unusual about the structure of this paragraph? (a) no topic sentence; (b) topic sentence at the end of the paragraph; (c) key question left unanswered.

**9.** How is this paragraph developed? (a) one single major example to prove the main point; (b) a solid array of different examples; (c) a chain of cause and effect.

**10.** Which of the following transitional expressions marks the major turning point in this paragraph? (a) *at the same time*; (b) *however*; (c) *whereas*.

# PA 1   WRITING THE PARAGRAPH

**Write the kind of paragraph that presents and supports one main idea.**

A paragraph is a group of related sentences that we expect the reader to take in at one time. In newspaper writing, paragraphs are often very short. There may be a paragraph break after every two or three sentences. In dialogue, a paragraph break signals a change from one speaker to another. In writing that explains things or argues with the reader, the paragraph is a solid, well-developed basic unit: The expository paragraph enables a writer to do justice to one point at a time.

A well-developed paragraph gives you a chance to show that you are serious about what you are saying. A passing remark about the advantages of solar energy is soon forgotten. It is not likely to change anyone's mind. But in a well-written paragraph, you can focus on one major advantage or one major application. For instance, you could describe houses where you have seen solar heating help meet the energy needs of a family. In such a paragraph, you have a chance to stay with one point long enough to show how things work, or to show what is involved. You have a chance to show what you mean—and, especially, to show what it means in practice.

Paragraphs differ in shape and purpose. A successful paragraph, however, answers some basic questions in the reader's mind.

- It focuses on one limited point or issue. (What are we talking about?)

- It presents an overall idea or conclusion. (What is the point?)

- It backs up the main point with examples or other supporting material. (What makes you think so?)

- It provides signals that help the reader see how you have arranged your material. (How is your paragraph laid out?)

## PA1a  Gathering Material                                      *dev*

**Use a paragraph to group together related material.**

The raw material for a paragraph is a group of related data or observations. As we focus on one limited area of a subject, we bring together different details that seem to be part of the same general picture. Reading about sharks, for instance, we may notice several things that explain how sharks appear mysteriously whenever there seems to be a chance of food:

| First observation | Sharks can smell blood from a quarter of a mile away, and they follow the faint scent to their prey. |
|---|---|
| Second observation | Sharks sense motion in the water with special sense organs. Something thrashing about in the water is for sharks a signal of food. |
| Third observation | Sharks are sensitive to bright light. They are attracted to bright and shiny objects, and to contrast between light and dark. |

These observations all relate to the same basic topic: the food-tracking equipment of sharks. They add up to a general conclusion: Sharks are well equipped for identifying and tracking down food. In the finished paragraph, this conclusion will serve as the central idea that holds the paragraph together. We usually put such a central idea early in the paragraph as a **topic sentence**. The finished paragraph might look like this:

*Sharks, known as voracious eaters, are well equipped for identifying and tracking down food.* As they prowl the water, they seem to sense the presence of unsuspecting prey from a considerable distance. There are several reasons why sharks are efficient at hunting down their prey. They can smell blood from a quarter of a mile away, and they follow the faint scent to a wounded creature. Sharks sense motion in the water with special sense organs; something thrashing about in the water is for them a signal of food. Finally, sharks are sensitive to bright light. Light reflected from something moving in the water alerts them, especially if it is the reflection from the shiny scaly surface of large fish.

Here is another set of related material drawn together for use in a paragraph:

| First observation | People who have never been on a horse spend hundreds of dollars for elaborately decorated Texas-style boots. |
|---|---|
| Second observation | They buy crafted leather belts with richly decorated silver buckles. |
| Third observation | Passengers march onto airplanes wearing broad-brimmed cowboy hats. |
| Fourth observation | Shirtmakers cultivate the urban-cowboy look. |
| Fifth observation | Blue jeans, once worn mostly by ranch hands, are now the national uniform of the young. |
| CONCLUSION: | *Everywhere we look today, we see city people wearing cowboy fashions.* |

When the material in a paragraph is related to the same basic idea, we say that it is **relevant**. It is to the point; it helps the writer make the point. The most basic requirement for successful paragraphs is the writer's ability to draw on a rich fund of material from observation, experience, and reading. When such material gives solid substance to a paragraph, what might have been a superficial opinion turns into a well-supported point that is worth taking in and worth thinking about.

## PA1b   The Topic Sentence                                  *foc*

**Use a topic sentence to sum up the major point of your paragraph.**

The most basic question in your reader's mind is: "What is the point?" It is true that sometimes we want our readers to think about an issue and to reach their own conclusions. But in most well-written paragraphs, we include a clear statement that tells our readers: "This is what I am trying to show. This is what I am trying to prove." A **topic sentence** is a sentence that sums up the main point or key idea of a paragraph. Often the topic sentence is the very first sentence:

TOPIC SENTENCE:   Some of the job areas most popular with students are very small.

Complete paragraph            *Some of the job areas most popular with students are very small.* No more than 1,000 foresters will be hired this year, although perhaps twice as many students may get forestry degrees. Only 2,700 new architects will be needed to design all the buildings sprouting on the landscape, and almost twice that number graduated in a recent year. Everyone wants to design things, but, according to the Department of Labor, only about 300 industrial designers are added to the labor force during an average year. Landscape architecture is appealing, too, because it combines creativity with outdoor work, but only 600 are expected to find jobs in the field this year.

Here is another example:

TOPIC SENTENCE:   Women have always been stuck with the sewing.

Complete paragraph

> *Women have always been stuck with the sewing.* The connection is there in Greek myth and legend—the Three Fates are women, and one of them cuts the thread of life. Penelope, famous for her patience, used weaving to put off her unwelcome suitors. American Indian women chewed hides and sewed them with bone needles. Farm women, with huge families and no servants, spent hours stitching—*after* all the other household work was done. Even in their leisure time, they quilted while they socialized. James Fenimore Cooper read novels to his wife in the evening while she sewed.

A topic sentence often carries its message most effectively if it is brief and to the point. A second (and perhaps a third) sentence may explain the main point in more detail. It may *restate* the main idea, explaining some key terms or spelling out important if's and but's. Then the paragraph will go on to the examples or details that back up the main point. These provide **illustration**—they show what the writer's idea means in practice. Sometimes the writer will restate the main idea in a "clincher sentence" at the end.

Study the way the following sample paragraphs vary this basic pattern of *statement–explanation–illustration*. The first paragraph is from an article about recent trends toward vocational or career-oriented education:

TOPIC SENTENCE:

Explanation

Striking example

Clincher sentence

*The new trend toward vocationalism is particularly counterproductive in an uncertain economy, when jobs are both scarce and changeable.* It makes slim indeed the chances of picking the right specialization years in advance of actual entry into the labor market. The writer of an article in the *New York Times Magazine* extravagantly extolling the virtues of New York's Aviation High School appeared unaware of its own ultimate contradiction: only 6 members of that year's 515-member graduating class reported that they had found jobs in the aviation industry. *The primary reason for youth unemployment is not lack of training but lack of jobs.*—Fred M. Hechinger, "Murder in Academe," *Saturday Review*

The second paragraph starts with a key question that is answered by the topic sentence. Note the expressions that help the reader follow the way the paragraph develops:

| | |
|---|---|
| Key question<br>TOPIC SENTENCE | Where do the terms of businesese come from? *Most, of course, are hand-me-downs from former generations of business people, but many are the fruit of cross-fertilization with other jargons.* Business people who |
| First set of<br>examples | castigate government bureaucrats, *for example,* are at the same time apt to be activating, expediting, implementing, effectuating, optimizing, minimizing, and maximizing—and at all levels and echelons within the |
| Second set of<br>examples | framework of broad policy areas. *Similarly,* though amused by the long-hairs and the social scientists, they are beginning to speak knowingly of projective techniques, social dynamics, depth interviewing, *and* sometime soon, if they keep up at this rate, they will probably appropriate that hallmark of the sound |
| Restatement<br>of key idea | sociological paper, "insightful." Businesese, *in fact,* has very nearly become the great common meeting ground of the jargons.—William H. Whyte, "The Language of Business," *Fortune* |

Sometimes we *delay* the topic sentence till the very end. This way we give our readers a chance to form a conclusion very similar to our own. They are then well prepared for our final summing up of the main idea. In such a paragraph, with the topic sentence last, we have to be especially sure that the details add up, so that the reader can follow our train of thought:

| | |
|---|---|
| Examples first | The shops of the border town are filled with many souvenirs, "piñatas," pottery, bullhorns, and "serapes," all made from cheap material and decorated in a gaudy manner that the tourist thinks represents true Mexican folk art. Tourists are everywhere, haggling with the shopkeepers, eager to get something for nothing, carrying huge packages and boxes filled with the treasures bought at the many shops. Car horns blare at the people who are too entranced with the sights to watch where they are going. Raucous tunes pour from the nightclubs, open in broad daylight. Few children are seen in the town, but some boys swim in the Rio Grande and dive to retrieve the coins that tourists throw as they cross the bridge above. People come for |
| TOPIC SENTENCE<br>last | a cheap thrill or cheap liquor. *A border town is the tourist's Mexico, a gaudy caricature of the real country.* |

Remember what a good topic sentence does for the reader:

(1) *A good topic sentence is like a promise to your readers.* It

gives them a sense of what to expect. In each of the following examples, the topic sentence steers the paragraph in a different direction. What additional details would you expect in each of these paragraphs?

Version 1: *The dormitory reminds me of a third-class hotel.* Each room has the same set of unimaginative furnishings: the same pale red chest of drawers, the same light brown desks. . . .

Version 2: *The dormitory reminds me of a big office building.* People who half know each other pass in the hall with impersonal friendliness. . . .

Version 3: *The dormitory reminds me of a prison.* The study room is enclosed by windows with lines on them, giving the student a penned-in feeling. . . .

(2) *A good topic sentence often hints at how the paragraph is going to be organized.* It often gives the reader a preview of the order in which points are likely to be covered. It hints at the procedure the writer is going to follow. Look at the program implied in each of the following topic sentences:

TOPIC SENTENCE: Just as traffic lights may be red, amber, or green, so job interviews may be classified according to their probable results as hopeless, undecided, or promising. (We now expect a description of the three kinds. We expect the kind of order that results from a sorting out into categories, or **classification**.)

TOPIC SENTENCE: During my high school years, I saw a major change in the way schools treated bilingual students. (We now expect an account of the situation first before and then after the change. We expect the kind of order that results when two things are lined up for **contrast**.)

Here is a paragraph that would follow up this last topic sentence:

TOPIC SENTENCE

Before

*During my high school years, I saw a major change in the way schools treated bilingual students.* In my grammar school days, the goal seemed to be to make everyone the same. English was the sole language spoken. A classmate of mine spoke only Italian at first, but in class she was allowed to speak only English. We

After

learned only American history, practiced only American traditions, and played only American games. In high school, however, the situation changed drastically. Special classes were established for groups that did not speak English. Many students graduated speaking English only imperfectly. We had frequent cultural weeks, when groups of students in different ways presented their cultural background. No effort was made to homogenize the students.

(3)   *In the theme as a whole, a good topic sentence moves the presentation or the argument ahead one essential step.* Then the rest of the paragraph fills in, illustrates, and supports the point made. Then the next topic sentence again takes a step forward. Part of an article on the influence of television on political campaigns might proceed like this:

### Smile—You're on Camera

Step 1:

*Television continues to change the look of political conventions.* Speeches are fewer and shorter. Sweaty orators, bellowing and waving their arms for an hour or more, have yielded almost completely to TelePrompTer readers, younger and brisker, some of them very slick and many of them no fun. Both parties have shortened sign-waving, chanting demonstrations. . . .

Step 2:

While many of the changes may be for the best, *there is something synthetic about this new kind of convention.* There is a lack of spontaneity, a sense of stuffy self-consciousness. There is something unreal about seeing a well-known newscaster starting across the floor to interview a delegate and getting stopped for an autograph. . . .

Step 3:

Nevertheless, *television coverage of conventions manages to get across to us a great deal about the way our political system works.* We are still a nation of different parts. The conventions are the occasions that bring various coalitions together every four years to pull and haul at one another; to test old power centers and form new ones; to compromise and, yes, to raise a little hell together in a carnival atmosphere. . . .

## PA1c   Developing the Paragraph                    *dev*

Build up your paragraph with a solid array of relevant detail.

In a well-developed paragraph, the topic sentence is backed up by details or examples. These details show what is behind the general idea summed up in the topic sentence. Well-chosen examples convince your reader that there is something to what you say. They make the reader feel, "I see what this means in practice" or "I see how you reached your conclusion."

Notice how much detail the writer has brought together in the following model paragraph. Notice how directly the details tie in with the point the author makes about Latin American culture:

*Latin American culture has been and is a dynamic element in the development of our own.* It has, for example, furnished more than 2000 place names to the United States postal directory. Its languages have influenced American English, as such simple examples as "rodeo" and "vamoose" indicate. Its customs are part of our "Westerns" on television. Its housing, its music, its dances, its scenery, its ruins, and its romance have been imitated and admired in the United States. One third of the continental area of this republic was for a long period, as modern history goes, under the governance of Spanish viceroys or of Mexico. The largest single Christian church in the United States is identical with the dominant church in Latin America.—Howard Mumford Jones, "Goals for Americans," *Saturday Evening Post*

If you chart the supporting material in this paragraph, you see a solid array of details that all point in the same direction: Much in our culture has roots or parallels in Latin American culture and history. Here is a rough chart:

Latin American Culture and Our Own

place names

Spanish words in English

"Western" customs

architectural styles, music, dances

former Spanish or Mexican territories

role of Catholic church

**243**

Here are some typical ways of backing up a topic sentence with convincing detail:

(1) *Follow up your topic sentence with three or four parallel examples.* The following is the kind of all-purpose paragraph that uses several different examples to illustrate the same general principle:

TOPIC SENTENCE

*The deep sea has its stars, and perhaps here and there an eerie and transient equivalent of moonlight, for the mysterious phenomenon of luminescence is displayed by perhaps half of all the fishes that live in dimly lit or darkened waters, and by many of the lower forms as well.* Many fishes carry *luminous torches* that can be turned on or off at will, presumably helping them find or pursue their prey. Others have *rows of lights* over their bodies, in patterns that vary from species to species and may be a sort of recognition mark or badge by which the bearer can be known as friend or enemy. The deep-sea squid ejects a spurt of fluid that becomes a *luminous cloud,* the counterpart of the "ink" of his shallow-water relative.—Rachel Carson, *The Sea Around Us*

First example

Second example

Third example

(2) *Use one exceptionally detailed example to drive home a point.* Sometimes one striking example or summarized case history is remembered where more routine examples would be forgotten. Study the following sample paragraph:

TOPIC SENTENCE

*Outside the Arctic, which is my second home, I find little comprehension of the remarkable skill, work, and endurance it takes for Eskimos to live off the land and sea in one of the world's most inhospitable climes.* The whale has traditionally been, and still is, a large and important part of the Eskimo diet. Even today, natives usually hunt it as their ancestors did—paddling up to the quarry in homemade driftwood-framed sealskin boats, then dispatching the giant with a hand-thrust harpoon or shoulder gun, the design of which was patented in the 1800's. As part of the hunt ritual, the Eskimos return the whale's skull to the sea to appease the spirit of the magnificent beast. Since bowheads are fairly wily, weigh a ton a foot, and sometimes grow to be 60 feet long, the crews require considerable courage. Their primitive method of

Key example
(the whale)

hunting definitely limits the take, which, until 1978, was unrestricted by law.—Lael Morgan, "Let the Eskimos Hunt," *Newsweek*

(3) *Follow up a major example with several parallel ones.* Often a detailed first example helps clarify the point. Then several additional examples show how generally it applies. The following paragraph illustrates this pattern:

| | |
|---|---|
| TOPIC SENTENCE | *Many Americans mindlessly oppose hunting, even in cases where animal populations are dangerously high.* |
| Detailed first example | In some areas of Alaska, wolves have become so prolific they are running out of hunting ground and prey heavily on moose, deer, and occasionally dogs. In the past, game managers curbed wolf populations by trapping and aerial hunting without wiping out the species. Still, whenever they propose to do this nowadays, they receive tens of thousands of letters of pro- |
| Second example | test. Growing deer populations in parts of California threaten to starve themselves out. Sea-otter colonies, |
| Third example | burgeoning along the Pacific coast, are fast running out of fodder, too, as well as putting commercial fishermen out of business.—Lael Morgan, "Let the Eskimos Hunt," *Newsweek* |

(4) *Draw on authentic detail from your personal experience.* The following could be a model for a paragraph in an **autobiographical** theme:

*My personal Mexican-ness eventually produced serious problems for me.* Upon entering grade school, I learned English rapidly and rather well, always ranking either first or second in my class; yet the hard core of me remained stubbornly Mexican. This chauvinism may have been a reaction to the constant racial prejudice we encountered on all sides. The neighborhood cops were always running us off the streets and calling us "dirty greasers," and most of our teachers frankly regarded us as totally inferior. I still remember the galling disdain of my sixth-grade teacher, whose constant mimicking of our heavily accented speech drove me to a desperate study of *Webster's Dictionary* in the hope of acquiring a vocabulary larger than hers. Sadly enough, I succeeded only too well, and for the next few years I spoke the most ridiculous high-flown rhetoric in the Denver public schools. One of my favorite words was "indubitably" and it must have driven everyone mad. I finally got rid of my accent by constantly reciting "Peter Piper picked a peck of pickled peppers" with little round pebbles in my mouth.—Enrique Hank Lopez, "Back to Bachimba," *Horizon*

245

(5) *Draw on relevant statistics to help drive home a point.* Many well-developed paragraphs use facts and figures to back up the key idea. The **statistics** in the following paragraph help show that the main point is not just one person's superficial impression:

> *Our democracy would be in trouble without quality public education.* Public schools are the driving force behind the high levels of social and economic opportunity in the United States. Fourteen percent of the people in the top leadership positions of our country come from the lowest socioeconomic groups—substantially higher than in other countries, where those rates hover around 3 to 4 percent. About 50 percent of working males are in jobs with a higher occupational status than their parents. Researchers have found that the occupational, educational, and income levels of previously low-income white ethnic and Asian minorities (such as Jews, Poles, Irish, Slavs, Italians, Japanese, and Chinese) are now equal to whites of native parentage—a tremendous change over the past decades.—Louis Honig, Jr., "The Case for Public Education," *San Francisco Chronicle*

# PA1d Transition *trans*

**Use transitional expressions to help your reader follow from step to step.**

A transition helps a reader "travel across" or move on from one point to the next. It provides a bridge from one idea or detail to another. **Transitional phrases** help your reader see how your paragraph is laid out; they help the reader follow from point to point.

Use transitional phrases to show where your paragraph is headed. A phrase like *for instance, for example,* or *to illustrate* takes the reader from a general point to a specific example. *Similarly, furthermore, moreover,* and *in addition* prepare the reader to continue the same line of thought. *However, but, on the contrary, on the other hand,* and *by contrast* signal that the argument is turning around. Objections or complications are about to follow. When you start a sentence with *it is true* or *granted,* you are ready to admit that an argument on the opposing side is true—you are making a concession; you concede or grant a point.

Here is a list of some of the most common transitional expressions:

| ILLUSTRATION: | for example, for instance, to illustrate |
| ADDITION: | too, also, furthermore, similarly, moreover |
| EMPHASIS: | indeed, in fact, most important, above all |
| RESTATEMENT: | that is, in other words |
| SUMMARY: | in short, to sum up |
| LOGICAL RESULT: | therefore, so, consequently, as a result, thus, hence |
| COUNTERPOINT: | however, but, on the contrary, nevertheless |
| CONCESSION: | it is true, granted, admittedly, to be sure |
| ALTERNATIVES: | on the one hand . . . on the other hand |

In the following sample paragraph, transitional expressions help prepare the reader for several similar examples, with the last one used to emphasize and reinforce the general point:

Many animals are capable of emitting meaningful sounds. Hens, *for instance*, warn their chicks of impending danger. *Similarly*, dogs growl at strangers to express distrust or hostility. Most of our pets, *in fact*, have a "vocabulary" of differentiated sounds to express hunger, pain, or satisfaction. . . .

The following sample paragraph uses transitional phrases to help the reader follow an argument. The writer first grants a possible objection—up to a point. But then the writer goes on to a counterargument that helps support the topic sentence:

Most of us are less tolerant than we think. *It is true that* we tend to be tolerant of things sufficiently remote, such as Buddhism or impressionist painting. *But* we lose our tempers quickly when confronted with minor irritations. My friends, *at any rate*, will rage at drivers who block their way, at acquaintances who are late for appointments, or at manufacturers of mechanisms that break down. . . .

The following sample paragraph traces several major factors that influence what we call intelligence: circumstances, time, motivation, training. Transitional phrases alert us that we are going on from one of these to another similar one, and that the last two are most important:

The fact that "intelligence" is a noun shouldn't delude us into believing that it names some single attribute we can attach a number to, like "height." In life, we face a variety of tasks and environments. Intelligence takes many forms: A machinist suggests a new production technique, a family manages in spite of inflation, a hustler helps build a huge conglomerate. *Similarly*, how intelligent a person's behavior is will vary

**247**

with time. Why should we suppose that these changes are fluctuations from some fixed, basic level? *Most important*, what people of almost any IQ can learn or do depends on what they want to do and on what kind of education and training they are given.

## PA 1e Coherence                                               *coh*

**Know how to improve coherence in a paragraph.**

A well-written paragraph has **coherence**; it "hangs together." The reader sees how the material in the paragraph relates to the main point. The reader can follow the major steps. In addition to clear transitions, use the following to strengthen coherence in your paragraphs:

(1) *Use recurrent or related terms to help hold a paragraph together.* In a well-focused paragraph, the same central term and various synonyms of it may come up several times. Such **recurrent terms** show that the paragraph is focused on a major idea. They help the reader concentrate on a major point or a key issue. In the following excerpt, notice the network of terms that relate to the idea of change:

> It is an ominous fact that in the long chain of evolution the latest link, man, has suddenly acquired alchemic powers to *alter* whatever he touches. No other species before has been able to *change* more than a tiny fraction of his habitat. Now there is but a tiny fraction that he has *left unchanged*. A bulldozer *undoes* in an hour the work of a million years. . . .—Paul Brooks, "Canyonlands," *Atlantic*

Notice how many words and phrases in the following paragraph echo the author's central point—the Victorian tendency to *avoid* discussion of sex:

> In Victorian times, when the *denial* of sexual impulses, feelings, and drives was the mode and one *would not talk* about sex in polite company, an aura of sanctifying *repulsiveness* surrounded the whole topic. Males and females dealt with each other as though neither possessed sexual organs. William James, that redoubtable crusader who was far ahead of his time on every other topic, treated sex with the *polite aversion* characteristic of the turn of the century. In the whole two volumes of his epoch-making *Principles of Psychology*, only one page is devoted to

sex, at the end of which he adds,"These details are a little *unpleasant to discuss....*" But William Blake's warning a century before Victorianism, that "He who desires but acts not, breeds pestilence," was amply demonstrated by the later psychotherapists. Freud, a Victorian who did look at sex, was right in his description of the morass of neurotic symptoms which resulted from *cutting off* so vital a part of the human body and the self.—Rollo May, *Love and Will*

(2)  *Use parallel structure to line up ideas of equal importance.* In both parts of the following paragraph, the repetition of very similar sentence openings signals to us that the writer is continuing the same trend of thought: "They are . . . They are . . . They tend . . ." Each of the sentences started in this way describes something that is part of the same basic attitude on the part of reviewers. Later, two sentences that are again similar in structure describe the contrasting attitude of ordinary readers:

With a few splendid exceptions, professional reviewers do not really read books. *They are* in the book business. And that makes a big difference. *They are* so bored and so jaded with the sheer volume of books which pass through their hands that if they manage to respond freshly to one, it's nothing short of a miracle. *They tend* to regard all books as guilty until proven innocent. But readers are different. *They regard* each book with optimism. *They expect* their lives to be changed—and often write to tell me that they were.

In the following paragraph, similarity in sentence structure helps us take in the two parts of a comparison:

Baseball does not pay its officials nearly as well as basketball does. *In basketball, an NBA official with ten years' experience* may make perhaps $600 per game, with over eighty games on the schedule. The official would make over $45,000 a season. *In baseball, an umpire with ten years in the majors* until recently made closer to $200 a game, with a schedule of about 160 games. . . .

# EXERCISES

A.  Write the missing topic sentence for each of the following paragraphs. In each of the following passages, *related material* has been brought together for a paragraph. However, the general conclusion suggested by the material has been left out. For each passage, sum up the general conclusion in a sentence that could be used as the topic sentence of the complete paragraph.

1. _____. Courses in ethnic studies began to appear in college catalogs. Community organizations representing ethnic groups appeared all over the country. Chambers of commerce in large American cities busily compiled lists of "ethnic" restaurants. Keepers of vital statistics records in many European towns and villages received requests for certificates of birth, baptism, or marriage from Americans engaged in the search for roots.

2. _____. The tribes of the Great Plains depended on the buffalo for much of their diet. A mixture of the dried and powdered meat with melted buffalo fat became pemmican, a concentrated and highly nourishing preserved food. In addition, the tribes used buffalo hides for their tents and as blankets. They used hides to make shirts, leggings, moccasins, and other articles of clothing. They stretched hides over willow or cottonwood hoops to make boats. Hunters used bows strung with the tough back sinews of the buffalo. The horns of the buffalo were the raw material for spoons and ornaments, and the hoofs became glue.

3. _____. In some arid countries, per capita consumption of water has risen tenfold thanks to improved sanitation. Underdeveloped countries need huge new water supplies for industrialization and irrigation. In the United States, many communities are facing water shortages. We have tapped most of the easily accessible sources of water in lakes, rivers, springs, and wells, and the fresh water that remains will often be prohibitively expensive to collect and distribute.

4. _____. People trying to protect whales have steered their small boats between the hunted whales and the sailors of catcher boats attempting to harpoon the animals. Other volunteers have harassed sealers on the harp seal breeding grounds on the ice of the Magdalen Islands. They have sprayed baby seals with organic dye that would make their pelts worthless for the hunters who club the defenseless cubs and then strip them of their fur. In one widely reported incident, an American released dolphins caught and penned up for slaughter by crews of Japanese fishing boats as threats to their catch.

5. _____. Many companies now employ private security guards to protect business property. The sales of burglar alarms and other security equipment for private homes have increased steadily over the years. Locksmiths do a booming business fitting entrance doors with multiple locks, dead bolts, and the like. Increasing numbers of private citizens buy handguns intended as last-ditch protection of their families and their property.

B. Study each of the following *topic sentences*. What kind of paragraph does it make you expect? How do you think the paragraph would be developed? What is the author's major point or intention? (Your instructor may ask you to write the paragraph that would follow up one or more of these topic sentences.)

1. Good friends of our family, after eighteen years of marriage, are getting a "civilized" divorce.
2. The rate of high school students going on to college has tripled during the last twenty years.
3. The modern "mature" style is for parents to punish a misbehaving child *after* they have cooled off.
4. Customs officials at an airport know how to make the traveler feel like a criminal.
5. When I went through high school, there were too many elective courses with little academic content.
6. The traditional American car had many features that had nothing to do with providing cheap and efficient transportation.
7. A major industry can shape the environment and determine the quality of life of a whole town.
8. The average person encounters many causes of frustration every day.
9. The student who causes trouble at school often has seen little but trouble at home.
10. Violence in movies is getting more realistic.

C. Practice writing the kind of *all-purpose paragraph* that follows up a key idea with three or four well-chosen examples. Choose one of the following topics for your paragraph:

1. We hear much about species endangered by the results of human technology or civilization. Choose three or four examples of animals (other than domestic animals or pets) that have survived well *in spite of* the onslaught of human civilization. Start with a topic sentence that makes a general point about the examples you have chosen. Then follow through with your examples.

2. It has been said that the flip side of progress is obsolescence. New inventions or technological breakthroughs gradually become old-fashioned and finally lose their usefulness. Choose three or four examples. Present them in a paragraph, using them to back up your topic sentence.

3. Several recent American Presidents have come from outside the East Coast political establishment. They were not Easterners; they did not have Ivy League degrees; they did not have names suggesting inherited wealth or influence. Choose your own examples. Use them to back up your topic sentence in a well-developed paragraph.

D. Practice writing the kind of paragraph that uses *one key example* to support a topic sentence. Choose a familiar stereotype about a group. Give a detailed account of one person from that group to show that the stereotype is misleading—or to show that there is some truth to the stereotype. Sum up your main point in a topic sentence. Here are some familiar stereotypes:

• Orientals: "studious, hard-working, very courteous, and more often than not shy"

**251**

• Irish: "hard-drinking, jolly but also capable of showing a furious hot temper, fond of sentimental old-country songs"
• German: "methodical and hard-working, humorless, tending to be cold and bossy"

E. Choose one of the following statements. Complete it two different ways, each time filling in a *different comparison*. Use each of the two statements as a topic sentence. For each, write the complete paragraph filling in the examples or details that follow through. Choose one:

A college is like _____.
A big city is like _____.
A small town is like _____.

F. Study the following *sample paragraphs* written by professional authors and student writers. Answer questions like the following about each:

(1) What is the key idea of the paragraph, and where is it stated in a topic sentence?
(2) Is any part of the paragraph a restatement or an explanation of the key idea?
(3) What supporting material is used to back up the key idea? What kind of material is it?
(4) How would you outline the overall pattern of the paragraph?

1.  Animals are always realists. They have intelligence in varying degrees—chickens are stupid, elephants are said to be very clever—but, bright or foolish, animals react only to reality. They may be fooled by appearance, by pictures or reflections, but once they know them as such, they promptly lose interest. Distance and darkness and silence are not fearful to them, filled with voices or forms, or invisible presences. Sheep in the pasture do not seem to fear phantom sheep beyond the fence, mice don't look for mouse goblins in the clock, birds do not worship a divine thunderbird.—Susanne K. Langer, "The Prince of Creation," *Fortune*

2.  People learning another language must completely immerse themselves in that language. I discovered this requirement after I studied French in junior high and high school. Much of the time, I spent five hours a week in the classroom speaking, writing, and studying French. In addition, I had on the average three hours of homework a week. I took French for four years before I made a long-awaited trip to France. I thought I had mastered the language and would have no difficulties with it. I did not realize how bad I was until I approached the natives and tried to speak with them. They could not understand me, and I could not understand them. I learned more French in the next three weeks than in all my years of schooling combined. The fact that everyone around me was speaking French and French only made all the difference.

3.  I was spending most of my time with a group from an orphanage down the block. I guess the orphan group was no more attractive than any other,

but to be an orphan seemed to me desirable and a self-made piece of independence. In any case, the orphans were more interesting to me than my schoolmates, and if they played rougher they complained less. Frances, a dark beauty of my age, queened it over the others because her father had been killed by the Mafia. Miriam, small and wiry, regularly stole my allowance from the red purse my aunt had given me, and the one time I protested she beat me up. Louis Calda was religious and spoke to me about it. Pancho was dark, sad, and, to me, a poet because once he said, *"Yo te amo."*—Lillian Hellman, *An Unfinished Woman*

4. When I was in grade school, I had many friends. They often invited me over to their houses. My parents would let me go if I asked politely. They sent me off with the usual warnings about not riding my bike in the middle of the street or being back in time for supper. One year my mother and I were looking at my class picture, and I pointed out a good friend of mine whose house I had often visited. Looking at his picture, my mother realized he was of a different race. I was never given permission to visit his family again. When I complained, I was told my friend was not a desirable influence. I believe that we are born with no natural instinct for prejudice but that we learn prejudices later in life from others.

5. The great majority of Americans favor some kind of registration or control of handguns. According to a recent Harris poll, almost 80 percent of the population favors a requirement that all handguns be registered with federal authorities. Advocates of such a measure point out that the easy availability of handguns is one of the major causes in the steady rise of violent crime. The homicide rate would go down if guns were not within easy reach of ordinary law-abiding citizens who lose their tempers. It is not robbers or burglars who commit most murders, but average citizens killing relatives or friends. A little more than 30 percent of murders are committed by robbers, rapists, or burglars. Forty-five percent of the murders in this country are committed among friends and relatives or between lovers.

6. We often retreat into the world of the imagination when we are not ready to face unpleasant reality. When I was in the fifth grade, my childhood was cut short by the sudden divorce of my parents. The ideal family of which I thought I was a part was suddenly dissolved. At the time, I started a diary that grew bulky over the months. It mapped out my weeks and told of special days when all of my family—my perfect family—went here and spent time there. I am not sure how long this make-believe continued. I do remember finding the diary later and reading the pages of those stories that had seemed so real to me at the time. I felt embarrassed at the thought of being caught with such fictitious tales. But at the time, I was merely protecting myself against reality, pretending I was growing up like my friends in families that had not known divorce.

G. In reading the following paragraphs, pay special attention to features that strengthen *coherence*. Point out any transitional expressions and show

how they help move the paragraph forward. Point out any recurrent or related terms. Point out any examples of parallel structure.

1. Recent census figures show that 53.7 percent of the college-age children of families with incomes of $15,000 and more were attending college. The proportion went downhill in direct relation to earnings until it reached a low of 12.7 percent for the same age group from poverty-level homes. In the past years, moreover, the percentage of college attendance among youths from lower-middle-class families has declined sharply. If this trend continues, young Americans from the old, established college "class" will increasingly dominate the campuses. Instead of helping to broaden the social and economic mix of the nation's leadership, higher education will then revert to its original restrictive function—to give children of inherited wealth an ever larger share of society's controlling positions.

2. Every time a man unburdens his heart to a stranger, he reaffirms the love that unites humanity. To be sure, he is unpacking his heart with words, but at the same time he is encouraged to expect interest and sympathy, and he usually gets it. His interlocutor feels unable to impose his own standards on his confidant's behavior; for once, he feels how another man feels. It is not always sorrow and squalor that are passed on in this way but sometimes joy and pride. I remember a truck driver telling me once about his wife, how sexy and clever and loving she was, and how beautiful. He showed me a photograph of her and I blushed for guilt because I had expected something plastic and I saw a woman by trendy standards plain, fat, and ill-clad. Half the point in reading novels and seeing plays and films is to exercise the faculty of sympathy with our own kind.—Germaine Greer, *The Female Eunuch*

3. All the evidence indicates that the population upsurge in the underdeveloped countries is not helping them to advance economically. On the contrary, it may well be interfering with their economic growth. A surplus of labor on the farms holds back the mechanization of agriculture. A rapid rise in the number of people to be maintained uses up income that might otherwise be utilized for long-term investment in education, equipment, and other capital needs. To put it in concrete terms, it is difficult to give a child the basic education it needs to become an engineer when it is one of eight children of an illiterate farmer who must support the family with the produce of two acres of ground.—Kingsley Davis, "Population," *Scientific American*

# PA2    KINDS OF PARAGRAPHS     *coh*

**Make your readers see a clear pattern in paragraphs that serve a special purpose.**

No two paragraphs are exactly alike. Often the organization of a paragraph is determined by its purpose: to describe a step in a process, to compare two related things, or to choose between alternatives. Study the way we lay out paragraphs that serve a special purpose.

## PA2a  Description, Narration, Process                    *coh*

**Make your paragraph follow a pattern appropriate to your subject.**

In description, in a narrative, in explanations, or in instructions, a paragraph often traces a pattern that is built into the subject matter. In such a paragraph, we do justice to what is there, to what we are writing about. At the same time, we make sure we take our readers along. We trace a pattern that they can follow:

(1) *Make a paragraph follow a clear pattern in space.* In describing a scene, lay out a pattern that the reader can easily visualize. The following model paragraph makes the eye travel gradually from what is close by (the house and its garden) to the far distance (the endlessly spreading tropical forest). We start at the top of a hill, go down cliffs to a river bed, and then go on to the opposite bank and beyond:

| | |
|---|---|
| TOPIC SENTENCE | *The house stood in what was certainly the best position in Mamfe.* It was perched on top of a conical hill, |
| (this side of gorge) | one side of which formed part of the gorge through which the Cross River ran. From the edge of the garden, fringed with the hedge of the inevitable hibiscus bushes, you could look down four hundred feet into the gorge, to where a tangle of low growth and taller trees perched precariously on thirty-foot cliffs. Round gleaming white sandbanks and strange, ribbed slabs |
| (river at bottom) (opposite bank) | of rock, the river wound its way like a brown sinuous muscle. On the opposite bank, there were small patches of farmland along the edge of the river, and |
| (distant forest) | after that the forest reared up in a multitude of colors and textures, spreading endlessly back until it was turned into a dim, quivering, frothy green sea by distance and heat haze.—Gerald M. Durrell, *A Zoo in My Luggage* |

(2)  *Make a paragraph follow a clear pattern in time.* In telling the story of something that happened, present major stages or major developments in **chronological** order—the way they followed one another in time. The following paragraph tells the story of a playground, from its opening to its gradual abandonment by the author and his friends. Notice that in a narrative the events often take shape without an introductory topic sentence. Notice the expressions and transitional phrases that help us follow the order of events in time:

(beginnings)         The orphanage across the street is torn down, a city housing project *begins to rise* in its place, and on the marvelous vacant lot next to the old orphanage they are building a playground. Much excitement and anticipation as *Opening Day draws near.* Mayor LaGuardia himself comes to dedicate this great gesture of public benevolence. He speaks of neighborliness and borrowing cups of sugar, and of the playground he says that children of all races, colors, and creeds will learn to live together in harmony. *A week later,* some of us are swatting flies on the

(later developments)  playground's inadequate little ball field. A gang of Negro kids, pretty much our own age, enter from the other side and order us out of the park. We refuse, proudly and indignantly, with superb masculine fervor. There is a fight, they win, and we retreat, half whimpering, half with bravado—my first nauseating experience of cowardice, and my first appalled realization that there are people in the world who do not seem to be afraid of anything, who act as though they have nothing to lose. *Thereafter* the playground becomes a battleground, sometimes quiet, sometimes the scene of athletic competition between Them and Us. But rocks are thrown as often as baseballs.

(end result)  *Gradually* we abandon the place and use the streets instead. The streets are safer, though we do not admit this to ourselves. We are not, after all, sissies—that most dreaded epithet of an American boyhood.—Norman Podhoretz, *Doings and Undoings*

(3)  *Make a paragraph trace a process step by step.* The following paragraph traces the major steps in a natural cycle. This kind of paragraph helps us understand how something works:

TOPIC SENTENCE    *Beavers often create forest ponds that for a time become the home of insects, reptiles, fish, otter, herons,*

(initial cause)

(new habitat)

(reason for
change)

(end of cycle)

*and other animals.* Beavers can transform a pine forest into an entirely new habitat by damming a stream. The pond will flourish for a short time—perhaps a few decades. The pond's creatures adapt to seasonal changes. In the winter, the pace slows beneath the frozen surface. Frogs and turtles bury themselves in the mud. But soon after the ice thaws, the natural rhythms accelerate. Dragonflies breed, fish spawn, and soon all the energies begin to prepare for another winter. But when the food supply is exhausted, the beavers will leave. Without their hard work and constant maintenance, the dam falls into disrepair and the water runs out. The area reverts to a swamp, then a marsh, a meadow, and finally a forest once again in this never-ending natural cycle.

(4) *Fit facts into a pattern that the reader can follow.* In presenting information, we often have several choices as we try to arrange the facts as part of an overall pattern that the reader can take in. One way to find a workable arrangement is to imagine the questions that might arise in the reader's mind:

TOPIC SENTENCE
(where observed)

(how produced)

(how ended)

*Comets strew debris behind them in interplanetary space.* Some of it is seen from the earth as the zodiacal light, which is visible as a glow in the eastern sky before sunrise and in the western sky after sunset. (It is brightest in the tropics.) Much of the zodiacal light near the plane of the earth's orbit is sunlight scattered by fine dust left behind by comets. Under ideal observing conditions, cometary dust also appears as the Gegenschein, or counterglow: a faint luminous patch in the night sky in a direction opposite that of the sun. Comets need to contribute about 10 tons of dust per second to the inner solar system in order to maintain this level of illumination. Over a period of several thousand years, the particles are gradually broken down by collisions with other particles, or are blown away by solar radiation.—Fred L. Whipple, "The Nature of Comets," *Scientific American*

# PA 2b  Comparison and Contrast                                   *coh*

**Use a paragraph to develop a comparison or contrast.**

We often use a paragraph to line up two things for comparison. Comparison can help a reader understand something difficult or new by showing how it is similar to something familiar. Contrast can alert the reader to important differences or distinctive features. Often comparison or contrast helps us evaluate things or make a choice.

The following paragraph follows the most common pattern for combined comparison and contrast. Similarities are shown first, and then differences:

TOPIC SENTENCE

Similarities

Differences

*People riding a moped should remember that it is not really a motorcycle but only a bicycle with a small motor attached.* The moped may look like a lightweight motorcycle, and it can weave through stalled traffic and crowded places like a motorcycle. Like a motorcycle, it is cheaper and easier to maintain than the bulky, gas-guzzling family car. *However,* the moped creates a real safety problem for people who ride it in ordinary traffic. It has much less weight and power than a real motorcycle. The driver depends on a very small, underpowered engine. The wind caused by a passing truck or bus can make the lightweight moped impossible to control.

The following paragraph develops a contrast between two sides of police work. The writer makes us see the contrast as her paragraph takes shape, without using an introductory topic sentence. As in other paragraphs tracing a contrast, a transitional expression like *however, but,* or *on the other hand* takes us from one major part of the paragraph to the other:

(First side)

(Second side)

Like any other job, police work falls into set patterns: patrol this sector, cover this assignment, check this complaint, interview this man, this woman, this child, investigate this company, work on this case. *But* always the unexpected, the sudden violent event, is also part of the routine. If there is an undue hardness in the voice of the traffic cop stopping an offender for a minor violation, it might be because he remembers, in some deep part of his brain, hearing or reading of some cop, somewhere—stopping a light-jumper, a speeder, an improper turner—a cop who, summons book in hand, was shot dead for no reason. If there is a dictatorial tone in the command of a policeman who tells a group of curious onlookers at some unusual event to move on, it might be because he has seen a curious crowd grow into a menacing mob.—Dorothy Uhnak, *Policewoman*

# PA2c Argument *coh*

**Write a paragraph that can serve as a step in an argument.**

When we reason with a reader, we try to present our points in such a way that a reasonable or objective reader would have to agree. We present major steps in the argument in such a way that the reader can reach the same logical conclusion. Here are several kinds of paragraphs that follow familiar logical patterns designed to take the reader along:

(1) *Write a paragraph that supports your point with convincing reasons.* In a well-developed paragraph, you can first take a stand and then present solid reasons for your attitude or position. In the following student-written paragraph, the author presents reasons showing that her attitude toward "convenience foods" is more than a personal dislike:

TOPIC SENTENCE

Reasons

*I object to convenience foods because they do not serve the cause of good nutrition.* These expensive, elaborately packaged, highly processed products are usually a combination of many ingredients, some of which have nothing to do with nutrition. Often the extra ingredients are there to provide long-term preservation and to improve coloring, texture, or taste. Refined sugar is one example of an often unnecessary ingredient. We eat too much sugar without realizing that much of the sugar we consume is hidden sugar. Almost every processed foodstuff contains sugar in some form: honey, molasses, sucrose, corn syrup, dextrose, and the like. Too much sugar plays a role as a cause of heart disease, diabetes, and high blood pressure. Salt is also abundantly used in processing beyond what is necessary for good health. The biggest argument against processed convenience foods is that during processing and packaging many of the original nutrients are lost and then artificially replaced by "enriching."

(2) *Trace a pattern from cause to effect.* We often explain something by first taking a look at its causes. Then we look at the results these causes have produced. The following paragraph has a simple **cause-and-effect** pattern:

TOPIC SENTENCE    *Europeans with time-honored experience in the technique of painlessly extracting cash from foreigners'
pockets have correctly gauged that Americans like to
travel abroad, provided they don't really have to leave
home.* They've seen the U.S. armed forces and U.S. oil
companies spend millions to give their personnel the
illusion of living in a European or African suburbia
filled with shopping centers, post exchanges, movie
houses, ice-cream parlors, juke boxes, and American-
style parking lots. Smart promoters now give Americans abroad exactly what they want. Hotel rooms are
furnished to please them, meal hours drastically
advanced to suit the American habit of eating dinner
at 6 P.M., arrangements made to satisfy the Americans'
affection for crowds, action, and noise.—Joseph
Wechsberg, "The American Abroad," *Atlantic*

Cause
(with specific
examples)

Effect
(with specific
examples)

In the following cause-and-effect paragraph, an author
writes about patterns of population growth earlier in this century. He traces two major causes and shows how they contributed to their combined result. Notice the transitional phrases
that help the reader follow the argument:

First cause    All the frontier industrial countries except Russia received
massive waves of emigrants from Europe. They *therefore* had
a more rapid population growth than their industrializing
predecessors had experienced. As frontier countries with
great room for expansion, *however*, they were also characterized by considerable internal migration and continuing
new opportunities. *As a result*, their birth rates remained
comparatively high. In the decade from 1950 to 1960, with
continued immigration, these countries grew in population
at an average rate of 2.13 percent a year, compared with 1.76
percent for the rest of the world.—Kingsley Davis, "Population," *Scientific American*

Second
cause

Combined
result

(3) *Use a paragraph to weigh alternatives.* We sometimes
start a paragraph by looking at one proposed solution or alternative and finding it wanting. We then go on to the more likely

or more promising possibility. The following paragraph first looks at a desirable alternative but then goes on to the more likely prospect:

|  |  |
|---|---|
| | History shows that wars between cities, states, and geographic regions cease once the originally independent units have amalgamated under the leadership of a single government with the power of making and enforcing laws that are |
| First alternative examined and rejected | binding upon individuals. *One might reason on this basis that if all of the industrialized and semi-industrialized regions of the world were to federate under a common government, the probability of another war would be greatly decreased. It seems likely that this conclusion would be valid if the resultant federation were as complete as was the federation formed by the original thirteen colonies in America. On the |
| Second alternative presented and supported | other hand,* it is extremely unlikely that such a highly centralized federation could come into existence at the present time; nationalistic feelings of individuals and groups, and conflicts of economic interests, are too strong to permit rapid transition. *Also,* those nations which have high per capita reserves of resources and high per capita production would be most reluctant to delegate their sovereignties to higher authority and to abandon the economic barriers that now exist.—Harrison Brown, *The Challenge of Man's Future* |

(4) *Use a paragraph to define an important term.* Often key terms related to a major political or social issue are vague or ambiguous. They mean different things to different people. When we define such a term, we mark off its boundaries; we show what we want to include and what we want to leave out. In the following **definition** paragraph, the author points to two different uses of the word *ethnic:* Sometimes people talking about "ethnic groups" seem to be thinking primarily of racial minorities. At other times, the emphasis seems to be on European immigrant groups other than the English. The author then states his own definition, which includes both of these uses and goes beyond them:

|  |  |
|---|---|
| TOPIC SENTENCE | *The word* ethnic *has come to have many different meanings during the years of the ethnic revival.* It is not that the word means nothing, but rather it means |
| First use | whatever the user wants it to mean. *Sometimes* it stands for "minority" and refers primarily to black, brown, native American, and Asian American, as in |

**261**

Second use           "ethnic studies" programs at universities. *Other times it is a code word for Catholics, as in* "the white ethnic backlash" or "white ethnic opposition to the candidate because of his Baptist religion." When the national news magazines or journals of opinion speak of ethnics, they mean Catholics, as when the *Nation* announced Daniel P. Moynihan as "ethnic." *When I*

Author's use       *use the word,* I normally refer simply to the variety of American subcultures, whether that variety be based on race, religion, nationality, language, or even region.—Andrew M. Greeley, "After Ellis Island," *Harper's*

(5) *Use a combination of familiar patterns where appropriate.* For example, we often present major causes in a chronological or historical order. We thus show how each cause in its turn contributed to the final result. The following paragraph summarizes the historical background of intercollegiate athletics. While doing so, it points out the major causes that have contributed to the current situation:

TOPIC SENTENCE    *In many American colleges, intercollegiate athletics has become a big business.* How did these institutions

Contrast with past    become as deeply involved as they are? *A hundred years ago,* athletic events at American colleges were true amateur events, with free admission. One of the

Milestone event    first big stadiums was built *in 1903,* when the Harvard class of 1878, to celebrate its twenty-fifth anniversary, offered the university $100,000 to build a stadium for track and football. As costs rose, specta-

Major factors    tors were *soon* charged for their seats. Institutions began to build bigger and bigger stadiums to outshine each other. Financial guarantees for visiting teams grew. The costs of scouting, recruiting, and traveling

End result    grew. *Today* a single large institution may employ forty coaches. The total athletic budget at a big football university may be between five and ten million dollars.

# EXERCISES

A. Write a paragraph that follows a clear pattern in *space or time.* Start with a topic sentence that sums up or previews what you describe. Choose a topic like the following:

- the layout of a baseball field
- building the foundation for a house
- disassembling the engine of a car
- the layout of your favorite park
- typing a letter on a word processor or computerized typewriter

B. Write a paragraph that develops a *comparison or contrast.* Start with a topic sentence that sums up the comparison. Choose a topic like the following:

- driving a car and riding a motorcycle
- organic and ordinary food
- downhill and cross-country skiing
- jogging and walking
- old-style and digital watches

C. Write a paragraph in which you take a stand and then *give reasons* for the position you have taken. Start your paragraph with a statement like the following: "I believe in _____ because _____." or "I object to _____ because _____." In the first blank in the sentence, fill in one of the following topics:

- large families
- stronger support for the U.S. military
- stricter speed limits
- rent controls
- religion in the schools
- health foods
- financial aid to minority students
- more financial support for women's sports

Use the rest of your paragraph to present your most important reason or reasons.

D. Write a paragraph whose major purpose is to explain *causes and effects,* or to weigh *alternatives,* or to *define* a key term. Here are some possible topics:

- the inflationary spiral
- affirmative action
- sensible diets

- protecting nonsmokers
- the causes of smog

E. Study the following *sample paragraphs*. Ask about each:

(1) What is the overall purpose of the paragraph?
(2) What is the main point, and where and how is it stated?
(3) What is the pattern of the paragraph—how is it organized?
(4) Does the paragraph serve a combination of purposes, or does it combine familiar patterns? Show how.

1. Three fourths of the world's people receive very little attention from American reporters. They are the peasants, the three billion people who are still traditional subsistence cultivators of the land. There should be no doubt that these people are worth our attention: all the major contemporary revolutions—in Mexico, Russia, Cuba, Angola—have involved peasant societies. In almost every case, the revolution was preceded by cultural breakdown out in the villages, because the old peasant ways and views of life no longer worked. The 450 or so American foreign correspondents only rarely report on these billions, because the peasants live in the world's two million villages, while the governments, wealth, and power—as well as telephones, cable offices, files, and typewriters—are in the cities.— Richard Critchfield, *Columbia Journalism Review*

2. Until as recently as a decade ago, the word *regulation* was applied almost exclusively to the government's attempt to control prices and licensing in such fields as transportation, electrical and gas utilities, communications, and oil. Today such agencies as the Civil Aeronautics Board, the Interstate Commerce Commission, and the Federal Communications Commission have this role. But the 1970's witnessed the growth of a new form of regulation that involves health, safety, and environmental protection. In less than ten years, Congress has created a federal bureaucracy employing 80,000 people, with the mission of protecting consumers or workers from harm. These new agencies act as agents for the public (including workers), which has no way of bargaining with business over product safety, pollution, or workplace hazards. We owe to these various organizations better air, less muck in our waterways, and fewer fatal mining accidents, among other achievements. Yet there are problems with this new "social" regulation. Thousands of highly detailed standards proved both confusing and costly. Automobile safety requirements have had no demonstrable effect on the highway death toll. A new program to make public transportation available to the handicapped costs more than providing them limousine service. The cost of social regulation has grown to vast proportions because society is billed for it indirectly.

3. I believe in large families because of the varied experiences each member of the family will encounter. I myself am one of five children, and the good times far outweigh the bad. I have always had someone around to be my friend, companion, and co-worker. Children from large families

have frequent dealings with other people and become aware of their occasional shortcomings: sloppiness, bad moods, laziness, and anger. However, the siblings also have opportunities to share many happy and joyous occasions, such as the birth of another child, many birthdays, a wedding, or a good deed being recognized. Growing up in surroundings where people cannot tolerate selfishness teaches the children common courtesies and acceptable social behavior. Learning to give and take, the child from a large family has a large lead over the children from small families.

4. Job opportunities for women have expanded considerably in one generation. When my mother graduated from college, the women she knew were expected to become secretaries or teachers. Knowing typing and shorthand was considered basic job insurance for a woman who wanted to work. In the last ten or twenty years, many of the stereotypes concerning women's work have begun to give way. Today, women are doctors, garbage collectors, truck drivers, plumbers, musicians, mechanics, and janitors. My best friend is a carpenter. It is true that it took her several months of defensive arguing and of being the butt of male jokes to become accepted. However, she worked as hard as any of the other carpenters and gradually became one of them. Ten years ago, she probably would not have had the chance to take the job and prove her competence.

5. There was in those days a great deal of optimism, shared by all levels of the black community. Besides a certain reverence for the benign intentions of the federal government, there was a belief in the idea of progress, nourished, I think now, by the determination of older people not to pass on to the next generation too many stories about racial conflict, their own frustrations and failures. They censored a great deal. It was as if they had made basic and binding agreements with themselves, or with their ancestors, that for the consideration represented by their silence on certain points they expected to receive, from either Providence or a munificent federal government, some future service or remuneration, the form of which would be left to the beneficiaries of their silence. And maybe because they did tell us less than they knew, many of us were less informed than we might have been.—James Alan McPherson, "On Becoming an American Writer," *Atlantic*

6. Immigration, exile, the tides of the Atlantic, the killing breath of famine, the murderous streets of Belfast had brought our parents to New York. We were to be the children of the second chance, living proof that a man can start over in his life and make something valuable out of that effort. But most of the time, that second chance had become warped by some grasping obsession with property. We began to visit friends who kept china closets filled with dishes that you were supposed to look at and admire but never sully with the fruits of the earth. People bought cars and two-family houses, and the dime-a-week insurance man vanished somewhere, and nobody needed credit at the corner grocery store anymore. The coal stove gave way to steam heat.—Pete Hamill, "Notes on the New Irish," *New York*

# PA3  REVISING WEAK PARAGRAPHS  *foc, dev*

**Revise weak paragraphs by bringing out the key idea more clearly and by strengthening the supporting details.**

In much student writing, paragraphs are not developed fully enough to drive home a point. They are not detailed enough to give the reader a good grasp of what is involved. Remember the following guidelines for revising weak paragraphs:

(1) *Revise paragraphs that lack a central focus.* Often a weak paragraph strays from one topic to the next. Remember that a good topic sentence gives unity to a paragraph. It can point out a logical connection that you previously missed or ignored:

RAMBLING:    San Francisco is a city of beautiful parks and public buildings. Golden Gate Park, with its spacious lawns and graceful ponds, enjoys international fame. The city's bohemian section became the national headquarters for jazz-age poetry and philosophy. Every tourist must visit Fisherman's Wharf and Coit Tower. The city is famed for its cultural events and conventions.

UNIFIED:    *Tourists and convention managers are irresistibly attracted to San Francisco.* Miles of varied waterfront, impressive public buildings, and spacious parks contribute to the city's unique appearance and cosmopolitan atmosphere. Fisherman's Wharf, with its seafood smells and colorful shops, attracts sightseeing crowds. Coit Tower affords a spectacular view of bay and city. Golden Gate Park, with its spacious lawns and graceful ponds, enjoys international fame.

(2) *Spell out a key idea that was previously only implied.* Anticipate the reactions of readers who want to know: "What does this prove? What does this show? What is the point?" In the revision of the following weak paragraph, the added topic sentence spells out what the readers would have had to conclude for themselves:

WEAK:    Last year I worked with a family that lives on a large Christmas tree farm. Much of what I saw there I found hard to believe. The children had to finish their chores, or they were not allowed to go out. Usually the father had them work Saturdays and Sundays on the farm. I can remember one incident that happened not long ago. The daughter, who is about thirteen, is a cheerleader. Her team was to attend a competition on a Saturday, but a Saturday that had been planned for work on the farm. Since she had already made the commitment to work on the farm, she could not go to the cheerleading competition.

POINTED: *In our modern permissive society, we sometimes see parents maintaining the stricter discipline of the authoritarian past.* Last year I worked for a man who was in no way permissive with his family. The family lives on a large Christmas tree farm. The father believes that if the children's chores do not get done, the children should not be allowed to go out. They usually spend their Saturdays and Sundays working on the farm. I can remember one incident that happened not long ago. His daughter, who is about thirteen, is a cheerleader. Her team was to attend a competition on a Saturday, but a Saturday that had been planned for work on the farm. Since she had already made the commitment to work on the farm, she could not go to the cheerleading competition. Even though I felt the father's attitude was very unfair, that was the way the family was run.

(3) *Build up the supporting material in weak paragraphs.* A basic weakness of many student-written paragraphs is the lack of concrete follow-through—a lack of specific scenes, incidents, and details. Readers need more than a general idea; they need things they can visualize and imagine. Whenever you start a paragraph, remember that your ideas will not become real for your readers unless you get down to specifics. Many unsuccessful paragraphs remain too general:

I was brought up rather strictly. I have learned to accept my parents' strict upbringing because I know they mean well. Having nice manners and being well groomed is an asset in almost any situation. People have always complimented my parents on how well behaved I am. . . .

A revision of this kind of paragraph might look like this:

I was brought up rather strictly. I have nice manners; I am well groomed; I am always punctual. People compliment my parents on how well behaved I am. I can remember being punished for one swear word, a chore not done properly, a messy room, playing music too loudly, and the like. As a result of being scolded for such minor offenses, I never dared to do anything really bad, such as breaking a window with a baseball, fighting with my little brother, crossing the street without looking both ways, or not doing my homework. . . .

In many weak paragraphs, the supporting material remains *too thin*. In revising such paragraphs, build them up by providing additional relevant detail. Notice how the following passage becomes more authentic through the filling in of detail from the author's experience:

THIN: I like politicians. I have spent a lot of time in their company. Mostly I have reported their doings, but on occasion I have assisted them. On the whole, they have proved better company than any other professional group I have had a chance to know well.

AUTHENTIC: I like politicians. *Ever since I started work as a city-hall reporter in New Mexico some thirty years ago,* I have spent a lot of time in their company—*in smoke-filled rooms, jails, campaign trains, shabby courthouse offices, Senate cloak-rooms, and the White House itself.* Mostly I've been reporting their doings, but on occasion I have served them *as speech writer, district leader, campaign choreboy, and civil servant.* On the whole, they have proved better company than any other professional group I've had a chance to know well—*including writers, soldiers, businessmen, doctors, and academics.*—John Fischer, "Please Don't Bite the Politicians," *Harper's*

Anticipate the reactions of the reader who will say: "Take a closer look!" Study the before-and-after contrast in the two versions of the following student-written paragraph:

SKIMPY: My grandparents' house is a typical Chinese household in the traditional mold. When visitors come to the house, the first thing they do is to remove their shoes. Around the house, the visitor sees souvenirs of trips back to Hong-kong—a dragon here, a painting over there.

BUILT UP: My grandparents' house is a typical Chinese household in the traditional mold. When visitors come to the house, the first thing they do is to remove their shoes. They may then put on a pair of house slippers if they wish. Walking through the house, the visitor sees many souvenirs of trips back to Hongkong. A dragon that is supposed to ward off evil sits on a shelf. Little white porcelain goddesses help protect the house. A picture made completely from shells shows a traditional landscape, with mountains in the distance. Almost any hour of the day, my grandmother is busy with the endless little chores that are expected of her as the traditional lady of the house.

# EXERCISES

A. For each of the following passages, write a topic sentence that would help turn the passage into a *well-focused, pointed* paragraph.

1. Raising four children does not leave much time for continuing an education. The desire was still there, but I felt fortunate to know who was running for President every four years. Upon moving back to my home state, I found myself enmeshed in a round of social luncheons, bridge games, and Girl Scout activities. While these were time-consuming, they were not satisfying to me, and I began attending discussion groups and an anthropology class at a nearby university. These were a new beginning. Realizing how little I know, I am once again in a classroom. This time I intend to take advantage of the opportunity.

2. Let us take a look at an average worker in an average American factory. Henry, an assembly worker, punches in at 8:00 a.m. alongside his co-workers. He places his lunchpail in his locker, takes off his jacket, and clothes himself according to regulations. On the assembly line, he tightens bolts on brake systems. In his years at the factory, Henry has seen and tightened more bolts than anyone could imagine. When the whistle blows at noon, he eats his lunch just as he did the day before. At five o'clock, after hours at his repetitive task, he punches out, changes his clothes, and heads home.

3. In many of my classes, teachers have asked me about my Irish heritage. Without my telling them that my father is Irish, they assume I am Irish from merely looking at my name. Many people admire the "fighting Irish" of the Notre Dame football team. On Irish holidays like St. Patrick's Day, many Americans share in the nostalgia for old customs and the old songs. Newspaper articles about the Irish often dwell fondly on their folklore and their love of song and story.

B. Practice *building up detail* in a multiple-example paragraph. Study the following paragraph as a model. Study its exceptionally ample use of relevant detail. (How many different examples can you identify?) Write a similar paragraph on a topic of your own choice.

*A person's touch makes what the other senses take in more real to the memory.* A wood carving appeals to the touch with deep grooves and parts that are rough as well as parts that are smooth. The fingers can interpret the richness of brocade and the rough warmth of wool. An ancient book becomes even older when one feels the fragile pages. A puppy tugging wildly at a leash feels like energy. Winter is felt in the hastily prepared snowball and the pine boughs that are brittle in the sharp air. A child must feel a hot stove before it becomes a thing to avoid touching. The energy of the sun becomes more apparent when one focuses a magnifying glass on one's fingers. A baby chick is something altogether new when one holds the cottonlike ball of feathers and feels its nervous heartbeat. An oil painting is only paint and canvas until one touches the swirls made by the artist's brush. A rose is only a flower until one holds it and pulls the petals from the intricate pattern. The surface of a rock is only light and shadow until one feels its ridges and ripples. Touching helps one to see and hear more clearly.

C. Choose a *weak paragraph* from a paper you have recently written. Revise it for clearer focus or more detailed development.

# 8

# The Whole Theme

# DIAGNOSTIC TEST

## INSTRUCTIONS:

This diagnostic essay will test your ability to write a well-focused, well-organized composition on a topic of current concern. The essay will test your ability to write serious written English, the kind of English appropriate for serious explanation or discussion of issues that are of general interest to educated readers.

Read the following theme topics carefully. Choose one that you can relate to your own observation, experience, and reading. Write an essay in which you draw on what you have seen, heard, and read. State your central idea or overall point of view early in your paper. Work out a plan of organization that your reader can follow. Use detailed examples to support your points.

Take a few minutes at the beginning to think, to gather material, and to prepare a working outline. If you wish, jot down some preliminary notes. Take a few moments at the end to correct spelling errors and punctuation problems. (You will not have time to copy over your complete paper.) Your essay should run to about 450 or 500 words.

Choose one of the following topics:

1. Many people feel that government today overregulates our lives. For example, we may be told how much gasoline a car may use or where we have to sit in a restaurant if we smoke. Where would you draw the line between necessary and unnecessary regulation of our lives?

2. Journalists often explain that news by its very nature deals with the unusual. What is ordinary is not news. Do you think television news programs today tend to exaggerate what is unusual, strange, or sensational in our society?

3. According to many observers, the types of people who are "untamed in the ways of society" and are therefore likely to commit crimes are increasing in proportion to the population as a whole. What in your opinion are the major reasons for this increase?

4. We are sometimes told that American advertising mirrors basic values of our society. What do current advertisements and commercials show about the values or expectations of Americans?

5. Some writers have claimed that young people in our society find few worthy objects or outlets for loyalty and devotion. They join groups ranging from neighborhood gangs to religious cults because they need something to be loyal to or something to believe in. How much truth is there in this claim?

## C1 GATHERING MATERIAL

**When writing a composition, start by gathering a rich fund of relevant material.**

What does it take to put a paper together? The finished composition is the result of a process. When you write an expository theme, you move through five closely related stages. These stages overlap, and writers do not always follow them in a neat order. But by fixing these five stages clearly in your mind, you can take some of the mystery and frustration out of writing. Think of writing as a process through which the finished product gradually takes shape:

(1) *You explore your subject.* You gather material; you mobilize your resources.

(2) *You bring your subject into focus.* You zero in on a key question or a major point. You limit yourself to what you can handle in detail.

(3) *You organize your material.* You sort things out and put them in order. You work out some overall strategy that suits your material and that fits your purpose.

(4) *You write your first draft.* You try to make sure that your ideas come through clearly, that they catch and hold the attention of your reader.

(5) *You revise your paper as necessary.* You fill in missing links or reshuffle parts that seem out of order. You proofread your final draft for spelling and punctuation and the like.

When you write your compositions, be careful not to neglect the first step. What you learn about organizing or polishing a paper will be of little use unless you have a rich fund of material to work with. Take time to work up your subject. Take time for *prewriting*—work up a rich supply of material to use in your finished paper. Draw on what you have observed, experienced, or read. Bring together from your memory and current observation whatever seems related to the topic at hand.

When you start discussing a topic, the first and most basic question in your reader's mind is going to be: "What do you know about it?" Jog your memory for incidents, details, and figures that tie in with your topic. Suppose you are writing a paper about welfare, or about the "welfare problem." Your first task is to sort out in your mind material that you might be able to use. Ask yourself questions like the following. Take rough notes on scratch paper, to use as raw material for your paper:

QUESTION ONE: "Where has welfare or the welfare problem touched my own experience?" Here are some ways welfare might have touched the lives of your family, friends, acquaintances:

• Elderly relatives were concerned about changes in Medicare. What were they worried about? What did they say?

• A neighbor is always complaining about people on welfare who are driving a sports car or spending their days on the beach. What details do you remember?

• A friend told you about his problems in trying to collect unemployment insurance.

• A friend of the family lost her job and tried to stay "off welfare."

To give your paper substance, be prepared to move in for a *close-up view*. Be prepared to talk in vivid detail about these people and their problems. Make your topic come to life by relating it to your own observation and experience.

QUESTION TWO: "What role does welfare play in current news and in current controversy?" When is the last time you read a newspaper report about investigations of alleged welfare chiseling? Have you ever listened to a political candidate who seemed to be running against the people on the welfare rolls? Have you heard someone present definite proposals for fighting poverty? Draw on current news and controversy to

• quote what officials and experts have *said*;
• cite striking *statistics*;
• mention a striking case or *case history*.

By drawing on this kind of material, you will be able to convince your readers that you are up to date on your subject, that you are aware of current problems and current arguments.

QUESTION THREE: "What reading have I done that would provide background for current discussion of welfare legislation?" In a classic like John Steinbeck's *Grapes of Wrath*, we see small farmers uprooted by an economy out of control. We see people willing to work but with no place to go. Books such as this vividly re-create the conditions that led to much of the welfare legislation with which we are familiar. They help explain why there are minimum wage laws, child labor laws, unemployment insurance, and social security.

The nature and extent of your preliminary exploration will vary for different assignments. Usually you will be able to draw on one or more of the following sources of material:

- Current *observation*—close firsthand study of scenes, people, objects, events.

- Past *experience*—the memory bank of everything you have experienced and read.

- Informed *opinion*—the views of others who have studied the same subject.

- Organized *research*—the systematic sifting of evidence from records, documents, and other printed sources.

# EXERCISES

A. Suppose you have been asked to write a paper on "Mainstreaming the Handicapped." What do you know about how our society treats the handicapped? Bring together from your own experience and observation what you remember about handicapped people. Ask yourself: What kind of people were they? What were their problems? How did they manage? What kind of encouragement or assistance did they receive?

For a preliminary collection of material, write *one paragraph each* about three handicapped people that you remember or that you have read about.

EXAMPLE:    I remember a teacher who was blind. He knew the campus well and insisted on walking without a white cane. He would often carry a coat draped over his arm. Holding the arm in front of him, he had some protection against unexpected obstacles. He read in Braille, and he had someone in his family read books or magazines and student papers to him. Discussing material in class, he knew all the relevant examples and details. He loved to tell stories or describe funny incidents and would laugh uproariously at his own jokes. Students knew they were lucky to have a good teacher; it was incidental that he was blind.

B.  Many teachers of composition today stress *discovery procedures* that help a writer explore a subject. Practice asking yourself questions that will help you discover what you already know about a topic. Suppose a topic requires you to express your views about the energy shortage. For a preliminary collection of material, write detailed responses for the questions listed under at least three of the following categories. (Your instructor may ask you to write responses for all five.)

1.  *The Popular Consensus*: What is the "conventional wisdom" or the theme of much current publicity on this subject? What are some of the things everyone says? What are some typical headlines? What do we read in typical newspaper or magazine articles?

2.  *Symptoms*: Where have you encountered signs of an "energy shortage" in your own experience? Where has the need for saving energy played a role in your own life or the lives of people you know? What incidents or experiences have brought you face to face with our energy needs?

3.  *Deeper Causes*: What are the major uses of energy in our society? What are the major sources? What major factors make the situation today different from that of earlier times?

4.  *Proposed Solutions*: What are some of the major alternatives or crucial choices facing us today? What unused or underexploited resources are there? What promising new developments have you read about? How would they work?

5.  *Dissent or Doubts*: What major uncertainties are connected with this subject? Are you aware of writers or officials who hold views radically different from those held by most people? Have you read any especially hopeful predictions or especially grave warnings?

C.  Suppose you have been asked to write about an especially meaningful or memorable event from *your own experience*. Perhaps you have witnessed a quarrel that taught you something about human nature or about the causes of violence. Or perhaps you have had a first serious encounter with the law. Or perhaps you have had a first serious experience with success or failure. For a preliminary collection of material, write responses to the kinds of questions listed under each of the five key headings that follow.

1.  *The Setting*: *Where* did the event take place? What was the setting? What were some of the sights and sounds that helped create the atmosphere of the place? Re-create the place and the time for the reader.

**276**

2. *The People*: *Who* took part? What kind of people were they? How would the reader recognize them? How did they look, act, or talk? Provide capsule portraits of the key individuals involved.

3. *The Situation*: *Why* could things happen the way they did? What relationships, or what events in the past, led up to the present situation? Fill your readers in on any background that is important for them to know.

4. *The Event*: *What* actually happened? How did things come to a head? Give the high points of the action in vivid detail.

5. *The Point*: What was the meaning of the incident for you? What did you learn from the experience? Why, when you look back, does it seem important? What did the experience seem to show or to prove? Explain the point of the story or the meaning of the incident to your reader.

D. Assume you have been asked to write about a vanishing institution: the farm horse, street cars, the passenger train, the corner grocery, the railroad station, or the like. Write down all you can remember about your experiences with it. Start from your earliest childhood memories. Write as fast and as much as you can. Follow a process of *free association*: let one thing lead to another as you write.

E. The following passages are a sampling of material used by student writers writing about the topic "Is Prejudice on the Decline?" For each of the passages, answer the following questions:

(1) What is the *source* of the material? Where did the writer turn for material?
(2) How *real* or authentic does the material seem to you? How convincing do you think it would be to readers, and why?
(3) Do you remember something from your own experience or observation that is *similar*? (Or do you remember something that points in a *different* direction?)

1. Prejudice and discrimination seem to be slowly fading out of our society. On radio and television, there are many shows with members of minorities in them. In department store catalogs, models are usually white, black, and Asian. There are more blacks in college now than there were ten years ago. There are also more black teachers. In sports, there never were black coaches or managers before. But some years ago, the first black manager in baseball was named by the Cleveland Indians. Black coaches made their appearance in professional basketball. People seem to keep their prejudices inside themselves more these days. We don't see prejudice out in the open anymore.

2. Discrimination toward Asian-Americans today is usually so unobvious that people of Asian ancestry may not be able to recognize the prejudices against them. I, personally, am very sensitive to verbal reactions. There is always the question "What are you?" The mere fact of being questioned makes me stiffen with resentment at the ignorance of those who felt that

they had to ask. There have been times when I have been completely at a loss for words on how to reply. I could answer, "American," "Japanese," and "Japanese-American," but somehow I feel unnatural and placed in an awkward situation. I do not consider myself totally American, because of obvious visible differences, nor do I think of myself as Japanese, since I was not brought up with the strict traditions and culture. Being thought of as a member of a minority makes me slightly uncomfortable, and responding to that question has made me sometimes regret my existence. I am a person, just like everyone else.

3. Every black person learns to steel himself for when he finds racial prejudice. As soon as he forgets, something like this happens: When I went to a big department store to buy something really slick with the accumulated loot from my birthday and a month of baby-sitting, a lady about sixty years old would not ring up on the register the items I wanted to buy until all the other people were taken care of. At first I didn't realize what she was doing until she snatched my things, rang them up, and wadded them in a bag. Then she abruptly turned away.

F. Many writers keep *journals* to record scenes, events, and ideas for future use. In a journal, diary, or log, we write down things as we remember them. We write down ideas as they come to mind. The writing that results is more candid and more spontaneous than a more carefully planned and structured theme. Start a journal. During the next two weeks, write in it at least three times a week. Record what you have seen, experienced, thought, or felt. Develop the habit of writing down in a rough preliminary form things that you might later be able to use as raw material for a more structured kind of writing. (Your instructor may ask you to continue your journal writing beyond the first two weeks.)

## THEME TOPICS 1

Write a theme of about 500 words on one of the following topics. Relate your topic to your own *observation, experience, and reading.* Include the specific details that will give your paper substance and make your points real for your reader.

1. How does our society treat the handicapped? What is it like to be handicapped in today's world?

2. Political candidates often talk about the "welfare problem" or the "welfare burden." What do you know about welfare or the welfare system in our society? What do you think a responsible voter should know or understand about welfare?

3. Women joining the labor force have often encountered traditional assumptions about what should be "women's work." To judge from your own

experience and observation, what new challenges have women taken on in recent years? In what new areas of work or responsibility have they been especially successful?

4. The traditional American "work ethic" encouraged people to do their work with a sense of pride and satisfaction. In recent years, well-known authors have claimed that many Americans are dissatisfied with their work or frustrated by it. Many Americans, we are told, hate their jobs. To judge from what you have seen of the world of work, how true are these charges? Draw on your own observation or experience.

5. A few years ago, observers of the American scene started to talk about the "nostalgia wave." They saw a return to the old-fashioned in dress, home furnishings, and popular entertainment. In recent years, have you seen such a return to old ways or old ideas in an area of our lives where it is not just a matter of superficial fashion? Describe the change, using detailed examples. Or do you know an area of our lives where there has been a major change toward the different and new? Describe the change with detailed examples.

6. At different points in this nation's history, various ethnic and religious groups have found themselves misrepresented by unflattering stereotypes. Such groups include the Irish, Jews, Catholics, Orientals, blacks, or Mexicans, among others. Choose one ethnic or religious group that you know well from firsthand experience as a member or as a close observer. Give the outsider a fair picture of what it would be like to be a member of the group. Pay attention to traditions, customs, or the like that have helped shape the common experience or shared way of life of the group. Describe real people and their way of life.

7. Is prejudice on the decline? Are the barriers of prejudice gradually breaking down in our society? Or are prejudice and discrimination merely taking new forms, with people being kept out in new ways? Answer the question on the basis of your experience and observation. Focus on one group of people who have been or still are the target of discrimination.

# C2  BRINGING THINGS INTO FOCUS

**Focus attention on one limited topic.**

A writer has to learn how to focus attention on one limited topic or on one major point. In practice, we do not write about birds in general, or about welfare as a large umbrella topic. We write because some part of our general subject is not well known, and we want to fill the gap. We write because an issue has come up, and we want to take a stand. We write because a question has come up, and we want to answer it.

Our reader wants to know: "What are you trying to accomplish? What are you trying to say?" This kind of question helps us bring a paper into **focus**. It helps us pull things together. The more clearly focused a paper, the better the chance that our point will sink in or that our information will be put to use. To bring your subject into focus,

- narrow the *area* to be covered;
- close in on one limited *question* to be answered;
- use your paper to support a *central thesis*.

## C2a  Limiting the Subject                                   *foc*

**Limit the area that you are going to cover in your paper.**

A writer has to learn to stake out a limited territory and then do it justice. No one could write a paper on a large general topic like "Education in America." Millions of Americans of all ages are in school, or attend at least some classes, or pursue various kinds of educational activities. Their goals, interests, and problems vary widely. If you want to write a paper about some part of American education, you have to bring this large, sprawling subject under control. You have to move in on some part of it so that you can take a closer look. You could narrow this general subject area in various ways in order to arrive at a manageable topic. You could focus, for instance, on a kind of education, or on a geographic area, or on a type of student:

| | |
|---|---|
| GOALS OF EDUCATION: | basic literacy, vocational training, education for citizenship, physical education, religious or moral education |
| GEOGRAPHIC AREA: | your home state, the inner city, a rural setting, the nation's capital, an Indian reservation in Arizona |
| LEVEL OF SCHOOLING: | preschool, grade school, high school, college |
| TYPE OF STUDENT: | gifted, handicapped, emotionally disturbed, bilingual |

By narrowing the general subject along these lines, you might arrive at a manageable topic like the following:

280

Space Age Science at Glenwood High
The English Language Is My Enemy
Mainstreaming the Handicapped Student
Busing: The Long Way to School
Prayer in the Public School

Often a large subject can be split into several medium-sized subjects. Each of these in turn may yield limited subjects narrow enough to serve as topics for short papers:

| | |
|---|---|
| GENERAL AREA: | Conflict Between the Generations |
| INTERMEDIATE: | Conflict over Drugs |
| | Different Attitudes Toward Sex |
| | Different Definitions of Success |
| | Different Attitudes Toward Progress |
| | Changing Views of Marriage |
| | What Happened to Patriotism |
| | Youth and the Military |
| | Religion Old and New |
| SUCCESS TOPIC | What Young People Look For in a Job |
| FURTHER BROKEN | Competition vs. "Working with People" |
| DOWN: | The Good Things That Money Can't Buy |
| | Making Do vs. Compulsory Consumption |
| | Staying Close to the Earth |

When you bring a topic into focus, remember that often "less is more." By narrowing the scope of your topic, you will be able to treat it in greater depth. You will be able to look at specifics. When you write on a topic of current concern, ask yourself: "How much narrowing should I do before I reach the level where people can see actual effects on their own lives? When would they begin to see what they themselves might be able to do about the problem?" Look at how the following general issue has been scaled down. The more specific topics make possible a paper that becomes specific enough to become real or convincing to your reader:

| | |
|---|---|
| VERY GENERAL: | Improving the Quality of Life |
| LESS GENERAL: | Cleaning Up the Environment |
| | Solving Chronic Unemployment |
| | Transportation Fit for Human Beings |
| SPECIFIC: | Bottles vs. Cans: A Problem in Ecology |
| | Plastics That Decompose |
| | The Psychology of Litterbugs |

**281**

## C2b   Choosing a Key Question                    *foc*

**Concentrate on a key question that your paper will answer.**

One way to make sure that your paper is unified is to think of it as your extended answer to one major question. The more specific the key question you choose, the more likely your paper is to have a clear focus. "How do crime comics shape their readers' attitudes?" is a very *general* question. Crime comics could affect the reader's attitude toward many things: police work, violence, minority groups, criminals, courts. Try to point your question at a more limited issue. Choose a question like the following:

- Is it true that crime comics equate ugliness with villainy, thus encouraging the reader to judge by appearances?

- Is it true that heroes look white, Anglo-Saxon, and Protestant, while villains look Latin, for instance, or Oriental?

- Is it true that in crime comics people are either all good or all bad?

- Do crime comics reveal the political sympathies of their authors?

A pointed question is more likely to produce a focused paper than a question that is merely exploratory. Avoid questions like "What are some of the causes of adolescent crime?" The "What-are-some" kind of question often leads to a paper in which many different things are mentioned but few of them studied in detail. Substitute a "What-is-the-most" or "What-is-the-best" kind of question:

KEY QUESTION:   What is the most serious obstacle to communication between teenagers and their parents?

KEY QUESTION:   What are three key features shared by successful television comedians?

KEY QUESTION:   What is the best source of alternative energy?

## C2c   Formulating a Thesis                    *foc*

**Sum up the major point of your paper in a thesis.**

The **thesis** of your paper is a statement that sums up in one sentence what the paper as a whole is trying to show. It summarizes the message of the paper or its central point. We lose the attention of an audience if we say a little something about many different points. We make an impact by concentrating on one major point and driving it home. Your thesis sums up your answer to the question raised in your paper. A well-stated thesis gives your paper a sense of direction, a sense of purpose. It satisfies the reader who wants to know: "What is the point? What are you trying to prove? What are you trying to show?"

A well-written thesis is a clear statement of a limited point. Whenever possible, state it in a single sentence:

TOPIC:    Urban redevelopment
THESIS:   Redeveloped neighborhoods lack the varied life of the grown neighborhoods they replace.

TOPIC:    What young people look for in a job
THESIS:   Young people today look for a job that has a personal meaning.

TOPIC:    Violence in movies
THESIS:   Too many of today's movies make killing seem quick and easy.

TOPIC:    Behind the Iron Curtain
THESIS:   People in Eastern Europe are fascinated by everything American.

In a short paper, the thesis typically appears at the end of a short introduction that raises the issue or brings the topic into focus:

**The Flip Side of the Coin**

Introduction    What do people envision when they hear about the "Americanizing" influence of education? Most likely, they envision a youngster who can barely speak English but who after a few years of school speaks fluent American and shares all the tastes and dislikes of his peers. This stereo-
THESIS          type is not always true, though. *Many young Americans continue to speak a second language on the playground and at home, and they retain many of the ways of their own group.*

The rest of this paper would present the observations, experiences, and information on which the author's thesis is based. It would *support* the thesis with relevant details, examples, or arguments. Often the conclusion of such a paper echoes or reinforces the central thesis in some way.

**283**

Remember:

(1)  *A good thesis pulls together your previous observations or available information.* Suppose you have observed handicapped students in your own classes and on your campus. You have observed changes designed to make buildings more accessible for such students. You have read about how schools are implementing laws about mainstreaming handicapped students. Everything you have observed and read will influence your final conclusion:

THESIS:    Everywhere in American education, handicapped students are playing a more visible and more independent role.

Not every conclusion you present as the major idea of a paper will be as positive or as clear-cut. Make sure your thesis reflects essential reservations or complications. The following thesis includes an important *if* about students in American schools who are learning English as a second language:

THESIS:    Most experts agree that children learn English fast—if the language of the playground and the neighborhood reinforces what they learn in school.

(2)  *A good thesis serves as a promise to the reader.* It serves as a program for the paper as a whole. It helps you decide what you need to include to satisfy the expectations of the reader. Suppose your thesis reads as follows:

THESIS:    Nineteenth-century American fiction often lacks strong female characters.

The reader is likely to say: "Let us take a look—maybe you are right." To keep your promise to the reader, you would have to take a look at several striking examples. Major paragraphs in your paper might be devoted to examples like the following:

First example:    In Mark Twain's *Huckleberry Finn*, the aunt is left behind, and the story revolves around the boy, his father, and Jim, the runaway slave. . . .
Second example:    In Melville's *Moby Dick*, we follow Ishmael and the all-male crew of the whaling ship in pursuit of the White Whale. . . .

Third example:   In Cooper's Leatherstocking novels, we move in a frontier world of hunters and scouts and braves. . . .

   (3) *A good thesis often hints at the overall plan of the paper.*
Thesis statements like the following give the reader a glimpse of
the ground plan of the paper that is to follow:

THESIS:   Contrary to familiar stereotypes, political opinion among college students ranges all the way from extreme conservative
through old-style liberal to the radical left.
(The reader will expect that major sections of the paper will
give examples or evidence under each of these three familiar
headings.)

# EXERCISES

   A. Suppose you wanted to write a paper relevant to a general topic of
current concern. How much *narrowing* would you have to do before you
reached the level where people could see actual effects on their own lives?
Note how the following general topic has been scaled down:

**VERY GENERAL:**   How Technology Runs Our Lives

**LESS GENERAL:**   The Spread of Automation
The Motorized Society
The Proliferation of Gadgets

**SPECIFIC:**   The Automated Assembly Line
Your Checking Account and the Computer
How Appliances Put the Customer to Work

   Provide a similar set of intermediate and specific topics for two of the
following general subjects:

   The Plight of the City
The Future of Marriage
Educational Opportunities for Minorities
Jobs for the Class of 2001
Freedom of the Press
Protecting the Consumer

   B. Of the *thesis sentences* presented in the following brief passages, select
the three that come closest to your own views. For each one, jot down briefly
what supporting material you could supply from your own experience and
reading to back up the point made.

**285**

1. *Students profit as much (or more) from a summer of work or travel as from additional course work in summer sessions.* Though such experiences are less systematic than academic learning, they are educational in the sense that they broaden the student's perspective. . . .

2. *The public schools do not fully practice the constitutional principle of separation of church and state.* Students, whether of Christian, Jewish, or agnostic parents, participate in Christmas plays and Easter pageants and sing religious songs. . . .

3. *Advertisers are reinforcing a stereotype of fun-loving, irresponsible American youth.* After watching the evening's commercials, we think of young Americans as smiling, tanned young people, forever playing ball and drinking soft drinks on a sunny beach. . . .

4. *Fear of violence restricts the activities of many Americans.* People stay away from public parks; older people are afraid to venture out into the streets. . . .

5. *Minority groups are becoming proud of their separate heritage.* Americans who used to feel like second-class citizens are asserting their separate identity. . . .

6. *Many of our older cities are making heroic efforts to create a livable environment downtown.* Redeveloped neighborhoods are designed to make people want to live closer to their downtown jobs; pedestrian malls are designed to bring customers back from the shopping centers in the suburbs. . . .

C. Study the following example of a *thesis-and-support* paper. How, and how well, did the student who wrote it support her thesis? How relevant is the material she provides?

## Success Is (Is Not) Having a Good Job

Introduction  For as long as I can remember, I have heard my parents say, "Money doesn't grow on trees" and "There is no free lunch." Every summer my father would ask, "What kind of kid doesn't have money jiggling in his pocket from his own efforts?" Last summer I worked in a real estate office, and my parents happily told all their

THESIS  friends about my first full-time job. *To many parents, success means security and a well-paying job, but young people today value people more than things.*

SUPPORT
First
example
  The parents of a girl I know have always wanted a son-in-law with a good job, making good money. The problem is that the boy she wants to marry is an auto mechanic. When she first started dating him, her parents objected because he was not "good enough" for her. They told her she would not be able to have all the things she wanted in life. She would not be able to travel or have

286

a new car. They told her he had no ambition (because he didn't finish college).

Her parents tried unsuccessfully to influence her feelings about her friend. They kept saying that his hair was too long. They mimicked his way of talking. She tried to tell her parents that she valued the person more than his job. Finally she gave up trying to defend her ideals. It is difficult for her to talk to her parents about anything, because they always bring up the subject of her friend.

Second example

A good friend of mine has a very similar problem with her parents. Her mother and father want her to marry someone who is in a profession—a doctor or a pharmacist. She was about to get married a year ago to a premedical student, but she never did. Her parents told her she had made a serious mistake in not marrying the boy. Their reasoning was simple. The boy was going to be a medical student, and he would be able to give her security.

Third example

My own parents constantly remind me that I should study hard and get a good job. As far back as grammar school, they were lecturing me about the virtues of hard work. My parents emphasized education so much that their children rebelled. My first semester in junior college, I was carrying twelve units. When my father found out about the number of units, he lost his temper completely. He kept asking why I was taking so few courses. I tried to explain that at the beginning twelve units was an average load, but he continued lecturing me.

The next semester, he again started to worry about whether I was taking enough classes. When I answered his questions, he called the school to check what I had told him. I realized I was losing my respect for him because of his lack of trust. I reached the point where I was losing interest in education.

Conclusion

There is indeed a gap between the young and their parents on the subject of success. One of the first things an older person wants to know about people is what they *do*. A younger person wants to judge people on the basis of what they *are*.

## THEME TOPICS 2

Write a theme of about 500 words on one of the following topics. Pay special attention to *limiting your subject* and *formulating a thesis*. Write a clearly focused paper and sum up your central idea as your thesis early in your paper. Support your thesis with specific details or examples.

1. Write a paper in which you support as fully as you can *one limited statement* about one of the following areas:

   - toys as a reflection of American society
   - the role of women in current American movies
   - images of childhood in American advertising
   - the image of the Indian in American Westerns
   - the treatment of conflict or violence in science fiction
   - guidance from teachers and counselors concerning jobs for women
   - teachers' attitudes toward children from bilingual backgrounds

2. The mass media are often accused of accentuating the negative. They are blamed for playing up everything that is unjust or sick in American society. What is *your* opinion? Give detailed examples to support your view.

3. Is intercollegiate athletic competition out of date in today's society? Does it perpetuate an image of American higher education as remote from the real problems and challenges of contemporary America? State your opinion in a thesis sentence early in your paper. Support your point of view with evidence or examples.

4. How much truth is there in the stereotype? Select one that you at one time shared or still in part share: the welfare chiseler, the militaristic ex-marine, the bookworm, the back-slapping Rotarian, the authoritarian father, or the like. Show how much or how little truth there is in the stereotyped picture. Sum up your conclusion in a thesis sentence early in the paper. Use detailed examples to back it up.

5. On subjects like the following, people often have strong personal views: the draft, sex discrimination, child abuse, integrated schools. On which of these do *you* have a fairly strong personal opinion? State your opinion as your thesis early in the paper. Then give an honest accounting of how you developed your opinion.

6. In the early seventies, about 50 percent of college freshmen felt "there is too much concern in the courts for the rights of criminals." Ten years later, the proportion had grown to 65 percent. What explains this shift in attitude? Where do *you* stand? Back up your point of view.

# C3 OUTLINING YOUR PAPER

**Work out a clear overall plan for your paper.**

The third major stage in the writing process is to organize the material that will support your thesis or main point. After

"What do I know about this subject?" and "What am I trying to prove?" you ask yourself: "How am I going to proceed? How am I going to arrange the material that I am going to use?"

A good paper provides a road map for your readers. It makes them feel that they are moving forward according to a clear plan. Your readers need to feel that you know where you are headed: As you write the first part of your paper, you already know your final destination. Before you start writing your first draft, work out the overall plan. Develop a general strategy that gives shape to your paper as a whole.

## C3a  Working Out an Outline                     *plan*

**Work out an outline that fits your subject and serves your purpose.**

When you write a paper that supports a central thesis, outlining the paper typically means marshaling the examples and the evidence that back up your central point. It means arranging your material in such a way that the reader can get a clear overview and will not get lost in the details.

Suppose you are writing a paper about what advertisers do to make products attractive to the consumer. You have decided that a few very basic appeals are used over and over. Again and again, we see ads and commercials that promise to make the customer's wishful thinking come true, or that reinforce basic fears. When you look over the ads and commercials that led you to this conclusion, your task is to sort them out in some convincing way. You need to group together those that seem to illustrate the same kind of wishful thinking, or the same kind of fear. We call this process of sorting things out **classification**. When you classify things, you establish basic categories, deciding what belongs together or what goes with what.

One major category or kind of advertising is familiar to all: A whole array of products—cosmetics, soaps, clothing, toothpaste, and even cigarettes—will, if we can believe advertisers, make us more attractive to the opposite sex. In this first category, we can place many examples of advertising that promises glamour and sex appeal. On the other hand, the sales pitch for homes or for cars often seems aimed at people who need to feel important. They need to feel they are somebody; they want to impress others. In a rough *working outline,* such differences might help you set up your first tentative categories:

—Attracting the other sex
    toothpaste commercials
    deodorants (?)
    fashions
—Status seeking
    car commercials
    real estate ads
—The easy way
    push-button appliances

Such a working outline is only tentative. It resembles an architect's preliminary sketches rather than a finished blueprint. As you explore your subject more, and as you start writing, you will complete the outline and change things around as needed. The final outline for your paper might look like this:

### The Art of Advertising

THESIS:   Much American advertising appeals to a few ulterior motives and basic anxieties.

  I.  Ulterior motives
    A.  Attracting the other sex
      1.  Toothpaste commercials
      2.  Cigarette ads
    B.  Status seeking
      1.  Car commercials
      2.  Real estate ads
    C.  Looking for the easy way
      1.  Commercials for push-button appliances
      2.  Commercials for "miracle" cleansers

 II.  Basic anxieties
    A.  The fear of rejection
      1.  Deodorant commercials
      2.  Commercials for antidandruff shampoos
    B.  The fear of disaster
      1.  Life insurance advertising
      2.  Accident insurance advertising

To arrange your major categories in an effective order, you may have to make some basic decisions about your strategy. You may decide to put the most striking or most interesting category first, in order to capture the attention of your readers. You may decide to leave the most important until the end, so that your readers will be left with a lasting impression. Often a writer will proceed according to the **order of difficulty**, going from what is most familiar or simple to what is new or difficult.

Suppose you wanted to discuss an important common element in books that have enjoyed great popularity with adolescents. You might first jot down titles as they come to mind:

> *The Pigman*
> *Catcher in the Rye*
> *Catch-22*
> *The Prophet*
> *Lord of the Flies*

To arrange these titles in a plausible order, you might decide to start with a *classic* example: *Catcher in the Rye*, the book about a "turned-off" adolescent that at one time everyone had read. You could then discuss outstanding *recent* examples, taking them up roughly in the order in which they became popular. Finally, you could discuss in detail a *personal* example—a book that meant a great deal to you as an adolescent. Your working outline might look like this:

> Classic example: *Catcher in the Rye*
> Recent examples:
>    *Lord of the Flies*
>    *Catch-22*
>    *The Pigman*
> My own favorite: *Slaughterhouse Five*

As this example shows, **chronological** order—the way things developed in time—often helps shape the writer's general strategy. The major divisions of the following outline reflect a familiar movement from "then" to "now," or from "traditional" to "modern":

### Generations in Conflict

THESIS:  The traditional conflict between parents and their teenage children is still with us.

> I.  The traditional generation gap
>    A.  Authoritarian fathers and rebellious sons
>    B.  Conformist mothers and independent daughters

II. Modern causes of conflict
   A. Freedom to be yourself
      1. Dress
      2. Hairstyle
   B. Unchaperoned outings
   C. Choice of part-time jobs
   D. Choice of friends and associates

Remember: Prepare an outline to help you work out and strengthen the organization of a piece of writing. Outlines help you visualize the structure of a paper; they help you confront and solve problems of organization. The more clearly you have outlined a paper in your own mind, the better your reader will be able to follow.

## C3b Writing the Formal Outline                    *plan*

**Use a formal outline as a final check on organization and as a guide to the reader.**

Your instructor may require you to submit a final outline with any paper that presents a substantial argument or a substantial body of material. Two major forms are common:

• The **topic outline** is most useful for planning a paper and for quick reference. It presents, in logical order, the topics and subtopics that a paper covers. Like other outlines, it often starts with a thesis sentence summarizing the central idea of the paper. Here is an example. Notice the use and placement of Roman numerals for the major categories, and of capital letters for the subdivisions:

                    To Join or Not to Join

THESIS: For today's realistic, cost-conscious college
        student, joining a fraternity or sorority
        makes sense.

   I. Academic benefits
      A. Inside information about teachers and classes
      B. Help with assignments

II. Social benefits
        A. Informal social life
        B. Organized activities
        D. Inside track in campus politics

   III. Economic benefits
        A. Current living arrangements
        B. Future business contacts

• In a **sentence outline**, we sum up, in one complete sentence each, what we have to say on each topic and subtopic. The sentence outline thus forces us to think through our material more thoroughly than the topic outline, which merely indicates the ground to be covered.

The following is a sentence outline for a paper that systematically surveys the factors that have helped or hindered women in their struggle for equal pay. Notice the use of Arabic numerals for the entries that further subdivide the first subcategory in the second major section of the paper:

### Why Women Earn Less Than Men

THESIS:  While some traditional causes of women's low earning power are becoming less important, current patterns of professional advancement will have to change before true progress can take place.

   I.  Some traditional causes for the low earning power of women are becoming less important as the result of social change.
       A.  Traditional prejudices about "men's work" and "women's work" are weakening.
       B.  Large differences in educational opportunities for men and women have slowly disappeared.
       C.  Traditional conceptions of women as short-term employees are changing as many women spend most of their adult lives in the labor force.

   II. Current patterns of economic success and professional advancement continue to work against women, nevertheless.
       A.  In most occupations, the years between age 25 and 35 are crucial to future success.
           1.  Blue-collar workers discover the job openings and training opportunities that lead to highly paid skills.
           2.  Corporations identify promising candidates for advancement in management.

**293**

      3.  Professionals finish advanced degrees and compete for promising jobs.

  B.  The years between age 25 and 35 are the most likely years for many women to be absent from the labor force or work part time because of family responsibilities.

III.  For women to achieve more nearly equal earning power, society must revise its patterns of promotion and advancement to provide greater opportunities for mature women reentering the labor force.

Check your finished outlines against the following guidelines:

(1) *Make sure your categories serve your purpose.* Let the subject of your paper help you determine appropriate categories. Writing about campus social life, you might divide students into Greeks, Co-op dwellers, and Independents. Writing about courses for vocational students, you might divide the students into nursing majors, engineering majors, police majors, and so on.

(2) *Avoid a confusing mixture of criteria.* It does not make sense to divide students into graduates of local high schools, disadvantaged students, and Catholics. There is no common principle of selection that would help your readers see how these categories are related. It would be hard for them to see how your mind jumped from one group to the next. It *does* make sense to sort students out according to geographic origin (local, rest of the state, out of state, foreign), *or* according to belief (Catholics, Protestants, Jews, agnostics), *or* according to social and economic background.

(3) *Avoid single subdivisions.* If there is a subdivision *A*, there should be a subdivision *B*. If there is a section numbered *1*, there should be a section numbered *2*. If a section covers only one major point or one major step, leave it undivided.

(4) *Avoid a long sequence of parallel elements*, such as *I–VIII*, *A–F*, or *1–8*. Try to split the sequence into two or three major groups.

(5) *Use parallel grammatical structure* for headings of the same rank, in order to emphasize their logical relation. For instance, if *A 1* reads "To revive the student's interest," *A 2* and

*A 3* should also be worded as infinitives: "To promote the student's participation"; "To develop the student's independent judgment."

(6) *In a topic outline, make each topic specific and informative. In a sentence outline, make each subdivision a complete sentence.* Make each sentence sum up an idea rather than merely indicate a topic.

# EXERCISES

A. Study the following example of a brief *classification paper*. In your own words, restate the author's thesis. Prepare an outline showing the three or four major categories that were set up by the author. Include subcategories where appropriate.

### A Life of Crime

"Lawlessness" and the "breakdown of law and order" have long been clichés of conservative political oratory. Candidates to the right of the political spectrum have often run against "crime in the streets." Today many Americans find that reality has caught up with rhetoric. Crime is everywhere becoming a familiar facet of everyday life.

According to police statistics, professional crime is steadily increasing. Burglaries are now an everyday occurrence in what used to be "nice quiet neighborhoods." In spite of television cameras and other safety precautions, bank holdups have tripled in number during the last ten years in many parts of the country. Increasingly, major robberies are planned commando-style and executed with military precision and ruthlessness.

Just as disturbing is the steady growth in personal moral laxity on the part of ordinary people: petty pilfering, routine stealing, "ripping off" the employer or the customer. Dresses put on the clothesline to dry disappear. Watches and wallets disappear from high school locker rooms. Recently a principal was caught stealing petty change from vending machines.

In many areas of our lives, we see a steady increase of personal aggressiveness and vindictiveness. Students threaten and bully teachers. Customers settle an argument with the bartender by firebombing the establishment. People taken to court vow to "get" witnesses who testify against them.

We see the same trend toward more lawlessness on the political scene, where it is projected onto a larger screen. Newspaper readers and television viewers have become accustomed to assassinations, bombings, and reprisals as part of the daily news. For many years, terrorism has been a major unsolved political problem in places like Northern Ireland, Italy, and the Near East. People are not allowed on airplanes until they have been searched for deadly weapons. High government officials drive to work surrounded by bodyguards.

As the result of these and similar trends, many ordinary citizens are losing faith in traditional law enforcement. People are ready to join vigilante groups and to "take the law in their own hands." Can you blame them?

B. The following interest inventory was adapted from a student paper. How would you *classify* the items in order to present them in a plausible sequence? Prepare a brief outline showing how you have sorted them out.

1. contact sports
2. coffee dates
3. religious retreats
4. taking a friend to the movies
5. work for worldwide disarmament
6. long hikes
7. beach barbecues
8. vacation trips
9. fellowship meetings
10. swimming
11. social work
12. student government

C. A student paper listed the following points as guidelines for parents. How would you sort out these points into *major categories*? Prepare an outline reflecting what you would consider the most plausible classification.

1. Parents should avoid swearing or vulgarity.
2. Parents should not contradict each other in the presence of their children.
3. Parents should provide encouragement when children do something constructive.
4. Punishment should be impartial when there are several children.
5. Parents should not shower their children with gifts.
6. One parent should not overrule the other in matters of discipline.
7. Parents should show affection, whether by a pat on the back or a good word.
8. Parents should respect children as individuals, letting them develop their own likes and dislikes.
9. Parents should not be overprotective.
10. Children should be allowed to learn from their own mistakes.
11. Parents should refrain from quarreling in the presence of their children.
12. Parents should teach good manners by example.
13. Parents should allow their children to choose their own friends.

14. Parents should not give vent to their frustrations or irritations by punishing their children.
15. Parents should not take notice of a child only when it does something wrong.

D. What is your favorite reading matter? Have you ever sorted it out into recurrent types? Choose one of the following: science fiction, detective novels, Western novels, historical novels, nineteenth-century British fiction, current American short stories, biographies, autobiographies, books on travel or exploration. Sort out the books you have read in this major category into a few major types. For each, write a short paragraph indicating the major features that examples of the type have in common.

E. Prepare both a *topic outline* and a *sentence outline* of a paper you have recently written. Observe conventional outline form.

## THEME TOPICS 3

Write a theme of about 500 words on one of the following topics. Pay special attention to working out a *clear overall plan* for your paper. Set up major categories and develop each well with relevant details or examples.

1. Write a paper in which you divide a *group of people* into three or four major categories. For instance, you might classify children as leaders, followers, and loners; or teachers as authoritarian, chummy, and withdrawn. Make sure to establish categories that reflect your own experience and that you can fill in with graphic detail.

2. Have you found that one of the following labels covers *different things*? Classify them, setting up several major categories and describing them as fully as you can. Choose one of the following:

   • crime comics
   • war movies
   • commercials
   • college courses
   • comedians
   • radicals
   • fads

3. Jobs vary widely in the rewards they offer or the qualifications they require. Write a paper about *jobs or careers*. Establish three or four major categories on the basis of what they offer the jobholder or what they require of the person. Use detailed examples.

4. Many different activities go on under the general heading of athletics. For instance, some people distinguish between sports that are mainly spectator

sports and other sports that allow wide participation by ordinary individuals. What do *you* think are the most important major kinds? What makes them different—what sets your major categories apart?

5.    What are major different styles of architecture in the American city? What are some kinds of buildings that we see over and over again? What sets the different kinds apart? Describe examples in vivid detail.


# C4    PATTERNS OF ORGANIZATION

**Know and practice organizing strategies appropriate to different writing tasks.**

Much of the organizing we do for a short paper fits under the general heading of **classification**. We sort things out to group together those that share common qualities setting them off from other groups. Suppose you are writing about the qualities that in your opinion are most important in an effective teacher. In sorting out material from your own observation and experience, you may set up three major categories:

• evidence that shows knowledge of the *subject matter*;

• evidence that shows *ability to organize* and to present things in an intelligible fashion;

• evidence of a friendly and encouraging *manner* with students.

Other subjects have natural subdivisions or obvious parts. A writer investigating the numerical strength of the nation's armed forces is likely to look first at the number of people on *active* duty, and second at the *reserves* of trained personnel.

Nevertheless, the plan you develop for a paper often depends on the purpose you are trying to accomplish. Often your overall plan will be shaped by the strategy you adopt for reaching the reader. Different patterns of organization and different organizing strategies become appropriate as a writer takes on different tasks.

# C4a Process　　　　　　　　　　　　*plan*

**Trace essential steps in the right order to make your reader understand how something works.**

To make a reader see how something works or how it came about, we often have to trace a **process**. We follow a process through its major stages so that the reader can understand it and see it as a whole. Writing of this kind trains us to use patient observation and good judgment. In tracing a process, we have to pay careful attention to how one thing leads to another. We have to decide what is essential and what is optional.

Describing the process of paper making, we trace the necessary steps that turn wood chips first into pulp, then into a paper web, and finally into sheets of paper. Describing the process of radio transmitting, we follow the newscaster's voice through microphone and transmitter to the receiving set and the listener's ear. What we learn from the process theme has many applications. We apply it when we

- explain a *scientific* process:
  How energy of motion converts into electricity
  How sediments build up on the ocean floor
  How a translation machine scans a sentence

- give *directions*:
  How to plant a lawn
  How to make wine from your own grapes
  How to make pottery

- trace a *historical* chain of events:
  How nomads became villagers
  How the railroad transformed rural America

The following instructions will help you write better process themes:

(1) *Pay careful attention to detail.* No one can make a machine work, or produce an enameled vase, who does not have a concern for the little things that add up to the whole. Take in details like those in the following paragraph. Note that they follow **chronological** order—step by step as they happen in time:

**299**

A black and white garden spider dropped down from one of the higher branches of the tree. He picked a flimsy, forked twig, covered with large drops of water from the rain, and swung in on it like a toy glider coming in for a landing. As he caught hold of it, it sagged under his weight, and several large water drops slid off to the ground below. The spider sat on the twig until it ceased vibrating. Then he carefully moved to the end of one of the forks. He first walked rather fast, but halfway down the twig fork, he slipped and turned upside down. He tried to right himself but failed, so he moved along the twig upside down, fighting both the vibrations of the twig and the large water drops. When the spider reached the end of the twig fork, he carefully fastened a silver thread to the end of the fork. Then he slowly righted himself on the twig. He proceeded to crouch in a peculiar position, somewhat like a sprinter set in his starting blocks. With a mighty leap, he jumped toward another twig fork, but he missed it. He swung down below the twig and hung by his silver thread until the vibrations and his swinging stopped. He climbed up the thread and repeated the maneuver, and again he failed. The third time he jumped, he caught the other twig and proceeded to fasten his silver thread to it. Running back between the two forks, the spider began to build his web.

(2) *Break up the whole sequence into major divisions, or emphasize the most significant steps.* An "and-then" sequence becomes confusing, because it gives equal emphasis to many parts, events, or operations. Suppose your paper follows the assembly line in an automobile factory: The basic parts of the body are welded together; the doors are hung; the body shells are dipped into a chemical solution; they are spray-painted; they are dried in ovens; electrical wiring is laid; door locks and other mechanisms are installed; glass is installed; interior lining is installed; and so on. Try to break up the body's progress into three major stages:

I. Building the body shell
II. Painting the body
III. Outfitting the painted shell

(3) *Do justice to one major stage at a time.* Give your readers a chance to concentrate on one essential step or one essential part of a procedure until it is clear in their minds. The faster you move on, the better the chance that you will leave your readers behind. The following might be a selection from safety instructions for drivers. The writer's task would be to fix steps like the following firmly in the reader's mind:

| First step: | To bring a skidding car back under control, you have to know how to use three different ways of controlling the movement of your car. *First*, turn the steering wheel as hard and fast as necessary. Use it to make your wheels point in the direction of the skid. Work your wheel rapidly if the skidding car keeps changing its direction. . . . |
|---|---|
| Second step: | *Second,* make use of your gas pedal to help you control the car. Ease your foot off the pedal when the car first begins to skid, but keep your foot hovering over it. Press down on the pedal lightly when your front wheels seem to be pointing in the direction of the skid. . . . |
| Third step: | *Third,* know when to use your brake pedal—and especially when not to use it. Do not use it until you feel you are fully in charge of the car. Press down on the brake gently to slow the movement of your car. . . . |

## C4b   Comparison and Contrast                        *plan*

**Use comparison and contrast to bring out similarities and differences.**

In writing that explains or clarifies, the writer often has to look at several related things and show how they are similar or how they differ. Such comparison or contrast presents a special challenge: The writer has to lay out the relevant details in such a way that the reader can follow the cross-references and take in the overall picture that emerges.

The need for comparison and contrast often arises when we are faced with a choice. We often compare and contrast to justify a preference. To justify our preference for a lackluster incumbent over a more dynamic challenger, we may compare their records on a number of crucial points. More basically, comparison and contrast help us notice things we previously took for granted. We learn to identify a style of architecture by noting the features it shares with other styles and those features that set it apart. We are more vividly aware of the American way of doing things after we spend a year in Mexico or in France.

For fruitful comparison and contrast, the author must *line up* the material so that one thing throws light upon the other. Here are the two basic ways of organizing the comparison-and-contrast paper:

(1)  *The author discusses two things together—feature by feature, point by point.* A **point-by-point comparison** takes up one feature of, say, an imported car and then immediately asks: "Now what does this look like for a competing domestic model?" A typical outline would look like this:

### Follow the Leader

THESIS:  It is becoming harder to tell a best-selling imported car apart from its closest domestic competitor.

    I.   Economy
        A.   Initial cost (data for both cars)
        B.   Cost of operation (data for both cars)
        C.   Resale value (data for both cars)

   II.   Comfort and convenience
        A.   Space for passengers and luggage (data for both cars)
        B.   Maneuverability (data for both cars)

 III.   Performance
        A.   Acceleration and speed (data for both cars)
        B.   Durability (data for both cars)

(2)  *The author discusses two things separately but takes up the same points in the same order.* Such a **parallel-order comparison** gives a coherent picture of each of the two things being compared. At the same time, it helps the reader see the connections between the two. The following is an outline for a parallel-order comparison of two of the most famous heroes of classical antiquity: Odysseus (or Ulysses) and Achilles. In organizing the material, the writer starts with a basic similarity but then goes on to important differences:

### Two Epic Heroes

THESIS:  Odysseus and Achilles are both great warriors, but they differ in the other qualities that make an epic hero admirable.

    I.   Odysseus as epic hero
        A.   Great warrior (unsurpassed in archery, etc.)
        B.   Accomplished orator (successful in pleading his own cause)
        C.   Shrewd counselor (carefully weighing facts and situations)
        D.   Very human character (loves good food and wine)

II. Achilles as epic hero
   A.  Great warrior (triumphs over Hector)
   B.  Not a great speaker (tends to be haughty and insolent)
   C.  Impulsive person (quick to yield to resentment)
   D.  Half divine (indifferent to food)

This outline looks at the same major categories or qualifications for both heroes, in identical order. The closely parallel structure keeps the paper from breaking up into two separate accounts. It prevents the kind of loosely organized comparison that finally forces the readers to find important connections on their own.

# C4c   Cause and Effect                                *plan*

**Explain things by tracing causes and their effects.**

We often feel we understand something after we see what caused it. As writers, it is often our task to trace a chain from cause to effect. In analyzing a problem, we often try to identify the causes that helped create it. Our readers will want to know: "What brought this on? What caused the present situation?" Once we sort out the major causes (or identify the main cause), our readers might be ready to listen to a possible solution.

The following might be a sentence outline of a magazine article on what has happened to the traditional family. The article would first trace major factors that have helped weaken the traditional structure of family life. It would then sort out some of the most important effects or results:

### The Family Out of Favor

THESIS:   Many forces in modern society weaken family ties and make people lose the traditional benefits of family life.

   I.  Many forces in modern society weaken or work against the traditional family unit.
      A.  In our upwardly mobile society, success often means opportunities for travel and entertainment from which families are excluded.
      B.  The modern city, cut up by freeways and requiring long commuting hours, has lost the network of small local

**303**

stores and local services that provided the framework for traditional family life.

C.   To many modern individuals, self-fulfillment means liberation from traditional ties and obligations.

D.   The mass media play up divorce statistics and play down the large number of lifelong marriages that continue to exist.

II.   The independent modern individual pays a price for the loss of traditional family ties.

A.   Many people lack the sense of trust and belonging that children used to acquire in a closely knit family.

B.   Many people today lack the network of kinship ties that used to be a source of economic and political support for many immigrant families.

C.   People outside the large traditional family do not experience the process of conflict and reconciliation that teaches mutual tolerance and mutual adjustment.

This outline reminds us of some of the features that make a careful analysis of causes and effects worth reading. It recognizes *several* major causes. We would often like to find one major root cause (and thereby simplify the matter). But in many situations, we have to recognize that several major factors may have contributed to a combined result. At the same time, we never lose sight of the major common thread. From the beginning, the author of the original article made it clear that he *regretted* the weakening of traditional family ties. This basic attitude, spelled out in the unifying thesis, is reflected or mirrored throughout the detailed points.

# C4d   Pro and Con                                        *plan*

**Weigh the arguments pro and con to reach a balanced conclusion.**

In a systematic argument, we take the reader along step by step to the desired conclusion. We present our thinking or our reasoning on a subject in such a way that our readers can arrive at the same logical result as we did. One effective way to structure such writing is to line up the arguments on two sides of an issue. We first discuss the advantages of a proposal or a program, and then the disadvantages. We first present arguments in support of a new method or approach; then we look at possible objections. Ideally, as the strengths and weaknesses of the opposing arguments become apparent, a balanced conclusion will emerge that reasonable people can accept.

The successful **pro-and-con** paper is effective because it follows an exceptionally clear overall pattern. We expect that the arguments in the first half of the paper will all point in the same direction. Roughly halfway into the paper, a link like *however* or *nevertheless* or *on the other hand* will signal that it is time to turn to the arguments on the other side. Toward the end, we expect some phrase like "Weighing the arguments on both sides, we must conclude that. . . ." The writer is ready for summing up and balancing off the opposing arguments.

The following excerpts show the structure of a pro-and-con paper on the relative merits of school and work:

### Dropping Out

Current proposal
    Recently pressures have built up to reduce the number of years of compulsory education. Students would be allowed to leave school earlier than is now legally possible. Students who want to go to work would have a chance to do so earlier. . . .

PRO
    *People supporting this trend point out the value of work for young people.* Students with strong mechanical aptitudes who would enjoy their work may find little in academic courses that is of interest to them. Earning a paycheck and developing a good attendance record on the job are responsibilities that are as educational as any the same student would encounter in school. . . .

CON
    *However, many students may later regret leaving school too early.* Many students eager to leave school are not yet able to pass basic proficiency examinations for such "survival skills" as written communication or mathematics. They will find themselves permanently handicapped in a more and more competitive world of work. . . .

Balanced conclusion
    *The solution might be to encourage students to become familiar with the world of work while they are still in school.* Many students would profit from current plans that allow them to combine school and work. Students would work part time. They would be given academic credit for work experience. In turn, their experience on the job would help them see how things the school has to offer are valuable to someone starting a career. . . .

When we deal with a controversial topic, the advantage of the pro-and-con paper is that it treats an issue as a genuine issue—as an open question worth thinking about. The following might be the outline of a pro-and-con paper on a subject of current controversy:

**A Difficult Choice**

THESIS: Many people are having second thoughts about the easy availability of abortions, considering abortion instead as a last resort.

I. Arguments in favor of abortion
    A. Social and political arguments
        1. Unwanted children as a social problem
        2. Large families as a cause of poverty
        3. The need for protecting victims of rape
    B. The right of women to control their own lives

II. Arguments against abortion
    A. Medical arguments
        1. Possibility of permanent physical damage
        2. Mental or emotional aftereffects
    B. Religious arguments

III. Abortion as a last resort
    A. Better birth control as an alternative
    B. Adoption as an alternative

*Note*: In writing a pro-and-con paper, you may anticipate your final conclusion by stating it as your thesis early in the paper. The thesis then serves as a preview of the logical conclusion the paper is going to reach. Or you may leave the issue open and *lead up* to your balanced conclusion at the end.

# C4e Definition     *plan*

**Trace the basic meaning or the most important ramifications of an important term.**

Sometimes your major task as a writer is to clarify an important term. What do we mean by "rehabilitation" when we argue about prison reform? What does the term *elitist* mean when it is applied to education? Before we can make up our minds on an issue, we often need a clearer understanding of the key terms that seem to sum up conflicting positions or opposing goals. A **definition** paper can help the reader see the common element in different and confusing uses of the same word. Or it can make the reader see the different uses that make a word vague or confusing.

Your major purpose in defining a term can help you shape the organization of a definition paper:

- Your major purpose may be to show the *common denominator* that underlies different uses or meanings of the same word. For instance, you may want to pin down the basic common element that is present when we hear the label *permissive* applied in many different areas of our society. You could sum up the common element early in your paper. You could then devote major sections of your paper to the application of the word in several major areas of contemporary American life.

- Your major purpose may be to show several *different meanings* of your key term. Major sections of your paper could explain and illustrate the most important different meanings and uses.

- Your major purpose may be to show how the *history of a term* helps explain its current uses. Major sections of your paper could show the most important stages in the development of the word. The following outline shows three major stages in the development of the word *democracy*:

### We the People

THESIS:  Over the centuries, the term *democracy* has moved away from its original Greek meaning of direct rule by the people.

   I.  Ideally, democracy gives people a direct voice and vote in the common business of the community.
     A.  The Greek beginnings
     B.  Early town meetings

   II.  In practice, participation in the political process is often indirect and ineffectual.
     A.  Parliamentary democracy
     B.  Checks and balances

**307**

III. In modern "popular democracies," an authoritarian leadership claims to exercise power in the name of the people.

In practice, an **extended definition** will often require some combination of these three major approaches. The following outline starts with a glance at the historical importance of a term. It then reviews the major competing, and sometimes confusing, uses of the term. It then points to the common denominator that nevertheless usually underlies these different uses.

### Who Is a Minority?

THESIS: In American politics, a minority is a group with a strong sense of shared identity and with common traditions rooted in a shared language, religion, race, or ethnic origin.

(Why important?)

I. In practical political terms, a minority is a group that feels discriminated against and seeks relief for past grievances.
   A. A history of discrimination
   B. Current efforts at correcting injustices

(Why difficult to define?)

II. Historically, the sense of a common identity that members of a minority share may derive from different factors.
   A. A common language (French Canadians, Hispanics)
   B. A common religion (Mormons, Catholics, the Amish)
   C. Common racial characteristics (blacks, Orientals, Native Americans)
   D. A shared ethnic or national origin (Irish, Polish, Lithuanian)

(What common denominator?)

III. A true minority shares common memories and cultural traditions that continue even when ties to an originally different language, religion, or old-country past weaken.

# EXERCISES

A. Identify the ten or twelve essential steps in a complicated *process* that is well known to you from firsthand observation or experience. Try to group the various steps into several major stages. Use the following outline form to report your findings.

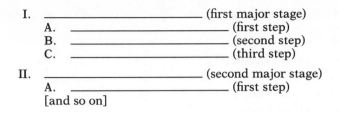

I. _____ (first major stage)
  A. _____ (first step)
  B. _____ (second step)
  C. _____ (third step)

II. _____ (second major stage)
  A. _____ (first step)
  [and so on]

B. In the following excerpt from a magazine article, the author describes what happened near "a small but growing city like many others around the country" after a planning commission was asked to approve a housing development on ten wooded acres just south of the city. The author vividly describes the process that turns a rural countryside into a modern suburb. He shows us several *major stages,* stressing how one thing leads to another. Outline and explain the major stages in your own words.

The three commissioners voted to approve the development. A few months after that, the city council, on the recommendation of the planning commission, agreed to annex the property to the city, thus guaranteeing that the subdivision would be provided with sewer, water, and electrical lines and police and fire protection. Then, because of a state law that forbade "islands" of noncity land within city limits, most of the property of owners who had fought against the development was automatically annexed to the city. Next came a flock of other developers, now assured of city services, knocking on the doors of once-irate residents, offering as much as $8,000 for an acre of land that—only months before—was worth $1,000 at best. The tax assessors came, too: Not only would tax rates be higher—to pay for the added services the city was obliged to provide all of its residents—but the assessed value of the property would have to be adjusted to reflect the change in market value. Almost overnight, property taxes jumped wildly. One by one, the residents, many of whom had owned their ten or twenty or thirty acres of green and wooded hillsides for a generation or more, sold. Those who didn't soon began receiving notices from the city asking for permission to cross their land with sewer or water lines to the new developments. If permission was refused, the city began "condemnation" proceedings to acquire an easement on, or title to, the land it needed. Legal fees soon became another major cost of owning the land. Meanwhile, earthmoving machines were leveling hillsides, bulldozers were uprooting trees, huge dump trucks were unloading their tons of gravel, steamrollers were packing the new asphalt streets, and four-lane thoroughfares were being laid over old country roads in anticipation of the traffic.
—Peter Meyer, "Land Rush," *Harper's*

C. Of the following topics, choose the one that to you seems most promising for fruitful *comparison and contrast*. Write two different outlines—one for a point-by-point comparison, the other for a parallel-order comparison. Choose one:

- old-style and current Westerns
- two people who influenced you strongly when you were young
- traditional home cooking and modern diet-conscious fare
- war movies old and new
- big old cars and small new ones
- high school and college
- commercial and public television

D. Study the following excerpt from a magazine article about nuclear energy. Summarize briefly the comparison and contrast that occurs early in this excerpt. Then find and outline the *point-by-point comparison* that the author uses later.

The simplest way of getting energy out of hydrogen is to combine it with oxygen—to let it burn and deliver heat. Such a process, however, involves merely the outermost fringe of the hydrogen atom and delivers only a tiny fraction of the energy store available at its compact "nucleus."

Something other than hydrogen-burning—something much more dramatic—takes place at the center of the sun. Under enormous gravitational pressures, the substance at the sun's core is squeezed together, raising the temperature there to a colossal 15 million degrees Centigrade (24 million degrees Fahrenheit).

At such pressures and temperatures, the very atoms of matter smash to pieces. Their outer shells break away and expose the tiny nuclei at the center, which then drive into each other at thousands of miles per second and sometimes stick. When hydrogen nuclei stick together to form the slightly larger nuclei of helium atoms, the process is called "hydrogen fusion."

Every second, 650 million tons of hydrogen are fusing into 645.4 million tons of helium at the sun's center. This process produces energy. Each missing 4.6 million tons per second represents the energy that pours out of the sun in all directions. A very small fraction is intercepted by the earth, and on that energy all life is supported.

Can we somehow take advantage of this process on earth? The trouble is we can't duplicate the conditions at the center of the sun in the proper way. . . . We want *controlled* fusion—the kind that produces energy a little bit at a time in usable, nondestructive quantities.

We still haven't reached controlled fusion. Still, at the rate we are going now, it seems that sometime before the mid-1980's, one or the other method will work. We have atomic power now in the form of uranium fission, but hydrogen fusion would be much better.

Fission uses uranium and plutonium as fuel—rare metals that are hard to get and handle. Fusion uses hydrogen, easy to obtain and handle.

Fission must work with large quantities of uranium or plutonium, so runaway reactions can take place by accident and cause damage. Fusion works with tiny quantities of hydrogen at any one time, so even runaway fusions would produce only a small pop.

Fission produces radioactive ash, which can be extremely dangerous and may not be disposed of safely. Fusion produces helium, which is completely safe, plus neutrons and tritium, which can be used up as fast as they are produced.

Finally, fission only produces a tenth as much energy as fusion, weight for weight.—Isaac Asimov, "Nuclear Fusion," *Parade*

E. Select three of the following topics. For each, make a preliminary list of possible or alleged *causes* for class discussion. Make your inventory as extensive or inclusive as you can. Choose three of the following:

- crime
- inflation
- success
- juvenile delinquency
- urban decay
- low birthrates
- unemployment

F. Sort out the following arguments *pro and con* for a paper on gun control. Prepare a topic outline (or sentence outline if you prefer) that would make use of all the ideas listed here.

1. The great majority of Americans are in favor of some form of gun control.
2. Children playing with their parents' guns or owners engaging in horseplay cause many fatal accidents.
3. The Second Amendment to the U.S. Constitution mentions the right of citizens "to bear arms."
4. The licensing of guns would require setting up a huge bureaucracy at great cost.
5. Gun owners kill themselves or others accidentally while cleaning their guns.
6. Enforcement of gun control is likely to take us a step further toward a police state, with police officers searching homes and frisking citizens for hidden guns.
7. Both the Harris poll and the Gallup poll have registered substantial majorities in favor of some form of gun control.
8. A large percentage of murders are impulse killings, made possible by an easily available, easy-to-use handgun.
9. Stricter gun controls might make guns harder to obtain for law-abiding

citizens, while doing little to keep guns from criminals ready to disobey the law.
10. Millions of the gun owners in this country might decide to defy new gun control laws, helping to create an atmosphere of disrespect for the law similar to that created by Prohibition.
11. Many murders are committed not with guns but with various kinds of other lethal weapons.

G. Each of the following *one-sentence definitions* could serve as the thesis statement of an extended definition of a familiar term. Each example first places the term in a general category (like "a feeling" or a "personal quality"). It then goes on to the specific features that help us mark off the term from similar or related ones. Study the examples and revise them or improve on them if you wish. Then write similar one-sentence definitions for five of the following:

| tolerance | dissent | conformity | backlash | censorship |
|-----------|---------|------------|----------|------------|
| apathy | vigilantism | ecology | pacifism | |

**Examples:**
1. Initiative is a personal quality that makes people attempt new and difficult things.
2. Privacy is the privilege of having one's own personal belongings, space, and thoughts free from intrusion.
3. Due process is a traditional set of legal procedures that protect us against swift and arbitrary punishment.
4. Respect is a feeling of concern and admiration that keeps us from putting down, exploiting, or abusing things or people.

## THEME TOPICS 4

Write a theme of about 500 words on one of the following topics. Pay special attention to working out the *strategy of organization* appropriate to your task.

1. Assume that your reader is a high school graduate with little detailed knowledge of science or engineering. Describe the *process* underlying one of the following: the operation of a television set, jet engine, or computer; the life cycle of a butterfly or frog; the manufacture of paper, sugar, or other product that goes through numerous stages in the production process.

2. Write *instructions* that will help your readers perform a difficult task well. Choose one requiring a skill that you have acquired but that is not generally shared. Preferably the task to be performed should require loving care: the

preparation of an unusual and difficult dish; the grafting of a bush or tree; the grooming of a horse.

3. Work out a *comparison and contrast* between two people who strongly influenced you: parents, relatives, teachers, friends, idols. Limit yourself to a few key features and illustrate them in authentic detail.

4. Write a paper developing a "then-and-now" *contrast* on one of the following topics:

   • old and new ways of treating children
   • an old-fashioned city neighborhood and today's city
   • traditional campus architecture and recent campus buildings
   • the American car then and now
   • war movies then and now

5. Write a paper in which you analyze the *major causes* (or the single major cause) of one of the following:

   • road accidents
   • long-lasting marriages
   • athletic success
   • frustration or depression among young people
   • charges of sex discrimination

6. Write a *pro-and-con* paper about a topic on which there is something to be said on both sides. Start with an introduction that raises the issue. Lead into the thesis statement that sums up your own balanced conclusion. Devote one major part of your paper to the arguments or the evidence on one side. Devote another major part of your paper to the arguments or the evidence on the opposing side. At the end, show how by weighing the pro and con you arrived at a balanced conclusion. Choose one of the following topics:

   • Should the government take steps to limit future immigration—legal or illegal—to this country?
   • Is divorce too easy in our society?
   • Should there be stricter gun controls to limit the easy availability of guns in our country?
   • Should the major aim of American public schools be to promote one common language and one common culture?

7. Write an *extended definition* of a term that we hear repeated over and over in our society. About which of the following do you feel strongly that the

word is more than just a cliché? Define the word or phrase in such a way that your readers will see why the term is important. Aim at the common element that underlies different uses of the term, or at its most important different or related meanings. Choose one:

bureaucracy     law and order     permissiveness
    exploitation      assimilation      the work ethic
      pluralism       equal opportunity

## C5   BEGINNINGS AND ENDINGS

**Get your readers' attention and leave them with a strong final impression.**

As a paper begins to take shape, we increasingly think of the audience. How can we attract and hold the readers' attention? How can we make clear to them what we are trying to do? How can we leave them with a strong final impression?

## C5a   Titles

**Use your title to attract the reader to your topic.**

Your title is your first chance to enlist the reader's interest and good will. A good title stakes out a topic and at the same time hints at how it is going to be treated. A good title is striking enough to compete with other claims on the reader's time. It often has a dramatic or humorous touch:

The Crime of Punishment
Looking for a Job Is a Job
God Helps Those That Help Each Other

Make sure that your title sounds like your personal choice, not like a ready-made, colorless general category. Here are some weak general titles, followed by a choice of improvements:

**BEFORE:**   Urban Decay
**AFTER:**   Neighborhood or Turf?
         No One Is Safe
         The Uncertainties of Gentrification

**BEFORE:** Business Success
**AFTER:** Red Ink, Black Ink
The Customer Is Rarely Right
Stretching Your Credit

# C5b Introductions

**Use your introduction to attract the reader but also to do important groundwork for your paper.**

An effective introduction creates interest; it hooks the reader into the essay or story. It sketches out the territory to be covered, often by narrowing down a more general subject. It sets the tone for the rest of the essay. Above all, it heads straight for the central idea to be developed in the rest of the paper.

You will seldom write a paper requiring more than one short introductory paragraph. Here are some typical examples:

(1) The writer may attract the reader's attention by relating the subject to a *topical event* or *current trend*:

### The Doom Boom

Until a few years ago, sex was a taboo topic; now death is being freed of its taboos, at least as a subject for frank talk. In a sense, death has come into fashion. In polite society, the act of dying no longer need be hinted at as "passing away." As opportunists discover that the hearse is a good bandwagon to jump on, the subject may even become over-exploited. But the abuses that occur are far outweighed by the benefits. . . .—*Life*

(2) The writer may start with *striking outward signs or symptoms* of the trend or situation that is going to be the subject of the paper:

### Patriotism Back in Style

Across the land, people are turning out in record numbers for holidays such as Flag Day and the Fourth of July. High school students are again entering patriotic essay contests sponsored by service organizations. ROTC programs, once scorned, are making a comeback on college campuses. Old-time patriotism is coming back into style. . . .

(3) The writer may start with a *dramatic case* that leads into a discussion of a more general situation or problem:

### The Return of the Moth

Everywhere trees stood defoliated, stripped of all leaves. Sticky little creatures hung from branches and created a sickly coating on roads. People rushed to their doctors with rashes on their hands and faces. Gypsy moth caterpillars had once again infested the Northeast in record numbers. Plagues like the gypsy moth remind us that the age-old war between human beings and the insects that destroy crops or vegetation is far from won. . . .

(4) The writer may approach a general subject *from a personal angle*, showing personal interest in or qualifications for the subject:

### The Immigrant's America

My grandparents, unknown to one another, arrived in America from the same county in Slovakia. My grandfather had a small farm in Pennsylvania; his wife died in a wagon accident. Meanwhile, a girl of fifteen arrived on Ellis Island, dizzy, a little ill from witnessing births and deaths and illnesses aboard the crowded ship, with a sign around her neck lettered "PASSAIC." There an aunt told her of the man who had lost his wife in Pennsylvania. She went. They were married. . . . I heard this story only weeks ago. Strange that I had not asked insistently before. Odd that I should have such shallow knowledge of my roots. . . .
—Michael Novak, *The Rise of the Unmeltable Ethnics*

(5) *An initial quotation* may serve as the keynote for the rest of the paper:

### Who Is Hamlet?

"It is a commonplace that the character of Hamlet holds up the mirror to his critics."[1] Shakespeare's *Hamlet* has been aptly described as the sphinx of the Western world, with each critic giving a personal and subjective answer to the riddle it proposes. . . .

(6) *Striking facts or statistics* may dramatize the issue to be discussed:

### Monolingualism Is Obsolete

Last year, only one out of ten American high school graduates had studied a foreign language. In spite of the publicity recently given to the teaching of foreign languages in primary and secondary schools . . .

(7) A *striking contrast* may heighten the point to be made:

### American Children Are Spoiled

Not too many decades ago, young children were early taught the difference between what they were, and were not, allowed to do. Today many American parents treat their children as if they could do no wrong. The most obvious manifestation of this change . . .

(8)  A *provocative statement* may challenge a familiar belief or ideal:

### Freedom Is Impossible

Freedom in society is impossible. When the desires of two people do not agree, both cannot be satisfied. Who is going to be free to realize his or her desire—the person who wants to walk down the street shouting and singing, or a neighbor who seeks peace and quiet? Those who want to build a new highway, or those who want to retain the unspoiled natural beauty of the land? . . .

(9)  An *amusing anecdote* may convey an important idea:

### Medical Journalism—With and Without Upbeat

As a veteran writer of medical and psychological articles for the mass-circulation "slicks," I have a fellow feeling for the violinist who rebelled after having been with an orchestra for thirty years. One day, so the story goes, he sat with his hands folded during rehearsal, and when the conductor rapped on the podium with his baton and demanded furiously "Why aren't you playing?" replied, with a melancholy sigh, "Because I don't like music." Sometimes I feel like sitting at my typewriter with my hands folded. I don't like popularization. It has gone too far. The little learning—with illustrations—which the magazines have been pouring into a thirsty public has become a dangerous thing. . . .—Edith M. Stern, *Saturday Review*

Some common ways of introducing a theme are usually *ineffective*:

- A *repetition*, often word for word, *of the assignment.*

- A *colorless summarizing statement*: "There are many qualities that the average college graduate looks for in a job. Most of them probably consider the following most important. . . ."

- An *unsupported claim to interest*: "Migratory birds are a fascinating subject. Ever since I was a little child, I have been interested in the migration of birds. Studying them has proved a wonderful hobby. . . ."

- *Complaints or apologies*: "I find it hard to discuss prejudice in a paper of 500 words. Prejudice is a vast subject. . . ."

**317**

# C5c   Conclusions

**Use your conclusion to tie together different parts of your paper and reinforce its central message.**

Avoid conclusions that are merely lame restatements of points already clear. Try making your conclusion fulfill an expectation created earlier in your paper. For instance, make it give a direct answer to a question asked in your title or introduction. Or tie it in with a key incident treated early in your paper.

Here are some examples of effective conclusions:

(1)   *A final anecdote that reinforces the central idea.* Close with an incident or a situation that helps make a general idea concrete:

> . . . My Nigerian friend looked out over the congested traffic as we sat in the stalled car. "Money," he said suddenly. "When you don't have it, it bothers you. When you get it, it worries you." He had summed up the story of his country, caught between ancient poverty and sudden wealth.

(2)   *Striking details that can serve as symbols of an idea or a trend.* For example, hobbies or styles of dress may become symbolic of more general attitudes:

> . . . In the shopping area across from the main entrance to the campus, head shops have been replaced by stores that sell roller skates and running shoes. Conservative styles of dress are coming back: tweed sports jackets and skirts. Some of the students dress up to go to the library.

(3)   *A strong final quotation.* Quote someone who has summed up your major point in a striking or memorable way:

> . . . As school boards order the removal of controversial books from libraries, it is time to remember what Henry Seidel Canby once wrote: "There will always be a mob with a torch ready when someone cries, 'Burn those books!'"

(4)   *A suggestion for remedial action*:

> . . . If the leading citizens in a community would make it a point to

visit their state prison, talk with the warden, then return to their communities with a better understanding of actual down-to-earth prison problems, they would have taken one of the most important and most effective steps toward a solution of our crime problem.—Erle Stanley Gardner, "Parole and the Prisons—An Opportunity Wasted," *Atlantic*

Here are some examples of *ineffective* conclusions:

- The *platitude*: "This problem deserves the serious attention of every right-thinking American."

- The *silver lining*: "When things look their grimmest, a turn for the better is usually not far away."

- The *panacea*: "The restoration of proper discipline in the nation's schools will make juvenile delinquency a thing of the past."

- The *conclusion belatedly raising problems* that weaken or distract from the point of the paper: "Of course, a small car has obvious disadvantages for a family with numerous children or for the traveler in need of luggage space."

# EXERCISES

A. Study the following *book titles* and rank the three best titles in order of their effectiveness. Explain what makes them effective. What kind of a book does each make you expect?

1. *George Washington, Man and Monument*
2. *Freedom in the Modern World*
3. *The City in History*
4. *The American Way of War*
5. *The Inner City Mother Goose*
6. *Number: The Language of Science*
7. *Lost Worlds of Africa*
8. *The Feminine Mystique*
9. *The Naked Ape*
10. *The Second Sex*

B. Look through recent issues of general-circulation *magazines* to find five articles whose titles you consider exceptionally effective. Defend your choices.

C. Describe the approach chosen in each of the following introductions. Evaluate the effectiveness of both *introduction and title.* Do they make the reader want to go on reading? Do they seem to lead clearly and directly into a specific subject? What kind of paper or article would you expect in each case?

1.                              **Ordeal by Fire**

Sooner or later, we may expect to see a candidate for the office of the President of the United States pitted against a bear. The engagement could take place in Madison Square Garden or any other arena convenient for the television cameras. Over the years, the presidential campaign has become an increasingly trying ordeal for the candidates and for the public. . . .

2.                              **Spoiling the View**

The boy, who was about seven years old, wrinkled his face in revulsion as he entered the subway car. The walls were thick with graffiti, and advertisements hung in shreds. "This is a dump train," he said loudly, glaring angrily at the other passengers. "Mama, why are we riding in a dump train?"

Vandalism in New York has leveled off in recent years, but the level is high and visible. . . .

3.                           **From Ghetto to University**

In the long and eventful history of the Jewish people, the year 1881 is a year to remember, for it marks a turning point both in the story of American Judaism and in the odyssey of the Jewish people as a whole. That was the year that the Russian government began to enforce a new policy aimed at its Jewish population, at that time the largest Jewish community in the world. . . .—Sarah Schmidt, *American Educator*

4.                           **The Demise of Education**

America is in headlong retreat from its commitment to education. Political confusion and economic uncertainty have shaken the people's faith in education as the key to financial and social success. This retreat ought to be the most pertinent issue in any examination of the country's condition. At stake is nothing less than the survival of American democracy. . . .—Fred M. Hechinger, *Saturday Review*

5.                    **"I Didn't Bring Anyone Here, and
                       I Can't Send Anybody Home"**

When I recently went back to the great yellow prison at San Quentin, it was, in a sense, to make good on a debt incurred twenty years ago. I'd started my career as a prison teacher with a good liberal's prejudice in favor of prisoners and against their guards. When I left, about five years later, I wasn't so sure of myself, for I'd met more than one prisoner who fully deserved to be locked up and more than one guard who turned out to be a decent human being.

The debt I'm talking about, then, was an obligation to report as truly as I could about the prison guard—or, as he's officially known in California, the correctional officer....—Kenneth Lamott, *Saturday Review*

6.                **More Catholic than the Pope**

While standing in the lobby of the administration building of a moderately sized Catholic college, I saw a recruitment poster for an order of nuns that said, in those light, slanty letters that are supposed to indicate modern spirituality: Are you looking for an alternative lifestyle?—Mary Gordon, *Harper's*

D. Examine the introduction or "lead" in three current articles from different general-interest magazines. Write a well-developed paragraph about each one. Describe the approach followed and evaluate its effectiveness.

E. Describe the function and estimate the probable effectiveness of the following conclusions:

1. (A paper describing the game of badminton)
   . . . Badminton can be very exciting. If you are ever looking for a good time, I suggest that you try this game. I know from experience that it can really be a lot of fun.
2. (A paper trying to demonstrate the futility of censoring comic books)
   . . . The parents can do most to counteract the comic-book habit. If they read to their children from good books, if they teach their children to treat good books as treasured possessions, if they make it a habit to talk about good books in the home, the positive attraction of good literature may prove more effective than censorship possibly can.
3. (A paper discussing several examples of "tolerance")
   . . . We thus conclude that by "tolerance" we mean allowing beliefs and actions of which we do not wholly approve. Since many of us approve wholeheartedly of only very few things, life without tolerance would be truly intolerable.
4. (A paper on race prejudice)
   . . . What can the individual do to combat racial prejudice? This question is very hard to answer, because nobody can predict the future.
5. (A paper on the democratic process)
   . . . The benefits society derives from the democratic process are often unspectacular, and slow in coming. Its weaknesses and disadvantages are often glaringly evident. By its very nature, democracy, in order to survive, must give its enemies the right to be heard and to pursue their goals. As Chesterton has said, "The world will never be safe for democracy—it is a dangerous trade."
6. (A paper on prison reform)
   . . . In spite of all the studies and reports done by numerous commissions

and panels, the U.S. lags behind other countries in the implementation of penal reform. What are we waiting for? New methods in use around the world have proven their value, and yet we drag our feet. We are made to wonder if our government is capable of dealing with more than one or two of the popular issues that are splashed over the headlines in each election year.

# THEME TOPICS 5

Theme topics like the following are used in colleges around the country for writing assignments designed to measure students' ability to meet college-level standards for written composition. Write a well-focused, well-organized theme of about 500 words on one of these topics. Pay special attention to beginning and ending. Provide an attractive but also informative *title*. Write an effective *introduction*, for example, one leading into the topic from a personal experience or from an event of current interest. Write a strong *conclusion* that does not merely repeat but instead reinforces your key point.

1. A writer discussing American schools divided students into two kinds: "answerers" and "questioners." The first kind always tries to give the right answer to the teachers' questions. The second kind asks questions that show curiosity and willingness to learn. To judge from your own experience, which of the two kinds of students receives more encouragement or reward in American schools?

2. Thomas Carlyle, a nineteenth-century British writer, wrote about the role of outstanding personalities in history. He once said, "Hero worship exists, has existed, and will forever exist, among mankind." What kinds of heroes do young Americans look for today?

3. One theory about people who get into trouble with authorities or with society is that there are born "troublemakers." According to this view, some people have a special aptitude for getting into trouble. How much truth do you think there is in this view?

4. Some people claim that differences in dress, hair length, and other matters of outward appearance are merely superficial. However, other people claim that such outward signs often show something important about the attitudes or values of a person. What is *your* opinion? Support or defend your point of view.

5. For a time, it was fashionable for writers about the future to stress how different the future was likely to be from anything we had known in the past. What qualities or aptitudes do you think will be most essential for people to help them succeed or survive in the years ahead?

# C6 COHERENCE AND TRANSITION

**Take your reader along from point to point.**

A paper has **coherence** when it takes the reader along. An effective writer knows how to make the reader follow from point to point. Provide the signals that tell your readers what to expect. Provide the signals that steer their attention.

## C6a Synonyms and Recurrent Terms          *coh*

**Use key terms and their synonyms to focus the reader's attention.**

In a coherent paper, we can often trace a network of related terms that help focus our attention on the key issue. Suppose you are reading an article on the psychological effects that over-crowding has on people in modern cities. If it is a well-focused article, you are likely to find many terms and phrases that echo the key term: "overpopulation," "penned up," "massive conges-tion," "great numbers," "rush-hour crush," "population density," "cramped quarters," and the like. Such synonyms or closely related terms show that the writer is never straying far from the central point.

Study the repetition of key terms like *work, toil,* or *labor* in the following excerpts selected to help you see the development of a long passage. In addition to such close synonyms, look at the other expressions that in some way paraphrase or echo the idea of work: "striving," "daily grind."

What elements of the national character are attributable to this long-time agrarian environment? First and foremost is the *habit of work.* For the colonial farmer, *ceaseless striving* constituted the price of sur-vival. . . .

The *tradition of toil* so begun found new sustenance as settlers opened up the boundless stretches of the interior. "In the free States," wrote Harriet Martineau in 1837, "*labour* is more really and heartily honoured. . . ."

One source of Northern antagonism to the system of human bond-age was the fear that it was jeopardizing this basic tenet of the American creed. "Wherever *labor* is mainly performed by slaves," Daniel Webster told the United States Senate, "it is regarded as . . ."

Probably no legacy from our farmer forebears has entered more deeply into the national psychology. If an American has no *purposeful work* on hand . . .

This *worship of work* has made it difficult for Americans to learn how to play. As Poor Richard saw it, "Leisure is . . ."

The first mitigations of the *daily grind* took the form of hunting, fishing, barnraisings, and logrollings—activities that had no social stigma because they contributed to the basic needs of living. . . .

The importance attached to *useful work* had the further effect of helping to make "this new man" indifferent to aesthetic considerations. . . .—Arthur M. Schlesinger, *Paths to the Present*

## C6b Patterns of Expectation *coh*

**Use a consistent overall pattern to guide the reader's expectations.**

If a writer sets up a clear-cut overall pattern, the reader is ready for the next step before it comes. Here are some familiar patterns that can help guide the expectations of a reader:

*Enumeration* Lining up major points in a numerical sequence makes for a formal, systematic presentation. In the following discussion of language, the key points gain force from marching across the page in a 1-2-3 order:

There are *five simple facts* about language in general which we must grasp before we can understand a specific language or pass judgment on a particular usage. . . .

*In the first place*, language is basically speech. . . .

*In the second place*, language is personal. . . .

*The third fact* about language is that it changes. . . .

*The fourth great fact* about language . . . is that its users are, in one way or another, isolated. . . .

*The fifth great fact* about language is that it is a historical growth of a specific kind. . . .—Donald J. Lloyd, "Snobs, Slobs, and the English Language," *The American Scholar*

*Order of Importance* Suppose an author is examining the causes of war. She takes up *minor* contributing causes first, as if to get them out of the way. She gradually moves on to major ones. The reader will be ready for a final central or basic cause coming as the **climax** of the article or the book.

***From Problem to Solution***  Study the logical pattern that helps move forward the following student paper:

| | |
|---|---|
| PROBLEM | In any family, there is a network of antagonistic desires. A young girl might want to practice her violin, while her brother insists that the noise interferes with his studying. . . . |
| SOLUTION<br>First<br>alternative | These situations must be solved or managed. If one parent dictates without consideration of the others, the family will be run in an authoritarian manner. Women used to bend to the wishes of an authoritarian husband. . . . |
| Second<br>alternative | If no authority figure guides and directs these daily decisions, the individuals in the family must create some method of living together. . . . |

# C6c Transition                                         *trans*

**Provide a bridge from one point to the next and from one subtopic to another.**

Effective writing provides smooth transitions—signals that help the reader move on from one part of a paper to the next. In writing but especially also in revising a paper, provide the links that help the reader follow:

(1) *Spell out the logical connection between one paragraph and the next.* Study the way experienced writers make the beginning of a new paragraph point back to what came before and point forward to what is to follow:

| | |
|---|---|
| THESIS | The diversity of higher education in the United States is unprecedented. . . . |
| First problem is taken up; one alternative is considered | *Consider the question of size.* The small campus offers . . . |
| Second alternative is considered | *Others feel hemmed in by these very qualities.* They welcome the comparative anonymity and impersonality of the big university. . . . |
| Second problem is taken up; first alternative is considered | *Another familiar question is whether* the student should go to a college next door, in the next city, or a thousand miles away. By living at home . . . |

Second alternative is considered

> *Balanced against this*, there are considerable advantages to a youngster in seeing and living in an unfamiliar region of the country. . . .

Alternatives are weighed

> *But this question too must be decided* on the basis of individual preference. . . .

(2) *Use transitional phrases to help the reader move smoothly from one point to the next.* The connection between parts of a paper is seldom as obvious as the writer thinks. **Transitional phrases** are directional signals that help the reader move along without stumbling.

Here are common transitional phrases:

| | |
|---|---|
| ADDITION: | too, also, furthermore, similarly, moreover |
| ILLUSTRATION: | for example, for instance |
| PARAPHRASE OR SUMMARY: | that is, in other words, in short, to conclude, to sum up |
| LOGICAL CONCLUSION: | so, therefore, thus, accordingly, consequently, as a result, hence |
| CONTRAST OR OBJECTION: | but, however, nevertheless, on the other hand, conversely, on the contrary |
| CONCESSION: | granted that . . . , no doubt, to be sure, it is true that . . . |
| EMPHASIS OR REINFORCEMENT: | indeed, in fact |

For more on transition, see **PA 1d**.

# EXERCISES

A. Point out all words that *repeat or echo* the ideas of fear and threat in the following passage:

What happened on the way to women's equality? What happened is a repetition of 1776, a rerun of the Fourteenth and Fifteenth Amendments and of the battles that defeated women's suffrage until 1920. The enemy is fear, and many of the fears are not irrational. Blue-collar and white-collar men, whose job security is already precarious, fear increasing competition from women for the same jobs. Other men, whose sense of identity has been heavily buffeted by a changing world, are threatened with loss of the faith that whatever may be their status among men, at least they are "better" than women. Women who are dependent upon men and cannot compete on equal terms fear that equality will force them into independence. Still other women and men fear equality as simply another unknown in a world already strewn with hidden pitfalls.—Shirley M. Hufstedler, *Women and the Law*

B. Read the following passage from Henry Steele Commager's *The American Mind.* Study it as an example of a passage clearly focused on a central topic, and supporting a clearly stated thesis. Answer the questions that follow it.

*The inclination to experiment was deeply ingrained in the American character and fortified by American experience.* America itself had been the greatest of experiments, one renewed by each generation of pioneers and each wave of immigrants, and, where every community was a gamble and an opportunity, the American was a gambler and an opportunist. He had few local attachments, pulled up stakes without compunction, and settled easily into new communities; where few regions or professions were overcrowded and every newcomer added to the wealth and the drawing power, he was sure of a welcome.

He was always ready to do old things in new ways, or, for that matter, to do things which had not been done before. Except in law, tradition and precedent discouraged him, and whatever was novel was a challenge. Pioneering had put a premium upon ingenuity and handiness, and where each man turned readily to farming, building, and trading, it seemed natural that he should turn with equal readiness to preaching, lawing, or doctoring, or combine these with other trades and professions.

The distrust of the expert, rationalized into a democratic axiom during the Jacksonian era, was deeply ingrained in the American character and persisted long after its original justification had passed. With opportunism went inventiveness, which was similarly invited by circumstances. Americans, who recorded at the Patent Office in Washington more inventions than were recorded in all the Old World nations together, likewise found more new roads to Heaven than had ever before been imagined, while their schools multiplied the seven liberal arts tenfold. Denominationalism and the inflated curriculum were monuments to the passion for experiment and inventiveness as well as to theological and secular learning.

1. How many words can you find in this passage that all echo or repeat the idea of "experiment"? Find all the synonyms or near-synonyms of this central term.
2. How many major instances of applications of the major thesis can you identify? Describe in your own words four or five *major kinds* of experiment that this passage maps out.

3. Select *one* of the major kinds of experiment mentioned here. Write a paragraph in which you fill in specific examples from your own reading or observation. Use a variety of transitional expressions. (Underline them in your finished paragraph.)

C. In each of the following pairs of sentences, a *transitional word or phrase* has been left out. Fill in a transition that will help the reader move smoothly from the first sentence to the second.

1. There are many special schools that should be considered by the young person who is not going on to college. The student who wishes to be an X-ray technician or a practical nurse, _____, will find many schools that offer the necessary training.
2. Apprenticeship systems are still operating in every industry and offer wide opportunities for ambitious youngsters. They must be warned, _____, that in some of the older crafts entry is jealously guarded.
3. The home environment is the largest single factor determining the grade school youngster's "scholastic aptitude." _____, how well children learn in school depends on what they have learned at home.
4. Rennie was lazy, self-indulgent, spoiled. _____, he did remarkably well in his favorite subjects.
5. The basic promise that American society has always held out to its citizens is equality of opportunity. The typical substandard big-city school, _____, is profoundly un-American.
6. Black athletes are not as pampered as some white sports fans seem to think. _____ the outstanding black athlete enjoys many privileges, but when a black and a white player are equally well qualified, coaches are likely to give preference to the latter.
7. The European system of education very early separates youngsters permanently on the basis of ability. The American system, _____, is designed to make possible numerous second chances.
8. In many Latin American countries, more young people study to be lawyers than are needed in their country. _____, in many underdeveloped countries, more young people study to be engineers than a preindustrial society could support.
9. A highly specialized skill limits a person's job opportunities. It _____ makes the specialist a potential victim of technological unemployment.
10. Our leaders are fond of the phrase "the free world." In actual fact, _____, societies that foster political freedom are the exception rather than the rule.

D. Prepare a rough outline of the following student paper. Is it hard to outline, or easy? How would you describe the overall pattern of the paper? What has the writer done to help the reader follow?

### No More Favors, Please

Many times in a conversation, I have heard it said that "a boss's son has it made." I doubt whether a person who makes that statement has ever worked for his father. At any rate, during the four years that I worked for my father's water softener firm, I was not treated nearly as well as were the other employees.

With them, my father was generous and tolerant. They received good wages for their standard forty-hour week. And if Jerry or Fred helped to sell a new water softener to one of our customers, he was awarded a twenty-dollar commission. Whenever Jerry asked for a little time off to go fishing, my father promptly granted his request. And once Fred got two days off to take a trip to Chicago, and Dad didn't even dock his pay. If Jack and Kenny botched an installation job, my father would reprove them in a kindly tone and explain how they could have avoided the mistake. Once Kenny failed to tighten a packing nut on a valve, and the water leaked all over the customer's floor. Father sent over a man to clean up the mess and just told Kenny to be more careful next time. On another occasion, Jack and Kenny dropped a softener down a customer's stairs, ruining the softener and damaging several steps. When they reported the incident to him with worried and anxious looks, Father calmed their fears and told them his insurance would cover the loss. If one of his men became involved in a dispute with a customer over a repair bill, it was his employee, and not the customer, who was always right.

But where I was concerned, my father was a close-fisted and harsh employer. My weekly paycheck was an unvarying fifty dollars, whether I worked forty hours or fifty-five, and the occasional salary raises the other employees enjoyed were never extended to me. I rarely received a commission on the sales I made; my father would either say that he couldn't afford to pay me any extra just then, or else that I wasn't really entitled to the money. If I wanted to take part in some school activity or go on a beach party with some friends, my father would not only refuse to give me time off, but he would often find extra jobs that would force me to work overtime. My mistakes called forth only anger from my father, never understanding. If anything went wrong with one of the company trucks while I was driving, he always assumed I had been driving like my "hot rod friends." If a customer complained about my service or her bill, my father bawled me out for giving him and his business a bad name. Once when I forgot to reduce the water pressure in the backwash machine and caused about twenty dollars' worth of mineral to be washed down the drain, he spent half an afternoon sarcastically analyzing my mistake and showing me, in minute detail, how my carelessness had "cut into the profits for the year." Insurance never covered *my* accidents; their cost was deducted from my salary, to teach me "to be more careful."

I don't know whether my father was so harsh with me because he didn't want to appear to be favoring me; but I do know that his constant criticism convinced me that the role of boss's son is a role I don't want to play for a lifetime.

## THEME TOPICS 6

Write a theme of about 500 words on one of the following topics. Pay special attention to the overall *coherence* of your paper. Provide the signals that steer your readers' attention.

1.  Write a paper in which a repeated key term, with its synonyms and related terms, helps focus the reader's attention. Choose one:

    - the spirit of competition in American life
    - leisure-time interests and the American economy
    - the political process and popular apathy
    - the legacy of segregation
    - the American tradition of being a good neighbor

2.  Write a paper in which you take up important categories, causes, or parts of a subject in order of importance. Lead up to the most important or most difficult part of your paper at the end. Choose one:

    - the benefits of education
    - the roots of happiness
    - what makes for true friendship
    - what is needed in a truly satisfying job
    - what is needed for good relations between police and community

3.  Write a paper in which you go from problem to solution. You may want to examine several possible solutions, settling for the most promising one at the end. Choose one:

    - vandalism
    - low academic achievement in the schools
    - low-quality television fare
    - the macho mystique
    - disrespect for the law

# 9

# The Research Paper

## R1   CHOOSING A SUBJECT

**Choose a limited subject that is worth investigating and that enables you to bring together evidence from different printed sources.**

In a research paper written for a composition class, you investigate a limited subject by bringing together information and comment from several printed sources. In your finished paper, you present something that was worth finding out—and worth sharing with others. A successful research paper sheds light on a question about which many readers might have only superficial or contradictory ideas. It provides solid, reliable information on a subject about which many readers have only vague general impressions.

Your first task is to settle on a subject that is of personal interest to you and that will make the time and energy you invest worthwhile. Remember the following general guidelines:

(1) *Focus on one limited part of a general subject.* The threat to animal life on our planet—the threatened extinction of endangered species—is a vast general subject. The following are some limited subtopics that you could investigate in detail:

- The passing of the American buffalo
- The threat to the American bald eagle
- The extinction of the passenger pigeon
- Saving the whales
- The war against the coyote
- Fact and folklore about wolves
- Why insects will inherit the earth
- The endangered habitat of the caribou

(2) *Make detailed use of several different sources.* Do not simply summarize information from one main source. You may want to start with an entry in an encyclopedia or a chapter in a textbook, but do not stop there. Do not simply follow the main outline of a single magazine article. An essential part of your task is to test one author's facts and figures against those of another. Weigh conflicting conclusions. Track down additional information where the readily available evidence is skimpy or inconclusive.

(3) *Stay close to the evidence you present.* When you write a research paper, your attitude toward the audience is: "Here is the evidence. This is where I found it. You are welcome to check these sources and to verify these facts." A research paper tests your ability to be **objective**—to follow the evidence where it leads, to revise tentative conclusions as it becomes necessary. A research paper does not exclude your personal conclusions or opinions, but it requires them to be backed up with a solid array of supporting material.

(4) *Stay away from highly technical subjects.* Recent discoveries about the nature of the universe or about the biochemistry of our bodies make fascinating topics, but you may soon need more knowledge of physics or mathematics than you and your reader can command.

The finished research paper differs from ordinary themes in outward form. It usually makes extensive use of quotation. It identifies the sources of quotations and of other material used by the writer. **Footnotes** (or end notes) give exact information about these sources, including the full title, date of publication, exact page numbers, and the like. Usually the sources are listed again in a **bibliography**, an alphabetical listing at the end of the paper. We call this exact identifying of sources the documentation for the paper. It makes sure the reader can check the material used by the writer—to see if the sources were quoted accurately or if the evidence was selected fairly.

Documentation helps the writer avoid **plagiarism**. Writers who plagiarize take over the results of someone else's research or investigation without acknowledgment. It is true that many facts and ideas are common property and need not be credited to any specific source. Major historical dates and events, key ideas of major scientific or philosophical movements—these are generally accessible in reference books. However, identify your source whenever you use information recently discovered or collected. Show your source whenever you adopt someone's characteristic, personal point of view. Never copy whole sentences or paragraphs without making it clear that you are quoting another writer. Never simply adopt someone else's plan or procedure without acknowledgment.

The following are general areas for research. Carve out a limited topic from a general area like the following:

(1) *Saving the animals*: the history of a major endangered species; the story of the disappearance of the buffalo or other nearly vanished animal; current conservationist efforts to protect endangered species of birds or other animals; the struggle to protect fur-bearing animals; in defense of the wolf or the coyote.

(2) *Alternative sources of energy*: the future of solar energy; the story of coal; wind power through the ages; fission and fusion; damming our last wild rivers.

(3) *The story of prison reform*: punishment vs. rehabilitation; the threat of prison riots; our overcrowded jails; what to do about juvenile offenders.

(4) *Fighting words in American history*: the abolitionist movement; the American suffragette; the tradition of populism; the story of segregation; the roots of unionism; robber barons or captains of industry.

(5) *The story of censorship*: controversial authors and the schools (Kurt Vonnegut, J. D. Salinger, Joyce Carol Oates); creationism and evolution; censoring the dictionaries; the definition of obscenity.

(6) *Bilingual Americans*: the pro's and con's of bilingual education; Hispanic vs. Anglo culture; the politics of a bilingual community.

(7) *Ethnic identity and the writer*: the search for roots (Alexander Haley, Maxine Hong Kingston); the search for black identity (Richard Wright, Ralph Ellison, Lorraine Hansberry, Maya Angelou); the immigrant's America (Willa Cather, Upton Sinclair, William Saroyan).

(8) *The American Indian*: the story of a forgotten tribe; the Cherokee nation; the Pueblos of the Southwest; the last wars; assimilating the Native Americans.

(9) *Changing attitudes toward age and the aging*: the passing of the youth culture; an aging society; traditional stereotypes about the aged; the changing self-image of senior citizens.

(10)  *A nostalgic look*: the vanishing passenger train; a short history of the stage coach; the passing of the American streetcar; ocean liners and their day of glory.

# EXERCISE

Write a tentative *prospectus* for a research paper in one of the general areas listed above. A prospectus outlines plans for a project or undertaking of some size. Describe whatever in your background or previous reading might help you with your chosen subject. Outline your tentative plans for limiting your subject: What aspects of the general topic, or what issues within the general area, interest you most? Outline any preliminary thoughts about how you might tackle your subject: What might be your overall plan of organization or your general strategy?

(Your instructor may ask you to delay your prospectus until you have had a chance to do a minimum of exploratory reading.)

## R2  GOING TO THE SOURCES

**Learn how to find and evaluate sources.**

The experienced investigator knows where to look. Writing a research paper gives you a chance to find your way around a library and to get acquainted with its resources. In the typical student research paper, you are likely to use three major kinds of printed materials:

- *encyclopedias* or other general reference works that provide a brief summary or overview of information;

- *magazine or newspaper articles* that deal with current developments or take a new look at a familiar issue;

- *books* that explore a subject in depth or include a section relevant to your topic.

Suppose you are writing about the era of the zeppelins that ended with the disaster destroying the airship *Hindenburg*. You are likely to find a survey article under the heading "Airship" in a standard encyclopedia. In a printed multivolume index to magazine articles, you are likely to find several articles published about airships in the years leading up to 1937, when their voyages and finally the last disastrous voyage of the *Hindenburg* were much in the news. Finally, you are likely to find several useful books when checking the general card catalog of your library under subject headings like "Airship" or "Zeppelin."

Remember that a successful research project depends on your perseverance and ingenuity in ferreting out usable material. Take time to familiarize yourself with sources and guides described in the following sections. When stymied, turn for guidance or information to people who might be able to help: librarians, subject-matter specialists, fellow researchers. When your college library fails you, try your public library. Remember that many libraries are turning into resource centers and service centers. Make use of services or facilities that allow you to obtain your own photocopies of a magazine or newspaper article (whether from a bound copy or from a copy on microfilm). Obtain xerox copies of important pages from a useful book.

# R2a  Using Reference Works

**Learn to use the reference tools available to every investigator.**

Every college library has a wealth of reference books that take stock of human knowledge. These are often imposing volumes ranging from updated versions of standard guides to ambitious new undertakings. Familiarize yourself with some of the best-known and most generally useful works of reference. Find more specialized reference works for a special field of interest in a guide like Eugene P. Sheehy's *Guide to Reference Books*, published by the American Library Association.

*Encyclopedias*  An encyclopedia is a good place to start—but not to finish—your investigation. The encyclopedia provides a convenient summary of what is generally known on your subject. The purpose of your investigation is to go *beyond* the encyclopedia—to take a closer firsthand look.

• The *Encyclopaedia Britannica,* now an American publication, is the most authoritative of the general encyclopedias. It is brought up to date each year by the *Britannica Book of the Year.* Although you would normally consult the most up-to-date version, you will occasionally find references to scholarly articles in earlier editions. A complete revision, called *The New Encyclopaedia Britannica,* was published in 1974. It has two major sections: a ten-volume quick-reference index (the *Micropaedia*) and a nineteen-volume guide to more detailed information on many subjects (the *Macropaedia*).

• The *Encyclopedia Americana* is sometimes recommended for science and biography. General subjects are broken up into short articles, arranged alphabetically. The annual supplement is the *Americana Annual.*

• *Collier's Encyclopedia* is another multivolume general encyclopedia, written in a more popular style.

• The one-volume *Columbia Encyclopedia* provides a bird's-eye view. It serves well for a quick check of people and places.

**Biography** In addition to the biographical entries in the major encyclopedias, most libraries have ample material for a paper about a famous person.

• *Who's Who in America,* a biographical dictionary of notable living men and women, provides a brief summary of dates and details on important contemporaries. (The original *Who's Who* is a British publication. Specialized offshoots of the same publication include *Who's Who of American Women.*)

• The *Dictionary of American Biography* (*DAB*) contains a more detailed account of the lives of important persons. (The British counterpart is the *Dictionary of National Biography.*)

• The *Biography Index* is a guide to biographical material in books and magazines. By consulting both recent and earlier volumes, you can compile a comprehensive bibliography of material on the married life of George Washington or on the evangelistic campaigns of Billy Graham.

**Literature** A library project on a subject from literary history may deal with an author's schooling or early reading, recurrent themes in the books of a well-known novelist, or the contemporary reputation of a nineteenth-century American poet.

• The fifteen-volume *Cambridge History of English Literature* and the *Cambridge Bibliography of English Literature* provide comprehensive information about English authors and literary movements.

• The Spiller-Thorp-Johnson-Canby *Literary History of the United States*, with its supplementary bibliographies, lists as its contributors an impressive roster of contemporary American literary scholars.

• *Harper's Dictionary of Classical Literature and Antiquities* is a comprehensive scholarly guide to Greek and Roman history and civilization. (Robert Graves' *The Greek Myths* and Edith Hamilton's *Mythology*, both available as paperbacks, provide an introduction to famous names and stories.)

*Other Fields of Interest*   Every major field of interest, such as science, business, education, or art, has its own specialized reference guides. People with an interest in the field are familiar with specialized encyclopedias, dictionaries of names or technical terms, or yearbooks reporting on current developments. Here is a brief sampling of specialized reference works that are frequently consulted:

• *American Universities and Colleges* and *American Junior Colleges* provide basic facts about educational institutions.

• The *McGraw-Hill Encyclopedia of Science and Technology* is kept up to date by the *McGraw-Hill Yearbook of Science and Technology*.

• The *Dictionary of American History* by J. T. Adams is a six-volume guide.

• Langer's *Encyclopedia of World History* is a long-established reference guide in one volume.

• The *International Encyclopedia of the Social Sciences* is a multivolume reference work.

• *Grove's Dictionary of Music and Musicians* is a traditional work for music lovers.

- The *McGraw-Hill Encyclopedia of World Art* has fifteen volumes.

- The Funk and Wagnalls *Standard Dictionary of Folklore, Mythology and Legend* is one of several well-known guides to basic themes in folk culture and folk tradition.

*Bibliographies* At the end of many encyclopedia entries, you will find a short bibliography—a list of important books and other sources of information. The encyclopedia may list only very general books, but these in turn will often contain more detailed bibliographical listings or direct you to book-length bibliographies. Any general survey of a subject is likely to provide information about more detailed studies. College textbooks often provide a short bibliography at the end of each chapter.

Take up first those books that a bibliography labels "standard," "indispensable," or "the best introduction" to your subject. If the bibliographies you have consulted merely *list* books, take up those that are most frequently mentioned. Study their tables of contents, prefaces, introductory or concluding chapters. Find out what each book is trying to do and whether all or parts of it would be useful for your project.

*Note*: The *Book Review Digest* contains short selections from book reviews written shortly after publication of the book reviewed. These can give you an idea of the intention and importance of books on subjects of general interest.

## R2b Finding Magazine and Newspaper Articles

**Know how to find articles in current and past issues of magazines and newspapers.**

Much information or comment is published in a vast variety of periodicals—publications that appear at regular intervals, ranging from the daily newspaper to monthly and quarterly magazines. Suppose you are writing a paper on the chances of survival for the American bald eagle or for the whooping crane. You might find useful articles in a whole range of periodicals that publish articles about our wildlife and the threats to its survival. These publications might include *National Geographic, National Wildlife, Audubon, American Forests, Outdoor Life,* and *Smithsonian.*

Most libraries have a compact catalog for all periodicals to which the library subscribes. (This catalog is separate from the general card catalog of the library.) For each periodical, this listing will show the location of recent issues (often on the shelves of a separate periodical room) as well as of back issues (usually in bound volumes in the book stacks of the library). However, to find individual magazine articles, you will have to consult specialized reference guides to periodicals.

***Periodical Indexes*** Magazine articles often mirror the full range of contemporary opinion on events of the past. For current issues and concerns, they help you bring up to date the information that you obtained from books. To find magazine articles that will help you with your subject, you may have to consult the periodical indexes in your library. These are published in monthly or semimonthly installments and then combined in huge volumes, each listing articles for a period of one or more years.

• The *Readers' Guide to Periodical Literature* indexes magazines written for the general reader. If you are writing on American policy in the Near East, the *Readers' Guide* may direct you to speeches by government officials reprinted in a publication like *U.S. News & World Report.* It may direct you to discussions of American foreign policy in such magazines as *Newsweek* and *New Republic.*

In the *Readers' Guide,* articles are listed twice—once under the name of the author, and once under a subject heading. If you are writing about robots or about space technology, you may know of some authors who are experts in these fields. You might find relevant material by looking for articles published during the last five or ten years by authors like Isaac Asimov or Arthur C. Clarke. More often, you will have to look for material under subject headings, ranging in the *Readers' Guide* from "Postage Stamps" to "Adult Education." These subject headings often have subdivisions. Headings like "Space Research" or "Space Stations" are likely to have subheadings like "United States," "Russian," and the like. (Some of the subject headings in the *Readers' Guide* are the names of individuals—scientists, political leaders, celebrities—who were the major subject of an article.)

Here is a sample entry from the *Readers' Guide*. You would find this magazine article under the subject heading. The article was written by B. Farber, is called "Mother Goes Back to School," and appeared in *Parents Magazine*:

> ADULT education
> Mother goes back to school. B. Farber. il
> Parents Mag 49:46-7+ Ja '74

(Further information included: The article appears in the issue for January 1974. The issue is part of Volume 49. The main part of the article appears on pages 46 and 47, but it is continued elsewhere. The article is illustrated.)

• The *Social Sciences Index* (formerly *International Index*) lists articles in more scholarly magazines. If you are looking for important studies of the black community, this index will direct you to articles in sociological and psychological journals.

• The *Humanities Index*, now a separate publication, was combined with the *Social Sciences Index* during the years 1965–1973.

Here is a list of periodical indexes for other specialized fields:

• *Applied Science and Technology Index* (see the *Industrial Arts Index* for years before 1958)

• *Art Index*

• *Biological and Agricultural Index* (called *Agricultural Index* before 1964)

• *Business Periodicals Index*

• *Education Index*

• *Engineering Index*

• *General Science Index*

Whatever index you use, read its introductory pages and study its list of abbreviations. Study the list of the periodicals indexed—it may not include a magazine that you have seen mentioned elsewhere and that you know to be important. Look at sample entries to study the listing of individual articles and the system of cross-references.

*Note*: Many fields publish **abstracts**—short summaries—of articles, usually collected and published several times a year. In many libraries, index information about periodicals is becoming available from data banks, accessible through computer outlets.

*Current Events*    A number of special reference guides are useful for papers on a political subject or on current events.

• *Facts on File* is a weekly digest of world news, with an annual index. It gives a summary of news reports and comments, with excerpts from important documents and speeches. It can serve as a convenient review of day-to-day happenings in politics, foreign affairs, entertainment, sports, science, and education.

• The *New York Times Index* (published since 1913) is a guide to news stories published in the *New York Times*. Look up an event or a controversy in this index to find the approximate dates for relevant articles in other newspapers and magazines.

• The annual index to the *Monthly Catalog of the United States Government Publications* lists reports and documents published by all branches of the federal government.

Note that magazines and newspapers are now often stored on **microfilm**, in miniature form. Familiarize yourself with the procedures for obtaining and viewing such materials.

## R 2c    Finding Books in the Library Catalog

**Learn to use the general catalog of your library efficiently.**

For the typical research paper in a composition class, you will be expected to find several book-length treatments of your general subject, or to find relevant sections or chapters in several books. An important part of your task is to find useful books in the central catalog of your college library. Traditionally, the central catalog has been a card catalog with rows and rows of drawers holding printed index cards in alphabetical order. As libraries become modernized, users will increasingly view computerized catalog information on screens. However, the kind and arrangement of the information provided to the user of the library are very similar under both systems.

In the typical library catalog, the same book is listed several times: by *author* (under the author's last name), by *title* (under the first word of the title, not counting *The, A,* or *An*), and by *subject*. At times, you will simply be tracking down a promising author or book on the basis of leads you already have. But often you will have to be persistent and imaginative in looking for possibly useful books under the right subject headings.

*Author Cards*  Author cards provide complete publishing information about each separate book by an author; cards for books by the same author are arranged in alphabetical order. (Such a set of several cards may be followed by catalog cards for books *about* the author.) Here is a sample author card:

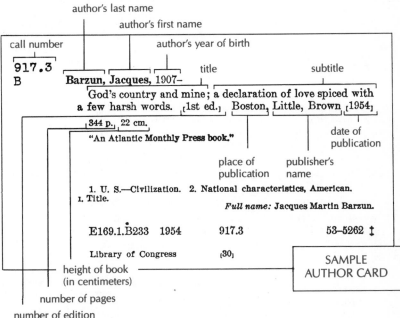

Look for the following clues to the nature of the book:

- *the number or description of the edition.* If the catalog lists both the original edition and another marked "2nd ed." or "Rev. ed.," generally choose the one that is more up to date.

- *the name and location of the publisher.* For instance, a book published by a university press is likely to be a scholarly or specialized study. The *date of publication* is especially important for books on scientific, technological, or medical subjects, where older information is often out of date.

• *the number of pages* (with the number of introductory pages given as a lower-case Roman numeral). It shows whether the book is a short pamphlet or a full-scale treatment of the subject. If the book contains *illustrations* or a *bibliography*, the card will carry a notation to that effect.

Often a card lists the several major *subject headings* under which the book can be found. For instance, a card for a sociological study of a Midwestern town may carry the following notation concerning various headings under which the study is listed:

1. U.S.—Social conditions.   2.   Cities and Towns—U.S.   3.   Cost and standard of living—U.S.   4. U.S.—Religion.   5.   Social surveys.   6.   Community life.

**Title Cards**   Title cards carry the same information as author cards. However, the title is repeated at the top for alphabetical listing. The following is an example of a title card. Instead of the traditional style of the printed card, it uses the slightly different style you are likely to see on a computer printout:

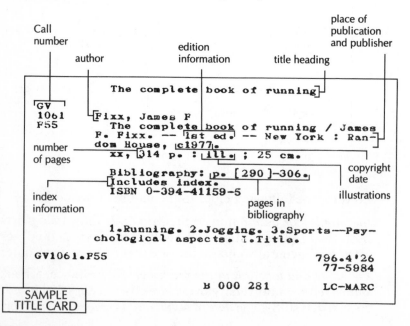

**Subject Cards**   Subject cards will often be your best hope for finding books related to your topic. Ask yourself under what headings material for your topic is likely to appear. For instance, books on the American Civil War might appear under *U.S.—History—Civil War*, under *U.S.—History—Military*, under *Slavery in the United States*, or under *Abolitionists*. Try to think of other key terms that might appear in the catalog: "Confederacy" or "Emancipation." Pay special attention to the cross-reference cards that often appear at the beginning of a set of related subject cards:

```
FISHES, see also

     Aquariums
     Tropical fishes
        (also names of fishes, e.g., Salmon)
```

Here is an example of a typed subject card from the card catalog of a special division of a college library:

```
978      MORMONS AND MORMONISM-HISTORY
S


     Stegner, Wallace Earle, 1909-

     The gathering of Zion; the story of the
Mormons, by Wallace Stegner.  1st ed.  New
York, McGraw-Hill, 1964

331 p. illus. maps 23 cm (American Trails
series)
```

|  |
|---|
| SAMPLE SUBJECT CARD |

```
Bibliography:  pp. 315-319
```

**Call Numbers**   Once you decide that you should consult a book, copy its call number. The **call number** directs you, or the librarian, to the shelf where the book is located. Your library may use either of two numbering systems: the Library of Congress system or the Dewey decimal system. The **Library of Congress system** divides books into categories identified by letters of the alphabet. It then uses additional letters and numerals to subdivide each main category. For instance, the call number of a book on religion would start with a capital *B*. The call number of a book on education starts with a capital *L*. The **Dewey decimal system** uses numerals to identify the main categories. For instance, 400–499 covers books on language; 800–899 covers books on literature. The 800 range is then further subdivided into American literature (810–819), English literature (820–829), and so on. Additional numerals and letters distinguish among individual authors and among individual works by the same author.

# R2d   Preparing a Working Bibliography

**Prepare your own inventory of promising printed sources for your project.**

From the beginning, record detailed accurate information about all sources that seem promising for your investigation. Your instructor will often suggest a minimum number of sources that you should consult. However, in your working bibliography, or preliminary listing of printed sources, you will have to include more than the minimum number, so that you can finally choose those that are truly useful.

For a brief research report limited to three or four sources, you may be able to record all information you need on an ordinary sheet of note paper. For a full-length research paper, prepare separate **bibliography cards** for each book, pamphlet, or magazine. Some of the information is mainly for your own use in locating the book or article: Copy the complete call number exactly, or note the place in the library where a periodical can be found. Other information will provide the basis for accurate and complete identification of a printed source in your finished paper.

Your bibliography card for a book may look like this:

HV
947
M58
1973

Mitford, Jessica. <u>Kind and
Usual Punishment: The
Prison Business.</u> New York:
Random House, 1973.

BIBLIOGRAPHY
CARD—BOOK

The typical card will include three kinds of information:

(1) *Full name of author or editor.* Put the author's *last name first* to facilitate alphabetizing. If a work has been collected or arranged by a person other than the author, you may start with that person's name, followed by "ed." for "editor." Ordinarily, however, the name of an editor or of a translator (followed by "trans.") comes after the title. If an article in an encyclopedia is identified only by the author's initials, you may be able to find the full name by checking the initials against a list of contributors.

(2) *Full title of the publication.* Include a subtitle, if any. (Separate it from the main title by a colon.) Underline the title of a book, pamphlet, or other work published as a separate unit. (Underlining in a handwritten or typed text corresponds to italics in print.) Put the title of an article or a poem in quotation marks to show that it was *part* of a larger publication. Then write and underline the title of the magazine or collection of which the article, story, or poem is a part.

(3) *The facts of publication.* For a book or pamphlet, these may include:

• The *number or description of the edition,* if the book has been revised or brought up to date since its original publication: "Rev. ed." or "3rd ed."

- The *number of volumes,* if a work consists of several, and all are relevant to your investigation: "2 vols."

- The *place of publication* (usually the location of the main office of the publishing house, or of the first office listed if several are given).

- The *name of the publisher,* leaving out such tags as "Inc." or "and Company": "Random House"; "McGraw-Hill."

- The *date of publication* (if no date is listed on the title page, use the latest copyright date listed on the reverse side of the title page).

- The *number of the specific volume used* (if only one volume of a larger work seems relevant to your investigation): "Vol. III."

Your bibliography card for an article will look somewhat different because it will include the title of the article *and* the title of the periodical where it appeared. A typical bibliography card for an article may look like this:

> Periodical Room
>
> Schorer, Mark. "D. H. Lawrence: Then, During, Now." *Atlantic* (March 1974), pp. 84–88.
>
> The author, one of Lawrence's biographers, traces Lawrence's reputation as a writer from its low point at the time of his death to its present "position of primacy among great twentieth-century prose writers in English."

> ANNOTATED
> CARD—ARTICLE

Note that this card is an example of an **annotated card**. Your bibliography cards will be especially useful to you if they carry brief reminders about the nature or content of the source.

Remember:

- For a magazine or newspaper article, the facts of publication ordinarily do *not* include the name of the publisher and the place of publication (though the latter is sometimes needed to identify a small-town journal).

- For articles in monthly or weekly magazines, and for articles in newspapers, write down the *date* of the issue and the complete *page numbers* for the article: "*Surfer's Companion,* Sept. 1980, p. 8." "*Milpitas Sentinel,* 10 Feb. 1982, pp. 17–19," Include the complete page numbers when an article is interrupted and then concluded later in the magazine: "pp. 12–17, 45–46."

- The pages of many professional or technical journals are numbered consecutively through the several issues of the same *volume*—usually all the issues published in one year. For an article in such a journal, record the number of the volume (in Arabic numerals), the year (in parentheses), and the page numbers of the article (leaving out *p.* or *pp.*): "*Modern Ornithology,* 7 (1982), 234–38."

- When page numbers throughout the different issues are *not* consecutive for the same volume of a technical journal, you may have to include the number of the issue: "*Birdwatcher's Quarterly,* 17, No. 3 (1979), 17–20."

- A newspaper may have more than one daily edition. It may have different sections, with pages not numbered consecutively throughout the issue. It may have a short article tucked away in one of many columns on the same page. Include all necessary or helpful information: "*Bogtown Herald and Gazette,* Late Ed., 20 March 1981, Sec. 3, p. 12, col. 3."

See **R 4e** for form of final bibliography.

# R 2e  Evaluating Your Sources

**Learn to choose authoritative sources and to evaluate conflicting evidence.**

Every investigator tries to find sources that are reliable and truly informative. When confronted with conflicting testimony, ask: "Who is talking? How does this writer know? What is this author trying to prove? What side is he or she on?" When you evaluate your sources, consider points like the following:

(1) *Is the author an authority on this subject*? If you can, find out whether a book was written by an economist whose specialty is Russian agriculture or by a columnist who spent four weeks surveying Russian agriculture from the windows of a train.

(2) *Is the work a thorough study or a sketchy survey of the topic*? Is it short on opinion and long on evidence? Does it weigh the findings of other authorities or ignore them?

(3) *Does the author settle important questions by going to primary sources*? **Primary sources** are legal documents, letters, diaries, eyewitness reports, transcripts of speeches and interviews, reports on experiments, statistical surveys, and the like. They take us close to unedited firsthand facts. They are often more reliable than **secondary sources**—other authors' accounts and interpretations of primary materials.

(4) *Is the author's treatment balanced or one-sided*? An early phase in the history of the American labor movement is likely to be treated one way in the success story of a famous industrialist. It will be treated another way in the biography of a labor leader. An objective historian will weigh both pro-business and pro-labor views.

(5) *Is the work recent enough to have profited from current scholarship*? If it was originally published ten or twenty years ago, is the current version a revised edition? Consider the possibility that an author's views may have been invalidated by new findings and changing theories in a rapidly expanding field of study.

# EXERCISES

A. Select one of the following subjects and compare its treatment in a general encyclopedia and in one of the more specialized reference works listed below. Choose one: atonality, surrealism, cybernetics, Zen, ESP, Savonarola, Hercules, Jacobins, Gestalt psychology, the Maccabees, Pan.

1. *Grove's Dictionary of Music and Musicians*
2. *Standard Dictionary of Folklore, Mythology and Legend*
3. *Comprehensive Dictionary of Psychological and Psychoanalytic Terms*
4. *Standard Jewish Encyclopedia*
5. *New Catholic Encyclopedia*
6. *Van Nostrand's Scientific Encyclopedia*
7. *Cambridge Medieval History*
8. *Cambridge Modern History*
9. *McGraw-Hill Dictionary of Art*
10. *Concise Encyclopedia of Living Faiths*

B. Interpret the following sample entries from the *Readers' Guide*:

**DIET**
Are we overdoing the diet thing? S.D. Lewis.
il Ebony 33:43-4+ F '78

**HAITIANS in the United States**
Forgotten heroes of Savannah; Haitian troops in
the American Revolution. C. Adrien. bibl il
Américas 30:55-7 N '78

**SPACE research**
United States
Long-range space policy advocated; remarks.
H. H. Schmitt. por Aviation W 109:63-4
N 13 '78; Excerpts. 109:7 S 25 '78
Routine utility in space; remarks. A. E. Stevenson.
Aviation W 109:11 N 6 '78
Year of the planets. il Time 112: 51 N 27 '78

**STARR, Bart**
Starr has a new bunch of stars. D. Jenkins. il Sports
Illus 49:32-3 N 6 '78*

**SOCIALLY handicapped children**
Education
Dealing with the disadvantaged; interview, ed by
A. Fryer, C. Adler. por Encore 7:36-7 Mr 6 '78

C. In the *Readers' Guide, Social Sciences Index,* or *Humanities Index,* find an article on one of the subjects listed below. Report on the intention of the author, level of difficulty of the article, and the author's use of sources. Choose one of the following general subjects:

- Supersonic aircraft
- Reevaluations of the CIA or FBI
- Freud and his disciples
- Birthrates and the schools
- Dissent in the Soviet Union
- Estimates of the world's fuel supply
- Testing in our public schools

D. Through the card catalog of your college library, find one of the following books. Study its preface, table of contents, bibliography (if any), and any other introductory or concluding sections. Study its treatment of selected entries or of one or two limited topics. Then prepare a brief report on the intention, scope, and possible usefulness of the book. Choose one:

1. H. L. Mencken, *The American Language*
2. Leo Rosten, *The Joys of Yiddish*
3. G. M. Trevelyan, *History of England*
4. Barbara W. Tuchman, *A Distant Mirror*
5. Kenneth Rexroth, *Classics Revisited*
6. Norma Lorre Goodrich, *Ancient Myths*
7. Margaret Mead, *Male and Female*
8. Alden T. Vaughan, *New England Frontier: Puritans and Indians*
9. Robert Coles, *Children of Crisis*
10. Thomas Pyles, *The Origin and Development of the English Language*
11. Mari Sandoz, *Cheyenne Autumn*
12. Margaret M. Bryant, *Current American Usage*
13. Linda Goodman, *Sun Signs*
14. Joseph Campbell, *The Hero with a Thousand Faces*
15. Simone de Beauvoir, *The Second Sex*

E. Study the arrangement of cards in the central card catalog of your college library in order to answer the following questions:

1. What are the major subdivisions for subject cards under the heading "Education"?
2. Where would you find a book by an author named John McMillan (under *Mc, Mac, Mi?*), George St. John (under *St., Sa, Jo?*), Antoine de Saint-Exupéry (under *De, Sa, St.?*)?
3. Do subject cards for books on the Civil War precede or follow cards for books on the War of Independence? Is the arrangement alphabetical or chronological?
4. Are books about George Washington listed before or after books about the State of Washington, or about Washington, D.C.?
5. Check under *John Keats*: What is the relative order of the author's individual works, his collected works, and books about the author?

F. Find and evaluate three major sources for a research report on changing attitudes toward one of the following: (1) nuclear safety; (2) prison reform; (3) age and aging. Your sources should include the following items:

- one book from the college or public library
- one magazine article indexed in the *Readers' Guide*
- one current magazine article

Prepare *bibliography cards* with full bibliographical information for your three sources. Include call numbers.

# R3 FROM NOTES TO THE FINAL DRAFT

In putting a research paper together, you face two major tasks. You collect material that bears on the question you are trying to answer, on the issue you are trying to explore. You then sort out and arrange these materials in a coherent presentation, supporting the conclusion or conclusions that your investigation has made you reach.

In the early stages of your project, your main worry is likely to be finding enough material. Will you be able to find usable articles and books? But with perseverance and luck, this worry is likely to change into its opposite: Will you be able to sort out all the material you have found? Will you be able to make sense of it? Can you present it in such a way that it tells a coherent story?

As you look at possible sources and read promising material, keep asking yourself what use you might be able to make of the material in your finished paper. Questions like the following will help you make the process of selection and organization productive:

- Am I personally *learning* something here about my topic?

- Does this help answer a *question* that has come up in my earlier reading?

- Does this point toward a major *subdivision* that should be part of my overall plan for organizing my material?

- Does this point toward a major *stage* in a chronological development or in a chain of cause and effect?

• Does this reinforce a major common concern that has played a role in my previous reading and that might point toward a possible overall *thesis* for my paper?

• What questions does this passage raise and leave *unanswered*—questions to which I should try to find the answer in my later reading?

## R3a Taking Notes

**Take accurate notes to serve as raw material for your first draft.**

For a short research report, you may be able to take notes on ordinary sheets of writing paper. But for a longer research paper, 3" × 5" or 4" × 6" note cards will enable you to shuffle and arrange your information as the overall pattern of your paper takes shape. Remember:

• Make sure *author and title of your source* (in shortened form) appear on each card, along with exact page numbers. Use the tentative subdivisions of your paper as the common heading for each group of related cards.

• Use each card for a *single piece of information*, for a single quotation, or for closely related material. This way you won't have to split up the material on the card later, to use in different parts of your paper.

• Include the kind of *specific detail* that you will need to support generalizations: selected examples, statistical figures, definitions of difficult terms.

• Make sure the material you select is *representative* of the source—not taken out of context. The person you quote should be able to say: "Yes, I'll stand behind that. That's more or less what I meant."

In taking notes, do not simply copy big chunks of material. Adapt the material to suit your purposes as you go along. Normally you will be using several major techniques:

(1) *Summarize background information; condense lengthy*

*arguments.* Here is a note card that condenses several pages of introductory information in John G. Neihardt's book *Black Elk Speaks*:

```
Last Battles

     In the fall of 1930, a field agent helped
Neihardt meet Black Elk, a holy man of the Oglala
Sioux who was a second cousin to Chief Crazy
Horse.  Black Elk was nearly blind and knew no
English.  Neihardt, speaking to him through an
interpreter, gained his confidence partly by re-
specting the holy man's long silences.  In the
spring of 1931, Black Elk took many days to tell
his life story, including the story of his share
in the defeat of General Custer, which Black Elk
witnessed as a young warrior.


Neihardt, Black Elk, pp. vii-xi
```

SAMPLE
NOTE CARD

(2) *Paraphrase much of the material that you are going to use.* In a **paraphrase**, we put information and ideas into our own words. This way we can emphasize what is most directly useful. We can cut down on what is less important. At the same time, we show that we have *made sense* of what we have read. The following sample note card paraphrases an author's statement and support of one key point:

```
Rehabilitation

     Trades or vocational skills taught in to-
day's prisons are often outdated or unrealistic.
In one case, a New York medium-security prison
provided detainees with a course in operating
diesel trucks.  The course was very popular and
was supported by local charitable organizations.
Ironically, after their release the prisoners
found that the law prohibited them from obtaining
a Class One driver's license for more than five
years in most cases.  In the interim, many re-
turned to the professions that had put them behind
bars in the first place.  As a result, over half
returned to prison.

Menninger, "Doing True Justice," p. 6
```

(3) *Make strategic use of brief, well-chosen direct quotations.*
When we quote **verbatim**, we quote directly word for word.
Quote characteristic or striking phrases. Quote sentences that
sum up well a step in an argument. Look for sentences that show
well the point of view or intentions of the quoted author. Apt,
brief direct quotations give your writing an authentic touch; they
show that you are staying close to the firsthand sources:

```
Indian Education

        Indian children were put in crowded boarding
schools and fed at the cost of 11 cents a day
(with their diet supplemented by food that could
be grown on school farms).  From the fifth grade
up, children put in half a day's labor on the
school farm.  They were taught "vanishing trades
of little or no economic importance."




"Breaking Faith," p. 240
```

(4) *Use more extended direct quotation for key passages.*
Quote at some length to let the original author sum up a major
argument. Quote the exact words when an author takes a stand
on a difficult or controversial issue:

```
Federal Policy

        "From the very beginnings of this nation, the
chief issue around which federal Indian policy has
revolved has been, not how to assimilate the
Indian nations whose lands we usurped, but how
best to transfer Indian lands and resources to
non-Indians."




Van de Mark, "Raid on the Reservations," p. 49
```

*Note*: In the actual finished paper, quotations running to several sentences, or to a paragraph or more, are usually set off as **block quotations**. (See chart, "Punctuating Quotations," on page 362.) Use such long quotations *sparingly*. Excerpt or break up quotations beyond paragraph length to keep the reader from merely skimming them or passing them by.

See **P 6c** on omissions from quotations.

# R3b   Using Quoted Material

**Use quoted material to good advantage in your own text.**

Learn how to work the material from your note cards smoothly into your own text. The following examples illustrate several legitimate ways but also an illegitimate way of using material from a source:

(1)   *Long quotation*—to be used sparingly:

In her biography of President Johnson, Doris Kearns

summed up the factors that weakened the role of the

traditional political party:

> The organization of unions, the development
>
> of the Civil Service, and the rise of the
>
> welfare state deprived the party of its
>
> capacity to provide jobs, food, and services
>
> to loyal constituents, thus severing its
>
> connection with the daily lives and needs of
>
> the people. . . . Technology provided access
>
> to new forms of amusement and recreation,

> such as movies and television, which were
>
> more diverting than party-sponsored dances
>
> and made it unlikely that people would
>
> attend political meetings and speeches for
>
> their entertainment value. During the
>
> 1960's, more and more people declined to
>
> affiliate themselves with a party and
>
> identified themselves as independents.[7]

In this example, the author's account of an important political change is quoted at some length. The excerpt is indented and set off as a **block quotation**—*no quotation marks.* The introductory sentence gives credit to the original author. The footnote numeral at the end directs the reader to a footnote that will give the title of the book and the exact page reference. The introductory sentence also sums up the point of the quotation. Readers easily become discouraged if they do not see the relevance and the point of numerous lengthy quotations.

(2) *Plagiarized version*—illegitimate, unacknowledged paraphrase:

The political party no longer plays its traditional

role. The growth of the unions and the welfare state

deprived the party of its capacity to provide jobs,

food, and services to people. New forms of amusement

and recreation, such as movies and television, were

more diverting than party-sponsored dances and made it

**358**

unlikely that people would attend political meetings

for their entertainment value. More and more people

declined to affiliate themselves with a party and be-

came independents instead.

Much **plagiarism** takes this form: The passage takes over
someone else's words and ideas in a slightly shortened, less
accurate form—*and without acknowledgment.* Even if the source
were identified, this method of adapting the material would be
unsatisfactory. Far too much of the original author's way of putting things has been kept—without the use of direct quotation.
The sentences have kept much of their basic structure. Much of
the wording has been copied: "deprived the party of its capacity,"
"more diverting than party-sponsored dances."

(3) *Legitimate paraphrase*—attributed to the original author:

As Doris Kearns reminds us, major changes in our

society weakened the traditional political party. The

old-style party had provided jobs, favors, and even

free food to the party faithful, but the unions, the

Civil Service, or the welfare state took over many of

these functions. People no longer depended on social

events sponsored by the party or on rousing political

speeches for entertainment; they had movies and televi-

sion instead. During the 1960's, fewer and fewer people

declared a party affiliation; many listed themselves as

independents.[7]

This **paraphrase**, documented by a footnote, keeps the essential meaning of the original. But the information is given to us in the adapter's own words, sometimes with the addition of touches that help make the point clear or vivid: "the party faithful," "rousing political speeches." The last sentence is parallel in structure to the original, but the other sentences are put together very differently. This is clearly an independent *interpretation* and adaptation of the original.

(4) *Part paraphrase, part direct quotation*—worked closely into the text:

In her biography of President Johnson, Doris Kearns traces the changes that weakened the role of our political parties. The growing labor unions, the expanding Civil Service, and the welfare state began to provide the jobs, the favors, and the free food that the old-style party had provided for the party faithful. These changes cut off the party's close "connection with the daily lives and needs of the people." Movies and television made the old-style party-sponsored dances and rousing political speeches obsolete as entertainment. During the 1960's, voters more and more "declined to affiliate themselves with a party and identified themselves as independents."[7]

Here the adapter explains the main points but at the same time keeps some of the authentic flavor of the original. Direct quotation is limited to characteristic phrases and key points. By using this technique, you can show that you have paid faithful attention to the original material and yet have made it truly your own. Use this method to break up the deadly "So-and-So says such-and-such" pattern of many research papers.

(5) *Legitimate summary*:

Doris Kearns shows how the unions, the Civil Service, the welfare state, and the mass media all helped weaken party affiliation. They provided the jobs, the favors, and the entertainment for which voters once turned to the traditional party organization.[7]

This **summary** gets at the gist of the passage. Such a summary is useful as a preview or an overview of major points, or as reinforcement of ideas developed in greater detail elsewhere in a paper.

# R3c  Introducing Quoted Material

**Know how to lead into quoted material in such a way that its source and its point are clear.**

In a well-written research paper, you move without abrupt or awkward breaks from your own statements and explanations to quoted material. As you lead up to a quotation or paraphrase, anticipate questions like the following:

- "Why is this material used here—what is it supposed to prove? What is the point?"

- "What is the source—who said this, and why is this person a good source? Why is this person worth listening to?"

**361**

## PUNCTUATING QUOTATIONS
### An Overview

DIRECT QUOTATION—quotation marks, introduced by comma or colon:

In the words of the report, "Engineering, medicine,

and law are no longer male bastions."

QUOTED WORDS OR PHRASES—*no* introductory comma or colon:

Like Horace Mann, Americans have long considered

education the "great equalizer" in society.

BLOCK QUOTATION—long passages set off and indented ten spaces, *no* quotation marks:

The article claims that most children today have

distorted ideas about older people:

> Most children have little contact with
>
> old people.  Their grandparents may be
>
> thousands of miles away or in nursing
>
> homes seldom visited.  As a result,
>
> young children's feelings about the el-
>
> derly and getting old tend to be negative
>
> and stereotyped. . .

LINES OF POETRY—When more than one line of a poem is part of your running text, use a slash—with one space on each side—to show where a new line of the poem starts. (Normally, set off *two or more* lines of poetry as a block quotation centered on the page.)

As Juliet says, it is Romeo's name that is her

enemy:  "That which we call a rose / By any other

name would smell as sweet."

Remember the following guidelines for introducing quoted material:

(1) *Link the material clearly to its source.* Give some indication of the nature of the source—book, newspaper article, report, interview, or the like. (Footnotes will provide the specifics for readers who may want to consult the original source.) Where appropriate, give some indication of the standing or background of the person you are quoting. Where necessary, put in tags like "According to the governor, . . ." or "As Erich Fromm has observed, . . ." When you quote several authors, make sure that references like "she" or "he" or "the writer" point clearly to the one you have in mind.

(2) *Steer your readers by telling them what the point of a quotation is.* Show how the material is relevant to your argument or to your line of investigation. Direct the attention of your readers by giving them a brief introductory summary of an important quotation:

According to William G. Nagel in his book *The New Red Barn*, we neglect our penal system because *it deals mainly with people who do not count in our society*: "The generally unsatisfactory condition of the correctional process reflects the lowly status of the people caught in it. . . . As long as the majority of offenders are poor, uneducated, and from minority groups, the correctional slice of the federal budget will remain small, and the overall response will be repressive."[2]

(3) *Know how to quote key words and phrases as part of your own sentences.* When a quotation becomes part of a sentence of your own, fit it into the grammatical pattern of your own sentence—without changing the wording of the part quoted directly:

WRONG: Pope Pius described a just war in this way: "If it has been forced upon one by an evident and extremely grave injustice that in no way can be avoided."

RIGHT: Pope Pius stated that a war is just "if it has been forced upon one by an evident and extremely grave injustice that in no way can be avoided."

**363**

Study the following two examples of how a writer leads into quoted or paraphrased material. Look at how each writer answers the questions in the reader's mind: "Why is this in here? Who said this? What is the point?"

**Example 1 (indirect quotation)**

Increases in out-of-state tuition are keeping students from Third World countries away from American colleges. Stephen Horn, president of California State University at Long Beach, told a meeting of educators that, of the 27,000 African students who attend college away from their home countries, 24,000 study in the Soviet Union. According to Horn, many of those students are the future leaders of their countries. The United States does not subsidize foreign students as heavily as the Soviets do and therefore attracts far fewer foreign students. In the opinion of the speaker, further increases in nonresident tuition would discourage all but rich foreigners from attending school in the United States.[4]

**Example 2 (block quotation)**

Many Americans feel a helpless anger about the proliferation of firearms in this country. They share the sense of outrage felt by the relatives of homicide victims and expressed, for instance, by David H. Berg, a criminal lawyer, in an article in <u>Newsweek</u>:

> A deputy sheriff held my brother's skull for a photograph that appeared in the center of the front page. . . . The suffering of my family is not unique. Someone is murdered by a gunshot every 48 minutes in America, about 10,000 people a year, a figure that has quadrupled since my brother's death in 1968. . . . Those of us touched personally by these grotesque statistics cannot even console ourselves. . . . We must live forever with an agonizing truth: that someone we loved was killed for nothing at all, and with a gun that was sold like groceries.[7]

## R3d Combining Different Sources

**Combine material from different sources in a coherent paragraph.**

Writing a research paper tests your ability to make things add up. A paragraph in your finished paper will often combine material from several different note cards. The paragraph will often begin with the general conclusion that the evidence on several related cards suggests. The rest of the paragraph will then present details selected from the cards.

Study the following three sample cards, which all focus on the same question:

**Card 1**

> Endangered Species—Counts
>
> The bald eagle became the national symbol in 1782, and there were nesting pairs in all the lower 48 states. The current bald eagle population has been estimated at 5,000 in the lower 48 states. As of 1975, only 627 nests remained active, and they produced approximately 500 young.
>
>
> Graham, "Will the Bald Eagle Survive?" p. 99.

**Card 2**

> Endangered Species—Counts
>
> "In 1948, the wild whooping crane population was up by just two from a decade earlier—to 31. The count sank to 21 in the winter of 1951-52, then rose gradually to an encouraging 74 in 1978-79. Last spring there were six yearlings to join the flight north. . . . The wild whooping crane count now stands at 76, an improvement deriving in large measure from protective practices at Arkansas."
>
> Wilson and Hayden, "Where Oil and Wildlife Mix," pp. 37-38.

**Card 3**

```
Endangered Species—Counts

    "Whooping cranes, the largest cranes inhab-
iting North America, are on the U.S. endangered
species list.  The big birds' population dwindled
to 14 in the late 1930s but is now estimated at
95."




Freedman, "Whooping Cranes," p. 89.
```

Study the way material from these note cards has been integrated in the following finished paragraph:

For years, nature lovers have been keeping an
anxious count of such endangered species as the bald
eagle and the whooping crane.  When the bald eagle
became the national symbol soon after Independence,
there were nesting pairs everywhere in what is now the
continental United States.  Two hundred years later,
Frank Graham, Jr., writing in <u>Audubon</u> magazine, reported
a current estimate of 5,000 bald eagles left in the
lower forty-eight states.  According to his figures,
only 627 nests remained active, and they produced approximately 500 young.[3]  In 1981, Steven C. Wilson and

Karen C. Hayden, writing in the <u>National Geographic</u>,
reported a count of 76 for wild whooping cranes left
in the United States, up from a dismal count of 21
thirty years earlier.[4] Another estimate puts the current population at 95.[5]

## R3e   Organizing Your Paper

**Go from tentative groupings to a definite outline for your
materials.**

You reach a crucial stage in your investigation when you go
beyond the first preliminary collecting of material and begin to
set up tentative major categories. From the beginning, look for
details and ideas that seem *related*—they bear on the same major
point, or they point toward the same tentative conclusion. In a
productive investigation, the collecting and the sorting out of
material go hand in hand. Remember the following advice:

(1) *Group together note cards that contain related material.*
Assign tentative common headings to groups of cards that deal
with the same limited question or the same part of a larger issue.
For a paper on prison reform, you might decide early that your
major groupings should include "Old-style penitentiaries,"
"Rehabilitation," "Experiments—U.S.," and "Experiments—
Abroad." As you continue your reading, additional headings and
subheadings will become needed.

Remember that your categories should grow out of your
material. They should reflect what you have found. At the same
time, they will help give direction to your further reading. They
will make you look for further supporting material where your
evidence still seems weak or confusing. Finally, they will begin
to suggest a rough overall plan for your paper.

Suppose you have been investigating charges that few Americans study foreign languages, and that the influence of the United
States around the world is seriously undermined as a result. You

have found evidence to support these charges in sources ranging from articles in the *New York Times* to specialized studies and government reports. As you sort out your evidence, you establish major groupings like the following. At the same time, these groupings begin to point toward an overall plan for your paper:

*"Statistics on Language Study"*

(The starting point for your paper may be comparative statistics on how many American students study foreign languages, compared with students in other countries. For instance, according to a former U.S. secretary of education, in the early 1980's there were almost ten million students of English in the Soviet Union but fewer than 30,000 students of Russian in the United States.)

*"U.S. Handicaps"*

(A major central portion of your paper may be devoted to specific shortcomings or handicaps that result from the failure of Americans to learn foreign languages. For instance, you may have collected many data about inadequate foreign-language preparation of people employed by the foreign service. Recently no one in the U.S. Embassy in India spoke Hindi, the native language most widely spoken by the local population. In 1979, the U.S. government did not employ anyone fully qualified as a simultaneous interpreter from Chinese to English—able to render Chinese into English while the speaker is talking.)

*"U.S. Isolation"*

(A major final section of your paper may be devoted to a growing isolation that is the result of our nation's neglect of the world's languages. A study in the *Washington Star*, for instance, claimed that Russian radio broadcasts reach listeners in eighty-five languages, whereas American radio broadcasts for foreign countries are broadcast in thirty-eight languages—for shorter periods, and with weaker signals.)

(2) *Work toward a unifying thesis.* Ask yourself: "What is this paper as a whole going to tell the reader?" Try to sum up in one sentence the overall conclusion that your research has made you reach. Present this sentence as your thesis early in your paper—preferably at the end of an effective but *short* introduction:

THESIS: The failure of Americans to learn foreign languages is producing a growing isolation of our country from the rest of the world.

If the results of your investigation are less clear-cut or more contradictory, make your thesis reflect the complications. Suppose you are writing a paper on the present state of gambling in the United States. To unify your paper, you concentrate on the legal aspects of gambling. You review in some detail the laws of Nevada as exceptions to antigambling laws in other states, the legal status of horse and dog races, the question of lotteries and games conducted for charitable purposes. Everything you say in the paper could support one single major point:

THESIS: Gambling laws in the United States are paradoxical and unpredictable.

(3) *Work out a clear overall plan for your paper.* Suppose you are writing about the threatened survival of the American bald eagle. You may early decide to group your note cards under major headings like the following:

Population counts
Dangers from pesticides
Dangers from sheep ranchers
Conservation measures

These headings suggest a plausible general strategy: You may want to start with a review of past history, go on to the discussion of current problems, and then conclude by discussing promising solutions. Here is a preliminary outline for a paper about the bald eagle as an endangered species:

```
THESIS:   The bald eagle will become extinct unless
          we come to understand and respect the special
          needs of this endangered species.

    I.    The history of the bald eagle

   II.    Dangers to the bald eagle
          A.   Pesticides used by farmers
          B.   Poisoned bait, traps, and bullets used
               by ranchers
          C.   Technological dangers
```

III. Steps toward improvement
  A. New eagle refuge
  B. Stricter control of poisons
  C. Better powerline structures

Your outline will enable you to decide which of your note cards contain irrelevant material and should be set aside. It will also help you to decide in which areas your notes need to be supplemented by further reading. A definitive outline preceding the final paper usually shows whether the paper has a unifying purpose, whether the major subdivisions of the paper contribute to that purpose, and whether unrelated odds and ends have been eliminated.

For forms of outlines, see **C 3b**.

# R 3f   Revising the First Draft

**Allow time for a final rewriting of your first draft.**

A first draft usually makes jerky reading. Important explanations may be missing. Links may be missing from one section to the next. Awkward repetition or backtracking may slow down the reader. In your final revision, do the following:

• Check for *clear overall intention.* Make sure your main points are not merely implied but clearly and fully stated. State them preferably at the beginning of the paper, following your introduction. Or, if more appropriate, state them toward the end of the paper in the form of a summary.

• Check for *adequate support.* Make sure you have the details and examples that your reader would accept as adequate evidence for your major points.

• Check for adequate *interpretation.* Many papers suffer from too much quotation, too much summary, and not enough explanation and comparison. Examine key terms to see whether they need to be more fully defined. Explain terms like *psychosomatic* or *monolingual.*

**371**

• Check for *coherence*. Make your reader see the relationship between different parts of your paper. Anticipate and answer the questions of a reader mired in a mass of details: "How did this get in here?" "Why do I have to study this particular set of statistics?" Make sure there is a clear **transition**, implied or stated, from paragraph to paragraph.

• Check for clear *attribution*. Make sure all material directly quoted is clearly identified. (See chart on page 362.)

# EXERCISES

A. Select a magazine article or a chapter in a book on one of the topics listed below. Assume that you are extracting information or opinions for use in a larger research project. Prepare five note cards illustrating various techniques of *note taking*: Include examples of summary, paraphrase, mixed indirect and direct quotation, and extended direct quotation. Choose one:

• the history of advertising
• secret wartime codes and how to break them
• the history of photography
• the Long March
• Hollywood's early stars
• the Cherokee nation
• the suffragette movement
• rape and the law
• space stations

B. Combine closely related material from different note cards in a finished *sample paragraph*. Prepare three note cards that all bear on the same limited point. Turn to sources that you have used for one of the previous exercises, or to sources related to your own current research paper project. Use the material on your cards in a sample paragraph that introduces the material clearly and helpfully to your reader. Hand in the note cards with your finished paragraph. (Omit the footnote numerals and footnotes that would accompany the paragraph in a finished paper.)

C. As you come close to finishing the first draft of your research paper, write a *one-page abstract* (double-spaced) of your project. Include your thesis and summarize the supporting material. Your instructor may ask you to add a tentative outline for your finished paper.

# R4    FOOTNOTES AND BIBLIOGRAPHIES

**Use footnotes and a bibliography to give full and accurate information about your sources.**

In a full-length research paper, you typically identify your sources twice. The first time you quote from a source or use information from it, you identify it fully in a numbered note keyed to the reference in the text. Then you identify it again in your final bibliography—your final alphabetical listing of the sources you have used. Your notes and your bibliography provide complete **documentation**. They enable your reader to identify, trace, and check your sources.

The purpose of documentation is to provide clear and accurate information in limited space. The style or form of documentation shown in the following sections is widely used by people doing research in modern languages and literatures. (In all essentials, the style recommended in this handbook follows the *MLA Handbook for Writers of Research Papers, Theses, and Dissertations.*) Follow this style unless told otherwise by your instructor. In preparing research papers in other academic fields, you may be required to follow a different style. (Other widely followed guides to style for documentation include the Chicago *Manual of Style* and Kate L. Turabian's *Manual for Writers of Term Papers, Theses, and Dissertations*, both published by the University of Chicago Press.)

## R4a    Using Footnotes

**Use footnotes to show the sources of facts, opinions, and examples.**

The most basic use of footnotes is to show the exact source of every direct quotation you use in your paper. You need to identify the exact source whenever you quote somebody or something word for word. But you also need to footnote indirect quotation—you need to identify your source when you merely paraphrase or summarize what someone has said. In addition, you need to show the source of all facts, figures, or ideas that are the result of someone else's effort or inspiration.[1]

A footnote is *not* necessary when you have merely repeated something that is widely known or believed:

NO FOOTNOTE:   George Washington was elected to the Virginia assembly in 1758.
               (This is "common knowledge," the kind of fact likely to be recorded in public documents and found in many history books.)
FOOTNOTE:      Samuel Eliot Morison describes Washington as "an eager and bold experimenter" in new agricultural methods.[17]
               (This is a judgment the historian made on the basis of firsthand investigation. The text already mentions his name; the footnote, not reprinted here, will give the exact source.)

Number your footnotes consecutively. Place the raised **footnote number** outside whatever punctuation goes with the sentence or paragraph. Indent the footnote itself like a paragraph, and start it with the raised footnote number. Capitalize the first word and use a period or other end punctuation at the end:

[3] Robin Northcroft, A Short Guide to British

Cooking (New York: Culinary Arts, 1979), p. 85.

Both in a typed manuscript and in a printed text, footnotes may appear in two different positions:

(1) *Most footnotes today are really end notes.* They appear at the end of a typed paper on a separate sheet, or at the end of a chapter or whole book. This system is easy and convenient for typist and printer, although less convenient for the reader. Follow this system unless otherwise instructed: Place your notes on a separate sheet at the end of your paper. *Double-space* your notes. (See the notes at the end of the sample research paper for an illustration of a separate page for notes.)

---

[1]Not all footnotes serve for documentation. **Explanatory footnotes**, of which this note is an illustration, may define technical terms unfamiliar only to some of the readers. They may provide information not necessary to the main trend of the argument.

(2) *True footnotes appear at the bottom of the page.* They are convenient for the reader but difficult to position for the typist.

# R4b First References

**Fully identify a source the first time you refer to it.**

The most common type of footnote gives full information about a source the first time you mention it or draw on it in your paper. The following sample footnotes illustrate the standard form for such a first reference, as well as the most important variations:

(1) *Standard reference to a book.* Give the author's full name, putting the first name first. After a comma, add the title of the book—*underlined* in typescript (italicized in print). Give the facts of publication in parentheses. (Include place of publication, name of publisher, date of publication.) After a comma, add the page reference ("p." for single page; "pp." for several pages: pp. 163–65):

[7] Mary McCarthy, Memoirs of a Catholic Girlhood

(New York: Harcourt, 1957), p. 23.

(2) *Newspaper or magazine article.* Enclose the title of the article in quotation marks; underline (italicize) the title of the newspaper or magazine: "How to Deep-Freeze Bait," *Angler's Monthly.* Give the date of issue, separated from what comes before and after by commas:

[3] "Environmentalists See Threats to Rivers," New

York Times, 15 July 1981, Sec. 1, p. 8, col. 1.

[19] Steven Weinberg, "The Decay of the Proton,"

Scientific American, June 1981, p. 67.

If page numbering is continuous through the several issues of an annual volume, add the volume number as an Arabic numeral. Enclose the year or month in parentheses. Then give the page reference *without* using *p.* or *pp.*:

> ⁷ Kenneth F. Weaver, "The Promise and Peril of Nuclear Energy," National Geographic, 155 (April 1979), 466.

(3) *Partial footnote.* If the text of your paper has given the author's full name, start your footnote with the title. (Do the same even if your text has given both name and title.) If your text attributes a quotation about American astronauts to Tom Wolfe as the author, your footnote might look like this:

> ² The Right Stuff (New York: Farrar, 1979), p. 376.

(4) *Work with several authors.* Give the full names of several authors who have coauthored a book or an article. If there are more than two, you may want to put *et al.,* Latin for "and others," after the name of the first author instead:

> ⁴ Renée Hausmann and Evelyn Taylor, A Practical Rhetoric for College Writers (Belmont, Calif.: Wadsworth, 1980), pp. 5-6.

> ¹¹ Noël H. Gale and Zofia Stos-Gale, "Lead and Silver in the Ancient Aegean," Scientific American, June 1981, p. 176.

> ¹⁷ Marie M. Stewart et al., Business English and Communication, 5th ed. (New York: McGraw-Hill, 1978), p. 194.

(5) *Work with subtitle.* Separate the subtitle from the title by a colon unless the original has other punctuation. Underline the subtitle of a book. Enclose both the title and the subtitle of an article in the same set of quotation marks:

[11] Bruno Bettelheim, <u>The Uses of Enchantment: The Meaning and Importance of Fairy Tales</u> (New York: Knopf, 1976), p. 65.

[6] Sarah Schmidt, "From Ghetto to University: The Jewish Experience in the Public School," <u>American Educator</u>, Spring 1978, p. 23.

(6) *Edited or translated work.* Insert the editor's or translator's name after the title, separating it from the title by a comma. Use the abbreviation "ed." or "trans." The editor's name may come first if the author is unknown, if the editor has collected the work of different authors, or if the editor has brought together an author's work from different sources:

[2] H. L. Mencken, <u>The Vintage Mencken</u>, ed. Alistair Cooke (New York: Vintage, 1956), p. 49.

[4] Alice Griffin, ed., <u>Rebels and Lovers: Shakespeare's Young Heroes and Heroines</u> (New York: New York Univ. Press, 1976), p. 80.

[6] Konrad Lorenz, <u>On Aggression</u>, trans. Marjorie Kerr Wilson (New York: Harcourt, 1966), p. 7.

(7) *Revised editions.* If a work has been brought up to date since its original publication, give the number of the edition you are using. Place it before the facts of publication. Separate it from what comes before by a comma:

<sup></sup>

² Albert C. Baugh, <u>A History of the English Lan-</u><u>guage</u>, 2nd ed. (New York: Appleton, 1957), pp. 7-8.

(8) *Work published in several volumes.* Show the number of the volume you are quoting. Use a capital Roman numeral. Insert it after the facts of publication, and separate it from what precedes and follows it by commas. Remember that after a volume number "p." and "pp." are omitted:

³ Virginia Woolf, <u>The Diary of Virginia Woolf</u>, ed. Anne Olivier Bell (New York: Harcourt, 1977), I, 17.

(9) *Article in a collection.* Identify fully both the article and the collection of which it is a part:

⁴ Carl R. Rogers, "Two Divergent Trends," in <u>Exis-</u><u>tential Psychology</u>, ed. Rollo May (New York: Random House, 1969), p. 87.

(10) *Encyclopedia entry.* Page numbers and facts of publication may be unnecessary for short entries appearing in alphabetical order in well-known encyclopedias or dictionaries. Date or number of the edition used, however, should be included because of the frequent revisions of major encyclopedias:

² M. J. Politis, "Greek Music," <u>Encyclopedia</u> <u>Americana</u>, 1956 ed.

⁴ "Aging," <u>Encyclopaedia Britannica</u>, 1974, I, 299.

(11) *Bible or literary classic.* References to the Bible usually identify only book, chapter, and verse. The name of a book of the Bible is *not* underlined or put in quotation marks. References to a Shakespeare play available in many different editions may specify act, scene, and line:

[4] Judges 13:5  or  [4] Judges xiii.5.

[3] <u>Hamlet</u> II.ii.311-22.

*Note*: You will have to specify the edition used if textual variations are important, as with a new translation of the Bible. No identification is necessary for well-known or proverbial lines: "To be or not to be"; "The quality of mercy is not strained"; "They also serve who only stand and wait."

(12) *Quotations at second hand.* Make it clear that you are not quoting from the original or complete text:

[5] William Archer, letter of October 18, 1883, to

his brother Charles; quoted in Henrik Ibsen, <u>Ghosts</u>,

ed. Kai Jurgensen and Robert Schenkkan (New York: Avon,

1965), p. 135.

(13) *Pamphlets and unpublished material.* Indicate the nature and source of the materials: mimeographed pamphlet, unpublished doctoral dissertation, and the like. Use quotation marks to enclose unpublished titles—publications duplicated informally for limited use:

[17] Calif. Dept. of Viticulture, <u>Grape Harvesting</u>

(Sacramento: State Printing Office, 1980), pp. 8-9.

[9] Fernando Lopez, ed., "Tales of the Elders" (Albu-

querque, mimeo., 1979), p. 82.

[23] Philip Latesta, "Rod McKuen and the Sense of

<u>Déjà Vu</u>," Diss. Columbia 1980, pp. 12-13.

(14) *Nonprint sources.* Give the information needed to describe such sources as interviews, lectures, recordings, or television programs:

[16] Personal Interview with Gene Silveira, 30 June 1981.

[7] Ottavia Massini, "The Art of Picasso," Valley Lecture Series, Los Angeles, 12 March 1982.

[11] Billie Holiday, "God Bless the Child," <u>Essential Billie Holiday</u>, Verve, 68410, 1961.

[3] <u>The Poisoned Earth</u>, narr. Sylvia Garth, writ. and prod. Pat Fisher, WXRV News Special, 23 Oct. 1979.

# R4c Later References

**Keep subsequent references short but clear.**

There is no need to repeat the full name and title or the facts of publication. Here are the most common possibilities:

(1) *Shortened reference.* Once you have fully identified a book, use the author's last name to identify it in later footnotes. Separate the name from the page reference by a comma:

[11] Baugh, p. 9.

When you are using *several works by the same author,* use the author's last name and a shortened form of the title:

[11] Baugh, <u>History</u>, p. 9.

(2) *One footnote for several quotations.* Avoid long strings of footnotes giving different page references to the same work. If several quotations from the same work follow one another in the same paragraph of your paper, put the page references together in a single footnote. Use this method only when *no* quotations from another source intervene:

$^{13}$ Harrison, pp. 8-9, 12, 17.

(3) *Page references in the text.* If all or most of your references are to a single work, you may put page references in parentheses in the body of your text: (p. 37). Identify the source in your first footnote and explain your procedure:

$^1$ Jerome S. Bruner, <u>On Knowing: Essays for the</u> <u>Left Hand</u> (New York: Atheneum, 1965), p. 3. All page references in the text of this paper are to this source.

*Note*: A different system for shortened reference is frequently found in earlier scholarship but is rarely used today. Instead of repeating, in a shortened form, the author's name or the title, the writer used *ibid.*, an abbreviation of Latin *ibidem*, "in the same place." When used by itself, without a page reference, it means "in the last publication cited, on the same page." When used with a page reference, it means "in the last publication cited, on the page indicated." Like other Latin abbreviations used in footnotes, *ibid.* is no longer commonly italicized. It can refer only to *the last source cited*:

$^1$ G. B. Harrison, <u>Introducing Shakespeare</u> (Harmondsworth, Middlesex: Penguin, 1947), p. 28.

$^2$ Ibid., p. 37.

If a reference to a *different* work has intervened, the author's name is followed by *op. cit.*, short for *opere citato*, "in the work already cited." (This abbreviation cannot be used when several works by the same author have already been cited.)

$^1$ G. B. Harrison, <u>Introducing Shakespeare</u> (Harmondsworth, Middlesex: Penguin, 1947), p. 28.

<sup>2</sup> B. Ifor Evans, <u>A Short History of English Drama</u> (Harmondsworth, Middlesex: Penguin, 1948), pp. 51-69.

<sup>3</sup> Harrison, op. cit., p. 37.

# R 4d  Abbreviations

**Know common abbreviations used in footnotes in scholarly books and articles.**

You will encounter a number of abbreviations and technical terms in addition to those you will regularly use in your own work. The meaning of many of these will be clear from their context or position: *anon.* for "anonymous," *ch.* and *chs.* for "chapter" and "chapters," *col.* and *cols.* for "column" and "columns," *l.* and *ll.* for "line" and "lines," *n.* and *nn.* for "note" and "notes." Others are not self-explanatory:

| | |
|---|---|
| © | copyright (© 1961 by John W. Gardner) |
| c. or ca. | Latin *circa*, "approximately"; used for approximate dates and figures (c. 1952) |
| cf. | Latin *confer*, "compare"; often used for **cross-references** instead of "see"; "consult for further relevant material" (Cf. Ecclesiastes xii.12) |
| et al. | Latin *et alii*, "and others"; used in references to books by several authors (G. S. Harrison et al.) |
| f., ff. | "and the following page," "and the following pages" (See p. 16 ff.) |
| loc. cit. | Latin *loco citato*, "in the place cited"; used without page reference (Baugh, loc. cit.) |
| MS, MSS | Manuscript, manuscripts |
| n.d. | "no date," date of publication unknown |

| | |
|---|---|
| passim | Latin for "throughout"; "in various places in the work under discussion" (See pp. 54–56 et passim.) |
| rev. | "review" or "revised" |
| rpt. | "reprint"; a current reprinting of an older book |
| q.v. | Latin *quod vide*, "which you should consult" |

# R4e   Final Bibliography

**In your final bibliography, include all the information needed to identify a source when it is first mentioned.**

Your final bibliography will be based on your bibliography cards. Its main purpose is to describe in one single alphabetical list all sources you have used. You may include sources that you have found helpful but have not actually quoted in your paper.

Entries in the bibliography differ from footnotes in form. The first line is *not* indented. The second line and additional lines are indented five spaces. Other differences:

(1)   *The last name of the author comes first.* This order applies only to the first author listed when a book has several authors. (The bibliography is an *alphabetical* listing.)

Brooks, Gwendolyn.   The World of Gwendolyn Brooks.

    New York: Harper, 1971.

Himstreet, William C., and Wayne Murlin Baty.   Busi-

    ness Communications: Principles and Methods.

    5th ed.   Belmont, Calif.: Wadsworth, 1977.

(If *no name of author or editor is known to you*, list the publication alphabetically by the first letter of the title, not counting *The, A,* or *An.*)

(2) *Major breaks are shown by periods.* The identification of
the author or editor is separated from what follows by a period.
The facts of publication for a book are not enclosed in parentheses and are separated from what precedes and what follows by
periods:

Silverberg, Robert, ed.  Science Fiction Hall of Fame.

    2 vols.  London: Sphere Books, 1972.

(3) *Entries for articles give the complete page numbers for the
entire article.* Entries for books do *not* include page references.
But entries for parts of a collection or for articles in periodicals
give the inclusive page numbers for the whole selection:

Berkowitz, Leonard.  "How Guns Control Us."  Psychology

    Today, June 1981, pp. 11-12.

Kelly, Orr.  "The Great American Immigration Nightmare."

    U.S. News & World Report, 22 June 1981, pp. 27-31.

When a periodical uses continuous page numbering through
the several issues of an annual volume, include the *volume number* as an Arabic numeral: "*PMLA*, 96 (1981), 351–62." (Omit *p.*
or *pp.*)

(4) *Do not repeat the author's name if you list several publications by the same author.* Substitute a line made of ten hyphens
for the name in the second and later entries:

Ibsen, Henrik.  A Doll's House and Other Plays.  Trans.

    Peter Watts.  Harmondsworth, Middlesex: Penguin,

    1965.

----------.  Ghosts.  Trans. Kai Jurgensen and Robert

    Schenkkan.  New York: Avon, 1965.

----------. <u>Three Plays</u>.   Trans. Una Ellis-Fermor.

Harmondsworth, Middlesex: Penguin, 1950.

The following might be the final bibliography for a paper on photography as social document. Study the different kinds of entries. (See also the bibliography at the end of the sample research paper.)

Bibliography

Capa, Cornell, ed.   <u>The Concerned Photographer</u>.

Vol. II.   New York: Grossman, 1972.
[the second volume of this work, listed under editor's name]

Capa, Robert.   <u>Images of War</u>.   New York: Grossman,

n.d.
[no date of publication available]

Dillard, Annie.   "Sight into Insight."   <u>Harper's</u>,

Feb. 1974, pp. 39-46.
[standard entry for article in a monthly magazine]

Eisenstaedt, Alfred.   <u>The Eye of Eisenstaedt</u>.   New

York: Viking, 1969.
[standard entry for book]

Evans, Harold.   <u>Pictures on a Page: Photo Journalism</u>

<u>and Picture Editing</u>.   Belmont, Calif.: Wadsworth,

1978.
[book with subtitle]

Gernsheim, Helmut, and Alison Gernsheim. <u>Creative</u>

  <u>Photography: 1826 to the Present</u>. Detroit: Wayne

  State Univ. Press, 1963.

  [book with two authors—last name is put first only for first author]

Kunhardt, Philip B., Jr. "Images of Which History Was

  Made." <u>Smithsonian</u>, July 1977, pp. 24-35.

  [standard entry for magazine article]

Nairn, Ian. <u>The American Landscape: A Critical View</u>.

  New York: Random House, 1965.

  [book with subtitle]

Ohlander, Frances. "The Haunting Image." West Valley

  Lecture, San Diego. 12 Dec. 1980.

  [nonprint source—unpublished lecture]

"A Photographer's Odyssey." <u>Oakland Herald</u>, 26 Aug.

  1980, p. 9, col. 3.

  [unsigned newspaper article (author unknown)]

Sontag, Susan. <u>On Photography</u>. New York: Farrar,

  1977.

  [standard entry for book]

# EXERCISES

  A.  Interpret the information in the following *sample footnotes*. Point out
special or unusual features.

⁵ Ray Bradbury, <u>The Stories of Ray Bradbury</u> (New York: Knopf, 1980), p. xiii.

¹¹ Tracy Kidder, "Flying Upside Down," <u>Atlantic</u>, July 1981, p. 55.

² Eileen Connell, "A Community View of Cable Regulation," in <u>Telecommunications Policy and the Citizen</u>, ed. Timothy R. Haight (New York: Praeger, 1979), pp. 204-05.

⁹ Euripides, <u>The Trojan Women</u>, trans. Richmond Lattimore, in <u>Greek Plays in Modern Translation</u>, ed. Dudley Fitts (New York: Dial, 1947), p. 161.

⁴ "Prison System Breaking Down?" <u>U.S. News & World Report</u>, 11 Aug. 1967, p. 61.

⁸ Kenneth Muir, ed., <u>Collected Poems of Sir Thomas Wyatt</u> (Cambridge, Mass.: Harvard Univ. Press, 1950), p. xx.

⁷ 1 Corinthians iii.18-20.

¹³ Simone Weil, "The <u>Iliad</u>, or The Poem of Force," trans. Mary McCarthy, in <u>The Mint</u>, ed. Geoffrey Grigson, No. 2 (1948), p. 85.

¹² Mary Jane Moffat and Charlotte Painter, eds., <u>Revelations: Diaries of Women</u> (New York: Random House, 1974), p. 10.

[3] Robert E. Spiller et al., <u>Literary History of the United States</u>, rev. ed. (New York: Macmillan, 1953), p. 1343.

[8] Paul Goodman, "The New Reformation," <u>New York Times Magazine</u>, 14 Sept. 1969, p. 14.

   B. Interpret the information provided in the following *sample bibliography entries*. Point out special or unusual features.

Adams, Virginia.  "The Sibling Bond: A Lifelong Love/Hate Dialectic."  <u>Psychology Today</u>, June 1981, pp. 32-47.

Churchill, Winston S.  <u>The Age of Revolution</u>.  Vol. III of <u>A History of the English-Speaking Peoples</u>.  New York: Dodd, Mead, 1957.

Epstein, Edward J., and Jeffrey Steingarten.  "Europe: The End of a Miracle."  <u>Atlantic</u>, July 1981, pp. 11, 18.

<u>Flight to the Stars</u>.  Writ. Bernard Grothe.  Dir. Jean Harmond.  PBS Science Special.  21 Oct. 1978.

Frost, Robert.  <u>Robert Frost Reads His Poetry</u>.  Caedmon, XC 783, 1952.

Komisar, Lucy.  "The Image of Woman in Advertising."  In <u>Woman in Sexist Society</u>.  Ed. Vivian Gornick and Barbara K. Moran. New York: New American

Library, 1972, pp. 304-17.

Norman, Jack, ed. <u>Stories to Teach and Delight</u>. New

York: Amsco, 1977.

"Trends to Watch in This Decade." <u>U.S. News & World

Report</u>, 22 June 1981, pp. 60-61.

Wells, Walter. <u>Communications in Business</u>. 2nd ed.

Belmont, Calif.: Wadsworth, 1977.

Yeager, Pat. "Beyond the Atom." <u>Physics Review</u>, 28

(1980), 878-95.

C. Draw on bibliography cards you have prepared for previous exercises or for your research paper. On a sheet of paper, write five *sample footnotes*. Include both books and articles. Then, on a second sheet of paper, arrange the same five sources alphabetically and present them as a *sample bibliography*.

## REVIEW EXERCISE: SAMPLE RESEARCH PAPER

Study the following sample research paper. Pay special attention to the way the author has adapted and worked into the text a variety of quoted material. Compare the different kinds of footnotes used. Contrast the way sources are identified in the footnotes and in the final bibliography. How successful has the author been in meeting the standards outlined in the preceding chapter?

Aging in America:

Is the Best Yet to Be?

by

Barbara Johnston

English 2, Section 5
Professor Lamont
May 11, 1980

Outline

THESIS:  American society needs to change its
          assessment of what aging is and how the
          aged should be treated.

Introduction:  The questioning of youth-worship

  I.  Growth statistics on the aging movement

 II.  Contradictory voices on the subject of age

III.  Areas of general agreement

      A.  The rejection of old stereotypes

          1.  How the stereotypes are perpetuated

          2.  How research and group pressure are
              destroying the stereotypes

      B.  The aged as leaders of the movement

      C.  The demand for choices

          1.  Choice in relationships

          2.  Choice in education

          3.  Choice in employment

Conclusion:  The idea of life as a continuum

Aging in America:

Is the Best Yet to Be?


In a famous poem, Robert Browning said, "Grow old along with me! / The best is yet to be."[1] [lines of poetry] Traditionally, American culture has not found this sentiment either comforting or believable. The idea that old age can be the "golden years" has been voiced by many but believed by few. A spot check of American magazines over the past decades reveals that Americans are a people obsessed with youth. The covers of magazines abound with titles such as "How to Stay Forever Young," "You Don't Have to Get Old," and "Closing in on the Fountain of Youth." Cosmetic firms make millions of dollars annually, peddling creams and cover-ups that promise to hide lines and wrinkles, those "telltale signs of aging," and hair dyes that will cover gray hair for both men and women. Soft-drink companies sell drinks by showing users of their product as suntanned adolescents, playing tag on a beach.

Recently thoughtful people have begun to

question America's worship of youth and fear of
age.  Increasingly, our popular magazines give
space to vigorous defenders of age who claim that
in the absence of illness there is normally little
decline in intelligence or memory and that the
blunting of abilities that we often notice "results
not from age but from put-downs, boredom, and exas-
peration."[2]  "Old age is a time whose topic has

partial
quotation

come," says David Fischer in an article entitled
"Aging:  The Issue of the 1980's."[3]  While modern

author and
title of article

writers and thinkers frequently disagree about the
nature of and solution to the problem of aging, one
common idea stands out:  American society needs to
change its assessment of what aging is and how the
aged should be treated.

THESIS

   Statistics show that significant changes are
taking place.  The percentage of older people in
our population has grown and is continuing to grow
rapidly.  In 1900, those over 65 made up some 4
percent of the nation's population.  Today they
make up over 10 percent.  They are 16 percent of
the voting-age population.  Some predict that those

summary
of
statistics

over 65 will soon make up 15 percent of the na-

tion's people.[4]  Those who are studying these

changes conclude that today we have an unprece-

dented situation:  "Large numbers of retired per-

sons, reasonably healthy, geographically separated

from their families, and relying on social insurance

programs for a living income are a comparatively

new phenomenon in this nation."[5]

direct quotation for key idea

The statement just quoted is from a journal

called the Gerontologist.  The very existence of

such a journal shows that important changes have

begun to take place.  Gerontology, the field of

research and service created to understand and aid

older people, has only recently had significant

impact.  In the universities, the formal study of

gerontology barely existed before World War II.

Today a national directory lists more than 1,275

educational programs on aging.  Political groups,

too, have grown.  Founded only twenty years ago,

The American Association of Retired Persons (AARP)

today has nine million members.  Together with the

National Retired Teachers Association, the National

summary of information

B. Johnston
Engl. 2, Sec. 5

Council of Senior Citizens, and several other
groups, it makes up a powerful "gray lobby" in
Washington.  In summing up, one observer said, "To
find lobbying skills equal to those of organizations
that represent the elderly, you have to go to someone with a gun——the weapons contractors or the
National Rifle Association."[6]

summary of information

It would be a mistake, however, to assume that
these statistics represent a unified movement with
singleness of purpose.  The ferment that is taking
place in our attitudes toward aging is characterized
by contradictory voices.  Rarely is there even
agreement over precisely what aging is.  The Encyclopaedia Britannica defines aging as "the sequential
or progressive change in an organism that leads to
an increased risk of debility, disease, and death."[7]

partial quote

Many today would take issue with such a definition,
arguing that debility and disease are not necessarily linked to aging.  Gerontologist Alex Comfort,
for instance, writes, "Modern research indicates
that a high proportion of the mental and attitudinal
changes seen in 'old' people are not biological

effects of aging.  They are the results of role
playing."[8]  A recent article in the <u>Smithsonian</u>
sets forth the opinion that an antiaging drug is
just around the corner and that "the fixed life
span of human beings is neither absolute nor immu-
table.  It will be up to us to choose how long to
live."[9]  The strong conflicting claims surrounding

partial
quote

aging may be evidence that major and lasting
changes in attitudes are ahead:

> It isn't easy to make sense of so
> many and such varied opinions.  But an
> interesting pattern begins to emerge if
> we study them <u>historically</u>, as events in
> their own right.  The great diversity of
> contemporary interest in aging becomes a
> unity of sorts if we understand it as
> <u>movement</u>, . . . as the latest of the
> great American reform movements, whose
> history is being repeated in new and
> important ways.[10]

block
quotation

When any great reform movement begins to stir

up set ways of thinking, confusion and contradiction are bound to result. But it is also possible
to find areas of general agreement within a movement, and we can pick out some general trends today
in the changing attitudes toward aging.

First of all, most people who have thought in
any depth on the subject agree that the traditional
stereotypes of old people have been mostly destruc-
tive, to young and old alike. They have distorted
reality and, by portraying old age as either ridiculous or awesome, have had the effect of dehuman-
izing the aged. Simone de Beauvoir writes:

> The purified image of themselves that
> society offers the aged is that of the
> white-haired and venerable sage, rich in
> experience, planing high above the common
> state of mankind. If they vary from this,
> they fall below it. The counterpart of
> the first image is that of the old fool
> in his dotage, a laughing stock for
> children. In any case, either by their

virtue or by their degradation, they
stand outside humanity.[11]

Research on the way old people are portrayed in
children's books supports what Simone de Beauvoir
is saying. Edward F. Ansello, associate director
of the Center on Aging at the University of Maryland, } credentials of authors
and doctoral student Joyce Letzler collected data
on the portrayal of old people in juvenile picture
books and easy readers. They found that three-
fourths of the old people have no discernible
function or position. For the most part, they
talk rather than act, and their actions are dull } paraphrase
and routine. Oldsters, they found, are not portrayed as flesh-and-blood characters, as problem
solvers, or as self-sufficient persons. They went
back as far as Beatrix Potter and Kate Greenaway
and found that even in the earlier children's
literature most old characters were portrayed as
"either passive bores or aggressive witches and
wizards."[12]

Modern research is blasting these old stereo-

types.  On the basis of seven years of studies of
older people at the University of Chicago, Bernice
Neugarten believes that real people simply do not
fit our conventional notions about them.  Most old
people are not lonely, neglected, or senile.  Old
people

> do not become isolated and neglected by
> their families, although both generations
> prefer separate households.  Old persons
> are not dumped into mental hospitals by
> cruel or indifferent children.  They are
> not necessarily lonely or desolate if they
> live alone.  Few of them ever show signs
> of mental deterioration or senility, and
> only a small proportion ever become
> mentally ill.[13]

Efforts to change the images of old people as
presented by the media and by textbooks are having
an effect.  Volunteers dedicated to the fight          paraphrase
against discrimination based on age have monitored
television programs and filed complaints about

those that foster negative images of old people.
They have complained about negative stereotypes of
old folks in certain comedy routines and the absence of older emcees and news anchor people.[14]
Consistent pressure on networks and publishers has
been getting results.

paraphrase

In discussing today's aging movement, we
should note that the aged themselves are leading
the way.  This active participation today contrasts
sharply with past decades when the aged were looked
at as the objects rather than the agents of reform.
Leafing through issues of popular magazines from
the forties and fifties, we find titles like
"Feeding Grandfather and Grandmother," "What Old
Person Do You Have to Support?", and "Use Old
People Wisely."  Such titles show that the reading
audience was assumed to be young or middle-aged.
The articles are directed to a younger audience
interested in the care and feeding of old people.
Today entire publications, such as Fifty Plus and
Retired Living, are directed at the older audience.
Maggie Kuhn, founder of the Gray Panthers, was one

of the first of the new senior leaders.  Forced

into retirement after twenty-five years of service

with the Presbyterian Church, she rebelled and set

out to organize other old people against mandatory

retirement.  She said:  "This is a new age, an age

of sweeping change and liberation, of self-deter-

mination; a new kind of freedom for all of us who

dare to take risks.  And I see us as a new breed

of old people."[15]

     key
     quotation

The common theme in what this "new breed of

old people" is demanding is freedom to choose:  to

choose relationships, to choose to work, to choose

to learn.  Older people today want the freedom to

choose their own relationships.  The popular stereo-

type is that of the old person clinging tenaciously

to relatives.  But Alex Comfort says that the real

need of older people is not so much for relatives

as it is for friends, chosen relationships.[16]

Maggie Kuhn has spoken with contempt of age-

segregated "sun-fun" communities, intended for

people who have "given up, copped out."[17]

     quoted
     phrases

Another choice being demanded by older people

today is the option to learn.  In an article enti-

tled "Education's Gray Boom," Edith Roth wrote,

"Because older adults are increasing faster than

any other segment of the population, educational

programs that attend to their special needs are

spreading like crabgrass."[18]  She described new

striking
short quote

educational programs for older people, such as

DOVES (Dedicated Older Volunteers in Educational

Services), a group of trained volunteers who worked

as teacher aides and tutors in the Los Angeles

Unified School District; and Elder-hostel, a pro-

gram that opened college campuses to older adults

for fifteen weeks out of the year and offered a

variety of college courses to elders at reasonable

prices.  Older people, who frequently lack formal

education, have proved themselves capable of doing

college-level work.  Roth said that the learning

skills of the older people remained sharp when

they were able to study what truly interested

them.  She called the idea that capacity for

learning shrinks with the years "an outworn notion

that has been generally discarded; in effect, the

reverse is true for those who have learned the skills of survival."[19]

However, the most vocal demand being made by elders is for the right to work. The trend over the last few decades had been toward earlier and earlier mandatory retirement. In 1900, people over 65 made up 36 percent of the labor force. Today, only 14 percent are over 65. Projecting on the basis of this trend, a recent report to a Senate sub-committee indicated that increasing mechanization might mean that in twenty-five years the economic life of most blue-collar workers would be twenty years.[20] In other words, people might be forced to retire at age 39. However, recent surveys have shown that many who are forced to retire would like to continue working. According to one survey, more than half of today's employees would prefer to continue working past their normal retirement age.[21]

Beneath the demand for greater freedom of choice for older people is a deeper demand: that we begin to see life not as a series of segments

summary of statistics

but as a continuous aging process. Old age does

not hit a person suddenly, like a catastrophe.

Instead, life as a continuum means that a person

gradually learns and grows through the years,

changing, yet maintaining his or her identity.

Learning and meaningful activity can be lifelong if

one chooses them to be so. In the words of Maggie

Kuhn, "Education has traditionally been deemed to

be for the young. Work is for the middle years,

and leisure for the later years." Life, which

should be a continuum, has been chopped up into     strong final
quotation
segments divided according to age. Instead,

"education, meaningful work, and leisure should

all be lifelong experiences."[22]

NOTES

¹ "Rabbi Ben Ezra," II. 1-2.  ⎤ lines of
⎦ poetry

² Alex Comfort, "Old Age:  Facts and Fancies," ⎤ article with
Saturday Evening Post, March 1977, p. 45.  ⎦ subtitle

³ New Republic, 2 Dec. 1979, p. 31.

⁴ Shana Alexander, "Getting Old in Kids'  ⎤ standard
Country," Newsweek, 11 Nov. 1974, p. 124.  ⎬ footnote
⎦ for article

⁵ David A. Peterson, Chuck Powell, and Lawne  ⎤ article with
Robertson, "Aging in America:  Toward the Year  ⎬ volume
2000," Gerontologist, 16 (1976), 264.  ⎦ number

⁶ Quoted in Fischer, "Aging," New Republic,  ⎤ quoted at
p. 33.  ⎦ second hand

⁷ "Aging," Encyclopaedia Britannica, 1974,  ⎤ encyclopedia
I, 299.  ⎦ article

⁸ A Good Age (New York:  Simon & Schuster,  ⎤ author's name
1976), p. 11.  ⎦ in text

⁹ Albert Rosenfeld, "In Only 50 Years We May
Add Centuries to Our Lives——If We Choose to Do
So," Smithsonian, Oct. 1976, p. 41.

¹⁰ Fischer, pp. 31-32.  ⎤ later
⎦ reference

[11] The Coming of Age, trans. Patrick O'Brian ⌉ translated
(New York:   Putnam's, 1972), p. 4. book

[12] Reported in Henrietta Wexler, "Ageism in
Children's Books," American Education, July 1978,
p. 29.

[13] "Grow Old Along with Me! The Best Is Yet ⌉
to Be," in Growing Old, ed. Gordon Moss and Walter │ article in
collection
Moss (New York:   Simon & Schuster, 1975), p. 114. ⌋

[14] Rebecca Blalock, "Gray Power:   Work of
Maggie Kuhn," Saturday Evening Post, March 1979,
p. 127.

[15] Quoted in Blalock, p. 34.

[16] A Good Age, p. 172. ⌉ second
reference
[17] Quoted in Blalock, p. 34.

[18] "Education's Gray Boom," American Education,
July 1978, p. 6.

[19] Roth, p. 6.

[20] Comfort, A Good Age, p. 14.

[21] "Early Retirement Rejected by Many," ⌉
newspaper
Christian Science Monitor, 24 April 1979, p. 19, │ article
col. 4.

[22] Quoted in Blalock, p. 32.

BIBLIOGRAPHY

"Aging." <u>Encyclopaedia Britannica</u>. 1974, I,     ⎤ encyclopedia

    299-304.     ⎦ article

Alexander, Shana. "Getting Old in Kids' Country." ⎤ standard

    <u>Newsweek</u>, 11 Nov. 1974, p. 124.     ⎦ entry: magazine

Blalock, Rebecca. "Gray Power: Work of Maggie     ⎤

    Kuhn." <u>Saturday Evening Post</u>, March 1979,     ⎦ subtitle

    pp. 32-34, 127.

Browning, Robert. <u>Poetical Works</u>. London:     ⎤ standard

    Oxford Univ. Press, 1967.     ⎦ entry: book

Comfort, Alex. <u>A Good Age</u>. New York: Simon     ⎤

    & Schuster, 1976.     ⎥ same author

----------. "Old Age: Facts and Fancies."     ⎦

    <u>Saturday Evening Post</u>, March 1977, p. 45.

de Beauvoir, Simone. <u>The Coming of Age</u>. Trans.

    Patrick O'Brian. New York: Putnam's, 1972.

"Early Retirement Rejected by Many." <u>Christian</u>     ⎤

    <u>Science Monitor</u>, 24 April 1979, p. 19, col. 4. ⎦ anonymous article

Fischer, David Hackett. "Aging: The Issue of the

    1980's." <u>New Republic</u>, 2 Dec. 1979, pp. 31-36.

Neugarten, Bernice.  "Grow Old Along with Me!  The

    Best Is Yet to Be."  In <u>Growing Old</u>.  Ed.

    Gordon Moss and Walter Moss.  New York:

    Simon & Schuster, 1975.

article in collection

Peterson, David A., Chuck Powell, and Lawne

    Robertson.  "Aging in America:  Toward the

    Year 2000."  <u>Gerontologist</u>, 16 (1976),

    264-75.

several authors

Rosenfeld, Albert.  "In Only 50 Years We May Add

    Centuries to Our Lives——If We Choose to Do So."

    <u>Smithsonian</u>, Oct. 1976, pp. 40-47.

Roth, Edith Brill.  "Education's Gray Boom."

    <u>American Education</u>, July 1978, pp. 6-11.

inclusive page numbers

Wexler, Henrietta.  "Ageism in Children's Books."

    <u>American Education</u>, July 1978, p. 29.

# 10

# Practical Prose Forms

## PR 1 SUMMARIES

**By writing summaries, train yourself to grasp the structure of written material and to concentrate on essentials.**

Practice in writing summaries will benefit you in important ways as a student and as a writer:

- It will give you practice in *close, attentive reading.* Too many writers are ineffectual because they have not learned to listen first, to think second, and to formulate their own reactions third.

- It will strengthen your sense of *structure* in writing. It will make you pay close attention to how a writer organizes material, develops a point, and moves from one point to another.

- It will develop your sense of what is *important* in a piece of writing. It will make you distinguish between a key point, the material backing it up, and mere asides.

In writing a summary, concentrate on three closely related tasks:

(1) *Make sure you grasp the main trend of thought.* Above all, you need to see clearly the organization of what you are asked to summarize. Identify key sentences: the thesis that sums up the major point of an essay (or section of an essay); the topic sentence that is then developed in the rest of a paragraph. Formulate in your own words major points that seem to be implied but not spelled out in a single sentence. Distinguish between the major steps in an argument and merely incidental comment.

(2) *Reduce explanation and illustration to the essential minimum.* Leave out passages that are paraphrase, restating a point for clarity or emphasis. Drastically condense lengthy explanations. Keep only the most important details, examples, or statistics. Reduce or omit anecdotes, humorous asides, and the like.

(3) *Use the most economical wording possible.* Where the original uses a whole clause, try to sum up the same idea in a phrase. Where it uses a phrase, try to use a single word. Where

several synonyms restate the same idea, choose the one that best gives the central common meaning. Cut out all grammatical deadwood.

Unless the original version is already severely condensed, a summary of about one third or one fourth the original length can usually preserve the essential points. The shorter the summary, however, the greater the danger of oversimplification or misrepresentation. Be careful to preserve essential conditions and distinctions: *if-* and *unless*-clauses; differences between *is*, *will*, and *might*; words like *only*, *almost*, and *on the whole*. Preserve the relative emphasis of the original, giving more prominence to a point treated at great length than to one mentioned in passing.

Study the following passage. The running commentary on the right suggests points you would have to note in writing an adequate summary:

We might characterize popular art first, as is most often done, with respect to its *form*. Popular art is said to be simple and unsophisticated, aesthetically deficient because of its artlessness. It lacks quality because it makes no qualifications to its flat statement. Everything is straightforward, with no place for complications. And it is standardized as well as simplified: one product is much like another. It is lifeless, Bergson would say, because it is only a succession of mechanical repetitions, while what is vital in art is endlessly variable. But it is just the deadly routine that is so popular. Confronted with that, we know just where we are, know what we are being offered, and what is expected of us in return. It is less unsettling to deal with machines than with people, who have lives of their own to lead. For we can then respond with mechanical routines ourselves, and what could be simpler and more reliably satisfying?—Abraham Kaplan, "The Aesthetics of the Popular Arts," *Journal of Aesthetics and Art Criticism*

(1) *Key idea*: Emphasis will be on *form* rather than content of popular arts.
(2) *Essential qualification*: "Most often done" and "is said to be" show this view to be widely held, but not necessarily fully shared by author.
(3) *Synonyms*: "Simple," "uncomplicated," "artless," "flat," "straightforward" all reinforce same major point.
(4) *Added step*: Popular art is "standardized" as well as "simplified."
(5) *Another added step*: It is "mechanical" rather than "variable."
(6) *Major transition*: The "mechanical" element in the popular arts is what makes them popular.
(7) *Explanation*: Why is "deadly routine" easy to live with?

Here is the summary you might write after close study of the passage:

Summary   According to a widely held view, popular art is simple and uncomplicated in form, and therefore "artless." It is standardized, and it lacks life because of mechanical repetition. But it is just the mechanical quality that is popular, because it is simple to react to what we know, but unsettling to deal with something that has a life of its own.

# EXERCISES

A. Study the differences between the full text and the summary in each of the following pairs. Would you have noted the same major points and essential qualifications?

**Original 1:**

The invention of the process of printing from movable type, which occurred in Germany about the middle of the fifteenth century, was destined to exercise a far-reaching influence on all the vernacular languages of Europe. Introduced in England about 1476 by William Caxton, who had learned the art on the continent, printing made such rapid progress that a scant century later it was observed that manuscript books were seldom to be met with and almost never used. Some idea of the rapidity with which the new process swept forward may be had from the fact that in Europe the number of books printed before the year 1500 reaches the surprising figure of 35,000. The majority of these, it is true, were in Latin, whereas it is in the modern languages that the effect of the printing press was chiefly to be felt. But in England over 20,000 titles in English had appeared by 1640, ranging all the way from mere pamphlets to massive folios. The result was to bring books, which had formerly been the expensive luxury of the few, within the reach of all. More important, however, was the fact, so obvious today, that it was possible to reproduce a book in a thousand copies or a hundred thousand, every one exactly like the other. A powerful force thus existed for promoting a standard, uniform language, and the means were now available for spreading that language throughout the territory in which it was understood.—Albert C. Baugh, *A History of the English Language*

**Summary:**

Printing from movable type, invented in Germany about 1450 and brought to England about 1476, had a far-reaching influence on all European languages. Within a hundred years, manuscript books had become rare. Though at first most printed books were in Latin, over 20,000 titles in English had appeared by 1640. Books were now within the reach of everyone and could exert a powerful standardizing influence upon language.

**Original 2:**
The tendency to erect "systems"—which are then marketed as a whole—affects particularly the less mature sciences of medicine and psychology. In these subjects, we have had a succession of intellectual edifices originally made available only in their entirety. It is as if one cannot rent a room or even a suite in a new building, but must lease the whole or not enter. Starting with a substantial contribution to medicine, the authors of such systems expand their theories to include ambitious explanations of matters far beyond the original validated observations. And, after the first pioneer, later and usually lesser contributors to the system add further accretions of mingled fact and theory. Consequently, systems of this kind—like homeopathy, phrenology, psychoanalysis, and conditioned reflexology (the last dominant for years in Russia)—eventually contain almost inextricable mixtures of sense and nonsense. They capture fervid adherents, and it may take a generation or several for those who preserve some objectivity to succeed in salvaging the best in them while discarding the dross.—Dr. Ian Stevenson, "Scientists with Half-Closed Minds," *Harper's*

**Summary:**
Medicine and psychology have produced a number of intellectual systems that one is asked to accept as a whole or not at all. The ambitious authors and adherents of such systems go beyond original valid findings to produce a mixture of truth and error that attracts enthusiastic supporters. Objective observers may not succeed in separating the valuable from the worthless till much later.

B. Select a passage of about 250 words from a history or science textbook. Prepare a *summary* running to about a third of the original length. Provide a copy of the original.

# PR 2 LETTERS

**Make your business letters suggest competence and efficiency.**

Correspondence creates special problems of manuscript form. In writing or answering a formal invitation, you will do well to follow forms suggested in a book of etiquette. In writing a personal letter, you may allow yourself considerable freedom, as long as you keep your handwriting legible and use presentable stationery. Between these extremes of formality and informality is the kind of letter that you may have to write to a teacher, to a college official, or to a future employer. In applying for a scholarship or for a job, follow a conventional letter form.

## PR 2a   Format and Style

**Make sure your business letters are neat, clear, consistent in format, and courteous in style.**

Study the samples of business correspondence on the following pages. Use them as models for spacing, indentation, punctuation, and the like. Remember the following points:

(1)  *Return address.* When you are not using the letterhead of a firm or an organization, type your return address above the date, as follows. Place it on the right side of the page:

```
                              138 South Third Street
                              San Jose, California   95126
                              January 12, 1982



        Ms. Patricia Sobell
        Personnel Manager
        San Rafael Gazette
        2074 Washington Avenue
        San Rafael, California   94903

        Dear Ms. Sobell:
```

(2)  *Inside address.* Write the complete address of the recipient. Use a courtesy title like *Mr.* or *Ms.* (the latter now widely replacing the traditional *Mrs.* and *Miss*). A woman may show her preference for one of the possible choices in the signature line of her own correspondence:

**414**

Sincerely,                                    Sincerely,

*Kate Gordon*                                 *Helen Freid*

(Mrs.) Kate Gordon                    (Ms.) Helen Freid


   (3)  *Salutation.* If you are writing to a firm or an organization rather than to an individual working there, use the greeting "Ladies and Gentlemen" or "Ladies or Gentlemen." (Use "Gentlemen" only if all the people in a group are male.)


INDIVIDUAL

```
Ms. Jane Day, President
The Waxo Company
225 East Elm Street
Walls, KS  76674

Dear Ms. Day:
```


ORGANIZATION

```
The Jackson Manufacturing Company
1334 West Devonshire Road
Bolivar, MO  65613

Ladies and Gentlemen:
```


   Use "Dear Sir or Madam" in writing to someone holding a position if you do not know the person's name:

```
              Personnel Director
              Wilson Chemical Company
              Hartville, KY  41052

              Dear Sir or Madam:
```

**SAMPLE 1: Standard Business Letter**

**CALIFORNIA STATE COLLEGE,**  letterhead
*809 East Victoria Street   •   Dominguez Hills, California 90247*

heading┤────► June 14, 1982

Dr. Dorothy King
Institute for Better Business Writing, Inc.
1000 University Way                  ◄────┤ inside address
Los Angeles, California   90025

Dear Dr. King: ◄──┤ salutation

I was happy to receive your request for information re-
garding business letter formats.

The format of this letter is the one most frequently used
in business.  It is called a modified block format.  With
the exception of the heading and the signature block, all
its elements begin at the left hand margin, even the first
word of each paragraph.  The body of the letter is single-
spaced, with double spacing between paragraphs.
──┤body
Typists generally like the block format better than the
older indented formats.  It has a clean and precise appearance, and is quicker to type—no indentations.

There are other formats in use, but the block format seems
to have the widest appeal.  You won't go wrong if you adopt
it for all your official correspondence.

                                    Sincerely yours,

      signature block
                                    *Walter Wells*
          complimentary
          close signature
          signature identification    Walter Wells
                                       Department of English
                                       ┌ IEC block
WW:mea                                  initials (of author and typist)
cc:  Dean Marion Carlota                enclosures
                                        carbon copies

**SAMPLE 2: Short letter, indented format**

# The Ironworks

2520 Eastern Avenue
Las Vegas, NE 89109

September 12, 1983

Mr. Perry Sneed, Manager
Green Thumb Nursery
3619 Kyrene Road
Tempe, Arizona  85282

Dear Mr. Sneed:

Your order for 3 dozen wrought iron potracks
was shipped today.

We appreciate receiving Green Thumb Nursery as
a new account.  Thank you for your initial order,
and we look forward to a pleasant business relationship.

Sincerely,

*Loraine Holloway*

Loraine Holloway
Sales Manager

fb

postscript—
last-minute
addition to letter

P.S.  We have just learned that some of our
shipments have been delayed briefly en route because
of a handlers' strike.  We apologize for any incon-
venience.

## SAMPLE 3: Business Envelopes

(Here are some examples of well-typed business envelopes. Remember: Accurate names and addresses are essential. Neatness counts.)

---

**Lawndale Pharmaceutical Company**
5170 Medina Road
Akron, Ohio 44321

SPECIAL DELIVERY

```
           Dr. Joan Coulton
           10372 White Oak Avenue
           Granada Hills, CA  91344
```

---

**United Bank of Iowa**
1640 Medina Road
Des Moines, Iowa 50313

```
       Attention Ms. Pat Corveau

               Schrader Lock Company
               624 South First Avenue
               Sioux Falls, SD  57104
```

---

*San Marcos Resort,*
*Country Club & Colony*
Chandler, Arizona 85224

```
        Confidential      Mr. Don Busche, President
                          Northridge Manufacturing Company
                          402 West Main Street
                          Northridge, Illinois  60162
```

**SAMPLE 4: Memo**

(A **memorandum**, or interoffice communication, is different from a business letter. It serves a different purpose—communication *within* an organization.)

---

Connecticut Life Insurance Company
# MEMORANDUM

To:      Harry M. Brown     Date: March 21, 19--
           cc:  Ben Siegel   File No.: 0010
                 Patricia Newman
                 Angela Millel

From:    Walter Wells

Subject:  A Word About Memorandum Format

      Memos can serve either an expository or a reaction-evoking function.  They can be long or short as need demands--but they must be clear, have an appropriate character, and be as impressive in format as any letter.

      Memo format is, of course, more tightly determined by its imprinted heading, as at the top of this memo.  Those headings come with minor variations, but this one is typical. Sometimes the <u>From</u> and <u>To</u> lines are positioned more closely together, and the "distribution" indicator is placed after the body of the memo rather than before it.  But in its essentials, this model is as good as any.

      As with your letters, you will be measured to a great extent by the memos you write.  So be sure to write them neatly, and write them well.

ms              *W. W.*

---

Try to write clearly and naturally. Do not use a special business jargon when you write a business letter. Avoid especially the following: a *stodgy*, old-fashioned businessese ("wish to advise that," "beg to acknowledge," "am in receipt of," "pursuant to," "the aforementioned"); a *breezy* "shirtsleeve" English ("give it the old college try," "fight tooth and nail," "give them a run for their money").

## PR 2b The Request

**State inquiries and requests clearly and positively, and aim them at the intended reader.**

Many of the business letters you write will ask someone else to do something for you: to provide information, to perform a service, or to correct a mistake. Make such letters clear, businesslike, and persuasive.

(1)  Make sure you state your request clearly and directly *early* in the letter. The basic question in your reader's mind is "What do you want?"

(2)  If you are making *several* requests in the same letter, or if several points need attention, make sure each stands out clearly. Consider numbering them for emphasis. Too often, only the first major point gets attention; other matters, buried later in a letter, are forgotten.

(3)  Whenever possible, relate your request directly to the *interests and responsibilities* of the person you are writing to. Avoid a "To-Whom-It-May-Concern" effect. Avoid using form letters if at all possible.

(4)  Even when you have a legitimate complaint, remain *courteous*. Emphasize the mutual satisfaction to be derived from a mistake corrected, rather than the mutual frustration occasioned when an error is first made.

The following sample letters attempt to put these principles into practice:[1]

---

[1]Most of the sample letters in this section are adapted from Walter Wells, *Communications in Business* (Belmont, Calif.: Wadsworth, 1977).

Letter 1

Dear Mr. Bliss:

Largely because of the success of <u>The Muse</u>, your new campus literary magazine, we at Colfax College feel the time is right for a similar publication on this campus. Your help on a few important questions would get us moving in the right direction.

We would like to know

> 1. How you went about soliciting manuscripts for your first edition.
> 2. How you decided upon the proportions of space to devote to fiction, poetry, criticism, reviews, and advertising.
> 3. Whether you use university or commercial printing facilities.
> 4. What mailing list you used to solicit charter subscriptions.
> 5. Why you decided to price <u>The Muse</u> at $1.75.

Our enthusiasm runs high over the possibility of a literary review at Colfax. Target date for the first issue is October 1 of this year. We have firm approval from the administration, and the faculty is solidly behind us. With your aid, we can be that much closer to realizing our goal--a first-rate campus publication capable of standing beside the best from the larger schools, <u>The Muse</u> most certainly among them.

> Sincerely,
>
> *Martha Gronowsky*
>
> Martha Gronowsky
> Student Body Vice-President

**Letter 2**

Dear Dr. Garcia:

I was surprised to receive your recent request for more transcripts to complete my application to the Graduate School. I will, of course, have them sent if absolutely necessary, but I do feel that your request penalizes me.

Upon coming to State as a transfer undergraduate in 1980, I paid two dollars, for transcripts in duplicate, to each of the three institutions I had previously attended. At that time, you informed me that all my papers were in order, and you admitted me. Now you request the very same transcripts in support of my graduate application.

Would it not be possible for you to refer to the transcripts already in your possession? Or if copies must be sent to the graduate advisor, could you not duplicate my transcripts and send me the bill? In either case, you would save me the time of recontacting each institution, and you would help me avoid possible delays in their responding.

I hope this request is in no way unjustified. It should be more expedient for both of us as you process my application.

Sincerely yours,

*Kenneth Darwin*

Kenneth Darwin

# PR2c  The Letter of Application

**Make your letter of application suggest competence, confidence, and a genuine interest in the position for which you apply.**

Employers look for employees who will prove an asset to their organization and who are at the same time good to work with and good to know. They shy away from applicants who seem to promise problems, trouble, or an overinflated ego. Remember the following advice:

(1)  *If possible, be specific about the position for which you apply.* Introduce the letter by mentioning the advertisement or the person that informed you of the vacancy (but do not mention leads that smack of the "grapevine").

(2)  *Stress previous training.* Point out any practical experience that you can show to be relevant to the job. Give a factual tone to the account of your qualifications, while at the same time presenting them to advantage.

(3)  *Give your letter character.* Establish your identity. Many job applications look very much the same. The anonymous, average applicant has little chance to be remembered—and to be preferred. If you have positive convictions about the work of the organization to which you apply, state them.

(4)  *If you want to list references, first get permission from those whose names you want to use.* Quietly drop from your list the names of teachers or former employers who show little enthusiasm when you tell them about your plans.

(5)  *Consider preparing a separate résumé.* If the account of your qualifications is extensive, put it on a separate "data sheet."

Study the following sample letters:

**Letter 3**

Dear Ms. Gabriel:

In answer to your advertisement, I wish to apply for
a post as general reporter.  My credentials are that
I am a journalism major, and I have had some practical
experience of working for a newspaper.

On February 1, I shall graduate from San Jose State
University.  While getting a degree, I have taken a
broad range of courses, representing all areas of
editing and reporting.  Also, I have been a general
reporter for the Spartan Daily for two years and a
feature editor for one year.  Last summer I worked
for thirteen weeks on the Santa Clara Journal, as an
intern sponsored by the Journalism Department of my
college.  I did general reporting and some photography.

The following people have agreed to supply references:

> Dr. Mary Jane Cahill
> Department of Journalism
> San Jose State University
> San Jose, CA   95116

> Mr. Thomas Bigelow, General Manager
> Santa Clara Journal
> 23 Roosevelt Avenue
> Santa Clara, CA   95052

> Mr. Richard H. James, Editor
> Los Angeles Examiner
> 481 Elvira St.
> Los Angeles, CA   90037

I am prepared to be interviewed when you find it
convenient.

> Yours truly,
>
> *Pat C. Romeros*
>
> Pat C. Romeros

**Letter 4**

Mr. Daniel Levin, Attorney at Law
Peale, Corman, Bishop, Levin & Dilworthy
80 Lomita Canyon Boulevard, Suite 7630
Beverly Hills, California 92025

Dear Mr. Levin:

Edith Winters informs me of an opening in your secretarial staff, a position for which I should very
much like to become a candidate.

I understand that you need a legal secretary with a
rapid stenographic skill and the ability to handle
a large volume of correspondence.  Along with my
degree in legal stenography from Foothill Junior
College, I have four years of secretarial experience
in retail dry goods and in insurance.  My shorthand
speed is 145 words per minute.  On my present job, I
handle between forty and sixty letters every day.
Both at Foothill and on the job, I have had training
sufficient to prepare me to handle routine letters
without supervision.

My present job at Southwestern Life & Indemnity has
been quite satisfactory, but, having taken my degree
recently, I seek the further challenges and rewards
of a top-flight legal firm.  Ms. Winters assures me
that I would like the job.  I hope the enclosed
résumé will help interest the firm in me.

I can be in Los Angeles for an interview any afternoon
convenient for you.  May I look forward to speaking
with you about the position you have available?

Yours sincerely,

Pat Edmondson

Pat Edmondson

<u>JEAN LAPORTE</u>

| | |
|---|---|
| Demmler Hall | Age:  23 |
| Valhalla University | Ht:  6-1  Wt:  170 |
| Kent, Ohio 26780 | Single |
| 613 KE 8 7600 | Willing to relocate |

## Education

B.S. in Industrial Engineering, Valhalla University,
June 1981; top 10% of class, with special course
work in statistics, motivational psychology,
business law, and communications.

Won U.S. Paint Company Scholarship 1980
Member of Industrial Relations Club
Elected Secretary of the Student Council
On Dean's Honor Roll since 1978

Also attended Colfax College, Colfax, Indiana,
1977-1979.

## Experience

Staff Supervisor, Cleveland Summer Camp, Kiowa, Ohio,
summer 1980; responsible for housing, activities
scheduling and occasional discipline of fourteen
counselors and 110 campers.

Camp Counselor, Cleveland Summer Camp, Kiowa, Ohio,
summers of 1976 and 1977.

## Personal Interests

Politics, world affairs, camping, chess, junior
chamber of commerce member, and volunteer
hospital worker.

## References

Will gladly be provided upon request.

# PR 2d   The Follow-Up Letter

**Keep interest alive, or reinforce a good first impression, by a timely follow-up letter.**

The follow-up letter serves important needs. It shows positive interest and thus reassures the recipient. It serves as a reminder, keeping alive an impression that is beginning to pale as other business calls for attention.

Study the following sample letter, written by an applicant *after* a job interview:

**Letter 5**

Dear Mr. Goodfellow:

Just a note of thanks for the many courtesies shown me during my interview on Monday. Seeing National Motors from the inside has, as I said then, made the Executive Training Program all the more attractive to me.

Incidentally, I located a copy of Michaelson's The Corporate Tempo and found his chapter on training programs as fascinating and as eye-opening as you did.

Needless to say, I am looking forward to hearing from you. After Monday's meeting, I am confident I can bring to the program the energy and ability for success at National Motors.

Sincerely,

*Sandra Weinmetz*

Sandra Weinmetz

## PR 2e   The Letter of Refusal

**Write letters of refusal that create good will rather than antagonism.**

There are many ways of saying no. The basic difference is between "No, thank you" and "No—and good riddance." A refusal that at the same time shows an appreciation of the interest expressed generates good will and at the same time leaves the door open for future contacts.

Study the following sample letter:

**Letter 6**

Dear Ms. Tibbins:

I want to thank you for your letter of July 20 and for your generous offer of the post as market-research analyst at Continental.

With reluctance and regret, I have decided to forego that offer and accept one made me by the Grollier Food Company of San Francisco. While the salary they offer is slightly less than Continental's, their market-research department is small, making possible, I feel, more rapid advancement. The decision was made quite difficult by the obvious attractiveness of your offer, not to mention the congeniality of your staff. Only time will prove if it's a wise one.

Once again, let me express my genuine thanks for all the consideration you and the Continental staff have given my candidacy.

Very sincerely yours,

Michael Henriques

Michael Henriques

# EXERCISES

A. In an effective business letter, as in all effective persuasion, we show our ability to imagine ourselves in the place of the reader. Compare and contrast the letters in each of the following pairs. Which letter in each pair is the more successful in this respect?

1(a) Enclosed is our draft in the amount of $31.90, which is the amount over your deductible for which Smith Motors, the garage of your choice, agreed to repair your automobile. You will also find enclosed a copy of the estimate on the basis of which they agreed to repair.

1(b) I'm happy to send you our draft for $31.90. It represents the repair cost for your car in excess of the deductible amount in your policy. The enclosed repair estimate was, as you requested, made by Smith Motors in Dalhart.

Smith will, I'm sure, get your car back into fine running order. I know you will be glad to be back on the road again.

2(a) Just what kind of outfit are you people running? We place a simple order, delivery takes forever, and when it finally gets here, half the pieces are broken. To top it all off, in the same day's mail we get our bill. Some joke!

We feel we can do without this kind of rotten service. There's no time left for us to place an order with a decent company (although we'd like to), so get on the ball and send us a replacement order right away.

2(b) On January 10, we placed an order with you for 500 pieces of glassware in various patterns. Yesterday the order arrived with only 234 pieces in salable condition. All the rest were chipped or broken.

**429**

You can understand our disappointment, I am sure.
Customers have been requesting your glasses, and we
have been promising them a prompt supply. Now some
of them will probably go elsewhere--their faith in us
destroyed, and our potential profit lost--unless you
take immediate action.

We ask that you send us an immediate duplicate order,
and allow us to adjust our payment to cover only the
salable glassware. We are confident that you will be
able to get this shipment to us as soon as possible.

B. Find a project or recent development that merits *publicity or support*.
Write a letter about it to the editors of a newspaper or magazine, to a legislator,
or to a responsible official. Observe conventional letter form.

C. Write a *letter of inquiry or request* in connection with some project in
which you are currently interested. Observe conventional letter form.

D. Write a *letter of application* for a position in which you have at one
time or another taken an interest. State the qualifications that you might have
by the time you are ready to apply for the position in earnest.

E. Write a *follow-up letter* or a *letter of refusal* in connection with some
business contact that you can imagine yourself being engaged in after your
graduation from college. Observe conventional letter form.

# PR 3 THE ESSAY EXAMINATION

**Learn to organize your thinking and marshal evidence in a
limited time.**

For many students, the most direct test of their writing ability is the essay examination. To improve your own performance
on such examinations, remember the following general advice:

- *Get a general picture* of the examination before you start writing. (If there are several questions or topics, work first on
  those that you feel best qualified to take up.)

- *Budget your time*, especially if there are several questions. If
  you gain five points by treating one question at great length,

and then lose twenty-five points by slighting the next two questions, you are twenty points behind.

- Take time to *outline your writing*—in your mind, or on a piece of scratch paper. An answer without a plan will be hard to read and hard to follow.

- *Write legibly.* The people grading essay examinations are only human, and they feel the pressure of time. By and large, they will prefer an answer that is short but well written to one that is scribbled and goes on and on.

- *Relax.* You will need a cool head to read the instructions without missing an important point.

## PR 3a   Analyzing a Passage

**Read carefully and organize your reactions when asked to analyze a selected passage.**

A test in a composition or literature class will often require you to interpret, and react to, a selected passage. You may be asked to analyze a passage of expository prose or a selection from imaginative literature. Such an exam tests your ability to read carefully and to organize your reactions. Remember to ask "What does it say?" before you ask yourself "What do I think?" Do not use the passage simply as a springboard for your own thoughts and feelings.

Suppose you are asked to explain a passage that the American poet Walt Whitman wrote in 1858 about capital punishment. You are then asked to react, showing where you agree or disagree with the writer, and why. Remember guidelines like the following when shaping your answer:

(1) *Show that you have taken in the author's key idea or central message.* Do not be satisfied with a vague general idea that a reader might gather while skimming the passage. Include important distinctions or reservations. Know how to sum up the position of a writer who does not simply answer yes or no to a key question:

In this passage, the author never says outright that he is for or against the death penalty for capital offenses. Instead, he attacks the system that *implements* the punishment. That system, according to Whitman, is riddled by indecision and contradictions. Whitman feels that society should make a definite choice—for or against the death penalty. Then it should act firmly on that resolve.

(2) *Organize your answer around major points.* If you can, structure your answer to reflect three or four major parts of an argument. Or identify several important stages in a historical development. The writer of the following passage takes up in order three major reasons for the poet's stand:

Whitman touches on at least three reasons why the contemporary practice concerning capital punishment is unsatisfactory. First, the application of the law is fitful and *inconsistent.* The law seems undecided whether to inflict capital punishment for murder, and the authorities often find ways to spare or pardon the offender. . . .

Second, the application of the law often seems patently *unfair.* When an execution does take place, as often as not the condemned prisoner belongs to a racial minority. . . .

Third, and above all, the authorities *procrastinate.* Any minor technicality can delay a case indefinitely. . . .

(3) *Respond to the author's style.* Show that you have reacted to whatever gives the author's writing force or personality. What makes the author's writing eloquent, or witty, or different? Quote striking or revealing phrases:

. . . Although Whitman does not state his own position on the justification of capital punishment outright, we can infer that he personally favors it from several remarks he makes in the passage. With a sarcastic tone, he refers to "soft-hearted (and soft-headed) prison philanthropists" who sympathize with convicted criminals. He refers to "penny-a-liner journalists" who write melodramatically about the plight of convicted murderers. He criticizes judges and lawyers who bend the law to give "the condemned every chance of evading punishment."

(4) *State your own position clearly and forcefully.* Draw on precedents or parallels that show your opinion is not merely improvised or superficial. If you can, refer to other reading for a parallel or for a contrast:

There are times when our anger makes us clamor for the death of an offender. But in our more thoughtful moments, we are likely to think differently. In Tolkien's *Lord of the Rings*, there is a passage that goes roughly as follows: "There are many who live who deserve to die. There are many who die who deserve to live. Can you give life? If not, do not be so quick to take it."

(5) *Support your position with reasons or examples.* Whether you agree or disagree with the passage you are evaluating, back up your own opinions or judgments:

My main reason for opposing capital punishment is that it is too arbitrary and unpredictable. Too much depends on the resourcefulness or incompetence of lawyers, on the private prejudices of a jury. . . .

Another reason is that the death penalty is irrevocable. If a mistake has been made, it cannot be corrected. . . .

## PR 3b  Writing About Your Reading

**Learn to write a structured essay examination that makes the best possible use of what you know.**

Many essay examinations require you to show your mastery of material that you have studied in preparation for the test. Students who do well on such examinations have learned to study with a sense of purpose and to write well under pressure. Remember the following advice:

(1) *Study not for total recall but for a writing test.* In studying the material, identify the key terms that might provide the focal point for a paragraph or short essay: *alienation, irony, agrarianism.* Fix firmly in your mind the three or four points you would cover if asked to trace the major steps in an argument or the key stages in a process. Then, for each key term or major point, try to retain *supporting detail* that would help you define or illustrate it. Do not merely memorize material; ask yourself practice questions that make you select and arrange materials in different ways to prove a point or to trace a comparison.

(2) *Memorize verbatim at least some key phrases, definitions, or short passages.* These will give an authoritative, authentic air

to your writing. Nothing more reliably identifies the well-prepared student than a sentence that follows a pattern like this:

Modern civilization, what D. H. Lawrence calls "my accursed human education," has alienated us from our roots in the natural world. . . .

According to Barbara Tuchman, dates are fundamental to the historian because they show order in time and thus make possible "an understanding of cause and effect." . . .

(3)   *Determine exactly what the instructions ask you to do.* Do not simply get a general notion of what the question is "about." Assume the question in a history exam is "What do you consider the most important difference between the fall of Greece and the fall of Rome?" Do not simply put down everything you can remember about the fall of Greece and the fall of Rome. Focus on the key word in the instructions: *difference.* What *is* the difference? How can you line up material that will bring out this difference as clearly and convincingly as possible? Look also for specific writing instructions: Are you being asked to *summarize,* to *define,* to *compare,* to *evaluate*—or merely, more vaguely, to *discuss*?

(4)   *No matter what the pressure of time, take time to structure your answer.* Come straight to the point. Especially in a one-paragraph answer, make your very first sentence sum up your key point or your answer to the question being asked. Then use the rest of a paragraph to explain, support, or argue your point. Select what is clearly relevant; try to avoid a mere rambling effect. Whenever you can, work from a brief *outline* jotted down on scratch paper before you begin to write.

Study the following essay exam, rated as above average by the teacher. The comments that follow it point out some features likely to have made a favorable impression on the reader.

EXAM
QUESTION:   *A common type of character in much contemporary literature is the individual who is trapped by a trick of fate, by the environment, or by his or her own nature. Choose such a character from a short story you have recently read. Define the trap in which the character is caught. Describe any struggle on the part of the character to become free.*

ANSWER:       Miss Brill finds herself trapped by her spinsterhood and the advancement of age. She is old, as the story tells us; she's as old as her out-of-date fox fur. She is alone, with no friends, relatives, or close neighbors. This is her trap. Like a bird that will create its own prison in its own territory, Miss Brill makes hers. She does not socialize, nor does she try to make something useful out of her life but rather preys like a parasite on other people's more interesting, colorful lives. In her own way, Miss Brill struggles to escape her prison. She daydreams. The world that she lives in is a fantasy world where all people are friendly and related. She "belongs" in this world, whereas in the other world, the real world, she actually belongs to no one.

      Quite successfully, Miss Brill loses the real world for a time, but she cannot escape the real world entirely. The real world sticks its head in, in the form of a boy who says "Ah, go on with you now." So she goes home, more aware than ever of her prison's boundaries and helpless (by her own nature) to do anything else. She can only fly on home to the security and solitude of her cold, dark nest.

Note the following points about this answer:

• It responds directly to the *key term or key idea* in the assignment. The assignment asks about a character who is *trapped*. Note how this word and its synonyms keep echoing throughout the student's answer: "trapped," "prison," "boundaries."

• The first sentence serves as a *topic sentence* for the answer as a whole. It gives the brief, clear definition of the "trap" that the question asks for.

• The point about the character's trying to escape through daydreaming responds to the *second* part of the question. But note that this point is worked organically into the first paragraph. The student has planned this answer; there are no afterthoughts, no "Oh-I-forgot" effect.

# EXERCISES

A. Study the following assignment for an essay examination and the two answers that follow it. One of the answers was rated good, the other poor. Which is which? Defend your choice in detail.

**Assignment:**    The following lines by Walt Whitman bear a close relationship to several ideas contained in essays you have read in this course.
Explore, in an essay of 300 words, the connections you see.

> When I heard the learn'd astronomer,
> When the proofs, the figures, were ranged in columns before me,
> When I was shown the charts and diagrams, to add, divide, and measure
>     them,
> When I sitting heard the astronomer where he lectured with much
>     applause in the lecture-room,
> How soon unaccountable I became tired and sick,
> Till rising and gliding out I wander'd off by myself,
> In the mystical moist night-air, and from time to time,
> Look'd up in perfect silence at the stars.

**Answer 1:**    Several points in Walt Whitman's lines are important in ex-
ploring the connections between his ideas and the ideas pertaining to
humanism in the essays we have read. First, we get the image of a man of
letters attending a lecture of a man of science. Secondly, the lecture material
consists of certainties—proofs and figures, charts, diagrams. Finally, we get a
feeling of complete isolation and peacefulness as Whitman stands outside in
the night air.

In his essay on "The Two Cultures," C. P. Snow states that our intellectual
society is divided into two sections—scientific and literary. Each section
believes the other is unaware of our human condition and shows no regard for
its fellow human beings. Each section believes it has the "right" answer for
society. Each section is so intense in its feelings that no communication is
possible between the two sections. C. P. Snow says that we must "rethink
education" to achieve a broad outlook on life, in contrast to the narrow outlook
that is the result of specialization and technicalities in science and in literary
studies. This is the thought that I get when Whitman attends the astronomer's
lecture.

The lecture material contains figures, charts, diagrams, to prove the astronomer's theories. I believe Whitman is putting across the same point as Saisselin
in his essay on "Humanism, or the Eulogy of Error." Saisselin claims that there
are no proofs or certainties for the humanist. Each of us is a single entity; we
live alone and die alone. This is our fate. We must recognize this isolation and
this potential for error. We must be flexible, but the astronomer suggests rigidity.
Furthermore, we must not confine ourselves to one area in life but must be
aware of the whole world about us. When Whitman steps outside into the
night air and gazes at the stars, he feels the vastness of the universe. The
astronomer looks at the universe to collect proofs and figures for his small
world of lecture and research. He does not comprehend our common fate.

**Answer 2:**    In the lines by Walt Whitman, I am given the general impression that this person cannot comprehend the meaning of the lecture, the
figures, or the charts and diagrams. It seems as though he is not scientifically

inclined in his thinking and cannot grasp even a thread of the knowledge the lecturer is trying to communicate to him.

In his discussion of "The Two Cultures," C. P. Snow points out some of the reasons for the division between the literary and scientific scholars. One of these reasons is a lack of communication. The literary scholars feel that they are an elite intellectual group and that they should not talk to such illiterates as scientists. The scientists, on the other hand, have a much more exacting knowledge and think they are doing more for the world than reading or writing books.

Remy Saisselin said that humanism can't be defined. It is lived. I think this is true, and it shows in Walt Whitman's poem. The lines don't say anything about wanting to learn a little about philosophy or art or literature. Walt Whitman just wanted to look around. He had no real reason. He didn't want to become educated for a reward. He merely wanted to explore and become educated in something besides strict science for his own satisfaction and enjoyment.

Students today are made to specialize, and this cuts down on a general well-rounded education. If one lives in a small world of one type of life day after day, he cannot fully enjoy life. Diversity makes for more enjoyment. By learning a little in both science and the arts, a person becomes more happy with himself and those around him.

B. Do you have a copy of an essay examination you have written recently? Select one or more passages totaling 250–300 words. Rewrite the material in accordance with the suggestions in this section. If you can, submit the original assignment, the original answer, and the improved version.

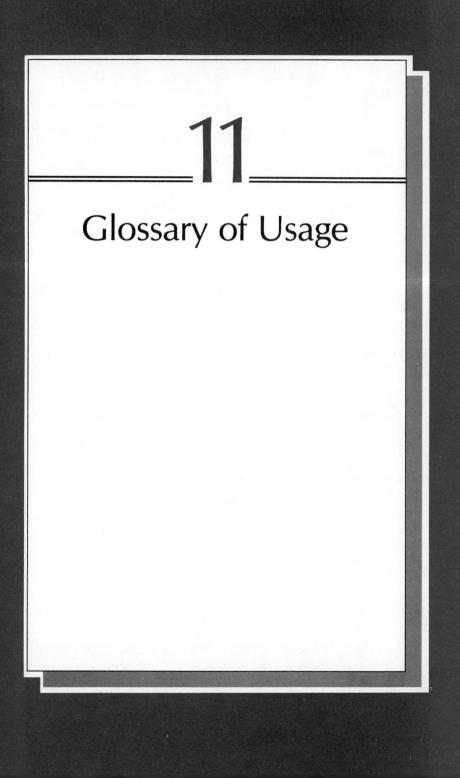

# 11

## Glossary of Usage

# DIAGNOSTIC TEST

## INSTRUCTIONS:

In each of the following sentences, which of the two italicized choices is appropriate for serious written English? Write your choice after the number of the sentence.

---

1. We assembled the unit exactly *as/like* the instructions said.

2. The governor's statement reported little progress *in terms of/concerning* new industries.

3. None of our so-called friends offered us *no/any* help.

4. Mario always rode his bicycle as if it *was/were* a high-powered motorcycle.

5. He dislikes *these kind of people/this kind of person.*

6. His vaguely worded letter *implied/inferred* that visitors would be unwelcome to him.

7. A psychic had warned the company of *a/an* accident.

8. The stadium was always filled with a large *amount/number* of people.

9. The reason Jim drove on the left side of the street was *that/because* he had grown up in England.

10. Cars *didn't use to/used not to* be permitted inside the park.

11. We had hoped the company would choose Phoenix over Houston, but it chose the *latter/later.*

12. Motorists *couldn't/could* hardly see the road in the dense fog.

13. Her new friend was *disinterested/uninterested* in restaurants that featured vegetable burgers and carrot juice.

14. The new manager always made people wait *several/a couple of* minutes in the outer office.

15. It was the kind of secret that is known to *most/almost* everybody involved.

16. The former owner had stubbornly refused to take anything *off of/off* the price.

**17.** *Being that/Because* fees are constantly going up, many students will have to reconsider their plans.

**18.** For some people, it is *cheaper/more cheaper* to lease a car than to buy one.

**19.** We were determined to continue *regardless/irregardless* of our collaborators' decision.

**20.** This year for the first time, we have had *fewer/less* applicants than the year before.

### Avoid expressions that many readers find objectionable.

The following glossary reviews the status of words, word forms, and constructions that are frequently criticized as careless, illogical, too informal, or otherwise limited in appropriateness and effectiveness. When in doubt, be safe: Choose the form that is widely considered acceptable in serious written English.

*Note*: Check **SP 1c** for confusing pairs like *accept/except*, *advise/advice*, *affect/effect*, *lose/loose*, or *than/then*.

*a, an*   The *a* should appear only before words that begin with a consonant when pronounced: *a desk, a chair, a house, a year, a C, a university.* The *an* should appear before words that begin with a vowel when pronounced (though, in writing, the first letter may be a consonant): *an eye, an essay question, an honest man, an A, an M, an uninformed reader.* In the latter position, *a* is nonstandard:

NONSTANDARD:   a ear, a accident, a automobile
STANDARD:      *an* ear, *an* accident, *an* automobile

*aggravate*   In writing, use to mean "make worse or more grave." Avoid its informal use in the sense of "annoy" or "irritate":

FORMAL:  When you *irritate* him, you *aggravate* his condition.

**ain't**  Nonstandard for *am not, isn't, aren't,* or *hasn't* (she *ain't* been seen since). Sometimes used in writing for a facetious or folksy effect.

**all right**  Spell as two words. (Although *alright* appears in some dictionaries, most of your readers will consider it a misspelling.)

**allusion, illusion**  An *allusion* is a brief mention that reminds us of a story or an event (the speaker's *allusion* to Watergate). An *illusion* is a deceptive appearance or false hope (the Vietnam war destroyed many *illusions*).

**a lot**  Always spelled as two words. "*A lot of* money" is informal; "*lots* of money" is slang:

FORMAL:  She owed us *a large amount of* money.

**already, all ready**  "They *already* (surprisingly early) had our equipment *all* (completely) *ready*."

**altogether, all together**  "It is *altogether* (completely) too late to bring these people *all* (every one of them) *together*."

**among, between**  See BETWEEN, AMONG.

**amount, number**  *Amount* is sometimes used loosely instead of *number* in reference to things counted individually and as separate units. Use *amount* only when thinking about bulk or a sum:

RIGHT:  A large *number* (not *amount*) of people were waiting.
RIGHT:  The *number* (not *amount*) of unsold cars on dealers' lots was growing steadily.

**and and but at the beginning of a sentence**  When *and* and *but* are used at the beginning of a sentence, they partly cancel out the pause signaled by the period. They can therefore suggest a sudden or an important afterthought. But many modern writers start sentences with *and* or *but* merely to avoid heavier, more formal connectives like *moreover, furthermore, however,* and *nevertheless*:

He was plagued by financial worries. But nothing could cramp his generous heart.—*Time*

**and/or**   *And/or* is an awkward combination sometimes necessary in commercial or official documents. Avoid it in ordinary writing.

**angle, approach, slant**   *Angle, approach,* and *slant* are overused as synonyms for "attitude," "point of view," "position," or "procedure."

**anyone, anybody**   *Anyone* and *anybody* stand for "any person at all." *Any one* singles out: "Take any one of those three." *Any body* refers to the physical body.

**anyways, anywheres, anyplace**   In writing, use *anyway* or *anywhere*.

**apt, liable, prone**   In informal English, *apt, liable,* and *prone* all appear in the sense of "likely." In formal usage, *apt* suggests that something is likely because of someone's aptitude ("She is *apt* to become a successful artist"). *Liable* suggests that what is likely is burdensome or undesirable ("He is *liable* to break his leg"). *Prone* suggests that something is almost inevitable because of strong habit or predisposition ("He is *prone* to suspect others").

**as**   *As* is nonstandard as a substitute for *that* or *whether* ("I don't know *as* I can come"). It is also nonstandard as a substitute for *who* ("Those *as* knew her avoided her"). As a substitute for *because* or *while, as* is often criticized as ambiguous, unemphatic, or overused:

As (better: "because") we had no money, we gave him a check.

**at**   Omit the redundant *at* in *where at.* Use "*Where* does he live?" instead of "*Where* does he live *at*?"

**attribute, contribute**   *Contribute* means "to give one's share" or "to have a share" in something. *Attribute* means "to trace to a cause" or "to credit to a source":

**443**

RIGHT:    He *attributed* the crossing of the letters in the mail to the intervention of a supernatural power.

**bad, badly**    Use the adjective *bad* after the linking verb *feel,* which shows a condition: "His resignation made everyone feel *bad."* Use the adverb *badly* to show how something is done: "She handled the assignment *badly."*

**being as, being that**    Nonstandard as substitutes for *because* or *since* ("*being that* I was ill").

**between, among**    *Between* is related to *twain,* which in turn is a form of *two.* As a result, grammarians have often restricted *between* to references to two of a kind (distinguish *between* right and wrong). They have required *among* in references to more than two (distinguish *among* different shades of color). *Between* is also appropriate when more than two things can be considered in pairs of two:

RIGHT:    He had sand *between* his toes.
RIGHT:    Bilateral trade agreements exist *between* many countries.

**blame for, blame on**    There are two idiomatic uses of the word *blame*: "He blamed the passenger *for* the accident" and "He blamed the accident *on* the passenger." The first of these is preferred in formal English.

**burst, bursted, bust, busted**    *Bursted* is a nonstandard form of *burst*: "The tank *burst* (not *bursted*) and killed two of the workers." *Bust* as a verb meaning "break" or "arrested" is slang.

**calculate, reckon, expect, guess**    In formal written English, *calculate* and *reckon* imply computing or systematic reasoning. *Expect* implies expectation or anticipation; *guess* implies conjecture. In the sense of "think," "suppose," or "consider," these verbs are informal or dialectal.

**can** and **may**    Formal English uses *can* in the sense of "be able to." It uses *may* to show permission. The use of *can* to indicate permission, common in speech and writing, is often considered informal:

**444**

FORMAL:    You *may* (have my permission to) take as much as you *can* (are able to) eat.

INFORMAL:    *Can* I speak to you for a minute?

***cannot help but***    Although occasionally found in writing, *cannot help but* is often criticized as illogical or confused. Use either *cannot help* or *cannot but*:

RIGHT:    I *cannot help* wishing that I had never met you.

RIGHT:    I *cannot but* wish that I had never met you.

***compare with, compare to***    We compare two cities *with* each other to see what they have in common. We compare a city *to* an anthill to show what a city is like.

***complement, compliment***    The first word means "complete" or "supplement." The second word means "say nice things, flatter." *Complementary* findings round out or complete a picture. *Complimentary* remarks flatter. *Complimentary* tickets are given free of charge to create a good impression.

***couple of***    In formal writing, *couple* refers to two of a kind, a pair. Used in the sense of "several" or "a few," it is informal. Used before a plural noun without a connecting *of*, it is nonstandard:

INFORMAL:    We had to wait *a couple of* minutes.

NONSTANDARD:    We had only *a couple* dollars left.

***credible, credulous, creditable***    Stories may be credible or incredible—easy or hard to believe. The people who read them may be credulous or incredulous—easy or hard to fool. An act that does someone credit is a creditable act.

***cute, great, lovely, terrific, wonderful***    Words like *cute, great, lovely, terrific,* and *wonderful* often express thoughtless or insincere praise; their use in formal writing can suggest immaturity. *Cute* is colloquial.

***data***    Though now often used as a singular, the word is originally a Latin plural (meaning "facts"):

FORMAL:    *These* data *are* part of a growing body of evidence.

**different than**   *Different from* used to be expected in formal English. Nevertheless, *different than*, widely used in speech, is becoming acceptable in writing ("Life in cadet school for Major Major was no *different than* life had been for him all along."— Joseph Heller, *Catch-22*). *Different than* is the more economical way of introducing a clause:

ECONOMICAL:      We tried a different method *than* we had used last year.
LESS ECONOMICAL: We tried a different method *from the one* we had used last year.

**disinterested, uninterested**   In formal English, *disinterested* means "unswayed by personal, selfish interest" or "impartial." *Disinterested* used in the sense of "uninterested" or "indifferent" is objectionable to many readers:

RIGHT:   We were sure she would be a *disinterested* judge.
RIGHT:   He seemed *uninterested* in our problems.

**double comparative, double superlative**   Short adjectives usually form the comparative by adding the suffix *-er* (*cheaper*), the superlative by adding the suffix *-est* (*cheapest*). Long adjectives, and adverbs ending in *-ly*, usually employ the intensifiers *more* and *most* instead (*more expensive, most expensive; more carefully, most carefully*). Forms using both the suffix and the intensifier are nonstandard (*more cheaper, most cheapest*).

**double negative**   Double negatives say no twice. The use of additional negative words to reinforce a negation already expressed is nonstandard: "I *didn't* do *nothing*"; "*Nobody* comes to see me *no more.*"

RIGHT:   I *didn't* do *anything.*
RIGHT:   *Nobody* comes to see me *anymore.*

Similar to double negatives are expressions like *couldn't hardly* or *couldn't scarcely*:

RIGHT:   I *could hardly* keep my eyes open during the talk.

**due to as a preposition**   *Due to* is generally accepted as an adjective: "His absence was *due to* ill health." "His absence, *due to* ill

**446**

health, upset our schedule." (In these examples, we could substitute another adjective: "His absence was *traceable* to ill
health.") As a preposition meaning "because of," *due to* is often
criticized:

OBJECTIONABLE:     He canceled his lecture *due to* ill health.
SAFE:              He canceled his lecture *because of* ill health.

**each other, one another**   Conservative writers distinguish between
*each other* (referring to two persons or things) and *one another*
(referring to more than two):

> Bride and groom had known *each other* since childhood.
> The members of his family supported *one another.*

**enthuse**   *Enthuse* is a "back formation" from the noun *enthusiasm.* It is informal or slangy as a shortcut for "become enthusiastic" and "move to enthusiasm." (Similar back formations,
like *reminisce* from *reminiscence,* have become generally acceptable. *Enthuse* still has a long way to go.)

**etc.**   *Etc.,* the Latin abbreviation for "and so on" or "and the
like," often serves as a vague substitute for additional examples
or illustrations. Furthermore, *ect.* is a common misspelling. "And
etc." and "such as . . . etc." are redundant. To avoid trouble, do
without *etc.* altogether.

**farther, further; all the farther**   A traditional rule requires *farther*
in references to space and distance ("We traveled *farther* than we
had expected"). It requires *further* in references to degree and
quantity ("We discussed it *further* at our next meeting") and in
the sense of "additional" ("without *further* delay"). *Further,* however, is now widely accepted as appropriate in all three senses.
   *All the farther* in the sense of "as far as" ("This is *all the farther*
we go") is nonstandard or dialectal.

**flaunt, flout**   We *flaunt* (show off) wealth or possessions. We *flout*
(defy or ignore) laws.

**flunk**   Slangy for *fail.*

447

**get, got, gotten**   The verb *get* is used in many idiomatic expressions. Some of these are colloquial:

- *have got* (for "own," "possess," "have available")
  I *have got* ten dollars; she *has got* blue eyes; you *have got* ten minutes.

- *have got to* (for "have to," "must," "be obliged")
  I *have got to* leave now; we *have got to* think of our customers.

- *get to* (for "succeed")
  I finally *got to* see him.

- *get* (for "understand")
  *Get* it?

- *get* (for "arrest," "hit," "kill")
  The police finally *got* him.

- *get* (for "puzzle," "irritate," "annoy")
  What really *gets* me is that he never announces his tests.

- *got* (instead of *be, am, was, were* to form the passive)
  He *got hit* by a truck.

*Note*: In American English, *have gotten* is an acceptable alternative to *have got* in the sense of "have obtained" or "have become." For example: "Her grandparents had *got* (or *gotten*) wealthy after the Civil War."

**hadn't ought to**   In formal English, *ought,* unlike some other auxiliaries, has no form for the past tense. *Hadn't ought* is informal, *had ought* is nonstandard:

INFORMAL:   You *hadn't ought* to ask him.
FORMAL:   You *ought not to have* asked him.

**he or she**   Many people now object to the "generic" *he* that is supposed to stand for either man or woman: "A writer must decide how *he* wants to approach *his* subject." *He or she* is more accurate but can easily sound awkward. Often the best solution is to make the sentence plural: "We *studied* writers to see how *they* solved their problems."

**hopefully**   When used instead of expressions like "I hope" or "let us hope," *hopefully* is considered illogical by conservative readers:

INFORMAL:   *Hopefully,* the forms will be ready by Monday.
FORMAL:   *I hope* the forms will be ready by Monday.

**if, whether**   Conservative readers object to *if* when used to express doubt or uncertainty after such verbs as *ask, don't know, wonder, doubt.* The more formal connective is *whether*: "I doubt *whether* his support would do much good."

**in, into**   Formal writing often requires *into* rather than *in* to indicate direction: "He came *into* (not *in*) the room."

**in terms of**   A vague all-purpose connective frequent in jargon: "What have you seen lately *in terms of* new plays?"

JARGON:   What did she expect *in terms of* salary?
BETTER:   What salary did she expect?

**infer, imply**   In formal English, *imply* means to "hint or suggest a conclusion." *Infer* means "to draw a conclusion on the basis of what has been hinted or suggested." A speaker implies something; the audience infers what is meant from the speaker's hints:

STANDARD:   The article *implied* that the mayor was dishonest.
STANDARD:   Her listeners *inferred* that she opposed the law.

**irregardless**   Used instead of *regardless, irregardless* is sometimes heard in educated speech but is widely considered nonstandard. Avoid it in speech and writing.

**it's me, it is I**   Grammarians require *it is I* on the grounds that the linking verb *is* equates the pronoun *I* with the subject *it* and thus makes necessary the use of the subject form. *It's me* is now freely used in informal speech. Avoid it and parallel uses of other pronouns (*us, him, her*) in your writing:

INFORMAL:   I thought it was *him.* It could have been *us.*
FORMAL:   It was *she* who paid the bills.

**449**

**judicial, judicious**   A "judicial" decision is a decision reached by a judge or by a court. A "judicious" decision shows sound judgment. Not every judicial decision is judicious.

**later, latter**   *Later* is the opposite of *earlier*. The *latter* is the opposite of the *former*. "Although both Alfred and Francis were supposed to arrive at eight, the former came earlier, the *latter later*."

**learn, teach**   In standard English, the teacher *teaches* (rather than *learns*) the learner. The learner is *taught* (rather than *learned*) by the teacher:

STANDARD:   They *taught* (not *learned*) us everything we know.

**leave, let**   In formal usage, *leave* does not mean "allow" or "permit." You do not "leave" somebody do something. Nor does *leave* take the place of *let* in suggestions like "Let us call a meeting."

**less, fewer**   *Less* is often used interchangeably with *fewer* before plural nouns. This use of *less* was once widely condemned. The safe practice is to use *less* in references to extent, amount, degree (*less* friction, *less* money, *less* heat). Do not use it in references to number (*fewer* people, *fewer* homes, *fewer* requirements).

**like as a connective**   In informal speech, *like* is widely used as a connective replacing *as* or *as if* at the beginning of a clause. Avoid this informal *like* in your writing:

INFORMAL:   Do *like* I tell you.
FORMAL:   Do *as* I tell you.

INFORMAL:   The patient felt *like* he had slept for days.
FORMAL:   The patient felt *as if* (or *as though*) he had slept for days.

In formal usage, *like* is acceptable as a preposition, followed by an object: *like* a bird, *like* a cloud. It is not acceptable as a connective that starts a clause, with its own subject and verb: *like* a bird flies, *like* a cloud had passed.

PREPOSITION:   Manuel looks exactly *like* his father.
CONNECTIVE:   We did everything *like* (should be *as*) the instructions said.

**moral, morale**   We talk about the "moral" of a story but about the "morale" of troops. People with good morale are not necessarily very moral, and vice versa.

**most, almost**   *Most* is informal when used in the sense of "almost" or "nearly": "*Most* everybody was there." "Mrs. Jones considers herself an authority on *most* any subject." In writing, use "*almost* everybody," "*almost* any subject."

**myself, yourself, himself, herself**   The *-self* pronouns are called reflexive pronouns because they usually "point back" to someone already mentioned:

> *I* blamed *myself* for the accident.
> *The woman* introduced *herself.*
> *He himself* gave me the key.

Conservative readers object to these pronouns when they do not "point back" but are used as simple substitutes for *I* or *me, he* or *him*:

FORMAL:   My brother and *I* (not *myself*) met him at the station.
FORMAL:   We have reserved seats for Jean and *you* (not *yourself*).

**nohow, nowheres, nowhere near**   *Nohow* and *nowheres* are nonstandard for *in no way* and *nowhere. Nowhere near* is informal for *not nearly*: "They were not nearly as clever as they thought."

**off of**   Nonstandard for *off* or *from*:

STANDARD:   Take if *off* (not *off of*) the table.
STANDARD:   She deducted two dollars *from* (not *off of*) the price.

**OK, O.K., okay**   All three spellings are acceptable, but the expression itself is informal:

FORMAL:   The mayor gave us her formal *approval* (not "her formal *OK*").

**on account of**   Nonstandard as a substitute for *because*:

NONSTANDARD:   When promoted, people may stop trying *on account of* (should be "because") they have reached their goal.

**451**

***plan on***   In formal usage, substitute *plan to*:

INFORMAL:   My parents had always *planned on* us taking over the farm.
FORMAL:   My parents had always *planned to* have us take over the farm.

***plus***   *Plus* is acceptable in writing when it means "added to" and is used in talking about figures, sums, and the like. Avoid using it as an informal substitute for *and* or *also*: "He dresses shabbily, *and* (not *plus*) he smells."

**possessives with verbal nouns**   A traditional rule requires that a verbal noun (gerund) be preceded by a possessive in sentences like the following:

FORMAL:   He mentioned *John's winning* a scholarship.
FORMAL:   I am looking forward to *your mother's staying* with us.

This rule is widely observed in formal writing. In informal speech and writing, the plain form is more common:

INFORMAL:   Imagine *John winning* a scholarship!

A combination of a pronoun and a verbal with the *-ing* ending may express two different relationships. In the sentence "I saw *him returning* from the library," you actually saw *him*. In the sentence "I object to *his using* my toothbrush," you are not objecting to *him* but merely to one of *his* actions. Use the possessive pronoun (*my, our, his, their*) when the object of a verb or of a preposition is not the person but one of his or her actions, traits, or experiences:

RIGHT:   We investigated the chances of *his* being elected.
RIGHT:   There is no excuse for *their* not writing sooner.
RIGHT:   I do not like *your* associating with the neighborhood children.

***predominate***   *Predominate* is a verb: "Shirt sleeves and overalls *predominated* in the crowd." *Predominant* is the adjective: "Antiwar feeling was *predominant*." "Democrats were the *predominant* party."

**preposition at the end of a sentence**   Teachers no longer tell students not to end a sentence with a preposition. The preposition that ends a sentence is idiomatic, natural English, though more frequent in informal than in formal use:

INFORMAL:   I don't remember what we talked *about.*
INFORMAL:   She found her in-laws hard to live *with.*

FORMAL:   Let us not betray the ideals *for* which these men died.
FORMAL:   Do not ask *for* whom the bell tolls.

**prepositions often criticized**   Look out for the following:

• *Inside of* (for *inside*), *outside of* (for *outside*), and *at about* (for *about*) are redundant.

• *Back of* for *behind* (*back of* the house), *inside of* for *within* (*inside of* three hours), *outside of* for *besides* or *except* (no one *outside of* my friends), and *over with* for *over* (it's *over with*) are colloquial.

• *As to, as regards,* and *in regard to* can seem heavy-handed and bureaucratic when used as substitutes for briefer or more precise prepositions:

AWKWARD:   I questioned him *as to* the nature of his injury.
PREFERABLE:   I questioned him *about* his injury.

• *As to whether, in terms of,* and *on the basis of* flourish in all varieties of jargon.

• *Per* (a dollar *per* day), *as per* (*as per* your request), and *plus* (quality *plus* service) are common in business and newspaper English but inappropriate in a noncommercial context.

***provided, provided that, providing***   *Provided, provided that,* and *providing* are interchangeable in a sentence like "He will withdraw his complaint, *provided* you apologize." However, only *provided* has escaped criticism and is therefore the safest form to use.

***reason is because***   In informal speech, *the reason . . . is because* often takes the place of the more formal *the reason . . . is that.* The former construction is often criticized as redundant, since *because* repeats the idea of cause already expressed in the word *reason.* Either construction can make a sentence unnecessarily awkward:

INFORMAL: *The reason* that the majority rules *is because* it is strongest.
FORMAL: *The reason* that the majority rules *is that* it is strongest.
LESS AWKWARD: The majority rules *because* it is strongest.

**shall, will**  In current American usage, *will* usually indicates simply that something is going to happen:

I *will* ask him tomorrow.
You *will* find it on your desk.
Mr. Smith *will* inform you of our plans.

The more emphatic *shall* often indicates that something is going to happen as the result of strong determination, definite obligation, or authoritative command:

I *shall* return.
We *shall* do our best.
Wages of common laborers *shall* not exceed twenty dollars a day.

*Shall* is also common in questions that invite the listener's approval or consent:

*Shall* I wait for you?
*Shall* we dance?

Formal English used to require *shall* for simple future in the first person: "I *shall* see him tomorrow." Current handbooks of grammar have abandoned this rule.

**so and such**  In *formal English, so* and *such* show that something has reached a definite point, producing certain characteristic results:

They were so frightened *that they were unable to speak.*
There was such an uproar *that the judge banged the gavel in vain.*

Informal English often omits the characteristic result. *So* and *such* then function as **intensifiers**: "I am *so* glad." "He is *such* a lovely boy." You can make such sentences generally acceptable in two different ways. Substitute an intensifier like *very* or *extremely*: "I am *very* glad." Or add a clause giving the characteristic result: "He is such a lovely boy *that everyone adores him.*"

**split infinitives**    Occasionally a modifier breaks up an infinitive, that is, a verbal formed with *to* (*to come, to promise, to have written*). The resulting split infinitive has long been idiomatic English and occurs in the work of distinguished writers. The traditional rule against it has been widely abandoned. However, a split infinitive can be awkward if the modifier that splits the infinitive is more than one word:

AWKWARD:    He ordered us *to* with all possible speed *return* to our stations.
BETTER:    He ordered us *to return* to our stations with all possible speed.

**subjunctive**    In *formal usage,* subjunctive forms point to possibilities rather than facts:

• After *if, as if,* and *as though,* use *were* instead of *was* if the possibility you have in mind is *contrary to fact or highly improbable*:

The bird looked as if it *were* a plane.
If I *were* you, I would try to improve my language habits.
He acts as if his name *were* John D. Rockefeller.

Use *is* or *was* if you are considering a genuine possibility:

If your brother *was* ill, he should have notified you.
It looks as if the plane *is* going to be late.

• Use subjunctive forms in noun clauses *after verbs indicating that something is desirable or necessary* but has not yet come about: "I wish I *were* (not "I *was*") a wise old man." Forms like *answer* instead of *answers, go* instead of *goes* or *went,* and *be* instead of *is* or *was* occur after verbs signaling a suggestion, a request, a command, or a resolution:

Her supervisor insists that she *spend* more time in the office.
We demand that he *repay* all his debts.
I move that this question *be* referred to one of our committees.

**superlative in reference to two**    In informal speech and writing, the superlative rather than the comparative frequently occurs in comparisons between only two things. This use of the superlative is often considered illogical:

| | |
|---|---|
| INFORMAL: | Which of the two candidates is the *best* speaker? |
| FORMAL: | Which of the two candidates is the *better* speaker? |

***take and, try and, up and***   *Take and* (in "I'd *take and* prune those roses") and *up and* (in "He *up and* died") are dialectal. *Try and* for *try to* ("I'd *try and* change his mind") is colloquial.

***these kind***   Agreement requires "*this kind* of car" (both singular) or "*these kinds* of fish" (both plural). "*These kind* of cars" and "*those kind* of cars" are informal.

**titles: *Dr., Prof., Reverend***   In references to holders of academic degrees or titles, *Dr. Smith* and *Professor Brown* are courteous and correct. *Professor* is sometimes abbreviated in addresses when it precedes the full name: *Prof. Martha F. Brown.* In references to clergy, *Reverend* is usually preceded by *the* and followed by the first name, by initials, or by *Mr.* (*the Reverend William Carper; the Reverend W. F. Carper; the Reverend Mr. Carper*).

***type, type of, -type***   Omitting the *of* in expressions like "this *type* of plane" is colloquial. *Type* is increasingly used as a suffix to turn nouns into adjectives: "an *escape-type* novel," "a *drama-type* program." Many readers object to such combinations. Often they turn simple ideas into fuzzy, wordy phrases: "A subsidy-type payment" says no more than "subsidy."

***unique, perfect, equal***   It is often argued that one thing cannot be *more unique, more perfect,* or *more equal* than another. Either it is unique or it isn't. Formal English therefore often substitutes *more nearly unique, more nearly perfect, more nearly equal.*

***used to, didn't use to, used to could***   *Used to* in questions or negative statements with *did* is informal and only occasionally seen in print ("the strident . . . antipolice slogans which *didn't use to* be part of the hippie mode"—*National Review*). Avoid it in writing:

| | |
|---|---|
| INFORMAL: | She *didn't use to* smoke. |
| FORMAL: | She *used not to* smoke. |

*Used to could* is nonstandard for *used to be able.*

**456**

**where, where at, where to**  In formal English, *where* takes the place of *where to* ("*Where* was it sent?") and *where at* ("*Where* is he?"). *Where* used instead of *that* ("I read in the paper *where* a boy was killed") is informal.

**who, which, and that**  *Who* and *whom* refer to persons ("the man *whom* I asked"). *Which* refers to ideas and things ("the car *which* I bought"). A *who*, *whom*, or *which* introducing a restrictive modifier may be replaced by *that* (but *need* not be):

The man *that* I asked liked the car *that* I bought.

A *whom* or a *which* that is the object in a restrictive modifier is often left out:

The man (*whom*) I asked liked the car (*which*) I bought.

*Of which* and *in which* can easily make a sentence awkward. *Whose* is therefore widely used and accepted in reference to ideas and things: "the Shank-Painter Swamp, *whose* expressive name . . . gave it importance in our eyes" (Thoreau).

**-wise**  People often change a noun into an adverb by tacking on *-wise*; this practice is common in business or advertising jargon:

JARGON:    The delay was advantageous *tax-wise*.
BETTER:    The delay was advantageous *for tax purposes*.

**without**  *Without* is nonstandard when used as a connective introducing a clause:

NONSTANDARD:    The owner won't let me stay *without* I pay the rent.
STANDARD:       The owner won't let me stay *unless* I pay the rent.

**you with indefinite reference**  Formal writing generally limits *you* to the meaning of "you, the reader." Much informal writing uses *you* with indefinite reference to refer to people in general; formal writing would substitute *one*:

INFORMAL:    In ancient Rome, *you* had to be a patrician to be able to vote.
FORMAL:      In ancient Rome, *one* had to be a patrician to be able to vote.

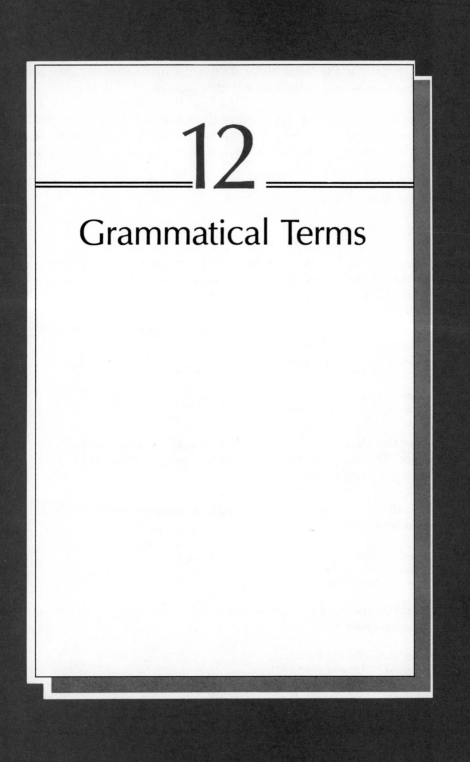

# 12

## Grammatical Terms

*Note*: Use the index to locate a fuller discussion of many of the grammatical terms listed in this glossary.

**absolute construction**   A word or phrase that is grammatically independent of the rest of the sentence. Typically, a verbal or verbal phrase: "*The guests having departed,* Arvin locked the door."

**accusative**   See CASE.

**active**   See VOICE.

**adjective**   A class of words that can point out a quality of a noun (or noun equivalent). They occur characteristically as modifiers of nouns ("the *happy* child") and as predicate adjectives ("The child was *happy*"). Most adjectives can show differences in **degree**; they have distinctive forms for use in comparisons:

| POSITIVE | COMPARATIVE | SUPERLATIVE |
|----------|-------------|-------------|
| tall | taller | tallest |
| happy | happier | happiest |
| cautious | more cautious | most cautious |

**adjective clause**   A dependent clause serving an adjective function: "The man *who had startled us* apologized." (The clause modifies the noun *man*.)

**adverb**   A class of words that answer questions like when, where, and how:

| WHEN: | now, then, today, yesterday, soon |
|-------|-----------------------------------|
| WHERE: | here, there, upstairs, downtown |
| HOW: | slowly, cautiously, rashly, clumsily |

Adverbs are used to modify verbs, adjectives, other adverbs, or a sentence as a whole:

| VERB: | She ran *quickly.* |
|-------|--------------------|
| ADJECTIVE: | He was *strangely* silent. |
| ADVERB: | She sang *moderately* well. |
| SENTENCE: | *Surprisingly,* he did not answer. |

**460**

Many adverbs show the distinctive *-ly* ending. Some irregular adverbs: *fast, much, well.*

**adverbial clause**    A dependent clause serving an adverbial function: "We left *after the rain had stopped.*" "We met *where the path ends.*" "*When the bell had ceased to ring,* I opened the door." (The dependent clauses answer questions like when, where, and how.)

**agreement**    Correspondence, mainly in number, between grammatically related elements. Use of matching forms of a subject and its verb (the *dog barks*—the *dogs bark*); choice of a pronoun matching its antecedent ("*Each girl* must be aware of *her* responsibility").

**antecedent**    The noun (or equivalent) for which a pronoun substitutes: "*Aunt Bertha* fell sick soon after *she* arrived."

**appositive**    A noun (or equivalent) placed as a modifier next to—usually after—another noun: "Mr. Brown, *the registrar,* proved most helpful."

**articles**    *A* and *an* (the **indefinite** articles) and *the* (the **definite** article), used as noun markers: *a* book, *an* honest man, *the* door.

**auxiliaries**    The helping verbs that are used in forming complete verbs: *be* (*am, is, are, was, were*), *have, shall* (*should*), *will* (*would*), *can* (*could*), *may* (*might*), *must, ought.*

**case**    Inflected forms of nouns and pronouns, signaling certain grammatical relationships within a sentence: the **possessive** of nouns (*George's* friend), the **subject form** (or nominative) and **object form** (or accusative) of pronouns: *I—me, he—him, she—her, we—us, they—them, who—whom.*

**clause**    A subject-predicate unit that may combine with other such units in a sentence. **Independent** clauses are grammatically self-contained and can be punctuated as complete sentences:

    I think; therefore, I am.
    I think. Therefore, I am.

**Dependent** clauses are grammatically subordinate to an independent clause (**main clause**):

> Arvin had a dog, *which barked all night.*
> *After the rain stopped,* we went home.

See also ADJECTIVE CLAUSE, ADVERBIAL CLAUSE, RELATIVE CLAUSE, NOUN CLAUSE.

**collective noun**   A group noun that is singular in form but may require a plural verb:

SINGULAR:   The *jury votes* tomorrow. (thought of as a unit)
PLURAL:   The *jury are* out to lunch. (thought of as individuals)

**comparative**   The form of adjectives and adverbs that is used to indicate higher degree: "Blood is *thicker* than water." "She speaks Spanish *better* than I do."

**complement**   A sentence element completing the predication of the verb. The complements, or completers, of action verbs are called **objects**:

> Edith called *the sheriff* (**direct** object).
> She wrote *my father* (**indirect** object) *a letter* (**direct** object).

The complement of a linking verb is a noun or an adjective describing the subject (**subject complement**):

> Her father was *a minister* (**predicate noun**).
> The boy looked *pale* (**predicate adjective**).

After some verbs, an object is followed by a description of the object (**object complement**):

> The editorial called the project *a failure.*
> Arvin labeled the charges *ridiculous.*

**conjunction, conjunctive adverb**   See CONNECTIVES.

**connectives**   Words that connect sentence elements or clauses, also called **conjunctions**. Three major kinds are **coordinating connectives**, or coordinators (*and, but, for, so, yet, or, nor*); **sub-**

ordinating **connectives**, or subordinators (*if, when, unless, because, though, whereas*); **adverbial connectives**, also called conjunctive adverbs (*however, therefore, nevertheless, moreover, indeed, in fact*).

**coordinate adjectives**  Two or more interchangeable adjectives that describe different qualities of the same noun, with a comma taking the place of *and*: "a *noisy, unruly* crowd."

**correlatives**  Paired connectives coordinating sentence elements or clauses: *either . . . or, neither . . . nor, not only . . . but also, whether . . . or.*

**declarative**  See SENTENCE.

**degree**  See ADJECTIVE.

**determiners**  Noun markers including **articles** (*a, an, the*), **demonstrative pronouns** (*this, these; that, those*), and **possessive pronouns** (*my, your, his, her, its, our, their*).

**elliptical constructions**  Constructions in which missing elements can be supplied to facilitate grammatical analysis:

> The paintings [*that*] he collected filled a large room.
> When [*she was*] interviewed, the actress denied rumors of an impending engagement.

**expletives**  The *it* and *there* used as mere introductory words in *it-is, there-is, there-are* sentences.

**finite verb**  A term used to distinguish a complete verb from a verbal, which cannot by itself function as a predicate.

**function words**  Words whose major function is to help establish grammatical relationships within a sentence: articles, auxiliaries, connectives, prepositions.

**gender**  The quality of nouns and pronouns that determines choice between *he, she,* or *it* (**masculine, feminine,** and **neuter**);

between *actor* and *actress, alumnus* and *alumna, fiancé* and *fiancée.*

**gerund**   See VERBAL.

**idiom**   An expression that may not conform to general grammatical patterns but that is the customary way of conveying a given meaning: *bear in mind, have a mind to, keep in mind.*

**imperative**   See MOOD, SENTENCE.

**indicative**   See MOOD.

**infinitive**   See VERBAL.

**inflection**   Changes in the form of words to reflect changes in grammatical relationships: the plural *-s* of nouns; the *-s, -ed,* or *-ing* of verbs; the *-er* or *-est* of adjectives. (Also changes in a word itself: *ring–rang; mouse–mice.*)

**intensifier**   Words that modify adjectives or adverbs and express degree, also called **intensive adverbs**: *very* hot, *quite* calm, *rather* young.

**interjection**   A grammatically independent element used to express attitude or emotion: *ah, oh, ouch,* and the like.

**interrogative**   See SENTENCE, PRONOUN.

**kernel sentences**   The minimum sentences from which more complicated structures are derived in transformational grammar. They are the **source sentences** from which actual sentences are generated by successive transformations.

**linking verb**   See VERB.

**modifier**   A word, phrase, or clause that develops or restricts the meaning of another sentence element or the sentence as a whole (see also ADJECTIVE, ADVERB). **Restrictive** modifiers contribute to identification and need no punctuation; **nonrestrictive** modifiers

provide additional information not essential to identification and are set off, normally by commas:

RESTRICTIVE:     The person *who returned my wallet* was a complete stranger.
NONRESTRICTIVE:  Mr. Norton, *who found my wallet,* is an old friend.

**modifying noun**   A noun that modifies another noun and takes the place usually occupied by an adjective: a *steam* engine, a *garbage* truck, a *labor* union.

**mood**   The classification of verb forms as **indicative** (plain or factual: "I *am* ready"); **imperative** (request or command: "*Be* quiet"); and **subjunctive** (hypothetical or contrary to fact: "I wish he *were* here!").

**nominative**   See CASE.

**noun**   A class of words that name or classify people, animals, things, ideas. They occur typically as subjects of clauses or as objects of verbs and prepositions. Their appearance is often signaled by noun markers like the **articles** (*a, an, the*). Many nouns add -*s* to the plain form to form the plural: *dogs, cars, houses, colleges.*
   **Common** nouns start with a lower-case letter (*car, college*); **proper** nouns are capitalized (*Ford, Yale*).

**noun clause**   A dependent clause taking the place of a noun: "*That he was late* does not surprise me." "We knew *why he was late.*"

**noun equivalent**   A sentence element (pronoun, infinitive, gerund, noun clause) that is grammatically equivalent to a noun and can replace it in a sentence.

**number**   Choice of appropriate forms to express **singular** (one of a kind) or **plural** (more than one).

**object**   See COMPLEMENT.

**object form**   See CASE.

**participle**   See VERBAL.

**parts of speech**   The eight major word classes listed in traditional grammar: noun, pronoun, verb, adjective, adverb, conjunction, preposition, interjection.

**passive**   See VOICE.

**past**   See TENSE.

**perfect**   See TENSE.

**person**   Choice of appropriate forms to express the person speaking (**first person**: *I know, we know*); the person spoken to (**second person**: *you know*); or the person spoken about (**third person**: *he knows, she knows, it knows, they know*).

**phrase**   A group of related words that function together as one grammatical unit—a main verb and its auxiliaries; a preposition or a verbal accompanied by its object or other related material:

| | |
|---|---|
| VERB PHRASE: | Craig *has been studying.* |
| PREPOSITIONAL PHRASE: | Irene sat *at the window.* |
| VERBAL PHRASE: | We should stop *hunting whales.* |

Verbal phrases may be further subdivided according to the verbal they use: infinitive (or *to* form), participle (form like *knowing* or *known* used as a modifier), or gerund (*-ing* form used as a verbal noun):

| | |
|---|---|
| INFINITIVE PHRASE: | He started *to call us names.* |
| PARTICIPIAL PHRASE: | *Breathing heavily,* we rested in the shade. |
| GERUND PHRASE: | The rules forbid *running near the pool.* |

A phrase, unlike a clause, does not have a subject and a complete verb.

**possessive**   See CASE.

**predicate**   The second basic element of the typical written sentence, making an assertion about the subject. The complete

466

predicate consists of a complete (finite) verb and its possible complements and modifiers:

Her brother / *makes sandals in Oregon.*

**predicate noun**   See COMPLEMENT.

**preposition**   A class of words that relate a noun (or equivalent) to the rest of the sentence: "Arvin left *after* dark." "Miriam worked *without* pay." The noun that follows the preposition is called its object; together they make up a **prepositional phrase**: *at night, in the morning, for your own good.*

**present**   See TENSE.

**principal parts**   The basic forms of a verb: simple present (*know*), simple past (*knew*), past participle (*known*).

**progressive construction**   Verb form expressing action in progress: "Fred *was frying* a fish."

**pronoun**   A class of words that can take the place of nouns, classified as **personal** (*I, you, he*); **possessive** (*my, your, his*); **reflexive** or **intensive** (*myself, yourself, himself*); **demonstrative** (*this, that*); **relative** (*who, which, that*); **interrogative** (*who, which, what*); and **indefinite** (*one, anyone, everyone*). See also CASE.

**relative clause**   A dependent clause related to the main clause by a relative pronoun: "The article *that I mentioned* begins on page 5."

**restrictive**   See MODIFIER.

**sentence**   A grammatically complete and self-contained unit of thought or expression, set off from other such units by end punctuation. The typical written sentence contains at least a subject and a predicate ("Birds sing"). The most common exception is the subjectless request or command, in which the subject is said to be understood ("Show him in").

Sentences may be statements (**declarative**), questions (**interrogative**), or requests or commands (**imperative**):

| | |
|---|---|
| STATEMENT: | My friends voted for Smith. |
| QUESTION: | Did you vote for Smith? |
| REQUEST OR COMMAND: | Vote for Smith! |

Sentences combining two or more independent clauses are called **compound**. Sentences combining an independent and one or more dependent clauses are called **complex**. A combination of the two types is called **compound-complex**:

| | |
|---|---|
| COMPOUND: | He hummed, and she sang. |
| COMPLEX: | He hummed when she sang. |
| COMPOUND-COMPLEX: | When they heard the news, he hummed and she sang. |

**source sentence**   See KERNEL SENTENCES.

**subject**   The first basic element of the typical written sentence, about which the predicate makes an assertion. The complete subject includes possible modifiers:

*The new assistant manager* starts tomorrow.

**subject form**   See CASE.

**subjunctive**   See MOOD.

**subordinate clause**   Another term for dependent clause. See CLAUSE.

**superlative**   The form of adjectives and adverbs used to express highest degree: "Maria is the *fastest* runner on the team." "She runs *fastest.*"

**tense**   The system of verb forms expressing primarily different relationships in time:

| | | | |
|---|---|---|---|
| PRESENT: | I know | PERFECT: | I have known |
| PAST: | I knew | PAST PERFECT: | I had known |
| FUTURE: | I will (shall) know | FUTURE PERFECT: | I will (shall) have known |

**transformation**   One of the successive steps by which more complicated structures are produced from simple ones in a transfor-

468

mational grammar. The reshuffling, addition, or deletion of grammatical elements needed, for instance, to turn present into past tense, active into passive voice, an affirmative into a negative statement, or a statement into a question:

SOURCE: The plane arrived.
TRANSFORMATION: *Did* the plane *arrive?*

**transitive**  See VERB.

**verb**  A class of words that signal the performance of an action, the occurrence of an event, or the presence of a condition. Verbs appear in typical verb positions: "Let's *leave*." "The boys *left* the scene." Most verbs can show a change in time by a change in the form of the verb: *bring* (present tense)/*brought* (past tense); *laugh* (present tense)/*laughed* (past tense). Verbs typically take an *-s* in the third person singular of the present tense (*asks, leaves, condones*). They use **auxiliaries** in forms consisting of more than one word (*have left, was asked, will be leaving, can talk, may have seen*).

Action verbs are modified by adverbs; **linking verbs** are followed by adjectives:

ACTION VERB: She *responded* quickly.
LINKING VERB: His response *seemed* quick.

**Regular** verbs use the same form for the simple past and the past participle:

REGULAR: I *laughed* | I have *laughed*
IRREGULAR: I *knew* | I have *known*

**Transitive** verbs normally require an object. **Intransitive** verbs can serve as the complete predicate:

TRANSITIVE: She *raises* chickens.
INTRANSITIVE: The sun *rises*.

See also TENSE, MOOD, VOICE.

**verbal**  A form that is derived from a verb but does not by itself function as a predicate: **infinitive** (*to* form); **present participle** (*-ing* form used as part of a verb, or as a modifier); **gerund** (*-ing* form used as a verbal noun); **past participle** (*-ed* form in regular verbs, irregular in others). Verbals appear as noun equivalents, modifiers, and *parts* of verbs:

| | |
|---|---|
| INFINITIVE: | The earth began *to shake*. |
| PRESENT PARTICIPLE: | They are *suing* the company. |
| | The *melting* snow feeds the river. |
| | *Smiling,* Pat started the car. |
| GERUND: | *Running* burns up calories. |
| PAST PARTICIPLE: | The tenants had *moved* the furniture. |
| | We looked at the *burnt* toast. |
| | He called it a *known* fact. |

See also PHRASE.

**voice**   The verb form that shows whether the subject is acting (**active**) or acted upon (**passive**):

| | |
|---|---|
| ACTIVE: | Manuel *feeds* the cats. |
| PASSIVE: | The cats *are fed* by Manuel. |

# Index

*Note:* In this index, entries for major categories in grammar, rhetoric, and mechanics have been boldfaced to facilitate reference to key terms. Page numbers followed by (gl) refer to an entry in the Glossary of Usage. Page numbers followed by (gt) refer to an entry in the Glossary of Grammatical Terms. The latter glossary often provides a more complete and more technical overview of terminology than the more selective and more gradual presentation in the teaching chapters of the text.

A separate listing of authors quoted or cited in *New English Handbook* follows this general index.

# Authors Quoted or Cited in *New English Handbook*

# ══Acknowledgments══

Cyrilly Abels for a passage from Warren Hinckle, "The Adman Who Hated Advertising" from *If You Have a Lemon, Make Lemonade*. Copyright © 1974 by Warren Hinckle III. Reprinted by permission of Cyrilly Abels, Literary Agent.

American Heritage Publishing Co., Inc. for a passage from Enrique Hank Lopez, "Back to Bachimba." Copyright © 1967, American Heritage Publishing Co., Inc. Reprinted by permission from *Horizon*, Winter, 1967.

*The American Scholar* for passages from articles by Joseph Wood Krutch, Donald J. Lloyd, and Philip M. Wagner.

Appleton-Century-Crofts, Inc. for a passage from *A History of the English Language*, Second Edition, by Albert C. Baugh. Copyright © 1957, Appleton-Century-Crofts, Inc.

Isaac Asimov for a passage from his article "Nuclear Fusion" in *Parade*, February 18, 1979.

*The Atlantic Monthly* for passages from articles by Saul Bellow, Paul Brooks, Oscar Handlin, Alfred Kazin, Vance Packard, and Joseph Wechsberg.

Beacon Press for a passage from *Notes of a Native Son* by James Baldwin. © 1955 by James Baldwin. Reprinted by permission of the Beacon Press.

William Collins & World Publishing Company for entries from *Webster's New World Dictionary of the American Language*, Second Edition. Copyright © 1974 by William Collins & World Publishing Company, Cleveland, Ohio.

Farrar, Straus & Giroux, Inc. for passages from Norman Podhoretz, *Doings and Undoings*. Copyright © 1953, 1954, 1955, 1956, 1957, 1958, 1959, 1962, 1963, 1964, 1965 by Norman Podhoretz.

*Fortune* for a passage by William H. Whyte (November 1950).

Harper & Row, Publishers, Inc. for passages from E. B. White, *One Man's Meat*; and from articles by John W. Gardner, C. P. Snow, and Dr. Ian Stevenson.

*Harper's* for a passage from *Land Rush* by Peter Meyer. Copyright © 1978 by Harper's Magazine. All rights reserved. Excerpted from the January 1979 issue by special permission.

Barbara Johnston for her research paper "Aging in America: Is the Best Yet to Be?"

Howard Mumford Jones for a passage from an article in the *Saturday Evening Post*.

Alfred A. Knopf, Inc. for a passage from Alistair Cooke, *One Man's America*. Copyright 1951, 1952.

The Macmillan Company for a passage from Arthur M. Schlesinger, *Paths to the President*. Copyright 1949.

McGraw-Hill Book Company for passages from *The Female Eunuch* by Germaine Greer. Copyright © 1970, 1971 by Germaine Greer. Used by permission of McGraw-Hill Book Company.

Newsweek, Inc. for a passage from "Let the Eskimos Hunt," by Lael Morgan in *Newsweek*, May 21, 1979. Copyright 1979 by Newsweek, Inc. All rights reserved. Reprinted by permission.

W. W. Norton & Company, Inc. for a passage from *Love and Will* by Rollo May, by permission of W. W. Norton & Company, Inc. Copyright © 1969 by W. W. Norton & Company, Inc.

Oxford University Press, Inc. for a passage from Rachel L. Carson, *The Sea Around Us*.

Random House, Inc. for entries from *The Random House Dictionary of the English Language*. © copyright 1966.

*The Reporter* for passages from articles by Michael Harrington and Ken Macrorie.

Virginia Rice for passages from Paul Horgan, "Pages from a Rio Grande Notebook," *The New York Times Book Review*. Copyright © 1955 by Paul Horgan.

*Saturday Review* for passages from articles by Fred M. Hechinger, James Michener, and Edith M. Stern.

*Scientific American* for a passage from "The Nature of Comets" by Fred L. Whipple. Copyright © 1974 by Scientific American, Inc. All rights reserved.